The Only Music That Mattered

# STUDIES IN PUNK

*The Only Music That Mattered: A Guide to Punk,
Post-Punk and Second Wave Ska, 1976–1983*
by John A. Zukowski (2025)

# The Only Music That Mattered
## A Guide to Punk, Post-Punk and Second Wave Ska, 1976–1983

JOHN A. ZUKOWSKI

**STUDIES IN PUNK**

*Series Editors* Christopher M. Innes *and* Andrew Wood

McFarland & Company, Inc., Publishers
*Jefferson, North Carolina*

LIBRARY OF CONGRESS CATALOGING-IN-PUBLICATION DATA

Names: Zukowski, John A. author
Title: The only music that mattered : a guide to punk, post-punk and second wave ska, 1976-1983 / by John A. Zukowski.
Description: Jefferson, North Carolina : McFarland & Company, Inc., Publishers, 2025. | Series: Studies in punk | Includes bibliographical references and index.
Identifiers: LCCN 2025024897 | ISBN 9781476697673 paperback ∞
ISBN 9781476655659 ebook
Subjects: LCSH: Punk rock music—Discography | Post-punk music—Discography | Rock music—1971-1980—Discography | Rock music—1981-1990—Discography | BISAC: MUSIC / Genres & Styles / Punk | LCGFT: Discographies
Classification: LCC ML156.4.R6 Z85 2025 | DDC 016.78242166092/2—dc23/eng/20250710
LC record available at https://lccn.loc.gov/2025024897

ISBN (print) 978-1-4766-9767-3
ISBN (ebook) 978-1-4766-5565-9

© 2025 John A. Zukowski. All rights reserved

*No part of this book may be reproduced or transmitted in any form or by any means, electronic or mechanical, including photocopying or recording, or by any information storage and retrieval system, without permission in writing from the publisher.*

Front cover image: Johnny Rotten performing with the Sex Pistols at the Paradiso club in Amsterdam on January 6, 1977 (Nationaal Archief)

Printed in the United States of America

*McFarland & Company, Inc., Publishers
Box 611, Jefferson, North Carolina 28640
www.mcfarlandpub.com*

# Table of Contents

Preface 1

Introduction 3

**The Guide: Punk, Post-Punk and Second Wave Ska, 1976–1983** 13

Appendix: Proto-Punk, Post-Punk and Second Wave Ska Influences 201

Chapter Notes 217

Bibliography 219

Index 223

# Preface

When I was young, I thought music could change the world. Or at least it could change your life.

Punk music was especially empowering to me when I first heard it because it came out during a dark time in American culture. It felt like the country was falling apart in the mid- to late 1970s and early 1980s. This is just some of what was going on: a U.S. president resigning after a scandal, a humiliating end to the controversial Vietnam War, gas lines, inflation, American hostages in Iran, the ritual of protests against America on the evening news every night, the ever-present fear of nuclear war that accelerated after the 1980 presidential election. What a mess.

At the time, listening to punk validated what it felt like to live then. But punk also provided some direction about how to navigate the disillusionment and chaos of this time period.

That was crucial because mainstream musical culture offered escapism like hard rock, arena rock, disco, and so-called soft rock. At a time when plenty of people—not only in America but also in the United Kingdom and elsewhere—wanted to flee reality, not face it, punk was a form of realism. So punk and its offshoots were mainly an underground phenomenon.

Decades later when I started putting this book together, I was stunned that this music for misfits is now sanctified and elevated as if precious remnants from a lost golden era. Records I remember selling for a couple of dollars are now worth hundreds and in some cases thousands. Why?

I believe it's because there's something inherently meaningful—deeply so—in the realism of punk that people still connect with. I realized that even more when I talked to young people. Many of them are fascinated by punk because it seems authentic to them. They are tired of faux authenticity more than just about anything, particularly celebrities pretending on social media that they're just like everyone else when they're not. It's a generation desperately wanting something genuine in an era of endless false and misleading content.

So, this book is both for people who need an introduction to this music and for those who want to refamiliarize themselves with the original punk era. And the book has two major goals. The first is to list the essential records from the era in a discography. The second is to analyze what this music means.

The discography features the best records from the era. It's an essential discography, not a comprehensive discography. If a song or album from this era isn't included, it's because I didn't designate it as essential.

These are the original vinyl releases. Many of these recordings were later rereleased on CD and MP3 formats with additional and alternative tracks. The catalog numbers are the original records from either the artist's country of origin or the country where the record was likely first released.

A record's exact release date is notoriously difficult to pinpoint. Unlike today, there often wasn't a hard release date. Release dates also can differ by country. They also often vary from source to source. Sometimes I had to review the release dates on a case by case basis to determine what source is most likely to be accurate. And sometimes even after exhaustive research I couldn't find an exact date. In some entries there is only a month and year or just a year of release.

I wanted to create a discography with critical commentary, not just trivia about the records. This kind of meaningful analysis exists elsewhere only for the most important artists of this era. One of the ideals of punk is that the one-off 45 on an indie label is just as important as the significant artist on a major label.

As I went deeper into the music, I concluded that the punk music from this time period can never be duplicated. One reason is the sound of the records. Like folk, blues, or gospel music recorded with more primitive equipment, punk just doesn't sound the same in the slicker and better produced settings that inevitably predominated as time went on.

The second reason is the content of the lyrics. The outrage and anger at unjust economic and political system would never be so consistent again. The target is the system itself. This broad political and cultural criticism isn't so popular today in a polarized culture where people point fingers at each other as the problem instead of upward to the overall power structure.

And the third reason is the purity of the punk genre. Although post-punk had much more flexibility in form than either punk or ska, there was still a certain adherence to remaining musically pure. It was somewhat tribal in the original punk era, but you knew who you were in your tribe. Today, it's generally considered too limiting to adhere to a specific genre like punk rather than appreciating many genres or blending genres together. I wonder how much this dilutes people's identities rather than expanding them.

Years after the ground zero of punk, and several years after compiling this book, do I think music changed my life? I'd like to think that there has been an inner teenager within me shaped by this music who remains as a moral barometer to what is real or true and what isn't. It's never too late to get back in touch with your inner teenager. So read about this music. Then start listening to it.

# Introduction

I always thought I was part of the baby boomer generation. But when I heard about Generation Jones, everything changed.

I realized how the perspective of Generation Jones, a generation designation I didn't know existed until later in life, helped shape my personality in my formative years. And some of that development came from punk rock, which I discovered shortly after it originated.

Years later, I feel that Generation Jones explains punk music and why it endures. If you're a punk fan, you've got to understand Generation Jones.

That's because the generation you grew up in matters. People remember events that happen during adolescence and young adulthood more than any other time of life.[1] And people are shaped not only by major personal events during their formative years but also by key events in the culture during that time.[2]

For most of my life I thought I was a baby boomer, born during the post–World War II period from 1946 to 1964. Social commentator Jonathan Pontell reevaluated this generation, however. He cut it in half and called the second half Generation Jones. For him, the boomer generation started slightly earlier (in 1942) and ended in 1953. Those born between 1954 and 1965 were not boomers but Generation Jones.[3]

This division was because of the vastly different experiences coming of age in those two time periods. The boomers grew up during economically prosperous times and were shaped by the hippie culture of the 1960s and early 1970s. Generation Jones was formed by the collapse of the hippie movement and the economic and political disintegration of the mid– to late 1970s and early 1980s.

It's a generation in a no-man's-land between the hippie and the yuppie. Generation Jones was born out of the tension between the fading hopes of the 1960s and the emerging pessimism of the 1970s.[4] Generation Jones refers not just to trying to keep up with the Joneses but also to *jonesing*, a longing for a way of living that can't be fulfilled, particularly in an era of economic decline.

Every other generation since has also grown up with the American Dream and economic heyday having passed. But for Generation Jones it was especially painful because the reality changed during our formative years.

Our childhoods witnessed economic prosperity and boomer-fueled optimism about changing the world. But sometime in adolescence our worldview changed. Because there was so much economic prosperity and idealism in the 1960s that either failed or dissipated, Generation Jones was angry and cynical about the boomers.[5] And for Generation Jones, the boomer generation was always connected to hippie culture.

This Generation Jones angst was the basis for punk and for Generation Jones's other major subculture, rap.[6] Rap emerged from the same downtrodden 1970s New York City as CBGB-era punk. Rap initially was associated with street reality and a prophetic critique of the culture, something that was also the basis for punk. And for a brief time in the early 1980s, an alliance of sorts formed between punk, post-punk, and rap.

Like punk, rap became more commercially viable over time. By the 1990s, a new crop of Generation X musicians achieved the financial success that had eluded most Generation Jones punks and rappers. The musical genres that were on the fringe during Generation Jones became the mainstream for Generation X.[7]

And with boomer idealism shattered, achieving commercial success posed less of an ethical dilemma for Generation X than it had for Generation Jones. Since the disintegration of ideals preceded the Generation X era, there was nothing to sell out from.[8] Generation Jones, in contrast, perceived the boomer generation as betraying their ideals—and felt a deep fear of selling out. As a result, for a period of time, punk and all of its subgenres were uncompromising and politically charged in a way that music never would be again so consistently.

Some of that was because of another facet of the Generation Jones era, which was the deindustrialization that accelerated in the mid- to late 1970s. Jobs were outsourced to where labor was cheaper. The working class who thrived in the manufacturing era had their once dependable livelihoods ripped from them. Many towns that were once part of the booming manufacturing age to this day lie in some state of ruin. Punk rock emerged from the ashes of this economic and cultural decay in both America and England in the 1970s. Some of this decline carried over to suburbia, which helped trigger the hardcore punk movement.

Disappointment and disillusionment with hippie culture and the economic decline associated with deindustrialization drove Generation Jones punks to question the entire political, cultural, and economic system. It was the beginning of a deep distrust and disillusionment with institutions that continues to this day. This burst of anger and outrage at systemic problems and their effect on young people wasn't something America wanted to hear. Punk was initially either ignored or maligned in America.

The punk movement that started in 1976 was in serious decline by about 1983, overshadowed by apolitical new wave bands embraced by the new video network MTV. Over the rest of the 1980s, a new generation of musicians toned down the anger and social observations and created a genre later called alternative music, which was much more eclectic than the more tribal punk music. But by the 1990s, the term alternative became irrelevant after grunge and so-called alternative music achieved mainstream success.

Years later, however, the Generation Jones era of punk, from 1976 to 1983, has rightfully become revered as a golden era for music, a time when there were no rules, no blueprint for success, and seemingly no desire for it.

After years of not listening to punk, I started listening to it obsessively again. As you age, you're inclined to examine what mattered to you when you were younger. Immersing myself in this music again was like contacting an old friend and finding a deep connection still intact.

I found that some common Generation Jones themes kept coming up in punk music. Collectively, we faced some of the same obstacles. There's outrage at systemic problems created by the government, big business, and the media. There was a deep fear of nuclear war along with a desire to reject mainstream culture. And there was a spiritual-like longing for deeper meaning than what the culture offered. These remain valid desires and feelings, which explains why punk still seems authentic to so many young people.

For several years, I was consumed with finding all the music that mattered from that golden era, for both those of us in Generation Jones who want to reexperience the music we grew up with and also the many young people drawn to the original punk era who need an introduction to it.

Even though some of the longest entries and the photos are of the best-known musicians from this era, let that be a gateway to the lesser-known music on indie labels because that's some of the best music from this era.

Put me in a room, or on a desert island, or anywhere with all these records, and I'll be happy.

But first, as either a review or an introduction, let's go over the three musical pillars of the Generation Jones era of music: punk, post-punk, and second wave ska, along with their subgenres.

## Punk

Because the first full-fledged punk singles were in 1976, many punks threw out music released before then.

Almost everything.

What wasn't discarded was music containing the seeds of punk. This was called proto-punk, the foundation for punk. It's now a genre of its own included in the appendix to this discography.

The ground zero of full-fledged punk and the dawning of a new era that came with it is the Ramones' debut album, released in April 1976. The Ramones established the main elements of punk, offering short, energetic songs that are fast but melodic. They are power chords played at an aggressive, fast tempo.[9]

Punk was also shaped by what is often called Johnny Ramone's buzz saw guitar, which with its distortion could sound somewhat like a chain saw. To this day, punk is associated with this sound. Johnny Ramone defined this as pure rock without the influence of blues or folk, which was the basis for much 1960s music.[10] It's a driving rhythm guitar sound with distortion and no solos.[11] This created an energetic and consistent drone. The chords meld into one another because they're played so fast that they make an urgent and constant rhythm.[12] Johnny Ramone also used a constant downstroke technique to play as fast and forcefully as possible. The lyrics were varied; there were gritty songs about New York, songs with horror movie imagery, songs about dancing, and even love songs.

The Sex Pistols and particularly John Lydon (Johnny Rotten), with his lyrics and stage persona, expanded punk's vision. For Lydon, everything was up for criticism: the monarchy, the nihilism of contemporary life, the music industry. He was the angry man who told the truth, the prophet who bluntly called out royalty, the voice of both a disenfranchised younger generation and the downtrodden working class.

If Johnny Ramone's buzz saw guitar was the embodiment of the energy of a new generation fed up with bland 1970s culture, Lydon's lyrics gave punk a social and political stance. He pointed out the problems of social conditions in a way that was liberating and felt like everything was possible.[13] It was music that felt like it could change the world, and as a result many other future punks were inspired by his voice, lyrics, and persona.[14]

The Ramones and the Sex Pistols were the one-two punch that created the new genre of punk, which was radically different from pop and rock music. While most pop music aims to relax listeners or provide them escape, punk is music of disruption.[15] Most pop and rock music is designed to distract listeners with fantasy and escape from reality instead of confronting them with reality, as punk music did.[16] Punks point out the corruption and destruction of society rather than offering romantic and utopian solutions as the hippie generation often did in their generation's music.[17]

## Subgenre: Pop Punk

Some punks didn't emphasize overt social commentary, however. Pop punk featured lyrics about relationships, emphasizing euphoria, disappointment, and anger.

The Ramones may have originated this subgenre with songs such as "I Wanna Be Your Boyfriend," "Uh-Oh I Love Her So," and "I Remember You." But the Ramones were so varied in subject matter that the Buzzcocks may have been the first significant band to acquire the pop punk label. Their punk pop wasn't lightweight, however. Although they lifted from melodic power pop at times, there was an underlying angst that in its own way is political and a product of an English working-class perspective. Many Buzzcocks songs are about how relationships in modern life create conflict and pain. Later in America, pop punk like the Descendents' *Milo Goes to College* reflected a suburban angst rather than the working-class anger of British pop punk.

Pop punk is distinctively different from power pop, which features jangle guitars rather than distorted guitar and less complex, happier songs about relationships in the tradition of traditional pop.

## Subgenre: Hardcore Punk

By 1978 punk faced a crisis.

Musically, punk's format was limited. The once liberating energy of punk seemed to exhaust itself.

How far can you go in a limited musical genre? How could punk continue without being a cliché of three-chord frenzy? Could it somehow evolve without selling out, without losing its soul?

And that led to a great divide. Punk split in two.

One direction was post-punk, which retains the angst and energy of punk but integrates it into a more adventurous musical style with more literary lyrical content. The other direction was a faster, rawer, more extreme version of punk called hardcore punk. It was partly a reaction against post-punk, which some punks considered too cerebral, too arty, and not primal enough.

Although hardcore punk scenes took off in many major U.S. cities, hardcore came to be initially connected with Southern California, a place associated with sunshine, mellow rock, and comfortable suburbia. Instead of the urban-fueled American punk from the East Coast or a British working-class perspective, hardcore punk was often about the downfall of suburban values and the emptiness of the paradise that was supposed to be California. During the mid– to late 1970s, the once comfortable and secure suburbs began to feel the effects of economic decline and shifting social trends. The disillusionment with what were supposed to be solid suburban values was at the center of hardcore. It was the sound of the American Dream gone wrong.

From 1979 to 1981, American punk bands were often a hybrid between more traditional punk and the newer, faster pace of hardcore punk. This new music expressed alienation, frustration, and angst. These were the songs of suburbanites who felt disenfranchised and dysfunctional and were labeled as underachievers, misfits, and slackers.[18] The music evolved over a few years, and it took the genre several years to attain the name hardcore punk, which may have come from the title of D.O.A.'s album *Hardcore '81*.

But once hardcore punk solidified as a genre, it became rigid in its structure. Part of what defines hardcore music and even the hardcore scene itself is remaining pure.[19] Musical virtuosity was considered a sellout because guitar solos were a distraction that diluted musical intensity and was too associated with traditional rock.[20] The speed in hardcore was about a band collectively playing fast, not showing off individualistic musical ability.[21]

## Subgenres: Oi!, Street Punk/UK 82, Crossover Thrash, Horror Punk

The British variation of more intense punk first came from Oi! music, named for the Cockney Rejects' song "Oi! Oi! Oi!" from British slang for "hey there!" Oi! was a transition out of traditional punk toward faster and harder music.

The foundation for the sound likely came from Sham 69, particularly the song "If the Kids Are United" with its chant-like chorus. Those choruses were essential to Oi! music. In some ways they recall the chants from glam rock songs or football cheers. But the sing-along structure goes back further. It originates in working-class folk songs with the crowd being encouraged to join in and sing as well as military and traditional work songs sung while marching or chanting.[22] The call-and-response vocals create unity among soldiers or workers leading to a sense of empowerment. Individual voices form into a single powerful call.[23] Other key components of Oi! include rejecting any sort of star system, celebrating working-class life, emphasizing manly virtue, and a British patriotism that sometimes crossed over into racism.[24]

The British version of faster punk was called street punk or UK 82, this name derived from a song by the Exploited, one of the major bands of the subgenre, and a nod to the year the sound solidified. Like Oi!, the new British punk was a working-class genre. It was influenced by American hardcore punk with less emphasis on the collective gang vocals of Oi! and more on a harder sound that sometimes verged on heavy metal, a genre that punk initially rejected. So, it was only a matter of time before those once opposing genres merged in what later was called crossover thrash.

Heavy metal was initially apolitical and formed out of blues-based late 1960s rock bands like Cream, Led Zeppelin, the Jimi Hendrix Experience and more progressive rock bands like Deep Purple.[25] The Ramones created a sound that was intentionally not blues-based, and the Sex Pistols injected social commentary into punk, so punk had little in common with heavy metal.

Heavy metal lyrics often focus on the macabre rather than the political. Heavy metal isn't grounded in political theory or working-class politics of class observation and liberation. Instead, it often uses horror imagery as a way of holding up a mirror to show how terrible things are for the individual rather than making social statements.

Punk invigorated the heavy metal genre by merging a political perspective with horror imagery and by making the music much faster rather than traditional, blues-based heavy metal. Punk influenced by heavy metal slowed down the punk sound into something thicker and more churning and at times incorporated some of the horror imagery of heavy metal.

Another punk mini-subgenre used so much horror imagery that it came to be called horror punk. It wasn't a widespread movement and largely centered on two bands, the Cramps and the Misfits. The horror imagery is more spoofy, likely influenced by B movie horror films. The Misfits formed a somewhat sludgier kind of high-energy punk, while the Cramps created their own genre, psychobilly, a combination of rockabilly and punk.

## Post-Punk

The other answer to the problem of punk's limited musical approach came from former Buzzcocks member Howard Devoto's new band Magazine. Magazine's 1978 song "Shot by Both Sides" retained the energy and vision of punk but was musically more adventurous. The song showed signs of the future by being dark and melodramatic rather than exhibiting the nihilism and aggressiveness with which punk was starting to become associated.[26]

Post-punk is a musically risk-taking, more experimental offshoot of punk. For the post-punks, punk at its core meant freedom. And that freedom meant going outside the punk rock structure while maintaining the punk energy and attitude. And it also dared to look inward, to portray how it felt to live within the chaos and uncertainty of the Generation Jones era. Public Image Ltd., Gang of Four, Wire, and Siouxsie and the Banshees were some of the first bands after Magazine to solidify this new direction.

Yet, the post-punk designation was deceptive. In 1977, before the term post-punk was in use or the abovementioned British bands made their mark, four American bands—Devo, Pere Ubu, Television, and the Talking Heads—released groundbreaking albums that would later be called post-punk classics.

Although there was no definitive proto post-punk sound, there were commonalities in post-punk at the beginning of the genre. There was often a rhythm guitar style inspired by reggae or funk.[27] The term most often used to describe this was either a nervous- or jagged-sounding guitar. Sometimes the bass drove the music. Perhaps it was featured prominently to distinguish the new sound from punk and rock music, where the bass was subordinate to other instruments.[28]

What post-punk bands also had in common was a thematic shift from punk. For some, the politics of punk were too overt and preachy. So post-punk songs were often about how power affects people personally in their everyday lives and how larger forces shape their feelings.[29]

Musically, that's shown in other characteristics of post-punk such as dour vocals with erudite lyrics, guitars that play texturally not melodically with sometimes a funk or dance groove, and a melodic bass line including echoing sound effects inspired by dub reggae.[30] While punk is characterized by simplicity and aggression, post-punk features a more complex, introverted aesthetic.[31]

## Subgenre: Post-Punk Traditionalists

The pioneers of this subgenre may be the Los Angeles band X. From nearly the beginning of their career, they incorporated rockabilly, country, and blues influences. While the Year Zero ideology rejected almost all previous pop and rock music, the traditional post-punk sound that X and other bands like the Gun Club made opened the door to past rock genres that many punks scorned.

This was different from most post-punk because it wasn't musically experimental. Instead, it looked to the past and asked: Is there anything we can incorporate to musically break out of the limits of the punk genre? Are there any kindred spirits we missed?

Most of the inspiration came from what later was called roots music or Americana music. This was American music that was purer and more basic, particularly rockabilly, country, and gospel. These post-punkers even reexamined the blues and traditional rock genres, something the original punks discarded. The goal in this post-punk subgenre was to eliminate the excesses of 1960s and 1970s blues and rock and strip those genres to their absolute basics.

## Subgenre: Goth

Goth music is influenced by Gothic literature from the Victorian era. It is not surprising, then, that the Goth subgenre of post-punk started in England , a country with a rich tradition of Gothic literature.[32]

The qualities that carried over into the Goth subgenre of post-punk include theatricality; anti-consumerism; a preoccupation with death; supernatural occurrences; unrequited, ill-fated, or all-consuming love; and living in the underground or on the fringes away from society.[33]

Gothic fiction was an escape from everyday industrial and modern English life into something more ancient containing ritual and ceremony as well as magic and mystery.[34] Similarly, Goth music was an attempt to find something more ancient, romantic, and spiritual to counteract the grimness, industrial decay, and economic downturn of the late 1970s.

Bauhaus, Siouxsie and the Banshees, Xmal Deutschland, the Birthday Party, Sisters of Mercy, and some songs by the Cure and Joy Division continued some of the traditional traits of Goth. In some cases, there was an emphasis on the supernatural, while other Goth songs fused the reality of everyday life with the dark vision of Goth. Musically, the songs could include cutting guitar sounds, high-pitched bass lines, hypnotic dirge-like beats that are sometimes tribal-sounding, and a droning vocal style.[35]

## Subgenre: No Wave

With its name a play on the term new wave, no wave was a deconstructionist form of music that was avant-garde using an abrasive minimalism rather than expansive experimentation. Rather than find a new format in post-punk variations, no wave musicians sought to destroy the form of anything punk or traditional rock and roll. Instead of using electronic instruments to get away from rock, they used conventional rock instruments to turn the rock genre against itself.[36]

This was yet another Generation Jones–era reaction to the grimness and disillusionment of the late 1970s. The collapse of musical form reflected the external collapse of

New York where no wave formed. Producer Brian Eno captured four of the best bands from this movement (The Contortions, DNA, Mars, and Teenage Jesus and the Jerks) in the legendary compilation *No New York*. But the true soul of the movement may be guitarist Glenn Branca, whose music contained a hypnotic, symphonic-like quality.

## Subgenre: Noise Punk

The decline of no wave didn't mean the end of the avant-garde and the subversive dismantling of conventional rock and punk. Out of the ashes of no wave came noise punk (also called noise rock). Unlike no wave, these songs are somewhat more conventional and not as reductionist. Still, bands like Sonic Youth, the Swans, and Big Black subverted traditional rock structures with dissonance and sometimes alternate tunings that created a disconcerting tone.

Central to this sound is playing guitars to squeeze out every noise possible or create as dirty a sound as possible. It's as if the guitar is an avant-garde instrument sabotaging and destroying the conventions of the listener's expectations. At times noise punk's goal is to create discomfort within a more structured song format.

## Subgenre: Jangle Post-Punk

Punk didn't just rebel against guitar hero blues-based rock music. It also eliminated what came to be called the jangle guitar. This bright sound was associated with 1960s bands such as the Beatles, the Byrds, and the folk-rock genre of the mid–1960s. For punks, guitars meant distortion, not the jangle guitar that became almost an electric version of folk guitar strumming.

But as post-punk unfolded, musicians looked for other sounds to break out of the limitations of the punk genre. A few bands reworked the once maligned jangle guitar, sometimes combining it with a post-punk edginess and an overall dirtier sound. This may have started with Scottish bands such as Josef K and the Fire Engines who integrated that sound with post-punk, but perhaps what solidified the new jangle punk was the Feelies' debut album, *Crazy Rhythms*, in 1980. R.E.M. later slowed down the frenetic pace of jangle punk on their *Chronic Town* EP, and the Smiths also integrated the jangle guitar into their eclectic sound.

# Ska

Punks rejected blues-based music. That's because blues was deeply assimilated into traditional rock, which punks distanced themselves from. But English punks embraced another form of music from Black culture: Jamaican music.[37]

Jamaican music was a byproduct of the influx of Jamaican immigrants to Britain in the post–World War II years. Because Jamaica was a British colony until 1962, Jamaican migrants came to Britain to meet the postwar labor shortage.[38] So Jamaicans integrated into working-class English towns. Because Jamaicans were in such proximity to the English, over time Jamaican music impacted the English working class more than American R&B or blues music.[39]

Three Jamaican musical genres ultimately influenced what came to be called second wave ska. That included not just the original era of ska but also rocksteady and reggae. Each one was progressively slower. The more upbeat, faster, and often instrumental genre of ska started in the late 1950s. In 1966, the medium-tempo rocksteady emerged, influenced by American soul music containing more emotion. In the late 1960s, the slower genre of reggae originated along with its subgenre of dub, which emphasized an echo-based sound.

In ska, there was a syncopation with accents on the offbeat or afterbeat, which gives the music a choppy feel.[40] The second and fourth beats of each bar are emphasized rather than the first and third as they are in rock music.[41]

Although the musical style of reggae was much different from punk, there was a social class consciousness in reggae missing from other contemporary music genres. This was largely because of the influence of the Rastafarian religion, which gave reggae a spiritual intensity and apocalyptic perspective that influenced punk.[42] Jamaican singers also often sang about economic oppression, crime, and societal corruption, which the punks also related to.

The challenge was how to integrate these two genres. The Clash used a punk foundation to incorporate reggae rhythms in songs like their cover of "Police and Thieves." The Specials formulated second wave ska by taking the staccato pulse of sixties ska and intensifying it with punk's energy.[43] This was the integration that led to a genre that combined Jamaican music with the energy of punk. The Specials bookended the genre's chart success with the release of their first album in October 1979 and their haunting single "Ghost Town" in June 1981.

Second wave ska diminished because ska faced the problem punk did after punk's initial blast of energy and influence. How do you transcend a limited format? Some bands tried. The Selecter's *Celebrate the Bullet* and the Specials' *More Specials* could have been the foundation for a kind of post-ska genre, an equivalent to how post-punk grew out of punk. But neither the media nor the public were as receptive as they were to the initial records by the second wave ska bands. The disintegration of second wave ska was also the result of the fickle music industry and music publications. They were on to something new: the image-conscious New Romantics and synth-pop bands.

## A New Era Emerges

Post-punk bands like Cabaret Voltaire, Throbbing Gristle, and Devo experimented with keyboards. But from 1978 to 1981, another synthesizer-based sound emerged. It used synthesizers not as a textural layer but as a melody instrument to give the song its "hook."[44]

The foundation of this music was the so-called krautrock of German keyboard-based bands such as Kraftwerk. But what came to be called synth-pop took this in a new direction. Despite the radical musical change of using keyboards, many of these songs in 1979 and 1980 still largely expressed a Generation Jones perspective, offering either social statements or a dark take on relationships. And as the punk guitar was basic, the keyboard sounds were simplistic in punk's DIY spirit. But from 1981 on, synth-pop become less challenging, more blatantly commercial, and changed the subject matter to love songs consistent with traditional pop.

That was largely fueled by the New Romantic movement with bands like Visage, Spandau Ballet, and Culture Club that embraced a glitzier image and a sound that mixed synth-pop with pop, glam, disco, and R&B. Duran Duran from Birmingham crafted an image of suave androgyny different from the more theatrical androgyny of London-based New Romantics. Duran Duran helped steer music away from the realism of punk, post-punk, and ska.

"There's been too much involvement in politics, and people trying to say things through music," Duran Duran bassist John Taylor said in a 1981 interview. "I hope now we're one of the main bands getting back to showbiz in the purest sense."[45]

"It's more escapism rather than commenting on what's going on," said Duran Duran's singer Simon Le Bon about the band's music. "It's more forgetting about what's going on and having a good time." He added that he lamented the punk era because "somewhere along the line somebody thought you got to learn from it, it's got to be educational, it's got to mean something, and that took all the fun out of it."[46]

Punk and post-punk didn't take off in America largely because of resistant radio, but from the beginning the new video channel MTV was ready to play the New Romantics.[47] This music wasn't just another trend. It reflected the ambition and individualism of the Reagan and Thatcher eras, the desire to stand out through fashion and being successful.[48] The new pop the New Romantics created wasn't rebellious and instead embraced the star system and desired success.[49] The emphasis on glamour, success, and indulgence helped usher in a new era of materialism, prosperity, and yuppie culture as the 1980s progressed.

By 1984, it was, to borrow the title of Dave Rimmer's book about the new 1980s pop, "like punk never happened." The punk, post-punk, and ska of Generation Jones started to decline in 1981 and were basically over by 1982, with some stragglers persisting into 1983. Over time, however, punk, post-punk, second wave ska, and their subgenres have come to be regarded as comprising a golden era with songs that remain relevant.

# The Guide
## *Punk, Post-Punk and Second Wave Ska, 1976–1983*

## 7 Seconds

***Skins, Brains, and Guts* 7" EP December 4, 1982 (Alternative Tentacles VIRUS 15) (USA)**

Detonating nine songs in 11 minutes, the Nevada band's first release is an early example of what came to be called positive hardcore. That's hardcore music that is more inclusive and a reaction against prejudice, apathy, and nihilism. In "Redneck Society" the band targets those who "believe in old time standards, like guns and bigotry." There are anti-racism songs such as "Racism Sucks" and "Anti-Klan." The EP culminates in the best song, "We're Gonna Fight" with its Clash-like declaration that "we're gonna fight the narrow minds."

***Committed for Life* 7" EP July 1983 (Squirtdown SQ 359) (USA)**

The band targets the hardcore punk scene itself in "Bottomless Pit," which condemns the aggressive mosh pits at hardcore punk concerts. The "macho thrash" moshers "can't be yourself, you're just an image of what's cool." "Drug Control" advocates a straight edge ideology, while "This Is the Angry" returns to a theme from their first EP: speaking for the oppressed.

**Genre:** Hardcore Punk

## 23 Skidoo

**"Last Words" b/w "The Gospel Comes to New Guinea" 12" September 1981 (Fetish FE11) (UK)**

This British band blends post-punk, funk, and world music with an emphasis on funk. "Last Words" features an infectious up-tempo groove. Even better is "New Guinea," an eerie instrumental piece propelled by a jazz drumming link with chants and a rumbling bass line that makes it a post-punk lament about colonization.

**Genre:** Post-punk

## 45 Grave

**"Black Cross" 45 August 7, 1981 (Goldar Records 1401) (USA)**

This California band with vocalist Dinah Cancer is basically hardcore punk blended with early versions of what eventually was known as crossover thrash, horror punk, and deathrock. The dramatic stops and starts make this memorable, as do Cancer's vocals, which mix punk and horror punk.

**Genre:** Hardcore punk

## 999

### "Nasty Nasty" b/w "No Pity" 45 October 21, 1977 (United Artists UP 37299) (UK)

Underneath the Johnny Rotten–style snarl is a condemnation of all things nasty, with the word "nasty" repeated twice for emphasis. Who's nasty? Hooligans looking for a fight, all types of liars, competition, and the media. The theme continues with the B-side "No Pity," another 1977 blast of energy.

### "Emergency" b/w "My Street Stinks" 45 January 13, 1978 (United Artists UP 36399) (UK)

The chorus verges on a pop punk sound. But it's a powerful song with a delivery at times that verges on a kind of pre-rap. "My Street Stinks" goes back to the straightforward energy of their "Nasty Nasty" single.

### "Homicide" 45 October 20, 1978 (United Artists UP 36467) (UK)

Perhaps the catchiest song with a word for murder in its chorus. It's a disturbing song about justification for murder and acceptance of violence. Universal enough that it could apply to other situations where violence seems to be expected.

**Genre:** Punk

## !Action Pact!

### *Heathrow Touchdown* split 7" EP November 1981 (Subversive ANARCHO ONE) (UK)

If this Brit band had released the same songs in 1977, they probably would have been acclaimed as one of punk's great bands. But time has been kind to this band, making their music now an overlooked treasure, including their debut record, which was a split 45 with two songs by Dead Man's Shadow on the other side.

Action Pact's two songs both have an anti-violent message. "London Bouncers" speaks out against excessive force used by bouncers. "All Purpose Action Footwear" is an ode to boots that are meant for good times and dancing. "London Bouncers" was later rerecorded and rereleased in 1983. But stick with this original punky version.

### *Suicide Bag* 7" EP August 29, 1982 (Fallout FALL 003) (UK)

The band builds on their first record by deepening their social observations starting with the menacing title track. "Stanwell" is about the oppression of their hometown, while "Blue Blood" condemns the elite. Features vocals from singer George Cheex, the stage name for Alison Roberts, one of this era's most animated female singers.

### *People* 7" EP March 1983 (Fallout FALL 010) (UK)

The band's third release is another gem that's perhaps their best EP. It expands their sound while still maintaining their energy. The title track calls out ambitious social climbers, while "Times Must Change" seems to criticize the trendy New Romantic

movement. "Sixties Flicks" disses nostalgia Brit 1960s movies from *A Hard Day's Night* to *Georgy Girl* as overrated and outdated while also dismissing 1960s fashion.
**Genre:** Punk

## The Adicts

### *Songs of Praise* LP October 29, 1981 (Dwed SMT 008) (UK)

The Adicts don't neatly fit into any category of punk. And that's a good thing. *Songs of Praise* combines and alternates between straight-ahead punk, pop punk, and with some Oi! around the edges in some of the choruses.

The album starts with the rousing anti-war song "England," "Distortion" critiques the media, and "Viva La Revolution" is about the nature of rebellion and power. "Calling Calling" asks a series of questions about why there is such injustice and trouble in the world. "Numbers" is about being enslaved and feeling like a number. Of the pop punk songs, the best may be "Hurt," which in Buzzcocks style is catchy pop punk.
**Genre:** Punk/Pop Punk

## Adolescents

### *The Adolescents* LP April 22, 1981 (Frontier FLP 1003) (USA)

This album captures California punk in the sweet spot between the initial blast of punk and hardcore. That means it's a faster, more intense punk, but not the full-blown hardcore punk that came to dominate starting in 1982. Because it's before the genre became so limited and rigid musically with hardcore, there's a variance in the tempos and styles of each song that makes every song memorable.

Many songs are about emerging from adolescence trying to make sense of the world. And what they see is disturbing. There's the Generation Jones boredom that always seems to lead to trouble in "Wrecking Crew." In "Rip It Up" there's the threat of violence the singer is fed up with. "Self-Destruct," "Losing Battle," and "No Way" all have a sense of despair. In "Creatures," the singer is partly in despair, partly angry from feeling like an outsider unable to fit in with any group. "Democracy" expresses the Generation Jones disillusionment with any possibility of political solutions. Political parties are all corrupt, and things are so bad it could all lead to World War III, which "Welcome to Reality" is also about.

With its power pop one-word chorus, "Amoeba" became the band's best-known song. The album's *tour de force*, however, is the epic "The Kids of the Black Hole," a dystopian communal living that's a punk rock *Lord of the Flies* where they live "carefree in their actions, as for morals they had none." The song shows that the hippie utopian ideal of a subculture living together isn't going to work, perhaps because in this generation young people are just too damaged.

### *Welcome to Reality* 7" EP October 1981 (Frontier FRT 101) (USA)

The band takes a sharp turn into darker territory. "Losing Battle" is so angst-filled the singer appears suicidal and questions a god "who'll damn you to hell then tell you to love." To emphasize this darkness, the EP's other two songs are slower and less frenetic, including the title track, which is an apocalyptic glimpse of end-times with imagery from the Book of Revelation.
**Genre:** Punk

## The Adverts

### "One Chord Wonders" b/w "Quickstep" 45 April 22, 1977 (Stiff BUY 13) (UK)

Both sides of this single are defiant songs about punk music detractors. "One Chord Wonders" (rerecorded for the band's first album) pushes back on an early common condemnation of punk: they were too DIY and not virtuoso musicians. But the Adverts repeat "we don't give a damn" to end the song. The B-side continues the early punk theme by saying the band was formed to escape oppression. Also notable for the picture sleeve with its now iconic image of bassist Gaye Advert.

### "We Who Wait" (B-side of "Safety in Numbers") 45 October 28, 1977 (Anchor ANC 1047) (UK)

A compelling song about the deprived and downtrodden who wait for a break and never get it. An almost spiritual psalm-like feeling of abandonment pervades. The agony of waiting is so painful that people turn to everything from apathy, anarchy, and anger to escape.

### *Crossing the Red Sea* LP February 17, 1978 (Bright BRL 201) (UK)

Seminal early British punk album. On songs like "Bombsite Boy," the band sounds like they're reporting from a war zone. Other times it sounds like a punk apocalypse with songs about crime, violence, and angry unrest. But within all of the distress are some songs that are so defiant they sound like anthems.

"Bored Teenagers" is another punk song that confronts boredom, the malady of the late 1970s. It's an affliction that produces such a void that it leads to alienation. "On the Roof" with its tempo changes is about a higher place of transcendence, a place to escape the crime on the street below. Other songs that turn into dystopian-like anthems include "No Time to Be 21," about an English underclass, and "Safety in Numbers," which describes the hope and demise of a new musical movement ("What about the new wave? Did you think it would change things?"). It ends with "Great British Mistake," the album's most complete vision of a declining dystopian England that uses horror imagery at times.

### *Cast of Thousands* LP October 12, 1979 (RCA PL 25246) (UK)

This album was largely dismissed after its release because it was so different from their first album, one of the great straight-ahead British punk albums. Like other punk bands, the Adverts faced the dilemma about how to go beyond the limited punk music structure. They did it very differently from other bands of their era. It's punk at times but also includes pop, almost theatrical music, and even elements of Goth. Yet it still has a punk spirit. It's one of the most unique and uncategorizable albums of its era.

The title track details an array of problems in society of corruption and crime in an almost subversive theatrical-like song. "My Place" is probably the catchiest song with a pop punk like chorus of a down-and-out-person, who, although he is "on the ropes, … live[s] on hope of better days." Another song with a catchy pop punk chorus but that includes an almost Gregorian-like chant in the background is "Television's Over." The most straight-ahead punk songs are the sarcastic "Love Songs" and "Male Assault," which contains some Cold War fear but also critiques the hypermasculine ideology behind war. It all ends with "I Will Walk You Home," an ambivalent mixture of reassurance and fear.

"Back from the Dead" (B-side of "Television's Over") 45 November 3, 1978 (RCA PB 5128) (UK)

A song about being at the edge of despair but deciding to go on. And about choosing life over death and hopelessness. This recalls the straight-ahead punk of their first album.
**Genre:** Punk

## Agent Orange

### "Bloodstains" on the *Rodney on the ROQ compilation* LP October 11, 1980 (Posh Boy PBS 106) (USA)

The band's best song was rerecorded for both their first EP and album. But this version is the fiercest. The yearning of American consumerism to live out a "stupid fantasy" of hedonism leads to a type of derangement.

### *Agent Orange* 7" EP October 18, 1980 (Agent Orange 245 T-1) (USA)

There's elements of the coming cowpunk and early hardcore music. And a heavy sense of disillusionment. "America" expresses disenchantment and sarcasm about patriotism, war, and the media. In "Bored with You" it's the punk scene itself that is endangered by fashion conformity and excessive drinking and drug use.

### *Living in Darkness* LP November 19, 1981 (Posh Boy PBS 122) (USA)

Along with the Adolescents' first album, this is one of the seminal California punk albums before California punk became mostly hardcore punk. It's almost Gothic-like in the lyrics with a sense of gloom and the weight of confused isolation. At times there's a despair with a post-punk sense of an emphasis on internal pain. Some of the songs are slower and somewhat sludgy-sounding to reflect the Gothic-like darkness.

The album starts with a sense of fear about what appears to be nuclear war in "Too Young to Die." But as this album consistently does, there's also a sense of inner distress. So the imagery could be what the singer imagines about his own life blowing up. In "Everything Turns Grey" the sense of dread continues, with the singer wishing the world could be different but realizing it can't be. "No Such Thing" expresses disillusionment with love, while "A Cry for Help in a World Gone Mad" is about discouragement with friends and with how punk hasn't changed the world as much as he hoped it would. "The Last Goodbye" is a goodbye to a world the singer can't understand. By the end of the album, on the title track, the singer is so disenchanted he has isolated himself from a world he can't successfully integrate into.

### *Bitchin' Summer* 12" EP September 1982 (Posh Boy PBS 1037) (USA)

Perhaps this EP is why the band is so associated with skate punk, where skateboards became an urban substitute for surfboards. The Revillos and B-52s incorporated surf guitar, but Agent Orange punked up three 1960s surf instrumentals. It also includes the frenzied "Breakdown," a song decrying commercialism.
**Genre:** Punk

## Agnostic Front

### *United Blood* 7" EP December 1983 (Agnostic Front AF 001) (USA)

New York City band injects their East Coast brashness to the hardcore punk genre that at first was dominated by California bands. It's all New York street attitude here. They're defiant and tough. They're largely short bursts of anger, most under a minute long. And it features a more heavy metal–influenced guitar sound.

**Genre:** Hardcore Punk

## Akrylykz

### "Smart Boy" b/w "Spyderman" 45 January 17, 1980 (Double R RED 2) (UK)

The ska phenomenon that dominated the British charts in 1979 and 1980 inspired some good indie ska singles. "Smart Boy" features an infectious Madness-like sax riff. Vocals are by Roland Gift, who would later be the singer in Fine Young Cannibals. The B-side is even better, with Gift doing some fast phrasing over a frenzied beat.

### "Ska'd For Life" (B-side of "J.D.") 45 June 27, 1980 (Polydor 2059 253) (UK)

This is up there with Madness's "One Step Beyond" as an instant dance party generator. There's an infectious saxophone and scratching guitar with some toasting over it. Although signed to a major label, rumor has it the band never recorded a full album because the label dropped them after the ska craze subsided. Too bad.

**Genre:** Ska

## The Alarm

### "Unsafe Building" 45 December 9, 1981 (White Cross none) (UK)

The Welsh band's first single contains a punk ethos largely within a traditional rock sound with post-punk guitar riffs around the edges. The lyrics use the metaphor of a condemned building as a symbol for the life of a young person who must establish a new identity or face demolition and destruction. The band later rerecorded this song. But find the indie 45.

**Genre:** Proto Post-punk

## Alley Cats

### "Nothing Means Anything Anymore" b/w "Give Me a Little Pain" 45 March 30, 1978 (Dangerhouse LOM-22) (USA)

One of the most important early California punk songs from Los Angeles trio. With its dark imagery and disturbing rockabilly-like vocal quivers, this sounds like an early version of the punk-meets-roots music that X and the Gun Club would also play. If William Faulkner wrote punk music, it might have sounded like this. The B-side is almost horror punk with its ironic chorus.

### "Too Much Junk" (from *Yes L.A.* compilation LP) April 12, 1979 (Dangerhouse EW-79) (USA)

Bassist Dianne Chai takes the vocals on this song with angst about politicians, the media, and the superficiality of popular dance music. There's just too much shallow junk culture everywhere, she declares. This version on the one-sided Dangerhouse compilation is better than the rerecorded version on *Nightmare City*.

*Nightmare City* **LP August 19, 1981 (Time Coast TC2201) (USA)**

Too much of the bite goes out of this band because of the production, which compresses the music and buries the vocals. Despite this, the best parts of this album rank as essential despite the production working against them. Until there's a remix of this album, we'll take this.

Like the band X, they unflinchingly portray the seedy underbelly of Los Angeles. There's an urban perspective that contrasts with some other Southern California punk and hardcore bands that put suburbia as their epicenter. As in some film noir, Los Angeles itself becomes more than a setting but like a character in the story.

The album sets its noir-like tone with the haunting opening song "Nightmare City," with its poetic description of the range of people who inhabit an urban underground. The lead vocals on the songs alternate between Randy Stodola and Dianne Chai, who provide different perspectives on their observations of the city. And everything seems immersed in a dark struggle on songs like "One More Chance to Survive," "King of the Street Fights," and "Black Haired Girl."

**Genre:** Punk

## Altered Images

### "Dead Pop Stars" b/w "Sentimental" 45 February 27, 1981 (Epic EPC A1023) (UK)

On their first album, this Scottish band led by singer and soon-to-be actress Claire Grogan took a direction into a quirky new wave pop band that incorporated some post-punk around the edges. But on the band's debut single, they were a bona fide post-punk band produced by Banshees bass player Steve Severin.

The A-side is a sarcastic take on the appeal of dead rock stars who are merchandised to a younger generation. Although performances of the song predated the death of John Lennon, that event prevented the song from having chart success. The moody B-side is even better with atmospheric guitar.

### "A Day's Wait" 45 May 8, 1981 (Epic EPC A1167) (UK)

Moody mysterious meditation on the implications of a late train. The long instrumental beginning adds to the anticipation. And Grogan's vocals get more agitated over the course of the song, adding more gravitas to it all.

**Genre:** Post-punk

## Alternative TV

### *The Image Has Cracked* LP May 5, 1978 (Depford Fun City DLP 01) (UK)

On their debut album, Alternative TV shows how they aren't going to play by the rules. Why not start the album with nine minutes of audience members being called onstage to say whatever they want? Why not record a cool-sounding riff for two minutes?

This album was also released when the heyday of original punk was ending and post-punk was emerging. So there's a fascinating overlap between the two genres.

At times it's more straight-ahead punk, like the sarcastic "Vive Le Rock and Roll" and the punked-up cover of the Mothers of Invention garage blues song "Why Don't You Do Me Right?" But there's also the shredding guitar post-punk of "Still Life" and the intoxicating three-minute Goth-like heavy riffing that ends "Nasty Little Lonely." "Action Time and Vision" is almost pop punk. As if there's no way to add up all the

pieces of everything that came before, the ending "Splitting in Two" is about an identity crisis. But the variety here is the strength of this album.
**Genre:** Punk/Post-punk

## Angelic Upstarts

### "I'm an Upstart" 45 April 6, 1979 (Warner Bros. K 17354) (UK)

Like Sham 69, the British punk/oi band with its foot-stomping football chant chorus over Ramones-influenced buzz saw guitar triumphs in the best of their singles. Lots of righteous working-class frustration here.

### "Teenage Warning" 45 July 26, 1979 (Warner Bros. K 17426) (UK)

A cautionary proclamation from the younger generation about how it's "no satisfaction, it's all frustration" and how punk bands feel alienated from the emerging new wave movement where "if you don't look right your days are numbered."

### "Never 'Ad Nothing" 45 October 20, 1979 (Warner Bros. K 17476) (UK)

A story that could come out of a gangster movie or a reggae song. A down-and-outer wants to use his gun for glory in the media. The sing-along pop chorus about someone who wants to "go out in a puff of smoke" makes it perhaps their catchiest song.

### "Kids on the Streets" 45 January 16, 1981 (Zonophone Z16) (UK)

Somewhat contrived but still an irresistible anthem. It's somewhat of a continuation of Sham 69's "If the Kids Are United." And the band distances itself from the white nationalism of some skinheads and Oi! bands. "All you kids black and white, together we are dynamite," the song commands.
**Genre:** Punk/Oi!/Street Punk

## Antidote

### *Thou Shalt Not Kill* 7" EP 1983 (Antidote ARI-1) (USA)

This solidified the New York hardcore sound and served as a blueprint for the future of hardcore punk and crossover thrash.
**Genre:** Hardcore Punk

## Anti-Pasti

### "Six Guns" 45 January 8, 1982 (Rondelet ROUND 10) (UK)

Transcends the standard English street punk/oi formula. The innovative guitar rhythms lead into a triumphant infectious Clash-like chorus. This is less cliché Oi! than a throwback to late 1970s righteous British punk.
**Genre:** Punk/Oi!/Street Punk

## Articles of Faith

### *What We Want Is Free* 7" EP November 1982 (Dub 002) (USA)

Chicago band starts their debut record off with the desperate "Everyday," an angry song about feeling trapped. It's a harrowing cry for help from someone tormented by deadening repetition. It's a blend of traditional punk, hardcore punk, and even some heavy metal and hard rock guitar.

It's followed by three hardcore scorchers. "My Father's Dreams" rebels against family expectations, while "Bad Attitude" is directed at those who've mislabeled the singer. "What We Want is Free" offers a solution to all the angst and ends the record with a declaration that entrapment awaits from being bought off by corporate demands. What the singer ultimately wants is what money can't buy.

### *Wait* 7" EP June 1983 (Affirmation none) (USA)

The outstanding song here is the opening "I've Got Mine," a Clash-like rocker with some reggae rhythms, blistering guitar, and swirling guitars. If production could be described as apocalyptic, this is it. It sounds like it was recorded in a war zone. The other two tracks—"Wait" and the frenetic anti-war song "Buy This War"—return to the straight-ahead hardcore punk of their first record.

**Genre:** Punk/Hardcore Punk

## The Associates

### *The Affectionate Punch* LP August 1, 1980 (Fiction 2383 585) (UK)

Scottish band has Berlin-era Bowie as an influence on this album, in the quirky music, the vocal phrasing, and the moody atmosphere of singer Billy Mackenzie's vocals, and the guitar of Alan Rankine, which is a constant force around the edges of the music, adding an important tension.

The record was rereleased two years later, however, with a slick 1980s remix and some new overdubs that particularly de-emphasize this innovative guitar playing to make it more listener-friendly for New Romantic–era listeners. Make sure to track down the original 1980 album or a rerelease of that mix.

In its original version, it's a post-punk record different from the more synth-pop direction they eventually would go in. One highlight is "Paper House," with a haunting vocal, a march-like drum part, and a ferocious guitar part. "Transport to Central" goes for a more mysterious sound, almost like a soundtrack to a post-punk science fiction film. The clever "A" ends the album with some Scottish jangle punk style guitar and Mackenzie's playful vocal delivery.

**Genre:** Post-punk

## Au Pairs

### *You* 7" EP October 1, 1979 (021 Records OTO2) (UK)

The ferocious "You" is a near punk song about a woman labeled as a fallen woman because of her past. The song contains a feminist theme that continues throughout most of the band's career: the depersonalization of women. "Domestic Departure," featuring a back-and-forth between male and female vocalists, introduces what will be another major theme in the band's work: the tension underlying traditional gender roles. "Kerb Crawler" is about how women feel vulnerable and afraid when out alone.

### "Diet" (B-side of "It's Obvious") 45 December 5, 1980 (021 Records OTO4) (UK)

Non-album flip side is about a housewife who takes pills to neutralize the oppression of traditional gender roles. More than acute pain, it's a loss of identity.

The oppression creates her descent from having no political views to having no views at all.

### *Playing with a Different Sex* LP May 13, 1981 (Human Records Human1) (UK)

There's more sophisticated production than their earlier singles and the album intensifies their version of funk-inspired post-punk. Singer Lesley Woods continues to explore people's motivations in relationships. Often it involves oppression of women. In "We're So Cool," a man approves of having an open relationship but wants to still be reassured that the woman will be dedicated to him. In "Love Song," a marriage is compared to a business deal. In "Set-Up," a woman must suppress her identity to please her husband. "Unfinished Business" depicts the shallowness of a casual affair where the woman feels used and unvalued.

Woods also sings about the forces that create these issues, such as in "Headache for Michelle" and "Armagh," which focuses on the torture and subjugation of women in a Northern Irish prison. The ending track, "It's Obvious," features a blistering post-punk guitar and a driving bass guitar line with its explosive chorus of "you're equal but different."

### "Inconvenience" b/w "Pretty Boys" 45 July 31, 1981 (Human Records HUM8) (UK)

The band revs up the funk for the danceable A-side about transactional sexual affairs. In this case it's adulterous ones that are "a break from monotonous monogamy." The funk groove is slower on the B-side over a sarcastic vocal about how both genders are defined by physical appearance.

**Genre:** Post-punk

## Avengers

### *We Are the One* 7" EP December 1977 (Dangerhouse SFD-400) (USA)

One of American punk's great early moments. In the title track, this Northern California punk band shows an idealism and hope influenced by Brit punk. Singer Penelope Houston sings "I am the one who brings you the future, I am the one that buries the past," and it sounds like she could lead a revolution. "I Believe in Me" features a chorus of self-empowerment interspersed with improvised verses speaking directly to doubters and haters who tell her not to believe in herself. "Car Crash" turns faster and bleaker in a song about sudden death possibly caused by self-destruction. America wasn't ready for this brilliant punk at this early stage of punk, so this EP was—shamefully—generally overlooked.

### *Avengers* 12" EP 1979 (White Noise WNR 002) (USA)

Two years after their initial EP, the band is still making righteous punk with piercing social observations. The standout track is "The American in Me" with its declaration of "ask not what you can do for your country, what's your country been doing to you?" "Uh-Oh" is a cautionary tale about a woman who is beautiful and mysterious but something disturbing underneath, while "Corpus Christi" contains religious imagery. The EP ends with "White N," with a raucous vocal about the white underclass that doesn't understand how oppressed and compromised they are.

**Genre:** Punk

# B-52s

***B-52s* LP July 6, 1979 (Warner Bros. BSK-3355) (USA)**

Like Blondie's first album, the B-52s lift 1960s musical tropes (surf guitar, garage band organ) to both play tribute to them and subvert them. But it's not retro-sounding. And without campiness or parody. They merge an avant-garde sensibility with a pastiche of pop musical styles.

Side one of this album is about as perfect as it gets. There's the mysteriousness of "Planet Clare," the girl group tribute female vocals of "52 Girls," and the haunting "Dance This Mess Around." The climax of the side is "Rock Lobster," a free-for-all account of beach life with almost a childlike observation of what one can find in the ocean. It's both fun and dangerous, a theme that would continue through some of the band's other songs. And it features the surf guitar meets avant-garde meets punk guitar of Ricky Wilson with his innovative guitar tunings. That sound would become one of the band's trademarks along with the back-and-forth between male singer Fred Schneider and vocalists Cindy Wilson and Kate Pierson.

The second side includes "Hero Worship," with some Yoko Ono–like yelps in a song about obsessive devotion, and "606–0842," about an inability to communicate with someone. Their version of Petula Clark's "Downtown" is both deconstruction and innovation. It shows the yearning for urban fun among bands of this generation rather than the utopia of country living that hippies sometimes elevated.

***Wild Planet* LP August 27, 1980 (Warner Bros. BSK-3471) (USA)**

The songs are generally shorter and less experimental than their first album. The result is more controlled with a punk-like succinctness. And what's brilliant is that underneath the danceable music is a sense of trouble and disturbance. It's there right from the beginning in "Party Gone Out of Bounds" with party-crashers provoking the question "Who's to blame when situations degenerate? Disgusting things you never anticipate." "Private Idaho" shows the self-isolation coming from paranoia about the outside world. That manifests in wanting to retreat from a swimming pool with too many people and a dangerous radium clock at the bottom.

At times there's a sense of desperation. In "Give Me Back My Man," the singer will do just about anything to get her lover back. In "Runnin' Around," there's a frantic search for someone. In "Quiche Lorraine," the singer feels like he's going insane when he loses his poodle to a Great Dane (likely symbols for people). But through it all, the music is fun and danceable. "Having a good time on a crummy day is our game," Schneider says in "Quiche Lorraine," in what could be the band's statement of purpose.

**"Mesopotamia" 45 June 1982 (Warner Bros. 7–29971) (USA)**

The disappointing David Byrne–produced EP this song came from was a misfire. The title track released as a single, however, is a gem, a sign of a new direction for the band. They use a post-punk groove perhaps even funkier than "Quiche Lorraine" from *Wild Planet*.

***Whammy!* LP April 27, 1983 (Warner Bros. 1–2389) (USA)**

This album takes the post-punk fun of the band's first two albums and combines it with a new wave–friendly sound. Some may say they've crossed over into new wave pop.

But they still retain enough of their post-punk sensibility. Even the songs that sound the most accessible have a murky undercurrent.

It starts with "Legal Tender," about counterfeiters on the run from authorities who print phony money with pictures of "gangster presidents." In "Whammy Kiss," the singer wants his object of attention to create an almost spell-like control over him. The band is creative and eccentric even in their love songs. "Song for a Future Generation" is about the wonder of mating to create life. Just what kind of baby and adventure will come from it? "Big Bird" is about an ominous bird flying over a house. What does it symbolize? Who knows? In "Queen of Las Vegas," a mother's dying wish is for her child to be a successful gambler and win a lot of money. In "Butterbean," the beans become a mystical-like substance in the American South that unites community.

**Genre:** Post-punk

# Bad Brains

### *Black Dots* recorded June 1979, released October 1, 1996 LP (Caroline CAR 7534) (USA)

The Bad Brains (named after a Ramones song), initially based in Washington, D.C., are probably the biggest architect of hardcore punk. They didn't technically release the first hardcore punk song (that's generally credited to "Out of Vogue" by the Middle Class). They did, however, develop a new type of faster punk. And their onstage presence from their constant touring inspired numerous other hardcore bands. They didn't put out a full-length album until 1982. And they later released this album of demos. As raw as they are, the stripped-down sound might be the best music they recorded.

The band is fast fast fast but also very tight. Vocalist H.R.'s voice is like an instrument as well. At times—in "Black Dots," "At the Atlantis," and "Send You No Flowers"—he sounds like the fastest jazz or rapper you've ever heard. They also record an experiment with reggae in "The Man Won't Annoy Ya," something they would later expand on.

The Bad Brains critiqued what they saw around them, including the punk movement itself, such as in "How Low Can a Punk Go." "Banned in D.C." is about how they were prohibited from playing clubs in Washington, D.C., because of their raucous live shows. "Redbone in the City" sounds like a parody of the Sex Pistols, particularly with H.R. rolling his r's. As an antidote to some of the negativity surrounding them is in "Attitude" with its idea of "P.M.A." (positive mental attitude), a concept they adopted from motivational writer Napoleon Hill.

### "Pay to Cum" 45 June 23, 1980 (Bad Brains BB001) (USA)

Released on their own label, this minute-and-a-half scorcher was a breakthrough in hardcore punk. And because of the straightforward bare-bones production (basically just get out the way and let the band rip), it might be their finest moment.

### *Bad Brains* cassette album February 5, 1982 (ROIR A106) (USA)

The production is more compressed and not as raw as their initial single or the demo songs released on *Black Dots*. But their 1982 debut album is still monumental music in the hardcore punk genre. The album was also initially released just on a cassette tape that came to be also known as *The Yellow Album* because of the color of the cassette packaging cover.

But no matter what form or format it's in, *Bad Brains* is revolutionary hardcore punk. The leadoff track "Sailin' On" feels like a kiss-off to someone who doesn't understand. And from there, the album is driven by social commentary and an anti-authoritative spirit in songs such as "The Regulator," "Fearless Vampire Killers," and "The Big Takeover." The band also plays three convincing reggae songs on the album. "The Right Brigade" comes closest to a heavy metal song without the thrash speed. These songs show that even in this era the band didn't seem to want to be pigeonholed.

### *Rock for Light* LP April 15, 1983 (PVC Records PVC 8917) (USA)

Because of their erratic recording career, the Bad Brains don't receive as much credit as they deserve for being hardcore punk's most influential band. They should have also been the most successful. But unfortunately, they weren't. This album produced by Ric Ocasek of the Cars isn't the best showcase for their sound. And it's likely an attempt to get them to be more accessible. But the Bad Brains are the Bad Brains. They're so good we'll take what we can get in any form.

Rastafarian-inspired lyrics feature in, among other songs, the album's first track, "Coptic Times." One of the album's best songs is the ferocious "Destroy Babylon," which aims to rally listeners: "Organize, centralize, it's time for us to fight for our lives." The title track combines a spiritual perspective with music saying that music can be a vehicle to fight violence and war and to be a force for good. This is to counteract the superficiality of the entertainment industry, denounced in the blistering "At the Movies." They also include three excellent reggae songs (the title track, "Rally Around Jah Throne," and "The Meek Shall Inherit the Earth").

**Genre:** Hardcore Punk

## Bad Manners

### *Ska N' B* LP April 11, 1980 (Magnet MAGL 5033) (UK)

This is way off the mountaintop of two tone ska. While Madness from the beginning incorporated ska with pop, there's almost a novelty aspect at times with Bad Manners. Other times, there's a pop ska synthesis that succeeds. There's a divided aspect to this band. Are they half a step away from being a wedding band? Or is this a legitimate fusion of pop and ska?

On this album there's both. Bad Manners is most like a novelty band when delving into covers. On "Monster Mash" and "Wooly Bully," they're in wedding band turf. The single "Lip Up Fatty," with some Caribbean influence, is likable ska pop. The highlight is "Inner City Violence," the band's one foray into ska with a social statement.

For better or worse, this was a significant progression in ska. The band's brand of pop ska would be the major influence on third wave ska bands of the 1990s that largely veered away from the social statements of two tone ska.

**Genre:** Ska

## Bad Religion

### *Bad Religion* 7" EP February 1981 (Epitaph JBG-1072) (USA)

California band's debut EP adds a dirty and sludgy-sounding edge in the guitar playing. The EP starts off aiming at their targets of religion and the government. But as it goes on, it becomes almost dystopian in tone. "Slaves" chronicles how life for most people is living like a slave to a ruling class of masters. "Drastic Action" is a desperate song about feeling that life is futile, while the ending track—"World War III"— shows the fear of nuclear war so prevalent during the Generation Jones era.

**Genre:** Hardcore Punk

## The Bags

### "Survive" b/w "Babylonian Gorgon" 45 December 1978 (Dangerhouse BAG 199) (USA)

The A-side by this short-lived Los Angeles punk band with Alice Bag on vocals begins with finger snaps and jazzy instrumentation like a deranged prelude to a musical. But it's soon followed by fast-paced punk where vocalist Alice Bag depicts a postapocalyptic vision of young people in a city where "survival is the game." The B-side is another winning early West Coast punk song that channels some ancient imagery in the name of female punk rock empowerment.

**Genre:** Punk

## Honey Bane

### "Girl on the Run" from *You Can Be You* 7" EP December 1979 (Crass Records 521984/1) (UK)

Former singer of post-punk band Fatal Microbes turns out a harrowing punk song. It's a tragic story of a runaway girl who goes to London but ends up being sexually assaulted. After returning home, she's rejected yet again and experiences more tragedy.

**Genre:** Punk

## Basement 5

### *1965–1980* LP August 11, 1980 (Antilles AN 7082) (UK)

Originally the singer of this English band was Don Letts, an important influencer in early punk. By the time of their first and only album, the band's vocalist was Dennis Morgan, who was also a photographer for the Sex Pistols and Bob Marley.

Before second wave ska, punk bands experimented with how to incorporate Jamaican music and punk. But during the era of second wave ska, Basement 5 did something different. Instead of reaching back to first wave ska for inspiration, they combined punk, post-punk, and reggae. The album was produced by Joy Division producer Martin Hannett, which emphasizes the post-punk elements.

That starts with the opening track, "Riot," which is an electrifying reggae-meets-rock sound. "No Ball Games" is a combination of dub and industrial, while "Immigration" blends reggae, jazz, and post-punk. The punkiest song is the fierce "Last White Christmas," which is one of the great overlooked songs of this era.

### *In Dub* 12" EP October 31, 1980 (Island IPR 2038) (UK)

Rather than duplicate the reggae dub sound, which some bands in this era did, Basement 5 adds experimental post-punk instrumentation and sound effects as well as some jazz-like undertones in the percussion at times. This created a more alternative dub sound that post-punk bands could draw from.

**Genre:** Post-punk

# Bauhaus

### "Bela Lugosi's Dead" 12" August 6, 1979 (Small Wonder TEENY 2) (UK)

At more than nine minutes, this ode to *Dracula* movie star Bela Lugosi created the post-punk subgenre of Goth. But rather than a frenetic sound associated with post-punk, this song utilized a reggae-like groove using drum rhythms, echo effects, and a bass line consistent with dub music. The scratching guitars create tension and an eerie fluttering effect. But perhaps the song stood out as Gothic just as much by the lyrics, which have an array of vampire imagery including bats, bleeding victims, virginal brides, dead flowers, and the chant of "undead."

### "Dark Entries" 45 January 16, 1980 (Axis AXIS 3) (UK)

After releasing a nondescript straight-ahead post-punk single ("Terror Couple Kill Colonel"), the band must have realized that the Goth imagery of "Bela Lugosi's Dead" couldn't be a one-time thing. They were on to something. In this song, they use seedy Goth imagery of city streets at night that are "avenues of sin" with sordid and exploitative sexual encounters. And instead of the dub-like structure of "Bela Lugosi's Dead," the song is all energetic post-punk.

### *In the Flat Field* LP November 3, 1980 (4AD CAD 13) (UK)

With the success of their first singles that were Goth-oriented, Bauhaus creates what is probably the first full-fledged Goth album. Although they use some post-punk rhythms, there's a disconcerting and dark quality to the songs. And a descent into impulses the singer can't resist. That's apparent from the first song, "Double Dare," an invitation to be brave enough to go into the darkness. The title track says that the "flat field," the reality that most people live in, isn't satisfactory.

The album contains other themes that would come to dominate the Goth subgenre of post-punk. "God in an Alcove" is a kind of pagan homage about how spirituality is no longer associated with the natural world and has been reduced to only a part of life rather than all of existence. "Stigmata Martyr" is about stigmata effects that become a "scarlet bliss." "Dive" celebrates living an underworld type of nighttime life away from the daylight and mainstream culture. It concludes with the ominous "Nerves," with both a melodic piano line and discordant sounds, which returns to the opening for a Goth-like perspective into life in a state where "the fabric of dreams is ripped apart."

### "Telegram Sam" 45 November 5, 1980 (4AD AD 17) (UK)

Want to quickly understand how the punk/post-punk revolution differed from glam rock? Check out this remake of this song by the glam band T. Rex. There's something menacing about the characters in the song, like "jungle-faced Jake" and "purple pie Pete." And something sarcastic in the vocals that almost at times make it seem like a semi-parody of glam rock.

### "Satori" (B-side of "Kick in the Eye") 45 March 19, 1981 (Beggars Banquet BEG 54) (UK)

Along with the Creatures' *Wild Things* EP, this is some of the great percussion-based music of this era. It's both infectious and eerie. Named after a Buddhist term for enlightenment that is beyond words, it makes sense that it's an instrumental.

### *Mask* LP October 16, 1981 (Beggars Banquet BEGA 29) (UK)

Bauhaus pretty much created the Goth music genre with their first album, but the band won't be typecast. This time, they tone down the more unsettling Goth overtones. But they're still there. The most notable example is "Hollow Hills," with its references to fairies, goblins, and witches that sounds like it could be an outtake from their first album. But most of *Mask* is an exercise in exploring the possibilities of post-punk. It's an adventurous undertaking that is perhaps their most satisfying album.

The album's standout tracks are probably the lead track, "Hair of the Dog," which, ironically or not, implies withstanding more of what's undesirable to ultimately transcend the pain. "Man with the X-Ray Eyes" is based on a 1960s horror film. There's a variety here that didn't come across on their gloomy first album. "Kick in the Eye" and "Muscle in Plastic" are funk-fueled Gang of Four and Talking Heads–like songs, while "In Fear of Fear" is almost a combination of ska and post-punk. "Of Lilies and Remains" is spoken word; "Dancing" is Iggy Pop–like anarchy meets post-punk.

### *The Sky's Gone Out* LP October 22, 1982 (Beggars Banquet BEGA 42) (UK)

After one album of Goth-soaked music and another emphasizing their brand of post-punk, Bauhaus both adheres to and transcends the conventions of both genres. The album isn't the variety of post-punk styles that *Mask* is, but it revisits them on the first part of the album and goes into territory beyond post-punk on the second part.

It starts with a bouncy cover of Brian Eno's "Third Uncle," the slower post-punk of "Silent Hedges," and then the faster post-punk of "In the Night," featuring an explosion of words at the end almost like a rap song. "Swing the Parade" returns to the style of their first Goth-laced album. But it all gets deconstructed, and the song structures are stripped to their core. The almost 10-minute and mostly instrumental "The Three Shadows" is like a tone poem. It's followed by the acoustic-based "All We Ever Wanted" and ends with "Exquisite Corpse," a postapocalyptic song that fluctuates between genres and even includes a reggae riff.

**Genre:** Post-punk (Goth variation)

## Beshara

### "When You're Wrong" 45 August 1, 1980 (Voyage VOY 0015) (UK)

This British reggae band crossed over into ska that's instructional and righteous. Be wise, responsible, and admit mistakes, the band advises. Great groove, vocals, and production. Too bad they didn't do more of this.

**Genre:** Ska

## Big Black

### *Lungs* 12" EP November 16, 1982 (Ruthless RRBB02) (USA)

In the 1990s, musician Steve Albini would be a polished producer for Nirvana, the Breeders, and PJ Harvey. But on his own first album, it's appealingly low budget; he uses a drum machine and plays almost all the instruments himself. He takes some inspiration from the duo Suicide and the DIY ideology of punk to make a record that's both punk electronic music and one of the first noise punk records.

The songs integrate horror imagery into profiles of real people. Most of the songs are dark stories of disturbed people with something primal and violent about them. Highlights include "Steelworker," about a menacing blue-collar hunter who can "rip you from limb to limb"; "Live in a Hole," about someone who tries to be as uncivilized as possible; and "Dead Billy," a macabre story of soldier.

### *Bulldozer* 12" EP December 1983 (Ruthless RRBB07) (USA)

The dominant use of the drum machine on Big Black's first record *Lungs* made the sound musically repetitive. Here, Albini benefits from using a band instead of playing almost all the instruments himself. The result is a fuller and better record.

Albini still sticks to his theme of mixing the horrible with the real in his lyrics. A group of men go to a slaughterhouse for entertainment and even help out in "Cables." Birds are poisoned in "The Pigeon Kill," and "Seth" is about a man who trains his dog to bite Black people. "Texas" is about the fear of blue-collar rednecks, while "I'm a Mess" and "Jump the Climb" both continue Albini's consistent theme that there's something primal and violent in human nature.

**Genre:** Post-punk

## Big Boys

### *Fun Fun Fun* 12" EP July 25, 1982 (Moment Productions BB-001) (USA)

In the early 1980s, many post-punk bands integrated funk into their music. Like the Minutemen, the Big Boys inserted funk into both hardcore punk and post-punk. And this Austin band goes further by doing a full-fledged funk and punk hybrid with "We Got Soul" and their version of Kool & the Gang's "Hollywood Swinging."

In "Fun Fun Fun," they declare they like punk bands Sham 69 and the Cockney Rejects but also post-punk groups Joy Division and Public Image Ltd. "even though that's not what I'm supposed to do." The post-punk influence is all over "Prison" with the Big Boys' own version of cacophony and chaos.

**Genre:** Hardcore Punk

## Big Country

### "Angle Park" (B-side of "Fields of Fire") 45 February 18, 1983 (Mercury/COUNT 2) (UK)

Haunting depiction of a park and the people in it who all seem to be searching for something or in the midst of trouble or agony. There's moody imagery of dimly lit statues and cracked water fountains. Features ex–Skids guitarist Stuart Adamson's piercing guitar playing.

### "All of Us" (B-side of "In a Big Country") 45 May 20, 1983 (Mercury/COUNT 3) (UK)

A thematic companion to "In a Big Country" about the longing for something transcendental. There's a desire to break free to a better place where dreams and possibility seem to exist. And there is another standout Adamson guitar solo over an intoxicating rhythm.

### *The Crossing* LP July 29, 1983 (Mercury MERH 27) (UK)

After the Scottish band the Skids ended, guitarist Stuart Adamson started a new band that blended traditional Scottish music, punk energy, and post-punk experimentation. Regarded as one of punk/post-punk's greatest guitarists, Adamson pays homage to traditional Scottish music by sounding like a Celtic bagpipe on "In a Big Country," "Fields of Fire," and "1,000 Stars," and like a plucking violin in "Chance." The instrumental passage in the middle of "Harvest Home" is almost a post-punk symphony.

Sometimes the songs are anthem-like; other times there's a tremendous sense of melancholy. Despite being up-tempo, "Inwards" is about inner turmoil. A sense of sadness comes through in "Chance," perhaps the most compelling song on the album about a young woman who marries thinking that she will finally achieve some independence from her oppressive working-class life. But the factory worker disappoints her, leaving her alone with their child. The chorus features a psalm-like lament of "Oh Lord, where did the feeling go? / Oh Lord, I never felt so low."

Adamson's guitar is big and bold on this album and one of the most distinctive sounds in this whole era of music and particularly 1983, when many bands were incorporating synthesizers and keyboards. This was big guitar music during a time when it was vanishing.

**Genre:** Post-punk

## The Birthday Party

***Prayers on Fire* LP April 6, 1981 (Missing Link LINK 14) (Australia)**

The band's previous album *The Birthday Party* (when the band was named the Boys Next Door) could fit in with other post-punk music. But on this first album released under the Birthday Party name, they go in a more experimental direction as if to show they will not be boxed in by post-punk clichés. At times it is chaotic, discordant, uneasy, and close to the deconstructionist direction of no wave.

The album starts with the experimental jazz-meets-funk of "Zoo Music Girl" followed by "Capers," which sounds like the Velvet Underground with a Louis Armstrong–like vocal. "A Dead Song" is a Goth-influenced funk song, while the ironically titled "Figure of Fun" is perhaps the album's highlight, almost a Goth version of a show tune about someone who is miserable but perceived as fun. The album ends with "Dull Day," about the darkness of alcoholism. At points on this album, vocalist Nick Cave often sounds like a soul in pain and torment. It's all very challenging music but also some of the most daring and distinctive songs of the post-punk era.

**"Release the Bats" b/w "Blast Off" 45 July 31, 1981 (4AD AD 111) (UK)**

Along with the Bauhaus song "Bela Lugosi's Dead" and Xmal Deutschland's "Incubus Succubus," the A-side may the most identifiable song from the post-punk subgenre of Goth. But this single is a demented rockabilly single, like the Cramps gone darker. The B-side is an especially frenzied Goth variation on rockabilly.

***Junkyard* LP July 10, 1982 (Missing Link LINK 21) (Australia)**

Less experimental than *Prayers on Fire*, this album is more Goth-like because of its lyrics presenting a grotesque view of life. Human motivations are linked with the criminal or the immoral. It's an effective mix of post-punk rhythms and a subversive blues sound. Cave's vocals are even more guttural and mixed down. This makes him sound as if he's removed from the outside world.

The album starts with the slow blues-like "She's Hit" followed by "Dead Joe," perhaps the standout track with its macabre lyrics about a car crash. "The Dim Locator" is a shockabilly-meets-blues and post-punk song, a formula also used in other songs. "Hamlet" contains some of Cave's most guttural vocals, emphasizing that someone is at their mental breaking point.

*Junkyard* also features songs about spiritual degradation, such as "Several Sins," a confession about the seven deadly sins, while "Kiss Me Black" is about someone descending into a sordid lifestyle. The album ends in complete degradation with the title track about the excesses of alcohol and sex. Yet in all this darkness is probably their most satisfying album. But it's relentlessly disturbing and challenging.

### *The Bad Seed* 12" EP February 2, 1983 (4AD BAD 301) (UK)

A dark record with imagery of death, darkness, and interior spiritual deterioration from start to finish. It begins with the up-tempo "Sonny's Burning," a dark rockabilly-influenced song, and ends with the sparse horror movie–like vision of "Deep in the Woods." The EP's standout track is "Wildworld," with its funeral-like tempo and a sweeping statement about the savagery of the dark spiritual battle of life itself.

### *Mutiny!* 12" EP November 1, 1983 (Mute Records Mute 29) (UK)

The band's last record starts with the stunning "Jennifer's Veil," with its twangy guitar over a dirge-like tempo. "Six Strings That Drew Blood" and "Say a Spell" are variations on blues songs, one with a fast tempo, the other one slower. "Swampland," with its imagery of being pursued through swamps, sounds like a Goth-inspired horror movie. The album ends with the frightening "Mutiny in Heaven," a firsthand account of a fallen angel.

Genre: Post-punk

## Black Flag

### *Nervous Breakdown* 7" EP December 18, 1978 (SST 001) (USA)

This is the debut record of one of the most important California punk and hardcore bands. Keith Morris (who would soon join the Circle Jerks) is the band's first vocalist. The first three songs—"Nervous Breakdown," "Fix Me," and "I've Had It"—chronicle the mental deterioration that comes from frustration with suburban life. This is young male angst so intense the singer sounds at times on the verge of suicide and mental collapse. The last song, "Wasted" (later recorded by the Circle Jerks), is about the regret of living a hippie lifestyle, which comes across as a kind of mental derangement.

### *Jealous Again* 12" EP August 4, 1980 (SST 003) (USA)

The band's second record features vocalist Ron Reyes and is a hybrid of the straight punk from the first EP but moving toward hardcore punk. The title track is a rare hardcore song about a romantic relationship. The most controversial song is "White Minority," about white flight, which may or may not be ironic. The highlight is "No Values," about the threat of a violent nihilist.

### *Six Pack* 7" EP June 13, 1981 (SST 005) (USA)

The music gets even faster with an angry view of contemporary America. It starts with a sarcastic cautionary tale about alcoholism in "Six Pack," then into the anti-authority anthem "I've Heard It Before" before concluding with the standout

**Henry Rollins of Black Flag crowd-surfs during a concert. After the initial blast of punk subsided, a more intense version of punk—called hardcore punk—emerged that created a subculture that broke down the barriers between the audience and bands (Sony Pictures/Everett Collection).**

"American Waste." It's a dystopian-like view of working-class life where "the world's got some plans for me: courthouse, jails, and factories."

### *Damaged* LP December 5, 1981 (Unicorn 9502 and SST 007) (USA)

Henry Rollins joins the band as the new vocalist, and Black Flag makes their first album, which is one of hardcore's definitive statements. While the Bad Brains largely laid the foundation for hardcore, and the early Black Flag EPs and the Circle Jerks cemented the genre, *Damaged* took it to another level. Musically, it's more adventurous than most hardcore punk. There's a sludgier heavy metal guitar sound rather than a straight buzz saw guitar, and there are even some guitar solos. Not all songs have the conventional hardcore punk breakneck speed.

Rollins heightens this intensity. His guttural and sometimes strained vocals at times sound like they're coming from a deep place of pain. This is the sound of someone broken by the difficulties of life. In songs like "Room 13," there are primal vocals pleading: "I need to belong," "I need to hang on," and "keep me alive." In "Damaged II," he's absolutely overwhelmed by his feelings, and the song is a true cry for help. Because it's so convincing, that's probably why the album resonated with so many disaffected Generation Jones teens and young adults and became arguably the most popular album in the hardcore genre.

Although there are some social statements, such as "Police Story" and the urge for self-empowerment in "Rise Above," most of the album is about extreme psychic distress that heightens the album's title. Some suffering comes from alcoholism, as in "Six Pack,"

"Thirsty and Miserable," and "No More." "Gimmie Gimmie Gimmie" is about feeling demands to be satisfied, which can also lead to addiction. "TV Party" is about addiction to both escapist television and alcohol. The enemy on this album more than any political entity is the threat of self-destruction, which is the subject of "Life Is Pain," where the singer watches someone else self-destruct. The hope is that he won't follow the same path.

*Everything Went Black* **LP June 1983 (SST 015) (USA)**

This collection of early demos and outtakes with the band's first three vocalists before Henry Rollins joined the band is overall hit and miss. The reason to have this album is the first nine songs sung by Keith Morris, the band's first vocalist who would leave to form the Circle Jerks. Before this release, his only vocals were on the band's first EP, *Nervous Breakdown*. But from these nine songs, it's clear that if there wasn't an entire album of high-energy punk there was definitely another EP or two. Everything's on fire here: the vocals, Greg Ginn's Ramones-style buzz saw guitar meets guitar hero playing, and the garage punk production.

Morris also sings a version of "Clocked In," the song Henry Rollins famously jumped onstage to sing that ended up being his gateway into the band. "Clocked In" is one of punk's great anti-work songs. The job leads to a kind of torture where the body is controlled and the mind is overcome with boredom. You're disempowered because you can't talk back to your boss. And you're trapped because you need the paycheck.

**Genre:** Hardcore Punk

# Blitz

**"New Age" 45 January 1983 (Future FS 1) (UK)**

They started as an Oi! band before radically transforming into a synth-based post-punk band with a pop influence. This sounds like they've finally found their voice. It's catchy and almost power pop, but the post-punk undertones save it from going into that territory.

**Genre:** Pop Punk

# Blondie

*Blondie* **LP December 9, 1976 (Private Stock PS-2023) (USA)**

A landmark pop punk album marking out a different terrain for pop punk. There's no Johnny Ramone buzz saw guitar here. But Blondie does nothing less than reinvent pop music by integrating their own brand of pop punk with a blend of keyboards and guitars.

It's partly at times subversive deconstructions/tributes to 1960s girl group music, like on the intro to "X Offender" and the ballad "In the Flesh." And there's a *West Side Story*-style subversion of the musical genre in "A Shark in Jet's Clothing." The brilliance of it is that it's not novelty. It's partly a tribute to pop culture conventions while infusing the band's own punk spirit.

Thematically, some of the album is about the dangers and illusions of love, including the underage infatuation leading to an arrest in "X Offender," the "groupie supreme"

**Blondie's Debbie Harry helped shape a type of pop punk different from guitar-based pop punk. Blondie subverted pop conventions with a punk perspective (Peter Mazel/Avalon Photoshot/Everett Collection).**

in "Rip Her to Shreds," and the karate-fueled object of fixation in "Kung Fu Girl." The album ends with a B movie style apocalyptic invasion in the rumba rhythm of "Attack of the Giant Ants." As groundbreaking as the music is, the band's impact also came from vocalist Debbie Harry. She was the template for punk female fashion, and her attitude was the forerunner of so many other punk bands with female singers.

### *Plastic Letters* LP February 4, 1978 (Chrysalis CHR 1166) (USA)

For their second album, Blondie scraps the more overt 1960s subversions and releases a monumental record that stretches pop punk further than their first album with an even wider variety of approaches. Without losing their quirkiness, they take different pop forms and inject their own pop punk sensibility. In the 1970s, when the emphasis was on serious, lengthy songs, they subvert that by taking a 1960s bubblegum song "Denis" and making it a pop punk classic.

As was true of their first album, there's a danger lurking underneath some of these songs, such as the Cold War–fueled "Contact in Red Square," an ominous submission in "I Didn't Have the Nerve to Say No," and an obsessive fan in "Fan Mail." There's an irony between the melodic songs and the underlying menace. Other songs are lodged in late 1970s life. "Love at the Pier" is about a missed romance at a sun-soaked bathing pier; "Detroit 442," with its Iggy Pop reference, is ultimately a sad song about a "concrete factory" where things don't change. "I'm on E" is about regretting giving up a car but trying to make the best of it because at least there's money saved during the Generation Jones–era gas crisis.

### *Parallel Lines* LP September 23, 1978 (Chrysalis CDL 1192) (USA)

Here's the difference between power pop and pop punk. Check out the original power pop version of the lead track "Hanging on the Telephone" by the Nerves (released in 1976). Then listen to how Blondie hijacks the song here and transforms it into a driving pop punk song. For the rest of the band's third album, however, producer Mike Chapman waters the band down to a more accessible sound. It takes away too much of what made the band so distinctive on their first two albums. Then there's the issue of the definitely non–pop punk "Heart of Glass," which is essentially a disco song.

Still, the other songs are strong and credible pop punk, although overall far less adventurous than their first two albums. Highlights include "Hanging on the Telephone," the moody "Fade Away and Radiate," the stalker saga "One Way or Another," and the bouncy "Pretty Baby." No matter what the production, Debbie Harry's energy comes through in these songs.

### *Eat to the Beat* LP September 28, 1979 (Chrysalis CDL 1225) (USA)

Blondie returns to form with an album that ditches the teenage lyrics of *Parallel Lines* for something more mature and even spiritual at times. And the band sounds much energetic here than on *Parallel Lines*. It all starts with Clem Burke's drum part in "Dreaming," which dominates the other instruments to the point of almost making it a post-punk rhythm.

"Dreaming" is about daydreaming as a form of transcendence or a gateway to spiritual insight. "Accidents Never Happen" and "Shayla" are also about moments of spiritual transcendence. "Atomic" is far superior to "Heart of Glass" as an electronic-based song that sounds more like a pop industrial song than the disco of "Heart of Glass." "Living in the Real World" and the title track return to the energy of their first two albums.

**Genre:** Pop Punk

## Blue Orchids

### "Work" b/w "The House That Faded Out" 45 March 14, 1981 (Rough Trade RT 067) (UK)

Former members of the Fall release a post-punk gem. "Work" features eerie keyboards and an ominous chorus of just the shouted word "work!" The song ends in an existential crisis, suggesting that it's more than just a job tormenting the singer. The B-side isn't as powerful, but it's still strong post-punk with scorching jagged guitar.

**Genre:** Post-punk

## The Bodysnatchers

### "Let's Do Rock Steady" b/w "Ruder Than You" 45 March 15, 1980 (2 Tone CHS TT9) (UK)

This all-female two tone band unfortunately didn't last long enough to make an album. But they released two great singles. One side of their first single is a fun and rambunctious cover of a 1960s rock steady classic. The other side is "Ruder Than You," a fun declaration of how women can be even cooler than their male ska counterparts. Singer Rhoda Dakar really lifts the energy.

### "Easy Life" b/w "Too Experienced" 45 July 19, 1980 (2 Tone CHS TT12) (UK)

The Bodysnatchers go beyond the standard ska sound to create a kind of feminist concept single that's still highly danceable and catchy. "Easy Life" questions gender roles in marriage, while "Too Experienced" is about a woman turning down a man's offer for marriage because she's "too experienced to let someone take my soul."

**Genre:** Ska

## Bow Wow Wow

### "C-30, C-60, C-90, Go" cassette single July 24, 1980 (TCEMI 5088) (UK)

Bow Wow Wow, with teen vocalist Annabella Lwin, was at the forefront of another trend in post-punk: a tribal percussion sound. This was influenced by a 1971 British hit called "Burundi Black" that sampled a recording of 25 East African Burundi drummers. Former post-punkers Adam and the Ants commercialized that sound so much they crossed over into a more image-based New Romantic–like band.

However, the use of tribal drumming in this song is the most potent of all the nouveau Burundi-influenced bands. And the lyrics turned out to be prophetic. This homage to cassette taping of songs to avoid paying for music escalated years later into free electronic downloads of songs.

### "Prince of Darkness" 12" July 28, 1981 (RCA RCAT 100) (UK)

The call-and-response between singer Annabella Lwin and guitarist Matthew Ashman is a reworked, extended version of "Sinner Sinner Sinner" from their *See Jungle!* LP. The band lets loose in a weird and wonderful extended version.

**Genre:** Post-punk

## David Bowie

### *Low* LP January 14, 1977 (RCA PL 12030) (UK)

*Low* was the first of what was later called Bowie's Berlin trilogy, three albums recorded with Tony Visconti and Brian Eno. *Low* is the most experimental, the most daring, and the boldest of the three albums (which included *Heroes* and *Lodger*). It creates a path for the post-punk genre, looking beyond punk into what will come next. *Low* was the bridge between krautrock and post-punk. It's a major inspiration for how to use electronic music in post-punk and also helped create the foundation for industrial music.

This is especially apparent in the instrumentals on side two, which create an atmosphere beyond most krautrock into something more eerie and ethereal. The haunting

"Warszawa" is both bleak and beautiful, while the ending "Subterraneans" is a contemplative lament. The album also contains the inner conflict that would come to be associated with post-punk. That persists through the album, even in the album's most accessible song, "Sound and Vision," about someone in isolation waiting for inspiration to take him out of his malaise. There's a sense throughout the album of waiting to be delivered from internal demons and oppression. That especially comes through in "What in the World" and "Be My Wife," which express desire for an end to loneliness and isolation.

**Genre:** Post-punk

## The Boys Next Door

### *Birthday Party* LP May 29, 1980 (Missing Link LINK 7) (Australia)

Australian band with vocalist Nick Cave progress from quirky pop punk on their first album, *Door Door*, into full-blown post-punk. It was such a drastic alteration that the band would change its name to the title of this album. And they would later rerelease this album under the name Birthday Party. On this album and their subsequent albums, Birthday Party would release some of the darkest and most challenging of all post-punk albums. But compared to what was to come, this was their most accessible album.

Although post-punk is the foundation, the no wave influences are worked into the songs. "Mr. Clarinet" and "Waving My Arms" feature more conventional post-punk structures with jerky jagged guitars and rhythms, while others, like "Hats on Wrong," implement more of the no wave influence. Nick Cave's vocals are like an instrument as well. At times, he seems to improvise with his voice like a jazz musician. On "Happy Birthday," there are guttural sounds and screeches that seem to express something from the subconscious beyond words.

**Genre:** Post-punk

## Glenn Branca

### *Lesson No. 1* 12" EP March 1980 (99 Records 99–001 EP) (USA)

Avant-garde and experimental guitarist whose work was vital to the no wave movement in New York City in the late 1970s and into the noise rock/punk of the 1980s. Little in post-punk was this experimental. But many bands were influenced by how Branca used his crescendo of layered guitars, which becomes like a no wave minimalist post-punk symphony.

### *The Ascension* LP November 1981 (99 Records 99–001 LP) (USA)

Branca builds on his first EP to create an even more daring and diverse symphony of guitar with five tracks instead of three. And it's a masterpiece. On a complete album, Branca branches out in a way he couldn't on his first EP. This is a basis for so much that will come after, including post-punk, noise punk, and alternative music. The guitar sound contains a beautiful gritty quality. And it has a kind of classical musical quality with a pattern of creating tension and then release.

Building a dramatic and bold new sound comes through, especially on the second half of "The Spectacular Commodity" and in "Light Field," where there's some resemblance to traditional song structures. On the shorter "Structure," it sounds more like a short, forceful wall of guitars. The ending title track brings the album to an eerie, mysterious finale.

**Genre:** Post-punk/No Wave

## Kate Bush

### *The Dreaming* LP September 13, 1982 (EMI EMC 3419) (UK)

For her first three albums, starting with the release of *The Kick Inside* in 1978, Bush was one of music's most unique and visionary artists. On her fourth album, there's a shift in her sound to something darker and more experimental. *The Dreaming* is more in the category of bands like the Cocteau Twins and Public Image Ltd. than what she previously released. And there's a more consistent sense of angst and experimentation. It's Bush's foray into the post-punk spirit.

The album starts with the explosive drumming of "Sat on My Lap," recalling everything from the Burundi drumming sound popularized by Bow Wow Wow to Public Image's "Flowers of Romance." The song is about a search for knowledge that is so difficult that it puts the singer in a state of distress. The pursuit of knowledge is seemingly unattainable, can go in many directions, and makes one aware of flaws and shortcomings. "Suspended in Gaffa" features an encounter with the mystical that leaves the singer feeling overwhelmed. "The Dreaming" uses a world music influence in a song about Indigenous Australian spirituality. "Houdini" is about a séance arranged by Houdini's wife to try to contact the spirit of the dead magician.

Other songs are about people desperate and on the downside of life, such as the bank robbers in "There Goes a Tenner" and the solider in "Pull Out the Pin," a frightening song about a Vietnam War solider. The most disturbing song, however, is the finale, "Get Out of My House," in which Bush uses a house as a metaphor for her internal state, where the house consists of mistakes, madness, and mess.

**Genre:** Post-punk

## Bush Tetras

### *Too Many Creeps* 7" EP September 21, 1980 (99 Records 99–02) (USA)

The title track is about harassment. It could express what happens when going outside of a punk subculture, or what women put up with on the streets of New York. Whatever it is, mainstream culture is not just indifferent but threatening. This is conveyed in a song with catchy riffs and an infectious chorus. But the entire EP has a looseness and a funk-influenced undercurrent prevalent in the New York downtown scene at the time.

### "Things That Go Boom in the Night" b/w "Das Ah Riot" 45 June 16, 1981 (Fetish FET 007) (UK)

Post-punk single that goes beyond the funky groove of the band's "Too Many Creeps" into darker territory with stormier, dirtier guitar and percussion. It's a nightmarish version of the same theme as "Too Many Creeps": it's a scary and threatening world out there. The B-side is the band's successful stamp of how to implement reggae influences into a post-punk format.

**Genre:** Post-punk

## Buzzcocks

### *Spiral Scratch* 7" EP January 29, 1977 (New Hormones 01) (UK)

One of the landmark events in punk, partly because it was released on an independent label. This encouraged many other bands from the punk and post-punk era to form their own record labels. It ignited an explosion of creativity and authenticity that would not have been possible if punk bands were forced to adhere to the demands of major labels.

It's more punk than the pop punk the band would become associated with after this EP. The band almost always conveys angst. But it's strong in songs like "Breakdown," where the singer describes himself as "a nowhere wolf of pain." The EP's highlight is "Boredom," with its famous two-note guitar solo that's a subversion of the guitar solo conventions of mainstream rock in the 1970s. It describes boredom as a state of spiritual deprivation, the inability to feel connected or engaged in the culture.

### *Another Music in a Different Kitchen* LP March 10, 1978 (United Artists UAG 30159) (UK)

After Howard Devoto left the band, singer Pete Shelley takes the group in a direction that came to be known as pop punk. But these aren't lightweight songs. Instead of a rush of elation about love, it's more often about romance gone wrong, whether it's unrequited love or just disillusionment. The approaches used on this album would be utilized repeatedly for decades by punk bands, particularly during the pop punk resurgence of the 1990s.

As with the Undertones, sometimes the melodic songs are an ironic juxtaposition to the lyrics, such as in "No Reply," which is about the pain of rejection. "I Don't Mind" features ironic choruses that seem to be a kind of apathy about identity loss. Because the Buzzcocks didn't use gender pronouns in their songs, there has been speculation that some of their songs—such as "Get on Your Own" and "Love Battery"—clandestinely feature references to gay relationships.

"Fast Cars" may be about the danger of fast cars, but it also seems to be a critique of the status symbol they symbolized in the 1970s. This subverts the ideology in rock music that since the 1950s has mythologized cars. "Fiction Romance" is about someone discouraged by real life romance because it doesn't match the version of romance in the media. "I Need" boils life down to a desperate-sounding list of demands.

### *Love Bites* LP September 22, 1978 (United Artists UAG 30197) (UK)

The band fine-tunes their pop punk sound with an increasingly darker view of personal relationships. When relationships don't work out, it triggers a despair that leads to questioning about self-identity, and sometimes questioning life in general. In "Nostalgia," the present is so troubled the singer longs for better future days. No wonder there's a song called "Operator's Manual" about needing an instruction booklet to navigate relationship dilemmas.

*Love Bites* includes one of the best-known songs, "Ever Fallen in Love (You Shouldn't Have)," rumored to be about a same-sex attraction. It also includes "Nothing Left," one of their more desperate songs with an almost post-punk like chaotic guitar solo and a driving guitar riff. For the Buzzcocks, to be shunned or unfulfilled in love leads to a state of utter despair. When salvation doesn't come through romance and love, it leads to painful desolation. Recorded fairly quickly after their first album, *Love*

*Bites* includes two instrumentals, "Walking Distance" and "Late for the Train." Both are atmospheric songs that embody the feeling the rest of the album conveys. There's a yearning pain around the edges of driving energy.

### *A Different Kind of Tension* LP August 11, 1979 (United Artists UAG 30260) (UK)

On their third album, the band generally sounds more grown up most of the time. But the angst is still there. The blast of energy on their first album, *Another Music in a Different Kitchen*, made it a significant album. But this may be their most satisfying album because it's so varied and lyrically ambitious.

On side one, "You Say You Don't Love Me" is an acceptance of a relationship that isn't going to happen, which seems to indicate some newfound wisdom. "Mad Mad Judy," which hearkens back to the energy of *Another Music in a Different Kitchen*, is about someone who experiences some kind of breakdown. The inability to make a positive connection in "Raison D'Etre" leads to a crisis of meaning and is a precursor to the adventurous side two.

Side two gets philosophical and more experimental lyrically. Their existential torment may be no more intense than in "I Don't Know What to Do with My Life," which continues in "Money," where Shelley confesses that he finds both himself and other people to be strange and concludes that "life is a zoo." The distress continues through "Hollow Inside," with its repeated declaration of "I was hollow inside, but I couldn't find out what the reason was." "A Different Kind of Tension" features an ominous guitar riff and a series of contradictory statements that create anxiety. "I Believe" is perhaps the band's most eloquent statement of all, with a litany of beliefs and a haunting chorus of "there is no love in this world anymore."

### *Singles Going Steady* LP September 25, 1979 (I.R.S. SP 001) (USA)

This is an essential collection of singles containing six non-album singles. That includes their debut single "Orgasm Addict" and "What Do I Get," one of the best-known songs. On the surface, "What Do I Get" is about unrequited love. But on a deeper level, it could be working-class frustration about not attaining the better things in life.

As with other Buzzcocks albums, the absence of love and all that can go wrong in relationships ultimately leads to anxiety about one's relationship with the world. In "Love You More," the singer is deeply in love but fears the possibility of abandonment. "Promises" is about disillusionment with not just romance, but about life's false promises. The only explanation is the painful realization that his former lover must have never cared at all, the song concludes. In "Everybody's Happy Nowadays," there's the haunting chant of "Life's an illusion, love is the dream" that points to the philosophical pop punk of *A Different Kind of Tension*.

*Singles Going Steady* includes some great B-sides, like "Whatever Happened To?" about the transitory nature of life both through emotions and objects. "Something's Gone Wrong Again" lists some of the frustrations of modern life, and "Why Can't I Touch It?" features what would be post-punk conventions of a funk groove and jagged guitar. "Oh Shit" is one of their most straightforward punky songs. It has a healthy kind of anger directed at the people who cause the singer's frustration.

### *Parts 1–3* 12" EP February 1, 1981 (I.R.S. SP-70955) (USA)

The band continues to grow with this collection of three singles released after *A Different Kind of Tension*. It starts off with the clever wordplay of "Are Everything," while

the middle single, "Strange Thing," is a desperate plea for the narrator to transcend frustrations and depression. Their last single, "Running Free," expands the instrumentation that points to an exciting new possibility for pop punk.
**Genre:** Punk/Pop Punk

## David Byrne and Brian Eno

### *My Life in the Bush of Ghosts* LP January 29, 1981 (Sire SRK 6093) (USA)

This collaboration between Talking Heads singer David Byrne and producer Brian Eno is a groundbreaking album for the layering of music (a combination of post-punk, electronica, and world music) with largely spoken-word samples. The unconventional use of vocals was enormously influential on how samples could be assimilated into music. It was also important for integrating experimental music into the genres of funk, electronica, and world music. Byrne and Eno built on the musical ideas on this album on the fourth Talking Heads album, *Remain in Light*, probably their finest album.

The samples come from radio broadcasts, sermons, chants, and even an exorcism. Although there's a world music feel to much of the album, there's particularly a Middle Eastern sound in several songs. "Regiment," "The Carrier," and "A Secret Life" use the vocals of Lebanese singers that sound like chants. "Help Me Somebody" and "Come with Us" feature parts of sermons from a Christian evangelist, while "The Jezebel Spirit" features an excerpt from an exorcism.
**Genre:** Post-punk

## Cabaret Voltaire

### "Nag Nag Nag" 45 June 14, 1979 (Rough Trade RT 108) (UK)

The band gained a reputation for their experimental and keyboard-based records, but on this single they blend punk attitude, post-punk music, and an emerging industrial music sound. The snarl in the vocals is all punk. They never sounded as on-target, dangerous, and punky.

### *Red Mecca* LP August 17, 1981 (Rough Trade ROUGH 27) (UK)

The band's first two albums fell more into the category of experimental music, but for their third album they introduce more solid song structures. The basis of this is experimental and sometimes features the most unpunk of instruments (aside from the acoustic guitar), which are keyboards. But the songs show a shift in direction that would turn it into a major work in the development of the industrial music subgenre of post-punk.

They use a compressed combination of rhythms, unorthodox vocals (sometimes just spoken), and percussion that give it a mechanical sound. A good example is the 10-minute "A Thousand Ways," with its buried-in-the-mix vocals, repetitive structure, and percussion sounds that sound like whips cracking. Although this album would expand the definition of post-punk into industrial music, this clearly uncommercial band would be an inspiration for some keyboard-based new wave bands that would borrow their unorthodox sounds in small doses and exploit their innovation.

### 2X45 double 45 May 12, 1982 (Rough Trade ROUGH 42) (UK)

With their purely experimental phase of their early records now definitely over, the band used song structures as an anchor for experimentation around it rather than having the entire song be experimental. For example, on "Protection" there's a danceable riff that serves as the foundation for a subordinate experimentation including a bebop-like saxophone and sinister-sounding spoken words. There's still an uneasiness about the sound that makes it not commercially viable. But it was the end of the most experimental and innovative era of the band's music. After the departure of Chris Watson, the band modified their sound on their next album, *The Crackdown* (1983).

**Genre:** Post-punk

## A Certain Ratio

### "Party All Night" 45 May 21, 1979 (Factory FAC 5) (UK)

Eerie, Goth-like pre-funk song with a reggae-inspired guitar line. Like other Goth-inspired post-punk, it's about dark places, dark thoughts, dark urges. In this case, it culminates in a crime. A unique song in the band's repertoire because it's so far from the funk sound they became so associated with.

### "Flight" 12" October 25, 1980 (Factory FAC 22) (UK)

This is probably the band's most accessible song. Although rooted in post-punk, it contains elements of dub, jazz, and early electronica music. The smoother groove makes the song more atmospheric than the band's other songs. This juxtaposition between voice and music, the song's intoxicating groove, and its influence on electronica music make this a seminal record.

### *To Each...* LP April 28, 1981 (Factory FACT 35) (UK)

Along with the Talking Heads album *Remain in Light*, this is one of the landmark mixtures of funk, post-punk, and world music. A Certain Ratio used elements of funk on their first album, but here it's much more pronounced. Although the bass line and percussion drive most of the album with its funk rhythms, the post-punk elements are still prominent. In "My Spirit," the band breaks out into a post-punk experimental midsection, while "Forced Laugh" features a foreboding bass and a soundscape of swirling sounds that have an almost Goth-like sense of menace. All of it comes with vocals mixed down so much they sound like they were recorded in the distance away from the band.

### *Sextet* LP January 27, 1982 (Factory FACT 55) (UK)

While their previous album *To Each...* used post-punk as the basis for the songs, the funk is definitely more blatant here. It's a more cleanly produced album with an immediate difference that the vocals are mixed up front. And vocalist Martha Tilton is featured prominently, with vocals that remain consistently different from those in conventional funk songs. In "Knife Slits Water," Tilton's somewhat ghostly vocals are double-tracked with a voice that almost sounds like a child's voice. Although *To Each...* was their most daring record, this album is another brave experiment.

**Genre:** Post-punk

## The Chameleons

### "In Shreds" 45 April 2, 1982 (Epic EPC A2210) (UK)

The debut single from this Manchester area band is a memorable cross between punk and post-punk. The singer is tormented because he feels he is "self-contradictory" since he has sold out to become "part of the machinery." This realization leaves him so fragmented that he feels as if his life has had no meaning. One of the many Generation Jones punk and post-punk songs about the fear of losing one's identity through selling out.

### *Script of the Bridge* LP August 8, 1983 (Statik STAT LP 17) (UK)

Instead of variations on their "In Shreds" single, the Chameleons go in a different direction and create their own variation on post-punk that would turn out later to be enormously influential in the post-punk revival in the 2000s. The more processed guitar sound created a kind of soaring atmospheric quality that blended in with the other instrumentation into a post-punk wall of sound. For much of the album the Chameleons also slow the pace down. Tension comes from the blend of the more processed guitars, sometimes in layers over vocals by Mark Burgess, which are a cross between melancholy, desperation, and outrage.

Among the album's standout tracks are "Less Than Human," a lament about feeling abandoned by God, and "Pleasure and Pain," with its beautiful melody. "Thursday's Child" is about a painful loss of innocence, while the album ends on a more transcendental tone with "View from a Hill," with its hopeful chorus of "you wait till your time comes round again." The best-known song is "Up the Down Escalator," about a ruling class that "sit at their tables and throw us the scraps." This album was largely overlooked at the time of its release. But it was another case of a band being so ahead of their times that their influence was recognized much later.

**Genre:** Post-punk

## James Chance and the Contortions

### *Buy* LP November 1979 (ZE Records ILPS 7002) (UK)

This is a funk-based album that showed the growing downtown NYC fascination with integrating funk into the post-punk genre. But it's much more than that. Chance was part of the no wave movement, and this album follows that movement's ethos by deconstructing the genre. It's stripped down to fewer instruments than other funk/post-punk fusions. But there's also a bebop jazz sound integrated into some songs. These frenetic, free-form jazz elements combine with the jerky nervous guitars associated with post-punk.

Somehow throwing this all together works. It's a masterpiece fusion of avant-garde funk and free-form jazz. Chance would continue to make albums that combined jazz and free-form jazz (with some disco as well). While they were interesting albums without the no wave reductionist tactics, they were more experimental funk/free-form jazz synthesis rather than something that grew out of post-punk.

**Genre:** No Wave

## Chandra

### *Transportation* 12" EP June 5, 1980 (Go Go Records GO GO 006) (USA)

One of the best of the more obscure and overlooked gems from this era. Twelve-year-old Chandra Oppenheim, the daughter of an artist associated with the NYC downtown art scene, writes her own lyrics and uses the post-punk NYC band the Dance as her backing band. And it captures something perhaps no other record does from this period does. That's the perspective of someone between childhood and adulthood.

And it's all channeled through a keyboard-driven post-punk sound with some no wave embellishments. The opening "Opposition" features keyboards far more sinister-sounding than the sterile, clean keyboards gaining popularity in England at the time with the growing synth-pop genre. "Let your feelings overtake you," Chandra sings with an encouraging tone. Even though they're scary you'll be tough enough to handle them. "Concentration" demands an almost spiritual focus on what's important. The second side has a punkier perspective. "Subways" turns a subway ride into a somewhat scary adventure into a more dangerous and confusing outside world. "Kate" is the angriest song, a jealous tirade against a popular girl with blonde hair showing the unfairness of life.

Genre: Post-punk

## Channel 3

### "Manzanar" from *CH3* 12" EP May 10, 1981 (Posh Boy 1018) (USA)

California punk group on the borderline between punk and hardcore punk unleashes a punk classic. The song is about the notorious internment camp for Japanese Americans on the West Coast during World War II. Conveys the sense of terror or a concentration camp that "wasn't in a country so far, in fact in your own backyard."

Genre: Punk

## Chaos U.K.

### *Burning Britain* 7" EP February 7, 1982 (Riot City RIOT 6) (UK)

Although sometimes compared to Discharge, on their debut record they are less heavy metal influenced and more punk. This guitar sound propels one of UK '82's punk's greatest moments before they would become more of a crossover thrash band.

Even on a punk record, however, Chaos U.K. uses the heavy metal convention of violent and horror imagery to express the distress and near paranoia of contemporary life in an oppressive state. This EP is a harrowing dystopian view of life in the early 1980s. It starts with the hardcore punk-like Cold War terror of "Four Minute Warning," with a frightening cry that "Hiroshima is here again!" And there's the ongoing threat from a militarized state that includes the British military in "Army" and the police in "Victimized."

Genre: Punk

## Chelsea

### "Right to Work" 45 June 1, 1977 (Step Forward SF 2) (UK)

The working-class anxiety over unemployment is not only about an economic crisis but also a moral and spiritual one that can lead to addiction and mental illness. A landmark record for addressing the necessity of work to survive in a capitalist society.

### *Chelsea* LP June 29, 1979 (Step Forward SFLP 2) (UK)

Underrated Brit punk band that recorded mostly social/political songs with catchy choruses. They're mostly in the spirit of bands like the Clash, Stiff Little Fingers, and the Jam but with some Buzzcocks-style hooks around the edges. During this period they never abandoned the punk approach despite the emergence of post-punk, Oi!, and hardcore punk.

The album's first two songs are a call to arms with "I'm on Fire" and the urgency of "Decide," a song that suggests finally making that decision that will change your life. It's not easy to determine whether "Your Toy" is about a relationship or resisting an oppressive societal force. But does it matter? The idea is still the same. Resist when you either feel used or someone is forcing you to sell out. "Government" features a reggae influence that's an effective hybrid of punk and reggae. The album concludes with "Trouble is the Day," a summary of obstacles.

### *Evacuate* LP April 5, 1982 (Step Forward SFLP 7) (UK)

In a year where original punk was being abandoned for Oi!, hardcore punk, crossover thrash, and post-punk, Chelsea sticks to the punk sound. With almost a completely new lineup from their debut album, the band adds some refinements in the approach and production without losing the band's energy. They are more focused and determined than on their debut album.

Highlights are the apocalyptic title track and the explosive "War Across the Nation." "Tribal Song" ventures into post-punk territory. But for most of the album the band rejuvenates punk with some Oi!-like catchy choruses on many songs. The concluding "Only Thinking" is contemplative, and with the alternation between reflective verses and a catchy chorus, it's a compelling search for meaning.

### "Stand Out" 45 October 2, 1982 (Step Forward SF 22) (UK)

An energetic anthem with a Joe Strummer–like vocal and an Oi!/football chant chorus: This band sounds like they're carrying the torch for the original punk spirit. In the second chorus they may be dissing either Goth rockers or New Romantics.

**Genre:** Punk

## Circle Jerks

### *Group Sex* LP October 1, 1980 (Frontier FLP 1002) (USA)

This album may not have created the hardcore punk genre, but it solidified and advanced it. Within 14 songs in 15 minutes, it's a rush of energy with little or no break between songs. It almost becomes like one continuous song or performance.

Some of the major themes in hardcore are also established. "Beverly Hills" ridicules mainstream culture, "Back Against the Wall" is about police harassment, and "Behind the Door" is a tour of the seedy urban landscape. There are songs about agitated outsiders and the angst of not being able to fit in, such as "World Up My Ass," and political and anti-authority songs such as "Paid Vacation," about the war in Afghanistan.

But there are also adolescent-tinged songs such as "What's Your Problem?" and "Group Sex." That would point to something beyond the political and outsider songs to something more juvenile. The album ends with "Red Tape," about bureaucracy, which seems to serve as a metaphor for the entire album of pointing out the obstacles the establishment puts up.

### *Wild in the Streets* LP March 4, 1982 (Faulty Products COPE 3) (USA)

Not as innovative or as varied as their first album, but more consistent and angrier. And Keith Morris may be hardcore punk's most nuanced and influential vocalist. There's more to than just the strained shouts that some other hardcore band singers employ. Morris knows how to dramatically alternate his vocal intensity for maximum effect.

The band doubles down on the themes in the first album and makes them more pronounced and effective. "Stars and Stripes" is about military escalation that could lead to nuclear war. "Meet the Press" criticizes the media. And there are more songs about working-class angst and oppression, such as the meaningless jobs in "Letter Bomb," "Forced Labor," and in "Leave Me Alone," where life is defined as "work, money, bills, reality, no spare time, no sanity." In "Trapped," Morris laments, "What did I do to deserve this?" It ends with the 1960s hippie anthem "Put a Little Love in Your Heart." It's not a gimmick but a way of showing how absurd the ideology in the song is in the midst of the anger and injustice that has been chronicled on the rest of the album.

### *Golden Shower of Hits* LP July 21, 1983 (LAX Records LAX 1051) (USA)

Yes, the production isn't punk enough. The sound is probably an attempt to make the band more accessible. But this is still one of the best hardcore bands at the height of their powers. It shows how singer Keith Morris helped shape hardcore punk's vocal style. Take, for example, the vocals in "High Price on Our Heads," with his declaration that there is "no way to get ahead in a loser's race." Even when the band takes a leap into a parody of heavy metal with "Rats of Reality" and parts of "Under the Gun," Morris's vocals give it all a menacing gravitas.

Like Minor Threat did with their *Out of Step* album the same year, this album takes a turn to the more personal effects of an unjust system and a sense of betrayal. That starts with "In Your Eyes," an anomaly of a breakup song within the hardcore punk genre. As the original hardcore bands progressed more into further adulthood, there was an examination of the damage that society took on them personally and how people grow apart and get more isolated as they get older. This comes through in "Product of My Environment," in which Morris recalls how he grew up where "events take place that will wipe the smile off your face," and in "Parade of the Horribles," which depicts an apocalyptic-like scene of people broken by society's oppression.

**Genre:** Hardcore Punk

## The Clash

### "1977" (B-side of "White Riot") 45 March 8, 1977 (S CBS 5058) (UK)

Nothing sounds, smells, or tastes more like 1977 than this B-side, which declares, "No Elvis, Beatles, or the Rolling Stones." The older generation's rock stars are no longer relevant, with the King of Rock and Roll dead, the Beatles not reuniting, and the Rolling Stones on a hiatus. Meanwhile there's poverty and danger on the streets, at least for those who don't have money, while the wealthy use the police to protect themselves from the uproar.

### *The Clash* LP April 8, 1977 (CBS 82000) (UK)

From the Class of 1977, only the debut albums by the Sex Pistols and the Damned are as influential. What makes this album so important is the everyman quality to the songs. It shows that punk can be not just political observations, but portray the ordinary lives of the downtrodden. It encouraged other punk rockers to write about their own lives, feelings, and experiences. The result is a blending of the personal and the political with truth and realism in these songs rather than rock clichés.

The Clash—(left to right) Topper Headon, Mick Jones, Paul Simonon, and Joe Strummer—were not only prophetic but also idealistic about the potential of the punk movement. They constructively examined the possibilities of rising above limitations (Parallel Film Productions/Film Four/Hanway Films/Nitrate Film/Alamy).

That this band was out to destroy those clichés, particularly the hedonism of rock and roll from the 1960s and 1970s, is there from the opening track, "Janie Jones." It represents the debauchery and excesses of rock that the Clash was an antidote to. Other songs are from the viewpoint of the alienated working class ("48 Hours," "Career Opportunities") or a young person trying to find his true identity ("What's My Name") or feeling a sense of evil in the world ("Hate and War"). "Police and Thieves" was one of the first forays (if not *the* first) into blending reggae and punk. The album ends with the statement of purpose—"Garageland"—about staying true to one's proletariat roots where truth is to be found.

### "Complete Control" b/w "City of the Dead" 45 September 23, 1977 (S CBS 5664) (UK)

A firsthand account of the frustrations of being a punk rock band with everyone seemingly working against you. The record company promises artistic freedom but doesn't deliver. Police hassle the band. The band's friends can't get in to see their concerts. The media smears them. This isn't at all different from the average person ("Joe Public") who is "controlled in the body, controlled in the mind." The B-side is also about being harassed and ostracized as a punk rocker.

### "Clash City Rockers" b/w "Jail Guitar Doors" 45 February 17, 1978 (S CBS 5834) (UK)

A call to arms to find purpose and drive in one's life or you'll be crushed. Deciding what to do about a meaningless job is a crossroads moment in life. This also depicts the combination of boredom and oppression that dominated late 1970s culture and nostalgia for glam rock. The criticism of out-of-date rock stars continues on the B-side, "Jail Guitar Doors," which mentions musicians recently busted for drugs.

### "White Man in Hammersmith Palais" b/w "The Prisoner" 45 June 16, 1978 (S CBS 6383) (UK)

Perhaps the greatest synthesis of reggae and punk released up until this time. The Clash covered Junior Murvin's "Police and Thieves" on their first album. But this is the first time they created a reggae punk fusion that's an original song. Consistent with what makes many of Joe Strummer's songs so powerful, it's a firsthand story that's a basis for broader social commentary. It's a story of a reggae concert at which the crowd hopes to hear something about their lives and social conditions but the pop reggae performers only offer escapist entertainment. The B-side uses the British TV show *The Prisoner* as a metaphor for the feeling of being trapped in an oppressively dull town.

### *Give 'Em Enough Rope* LP November 10, 1978 (S CBS 82431) (UK)

When this album was initially released, it was a disappointment after the band's revolutionary first album. Most of it is because of the album's production by Sandy Pearlman, who produced the hard rock/heavy metal band Blue Oyster Cult. The album has a kind of sludgy, muddy quality to it that takes away the band's energy. Most of the songs also move away from the band's trademark lyrical approach, which was first-person accounts of life under the oppression of late 1970s urban English life.

This time it's more about branching out into other topics other than life on the streets in England. That includes a firsthand glimpse at crime-ridden Jamaica ("Safe European Home"), terrorism ("Tommy Gun"), and gun violence ("Guns on the Roof"). The ending trilogy of songs ("Stay Free," "Cheapskates," and "All the Young Punks") recalls their first album with firsthand accounts of life, with these songs about male friendship and their perspective on fame. Despite the counterproductive production, most of these are strong songs. And perhaps one day we'll get a remix of the album that sounds more punk than 1970s hard rock.

### "Pressure Drop" (B-side of "English Civil War") 45 February 23, 1979 (S CBS 7082) (UK)

The Clash took several different approaches to integrating reggae and punk. For the first part of their career, they integrated reggae elements into punk songs. And this is their most outright punk-driven reggae-influenced song, a rousing version of the Toots and the Maytals song.

### *Cost of Living* 7" EP May 11, 1979 (S CBS 7324) (UK)

The first side of this EP smashes 1960s ideology. First, they commandeer Bobby Fuller Four's "I Fought the Law," turning a jangly garage rock song into one of punk's great cover songs with a sense of danger lacking in the original. Then they mock 1960s nostalgia amid societal unrest in "Groovy Times." On side two, "Gates of the West" celebrates making it out of poverty in London and the freedom and adventure it brings in New York City. "Capitol Radio" is perhaps the most piercing anti-radio song of many from this era.

### *London Calling* LP December 14, 1979 (CBS CLASH 3) (UK)

Not many bands radically expanded a musical genre twice in their career. The first Clash album enlarged the punk perspective by showing how punk can merge the political and the personal. Their third album is a manifesto that also moves punk forward.

It provides a solution to a problem punk presented not long after it started: how do you transcend the limited musical form of punk and still retain the energy?

The Clash's answer is that the punk spirit can be put not only into other genres like ska ("Rudie Can't Fail" and "Revolution Rock") and rockabilly ("Brand New Cadillac") but also in a blend of punk and rock. Rather than the experimentation of post-punk, this is another approach to take punk out of the Ramones-influenced genre of fast buzz saw guitar that dominated the genre.

The result is just as exciting as the beginning of punk. It starts with the title track, which slows the pace down from their first album but still conveys an almost apocalyptic-like urgency. Songs like "Clampdown" and "Four Horsemen" focus on self-empowerment by resisting oppression rather than the almost desperate feeling of entrapment on their first album. Because of its broad vision, it's one of the most important albums released during the Generation Jones era.

### *Sandinista* LP December 12, 1980 (CBS FSLN 1) (UK)

As *Give 'Em Enough Rope* was a disappointment after the first album, similarly *Sandinista* was at the time of its release a letdown after the colossal statement of *London Calling*. The punk approach pretty much vanished, only really emerging on the cover of "Police on My Back." For many Clash fans, it was too much of a change of direction too soon. And it might have been better received if the weakest album's worth of material were removed and it were a double album instead of a triple album. This is, however, a Clash album that has been reevaluated much more favorably than it was received at the time of release.

Years later, it has become a landmark album in the tradition of post-punk taking the punk spirit and injecting it into other genres. The Clash have always played reggae convincingly, and some of the best of this album is either reggae or reggae-influenced. But they succeed in other genres, too, including rap ("The Magnificent Seven"), gospel ("The Sound of Sinners"), jazz ("Look Here"), and Caribbean music ("Let's Go Crazy"). This is a band that does not want to be trapped in the limitations of punk.

### "This Is Radio Clash" 45 November 20, 1981 (CBS A1797) (UK)

During the height of post-punk's fascination with funk, the Clash commandeer the funk/post-punk hybrid and inject their own brand of fiery street politics (along with some rap influences). While much of *Sandinista* wasn't that energetic, this is a revolution you can dance to. This is an apocalyptic-like vision of war, poverty, and police brutality.

### "Know Your Rights" 45 April 23, 1982 (CBS A2309) (UK)

By *Combat Rock*, their final album in the band's original lineup with Mick Jones, the band seemed lost. Aside from a shockingly blatant pop song ("Should I Stay or Should I Go"), it was riddled with variations on *Sandinista*-style experimentations that largely fall flat. But the kickoff track on the album is the last classic Clash song. Its inspiration goes back further than *Sandinista* and *Combat Rock* to the band's punk origins.

**Genre:** Punk/Post-punk

## Cock Sparrer

### "Running Riot" 45 June 3, 1977 (Decca FR 13710) (UK)

Like the Clash's "White Riot," this is a call for taking to the streets. The song's title is British slang for going on a wild rampage. And that would have sounded like a threat during the time of the song's release, when there were riots and insurrections across economically ravaged England.

**Genre:** Punk

## Cockney Rejects

### *The Power & the Glory* LP July 13, 1981 (EMI ZONO 105) (UK)

After more than a year of churning out formulaic and cliché Oi! songs (including the song "Oi, Oi, Oi," which the Oi! genre was reportedly named after), the band made an album for grown-ups. What they create is the finest album from a band associated with the Oi! movement. The pace is somewhat slowed down, the production is more polished without being too polished, and thematically there's an homage to the original era of punk rather than the naive and sometimes nationalistic Oi! formula.

While the album features the trademark football-influenced chant choruses that people associate with Oi!, the songs are heartfelt tales of being an outsider and trying to find a better way. "The Power and the Glory" starts the album with an anti-war song that condemns the politicians who send young men to go to war. "Friends" is about the pain of betrayal, while "On the Run" is a compelling story of being an outsider. And as if to say they won't be bound by the limitations of Oi!, there's a short acoustic piece and the contemplative instrumental "BYC" features a synthesizer and sounds like it could be from a soundtrack of a film. It ends with "The Greatest Story Ever Told," which follows in the pattern of the Clash and Stiff Little Fingers indicating that they won't be discouraged by naysayers and critics.

**Genre:** Punk/Oi!

## Cocteau Twins

### *Garlands* LP July 14, 1982 (4AD CAD 211) (UK)

The Cocteau Twins put their own unique stamp on the Goth-influenced post-punk of this period. Over a drum machine are guitars that sound more experimental than anything resembling a pop song. Elizabeth Fraser's vocals are almost like an instrument, with a twisting of phrasing that on some songs makes it difficult to distinguish if it's sung in English.

From what lyrics can be distinguished, some of the songs have an earth-based spirituality to them. The juxtaposition of this with the sometimes mechanical-sounding drum machine creates a kind of tension between the worldly and the mystical. In an era where post-punk offered all kinds of possibilities, this album showed yet another direction it could go in. It still has some of the disconcerting uneasiness of post-punk, but at the center of it is Fraser's ethereal voice.

### *Lullabies* 12" EP September 18, 1982 (4AD BAD 213) (UK)

This ironically titled EP sounds like anything but lullabies. During these three songs Elizabeth Fraser's vocals go in an even eerier direction than on *Garlands* and she enunciates the words as if she's singing in a non–English language. It's almost like a more melodic version of speaking in tongues. But as the lyrics from the EP indicate (on the band's website), she does indeed sing in English. It all gets swept up into the music, with Fraser's vocals more out front and without the drum machine so omnipresent on their debut album.

*Head Over Heels* LP October 24, 1983 (4AD CAD 313) (UK)

Just try describing this band without using the word ethereal. That's mostly because of Elizabeth Fraser's vocals, which glide over the music, at times almost in a Goth-like ghostly tone. Sometimes she repeats lines or phrases things in a distinct way that also gives her voice an otherworldly quality.

The band makes a change on this album where the songs are generally slowed down into a more integrated wall of sound. It's a softer kind of post-punk with layered and processed guitars in some ways similar to what the Chameleons did the same year with their landmark album *Script of the Bridge*. Not only is *Head Over Heels* produced differently with a wall of sound, but the songs are also generally slower. An exception is "In Our Angelhood," which has the energy of most post-punk even with the more compressed sound.

**Genre:** Post-punk

## Comsat Angels

*Sleep No More* LP August 21, 1981 (Polydor POLS 1038) (UK)

This British band's first and third albums blended post-punk with new wave, synth-pop, and pop but couldn't quite find the right groove. But their second album is a post-punk gem. It's fueled by a jagged, agitated, and expressive guitar with a melancholy and darker tone to the vocals and lyrics. Unlike some other post-punk, there isn't an avant-garde quality to it. It's catchy without being compromising.

A persistent sense of dejection on the album comes from a sense of loss and change. "The Eye Dance" asks the pleading question "Would you think it over?" showing that the singer wishes things could be different. "Gone" is even more blatant about a loss of innocence, asking "What happened to you?" before declaring "you got lost" to someone who "used to be so young." "Dark Parade" goes in a Goth direction with ominous drums and screeching guitars. In "Light Years," there's a lament of spending "years of life waiting for what might have been." Yet it ends with "Our Secret," a defiant refusal to give up hope. Along with U2's *Boy*, this is post-punk's chronicle of a loss of innocence and its effect on one's spirit.

**Genre:** Post-punk

## Conflict

*The House That Man Built* 7" EP September 1, 1981 (Crass Records 221984/1) (UK)

Debut record from British anarcho-punk band conveys their political perspective succinctly in four songs. "Conflict" shows the pointlessness of being on either side in a war, while "War Games" cautions young men from joining the army and carries the military ideology through to the terrors of nuclear war. "I've Had Enough" calls out the patriarchy, and the ending song "Blind Attack" sums up their anarchist ideology.

*It's Time to See Who's Who* LP March 1983 (Corpus Christi CHRIST IT's 3) (UK)

In the post UK 82 landscape, British punk intensified, and this album shows that. "1824 Overture," "One Nation Under the Bomb," and "Vietnam Serenade" are frenetic and rival American hardcore punk for speed. But the songs don't have the dystopian bleakness other British punk had during this period. Because of their anarcho-punk roots, the band seeks to educate and inspire rather than relentlessly show the horror of modern life as some other punk bands did during this time.

"Bullshit Broadcast" aims at career-conscious journalists who are irresponsible to the public, and the song ends with a question: "Can't you see the damage that you do?" "Exploitation" ridicules the punk band the Exploited for appearing on *Top of the Pops* and for their music. The band makes clear their preference for the politics of anarchy in "Blood Morons" and "Crazy Governments." In "The Guilt and the Glory," the band condemns traditional politics, criticizing both "the left-wing manifesto" and "the right-wing sham."

### *To a Nation of Animal Lovers* 7" EP 45 August 1983 (Corpus Christi CHRIST IT'S 4) (UK)

This is probably the first punk record completely devoted to animal rights. The band expands on "Meat Means Murder" from their album over three songs that cover eating meat, animal testing, wearing fur, and other animal rights issues. For the anarcho-punk band, this is an extension of standing up for the oppressed. "Human freedom, animal rights, it's one struggle, one fight," the band sings in "Whichever Way You Want It."

**Genre:** Punk

## Elvis Costello

### "Watching the Detectives" 45 October 14, 1977 (Stiff BUY 20) (UK)

Costello unintentionally helped create the second wave ska phenomenon by using drums, bass, and keyboard sounds that showed a way to blend punk and reggae. Perhaps it was because of this sound that Costello produced the first Specials album, the record that launched second wave ska.

**Genre:** Ska (influence)

### *This Year's Model* LP March 17, 1978 (Radar RAD 3) (UK)

The long-lasting Costello is perhaps music's greatest chameleon. He seems to go through a different musical genre with every album. As Costello's involvement in punk goes, this album is it. Mixing power pop and punk, the bulk of the album is an angry, scathing critique of contemporary culture. It was also groundbreaking for using keyboards prominently rather than just the standard electric guitar used in punk rock. This may have influenced the keyboard-laced new wave music to come.

Much of the album is about consumerism of people, experiences, and products that end up leaving one in a depleted and meaningless void. "The thrill is here but it won't last long / You'd better have your fun before it moves along," he says in "Living in Paradise," an insight that carries through for the entire album. "This Year's Girl" is about the merchandising of women to appeal to male fantasies. "Pump It Up" is almost Devo-like about the futility of sex, which is a primal urge causing all kinds of problems. The songs about relationships are all cynical, like "No Action," or depict interactions that have no real human quality to them, as in "You Belong to Me."

### "Radio Radio" 45 October 20, 1978 (Radar ADA 24) (UK)

Originally released on the U.S. version of *This Year's Model*, "Radio Radio" is about how radio and the media in general exists to "anesthetize the way that you feel" and where, in his truest punk rage, Costello wants to "bite the hand that feeds [him]."

Costello had his best-known punk rock moment when on a 1977 episode of *Saturday Night Live* he stopped playing the song "Less Than Zero" and launched into "Radio Radio."
**Genre:** Punk/Pop Punk

## Wayne County and the Electric Chairs

### *Storm the Gates of Heaven* LP August 26, 1978 (Safari Records GOOD 1) (UK)

Band led by punk's first transgender singer Wayne County (later Jayne County). County had one foot in 1970s rock (particularly Iggy and the Stooges) and the other in campy performance art–influenced songs. As a result, much of County's band's material tends to be not quite punky enough or songs that are potty-mouthed and almost novelty songs such as "Toilet Love." And in the late 1970s, County was sometimes more well-known for outrageous and daring live shows than music.

But everything seemed to click on this album. There's a seriousness, a sense of urgency, and a righteousness that together put this more squarely in the punk category. There's social commentary that doesn't have the campiness of some of County's other material. County tried Stooges-like rockers before, but nothing in that vein is as effective as "Speed Demon." There's the condemnation of conformity in "Mr. Normal" and what is probably punk's first song about transgender issues ("Man Enough to Be a Woman"). "Trying to Get on the Radio" sounds like a cross between a song that could have been on the *Rocky Horror Picture Show* soundtrack and an actual attempt to subversively write a radio hit.
**Genre:** Punk

## The Cramps

### *Gravest Hits* 12" EP June 20, 1979 (Illegal/I.R.S. SP-501) (USA)

This band basically invented psychobilly, a mash-up of rockabilly, punk, surf music, blues, and R&B. But this is no revival band. The Cramps put their own Gothic stamp on these musical genres, making it partly sinister but not losing the sense of liberating fun. This EP includes all the tracks from their first two 45s with an added song.

The Ramones covered "Surfin' Bird" earlier on their *Rocket to Russia* in 1977. But the Cramps give this complete psychobilly treatment with an explosive jam at the end. "Domino" features a Duane-Eddy-meets-punk-rock guitar part, while "Human Fly" is slower with a combination of B horror movie soundtrack and rockabilly. Surprisingly effective is the stripped-down cover of Ricky Nelson's "Lonesome Town," which sounds chillingly desperate and desolate.

### *Songs the Lord Taught Us* LP March 21, 1980 (I.R.S. SP 007) (USA)

On their first full-length album, this band goes through variations on the psychobilly sound. As a result, the psychobilly subgenre becomes solidified as part of horror punk, apparent in "TV Set" with its gory imagery as well as the mystery of "What's Behind the Mask." More fun is "Zombie Dance," which blends horror punk imagery with their trademark rockabilly-inspired influence.

The album also includes frenzied variations on rockabilly in "Rock on the Moon," "The Mad Daddy," and "Tear It Up." But they're not revivalist rockabilly at all. The Cramps add a dark punk and post-punk tone to songs like "Sunglasses After Dark." The nervous vocals of Lux Interior and the twangy guitar of Poison Ivy give the songs a dangerous quality even in what could be a lightweight song such as "I Was a Teenage Werewolf." There's an outsider punk persona in "Mystery Plane" of either an alien or someone who feels like one. Best of all may be "Garbageman," a first-person account of a garbageman, whether it's all literal or metaphorical. Their eclectic hybrid of influences and sounds made them one of the most influential bands on post-punk, horror punk, and alternative American roots music of the 1980s and beyond.

### "Goo Goo Muck" b/w "She Said" 45 May 8, 1981 (I.R.S. IR 9021) (USA)

With its melodic guitar riff, "Goo Goo Muck" is probably the band's most accessible song. But this psychobilly pop about a teenage monster with zombie tendencies still has an edge of danger to it with Lux Interior saying, "The city is a jungle and I'm a beast." With its marble-mouthed vocals, the B-side is on the verge of being a novelty song. But the tribal-type drumming during the verses into the rockabilly/surf guitar–fueled choruses is madcap fun.

**Genre:** Punk/Post-punk (Psychobilly)

## Crass

### *The Feeding of the 5,000* 12" EP January 18, 1979 (Small Wonder Weeny 2) (UK)

This album was probably the most important album in what is called anarcho-punk for its sense of chaos. And for targeting pretty much everything. There's something ragged in this music, particularly in the drums, which at times sounds more like a school band drummer trying to keep up more than a punk drummer. It deconstructs the punk music form even if it tries to uphold the spirit of punk. And the vocals don't adhere to conventions. The singers use thick, proletariat accents, singing lyrics that are often nearly indecipherable. In anarcho-punk there's something less warm about it, as if too much brightness would be too bourgeois.

The band in its anarchist intentions seems to want to destroy or criticize everything, including punk rock itself. In "Punk is Dead" some of the icons of punk are targeted, including Steve Jones of the Sex Pistols (for having the pretensions of a rock star), the Clash (for signing with CBS), and Patti Smith (for liking the poet Rimbaud). Among the other targets are some standard punk subjects including the military, consumerism, and the Cold War–era fear of nuclear destruction. Within all the fury, the standout track is "Do They Owe Us a Living?" which answers the question with the simple chant: "Of course they do!"

### "Rival Tribal Rebel Revel" 45 January 1980 (Flexi 421984/6F) (UK)

Could very well be a condemnation of the violent and nationalist tendencies of some of the Oi! movement. It's from the point of view of someone who views life as a battle who says, "Dealing out pain is my kind of fun." A bit of a turn in direction for them away to singing from the point of view of someone with an ideology they don't agree with. Yet within all of this is one of their catchiest and most accessible songs.

### "Big A Little A" (B-side of "Nagasaki Nightmare") 45 February 15, 1981 (Crass Records 421984/5) (UK)

One of Crass's most raucous songs and one of their best known. The song alternates between what they call oppressive forms of "external control." So there are the points of view of God, the Queen, and "the Prime Sinister" (then British Prime Minister Margaret Thatcher). The antidote is to break away from conformity to individualism to "be exactly who you want to be, do what you want to do" because "you're the only you."

### *Penis Envy* LP June 7, 1981 (Crass Records 321984/1) (UK)

After a second album, *Stations of the Crass* (1979), that was too derivative of their first album, the band radically changed direction. Using exclusively the vocals of Eve Libertine and Joy De Vivre, the result is a revitalized band and one of the most daring and important feminist punk albums ever made.

It starts with "Bata Motel," about a woman willing to be exploited sexually. And most of the rest of the album is about exploitation from a woman's perspective, whether it's the oppressive family life in "Systematic Death," marriage in "Berkertex Bribe," and even the nature and dynamics of relationships in "Smother Love" and "Dry Weather."

As with anarcho-punk, there's a relentless criticism of society's institutions that is sometimes done through shock and sometimes blatantly disturbing lyrics. The album ends, however, with another approach in the saccharine-sounding "Our Wedding," which on the surface sounds like a sincere ode to marriage. But the band ended up pranking a teen magazine into giving it away as a flexi disc.

**Genre:** Punk

## The Cravats

### "Precinct" 45 August 27, 1980 (Small Wonder SMALL 24) (UK)

Ominous song with the speed of punk and the frenzy of aggressive post-punk. It's propelled by a tribal beat and a nervous saxophone. The song is a menacing view of a society filled with injustice, consumerism, and oppression by the wealthy.

**Genre:** Punk/Post-punk

## The Creatures

### *Wild Things* double 45 September 29, 1981 (Polydor POSPG 354) (UK)

Siouxsie and the Banshees side project features vocalist Siouxsie, drummer Budgie, and an array of percussion. With one of post-punk's most important bands stripped to these basic components, there's a primal quality to the music in "So Unreal," "Mad Eyed Screamer," and "But Not Him." And it includes a subversive version of the 1960s tired warhorse "Wild Thing," which includes the lyrical twist of "wild thing I think I hate you!" The ending track—"Thumb," about hitchhiking—is a haunting post-punk version of a torch song.

### *Feast* LP May 20, 1983 (Wonderland/Polydor SHELP 1) (UK)

Siouxsie and Budgie record a full album of their offshoot group. Although there's still the tribal-like drumming from their *Wild Things* EP, there's also more of an emphasis on world music. Perhaps this is part of the Goth perspective of reverence for non–Western cultures, as if there's some truth in them through something more primal and less rational and not hindered by Western values. As with *Wild Things*, it's fascinating hearing Siouxsie's vocals in a more minimalist format as if Western instruments would destroy the ambiance.

"Inoa Ole" starts with a world music chant leading into Siouxsie's vocals that sets the tone for the rest of the album. There's also an emphasis on the exotic in songs like "Gecko." "Sky Train" features a very fast beat with sound effects and Siouxsie's chants. It's a somewhat eerie mix of the disturbing and the transcendent. "Festival of Colors" and "A Strutting Rooster" use some Hawaiian words (the album was recorded in Hawaii). "Dancing on Glass" features an infectious beat over the drums, some swirling keyboards, and handclaps.

It ends with the disturbing song "Flesh," about what appears to be exploitation of native cultures by Westerners and the decadence of Western rituals seen through a cocktail party. This isn't just a band immersing themselves in world music as a novelty. They try hard here to be authentic and reverent.

**Genre:** Post-punk

## The Cure

### "Killing an Arab" b/w "10:15 Saturday Night" 45 December 21, 1978 (Small Wonder SMALL 11) (UK)

Unfortunately, the A-side is still controversial because of its title. The song is, however, based on Albert Camus's existentialist novel *The Stranger*, in which the protagonist kills a man known only as "the Arab" on a beach. The point is the indifference of the act reflecting the protagonist's feeling that we all inhabit an indifferent world. Too bad the band didn't call the song something else because the song is often overlooked because it's so misunderstood. The B-side is a lament of someone waiting for someone to return. The protagonist is stuck in a specific time as he listens to the sound of a dripping faucet, and the music reflects the repetition of what he hears.

### "Jumping Someone Else's Train" 45 November 2, 1979 (Fiction FICS 005) (UK)

A song about adapting to trends rather than being an original. It refers to someone who wants to be part of "the latest wave," which could mean any number of musical trends occurring during this time. But it's about losing oneself in a world where "you'll have to adapt or you'll be out of style." The whole song is propelled by an infectious driving rhythm.

### "A Forest" 45 April 4, 1980 (Fiction FICS 10) (UK)

Haunting song with lyrics about someone drawn to the sound of a girl's voice in a forest. But the song's narrator realizes that he is "running toward nothing" and then repeats a refrain of "again and again." The symbolic implications for what it all means are enormous. But the band also found its musical groove here with something more ethereal and mysterious.

### *Faith* LP April 17, 1981 (Fiction fix6) (UK)

The band's first album, *Three Imaginary Boys*, was a diverse collection of songs and styles, as if they were trying to find their identity. In their second album, *Seventeen Seconds*, they were moving toward a more definitive sound, but it didn't sound quite complete. On this third album they make a breakthrough that defined the tone of this band for their career. The album centers around a crisis of faith, a search for something definitive and reassuring. Despite the somberness there is a beauty that comes through in the songs, which have an earnest search for meaning.

Religious symbolism starts on side one in "The Holy Hour," where the singer stays in a religious sanctuary because he feels it might offer some "promise of salvation." This initiates the searching theme in the album. After this comes "Primary," a song about being discouraged when age does not provide the wisdom that one hoped for. "Other Voices," with its memorable bass line, contains a theme of sin and confusion, a theme that would become dominant in their next album, *Pornography*. The theme of confusion continues with "All Cats Are Grey" with its ambiguity between black and white. The long meditative introduction is one of post-punk's great contemplative moments.

Side two starts with loss, memories, and emptiness provoked by the death of loved ones in "The Funeral Party." It's followed by "Doubt," which directly addresses doubt and hopes to destroy it. The album's closing songs seem to present two different conclusions. "The Drowning Man" ends in despair and tragedy, while "Faith" offers a more hopeful conclusion to the album's search. Staring at the abyss, the singer chooses to have faith, repeating the line "I went away alone with nothing left but faith."

### *Pornography* LP May 4, 1982 (Fiction FIXD7) (UK)

This album features a much more agitated and desperate melancholy than their previous album, *Faith*. The first line in the first song, "One Hundred Years"—"It doesn't matter if we all die"—shows the despondent feeling that permeates much of this album. The album also sounds much different from *Faith* with a compressed feeling, tribal-like drumming at times, and singer Robert Smith's voice sounding remote and almost disembodied at times. Rather than the quiet somber search of *Faith*, *Pornography* is a descent into a cruel and exploitative world. "I will never be clean again," Smith sings in "The Figurehead," as if he's a lost soul in an immoral world. *Pornography* is the Cure's gloomiest album with deep disillusionment and sometimes disturbing imagery of meaninglessness, exploitation, and violence.

Death, suffering, and disorientation are dominant themes, starting with the opening "One Hundred Years" introducing suffering in life and the specter of death. The rest of the album is a nightmarish tour through human motivations. Sex becomes a kind of primal motivation using animal imagery in "The Hanging Garden," while the theme of initial sex in "Siamese Twins" has a sense of disappointment with singer Robert Smith asking, "Is it always like this?" "A Strange Day" could be metaphorical about something that feels like the end of the world, or another Generation Jones–era imagining of the terror of sudden nuclear war. On the album's final song, "Pornography," Smith sings "I must fight this sickness, find a cure," as if searching for a way out of the darkness.

**Genre:** Post-punk

## Rhoda Dakar with Special AKA

### "The Boiler" 45 January 8, 1982 (2 Tone CHS TT18) (UK)

This narration of a date rape is terrifying. Rhoda Dakar, former singer for the ska band the Bodysnatchers, tells the frightening story with a backdrop of ska-influenced music that also sounds like it could be a movie soundtrack. A man asks out a woman who describes herself as a "boiler" who has "been left on the shelf." She dresses up; they go dancing. Afterwards she wants to get a cab to go home, but he invites her back to his place. He gets mad at her; they walk on through desolate alleyways and railway bridges. Then he takes her down an alleyway, starts to hit her, and tries to sexually assault her. The song ends with a bloodcurdling shriek.

**Genre:** Ska (variation)

## The Damned

*Damned Damned Damned* **LP February 18, 1977 (Stiff ZSEEZ 1) (UK)**

An enormously important punk album. Unlike the Clash and the Sex Pistols, their music is usually not overtly political. So it actually broadened the subject matter of punk songs. And the Damned generally play faster than the Sex Pistols or the Clash. Or just about anyone in 1977. The Damned also toured the United States in the spring of 1977 before either the Clash or the Sex Pistols' final show in San Francisco. For some Americans, the Damned was their first live exposure to English punk music. So they had an enormous influence on early West Coast punk and hardcore punk bands.

It all started with their energetic song "New Rose" in 1976, released between the first Ramones album and the Sex Pistols' "Anarchy in the UK." On first listen it may

The Damned—(left to right) Captain Sensible, Brian James, Rat Scabies, and Dave Vanian—were innovative and maintained their punk sensibility no matter what they played. They helped expand and define the genres of punk, hardcore, pop punk, Goth, and more (LFI/Photoshot/Everett Collection).

sound like it's about a romantic relationship. But band members said years later that it was at least partly about the punk scene itself. Preserved on this album, it's one of the most ferocious and exciting songs in all of punk. Another key track, "Neat Neat Neat," is also another song at breakneck speed with obscure lyrics that appears to be about a woman who is defenseless while chaos, crime, and apathy go on around her. There's also a darkness on some of the album that points to their later Gothic influences and also hints of what came to be known as horror punk. Recorded in just three days, this offering has an energy and ferocity found in few other punk albums.

**"Problem Child" 45 September 30, 1977 (Stiff BUY 18) (UK)**

On *Music for Pleasure*, the Damned suffered from the second album syndrome. They didn't want to repeat their first album or change so much that they would alienate their audience. So the album ended up being a no-man's-land. There isn't the energy of their first album. But there's also not the broadening and variation that rebuilt their sound on their third album, *Machine Gun Etiquette*. There is, however, this satisfying single from the album about an alienated outsider child.

*Machine Gun Etiquette* **LP November 2, 1979 (Chiswick CWK 3011) (UK)**

The Damned's disastrous second album, *Music for Pleasure*, was produced by Nick Mason of Pink Floyd (how did that happen?). So much of their energy was eliminated that it led to the band temporarily breaking up. But the band revived themselves with this album. This album is dynamic like their first album but incorporates other elements from pop, hard rock, and even elements of the emerging Goth subgenre of post-punk. As forceful and important as their first album is, *Machine Gun Etiquette* may have had more lasting impact because it expands the punk sound with a variety of approaches and styles.

The title track is basically a proto-hardcore song with its ultrafast speed and its call-and-response vocal structure. "Looking at You" has a similar fast pace. There's a Goth-like ominous quality to "I Just Can't Be Happy Today" with its dystopian worldview that may be a metaphor for contemporary society. "Plan 9 Channel 7" is about the actress Vampira, who appeared in Ed Wood's so-bad-it's-good sci-fi movie *Plan 9 from Outer Space*. The album ends with the anti-hippie song "Smash It Up," a new kind of pop punk with a simple keyboard part.

**"Rabid" (B-side of "White Rabbit") 45 June 2, 1980 (Chiswick 2C 008–63.938) (France)**

Energetic song using B movie horror and sci-fi imagery in its lyrics. No other band this side of hardcore punk does fast punk as well as the Damned. But they build on their breakneck speed by using a keyboard around the edges, a football chant of "rabid" during the chorus, and some pop harmonies. This is fun.

*The Black Album* **LP November 3, 1980 (Chiswick CWK 3015) (UK)**

The Damned continue to progress and show why they are one of the great bands of this era. Singer Dave Vanian always had a Goth persona, and now it comes through in the punk genre with some pop flourishes. In the opening track, "Wait for the Blackout," there's almost a vampire-like yearning to get away from society because "the darkness holds a power you won't find in the day." In "Lively Arts" there's a punk-like declaration that "culture's just a bore when you're angry, young, and poor." And they still can pull out the rapid-fire punk with the ferocious "Hit or Miss" and "Sick of This and That."

The pop embellishments in songs like "Drinking About My Baby" seem to sustain rather than dilute. The album could have been one album instead of two, however. Side four contains live tracks, and side three is taken up with the 17-minute "Curtain Call." There is an extended instrumental section that just seems to take up space. But this is a band showing they want to transcend the structural limitations of punk.

### "I Believe the Impossible" (B-side of "The History of the World Part 1") 45 September 22, 1980 (Chiswick CHIS 135) (UK)

The Damned at their most idealistic. Perhaps. There's a hope for a world without lying politicians or criminals and with full employment. But the second half of the song slows the pace down with an eerie keyboard that sounds like a Gothic-influenced church organ. So is it all ironic? Is it actually an impossible dream after all?

### "Dozen Girls" b/w "Take That" 45 October 1, 1982 (Bronze BRO 156) (UK)

This version of "Dozen Girls" is superior to the rerecorded version for the *Strawberries* album. And it contains the outgoing reciting of the names of a dozen girls rather than the somewhat bizarre "thermal underwear" chant on the album version. Like the songs that would dominate the *Strawberries* album, it is the band's own impressive take on punk with some pop overtones. The B-side is more like the straight punk from the band's early days and is a warning from a down-and-out person: "I'm going to take your throne." Is it the voice of the underclass? Or a criminal?

### *Strawberries* LP October 1, 1982 (Bronze BRON 542) (UK)

The album starts off with the punky fury of "Ignite." But the rest of the album is a deepening experiment in expanding their punk sound with pop embellishments. It's the band's unique way of reconfiguring the punk spirit into other formats. In this way the band becomes like more traditional post-punk bands. They don't use the experimentation of most post-punk but instead use more traditional pop and rock formats to embody the punk spirit.

There are horns in the soul-influenced "Stranger on the Town." But the band doesn't compromise like so many other bands did. Songs like this have a feeling of the punk outsider. "The Dog" is a Goth-like story of a woman named Claudia (perhaps a vampire?) who remains "undecayed for all eternity." "The Pleasure and the Pain" is about the ambivalence of being in love. "Life Goes On" is about ambivalence about life itself but seems to reach some resolution and acceptance of its contradictions and disappointments. Not everything works on this album, but most songs do. And it shows one of this era's very best bands consistently reinventing their sound while still retaining a punk perspective.

### "I Think I'm Wonderful" (B-side of "Lovely Money") 45 July 2, 1982 (Bronze BRO 149) (UK)

Is it a song of self-empowerment? Or it is the thoughts of a misanthropic criminal? It's to the band's credit that there are multiple interpretations to some of their songs. It's the band's biggest experiment to date to go beyond their punk sound.

**Genre:** Punk

## The Dance

### *Dance for Your Dinner* 12" EP 1980 (Go Go Records R003) (USA)

Although mostly propelled by downtown New York City post-punk funk, there's elements of no wave, Latin music, and jazz. It almost sounds like a collage of music you might hear walking through Greenwich Village in the Generation Jones time period. What holds this eclectic mix together is vocalist Eugenie Diserio, who can sound playful, defiant, jumpy, and a whole lot more.

She stretches her vocal phrasing in "She Likes to Beat" to give a disturbing aura that is an effective ironic juxtaposition to the music. In "Do Dada" she alternates between jazz scat singing and almost a punk-like snarl in the choruses. "Dance for Your Dinner" features a sarcastic-like vocal that's almost rap or sprechgesang. "Slippery When Wet" features a manic funk groove with world music flourishes.

**Genre:** Post-punk

## Dead Boys

### *Young Loud and Snotty* LP August 31, 1977 (Sire SR 6038) (USA)

This band formed in Ohio, moved to New York City, and landed in the downtown CBGBs punk rock scene. They seem to be both influenced by proto-punk and also building on the emerging punk movement. However, lead singer Stiv Bators had a more desperate and disturbing stage persona and lyrics than either proto-punk or punk bands. The band's debut album is crammed with sexism, violence, and at times hedonism and nihilism. Although the album hasn't aged well in some ways, it's still a testament to its time and to a different type of punk rock. It doesn't have the political and social consciousness of British punk or the sense of fun and liberation of the Ramones.

The highlight is the first track, "Sonic Reducer," which is an anthem-like pledge to being nonconformist but being confident that that is the best way to live. "Not Anymore" is about the underside of downtown New York life where someone who sounds like they could be homeless just tries to find some place to temporarily stay. "Ain't Nothing to Do" is another song about boredom with the media, and the album ends on a somewhat nihilistic feeling with "High Tension Wire" and "Down in Flames," which both have a resignation to them.

**Genre:** Punk

## Dead Kennedys

### "California Uber Alles" b/w "The Man with the Dogs" 45 June 19, 1979 (Optional Music OPT 2) (USA)

San Francisco punk band's debut single. "California Uber Alles" is another imagining of a punk dystopia. Then California Governor Jerry Brown becomes a new kind of fascist president, a liberal hippie dictator. "Mellow out or you will pay," the song warns. This version is rawer and stronger than the rerecorded version on their first album. The B-side is a strange and disturbing song about an outsider figure who imitates others and seems to have a sense of rage within him.

### "Police Truck" b/w "Holiday in Cambodia" 45 May 29, 1980 (Optional Music OPT 4) (USA)

Surf guitar style propels "Police Truck" with its ironic use of the phrase of "let's ride" about corrupt police on the prowl to cause damage. They claim to the supervisors they're just writing tickets. But they drink beer, beat up drunks, and force prostitutes to perform sexual favors for them. "Holiday in Cambodia" chastises wealthy college students who are ignorant about foreign policy. Like "California Uber Alles" it was rerecorded for their first album.

## 62    Dead Kennedys

*Fresh Fruit for Rotting Vegetables* LP September 2, 1980 (Alternative Tentacles VIRUS 1) (USA)

San Francisco punk bands like the Dead Kennedys were different from the Southern California punk bands emerging in the early 1980s. Although bands from both areas

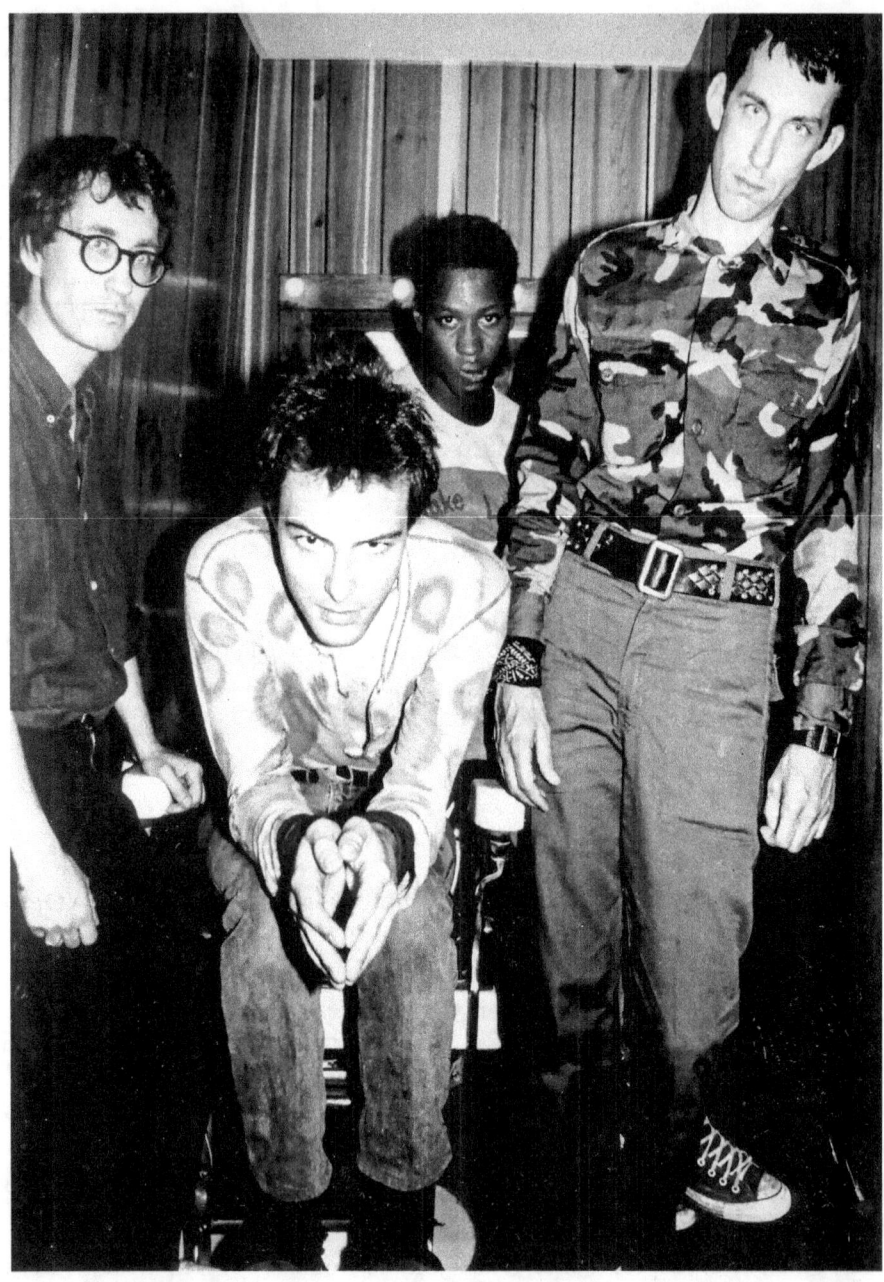

The Dead Kennedys—(left to right) Klaus Flouride, Jello Biafra, D.H. Peligro, and East Bay Ray—helped develop California punk and hardcore punk into a genre deeply associated with political and social commentary. They also added a satirical quality to the punk genre (Pictorial Press Ltd./Alamy).

could be political, Los Angeles area bands seemed to specialize in teen angst and the feeling of being an outsider. They chronicled the inner pain brought on by authority and the feeling of being a misfit. The Dead Kennedys, however, focused on the external. They utilized politically charged satire in a way that was sometimes almost theatrical. They were so influential that it became almost obligatory for every hardcore band to have at least some political perspective in their music.

The album starts with the satirical "Kill the Poor," about exterminating the troublesome poor by using the neutron bomb, which kills people but doesn't damage buildings. The Cold War–themed songs continue in "When Ya Get Drafted" about the recently reinstated draft registration. The album goes on to tackle contemporary problems like greedy landlords ("Let's Lynch the Landlord"), the effects of consumerism ("Drug Me"), and anger at the affluent ("Chemical Warfare").

### "In-Sight" (B-side of "Kill the Poor") 45 October 20, 1980 (Cherry Red Cherry 16) (UK)

Sung from the point of view of career-minded high school students who bully and harass an outsider student they label as weird. The loner student keeps to himself, alternating between bold resistance and bored withdrawal. A song of understanding for those who felt like misfits in high school.

### "Nazi Punks Fuck Off!" b/w "Moral Majority" 45 October 24, 1981 (Subterranean Alternative Tentacles VIRUS 6) (USA)

An ultrafast song that speaks out against the growing violence at hardcore punk shows. It also lashes out against punks who use Nazi symbolism and don't understand the nature of fascism. The B-side is a rant against the conservative religious movement Moral Majority, which helped propel Ronald Reagan to victory in the presidential election the previous year.

### "Bleed for Me" b/w "Life Sentence" 45 August 5, 1982 (Alternative Tentacles VIRUS 23) (USA)

"Bleed for Me" is fiercer with grittier guitars than the version on *Plastic Surgery Disasters*. It intensifies the song's view of torture and violence initiated by CIA-trained entities. Like "Holiday in Cambodia," the B-side is about college students. This time it's about those who graduate and then lock themselves into jobs that feel like prison sentences they can't escape from.

### *Plastic Surgery Disasters* LP November 23, 1982 (Alternative Tentacles VIRUS 27) (USA)

Since their first album released two years earlier, hardcore punk became a full-fledged genre and got a lot faster. And this album is distinctly hardcore punk rather than a combination of punk and hardcore punk as on their first album. This is full-on hardcore punk such as the ultrafast "Riot." Singer Jello Biafra returns to some of his usual targets. One is college students, in "Terminal Preppie." Then there's the affluent in "Forest Fire" and the brutality of imperialism in "I Am the Owl."

Like the first album, it's a tour through the problems of contemporary America. And it's mostly handled through satire. There are the professions that cheat people, such as "Trust Your Mechanic." The album's two ending songs slow down the pace in a kind

64    Deep Wound

of despair about apocalyptic-like conditions. In "Dead End," "profits are better than life," and in "Moon Over Marin," an oil spill produces environmental disaster.
**Genre:** Punk/Hardcore Punk

## Deep Wound

### *Deep Wound* 7" EP 1983 (Radiobeat RB002) (USA)

Massachusetts band with future Dinosaur Jr. member J. Mascus puts their innovative stamp on hardcore. At times there are chaotic and experimental song structures far beyond standard hardcore. Sounds at times like it's on the verge of going off the rails into something free form but stays powerfully on course.
**Genre:** Hardcore Punk

## Delta 5

### "Mind Your Own Business" 45 December 2, 1979 (Rough Trade RT 031) (UK)

With two bass players and duel female vocals, this Leeds band put their own unique stamp on the post-punk genre. In this song (as in most of their songs) there's a funk influence in the bass parts with jagged guitars consistent with the post-punk genre. But it's the doubling of female vocals that gives this band their strongest identity. The band's best-known song appears to be a feminist slap down of those that are too intrusive, demanding, and misunderstanding.

### "Anticipation" b/w "You" 45 April 7, 1980 (Rough Trade RT 041) (UK)

Instead of the jagged guitar of "Mind Your Own Business," this song uses a swirling flanger guitar. Many of the songs on the band's early singles are about disillusionment. The reality fails to live up to the promise and the potential. And it's all danceable, with an almost disco beat with the percussion. The B-side features some yelping vocals, a prominent driving bass line, and lyrics exposing the limitations of a partner who leaves her disappointed.

### "Try" b/w "Colour" 45 November 26, 1980 (Rough Trade RT 061) (UK)

The A-side is about someone who can never understand her point of view with its repeated refrain of "you don't see what I see." The B-side effectively adds some brass to a continuation of the theme in "Try" about being marginalized and misunderstood.
**Genre:** Post-punk

## Descendents

### "It's a Hectic World" (B-side of "Ride the Wild") 45 1980 (Orca Productions 001) (USA)

Pop punk with some quirky rhythms and jangle guitars instead of standard punk buzz saw guitar. But even in a band with strong pop elements, the Generation Jones perspective on oppressive work and conformity defines work as a competitive, anxiety-producing rat race.

### *Fat* 7" EP May 10, 1981 (New Alliance NAR-005) (USA)

The California band finds its groove with a mixture of punk, pop punk, and hardcore punk. It's all much faster than their debut single, with five songs performed in less than five minutes. There are two very short songs about food, one about teen anger over parents (something that would resurface on their debut album *Milo Goes to College*). However, the two longest songs—"Mr. Bass" and "Hey Hey"—point to a new direction. "Mr. Bass" is a cartoonish song about a fishing voyage, while "Hey Hey" contains the kind of angst of "It's a Hectic World" with a sense of torment and confusion.

### *Milo Goes to College* LP September 4, 1982 (New Alliance NAR-012) (USA)

While their *Fat* EP was more cartoonish, there's a lot of anger here. And it was a landmark album in redefining pop punk. This record wasn't the purer pop punk of the Buzzcocks, the Undertones, and the Dickies. Instead, the Descendents integrate pop punk, punk, and hardcore punk. Although there is some political and social commentary like the anti-military "M-16," and the questioning of American values in "Statue of Liberty," most of the album shifts the perspective to teen angst. This association of punk with an angry teenage persona along with the hybrid of punk, hardcore punk, and pop punk greatly influenced 1990s pop punk.

The album has a suburban American teenage-like perspective with a rage and sense of rebellion. "Suburban Home" is a satire about conformity to suburban living, but there is some recognition of social class, primarily through viewing the more privileged in "I'm Not a Loser." Following the pop punk convention, there are some songs about relationships. "Kabuki Girl" is about an exciting infatuation, but there's mostly a darker tone to relationships, such as the rage and pain in "Hope" and "Mysage." Anger about being pigeonholed into a punk tribe comes out in "I'm Not a Punk," which condemns stereotypes of the punk movement, as well as punk posers in "Tonyage." The album ends with its darkest moments with songs about how young people can be destroyed, like the 15-year-old junkie prostitute in "Bikeage" and the suicide victim in "Jean Is Dead."

**Genre:** Punk/Pop Punk/Hardcore Punk

## Desperate Bicycles

### "The Medium Was Tedium" 45 July 19, 1977 (Refill RR2) (UK)

With a cheap-sounding keyboard, shuffling percussion sounds, and an unorthodox-sounding vocalist, this song became a punk DIY anthem. There's an encouraging cry to "go and join a band" and the song's famous declaration "it was easy, it was cheap, go and do it!" While the song's theme is all DIY punk, the song structure itself is an unusual and interesting minimalism.

**Genre:** Punk/Post-punk

## Destroy All Monsters

### "Bored" b/w "You're Gonna Die" 45 February 1978 (IDBI EEE1) (USA)

At the beginning of the punk era former Stooges guitarist Ron Asheton joined this Michigan band featuring artist and singer Niagara on lead vocals. The first of three singles the band released during this period confronts a major affliction of the late 1970s: boredom. Niagara sings about boredom as if it's a disease that can't be cured. The B-side is an ominous song about what sounds like curses that are put onto the singer. And there's a feeling of anarchy in Niagara's vocals, which, along with the screeching saxophone, sounds at time like a no wave experiment.

**"Nov. 22" b/w "Meet the Creeper" 45 June 19, 1979 (IDBI MONZ-2) (USA)**

The A-side is about the assassination of President John F. Kennedy described as if it's a horror movie. And it shows an essential distrust and disillusionment of the government and the media. The B-side is their most accessible and perhaps most straight-up punk song with one of Asheton's greatest guitar riffs. It also is one of Niagara's best vocals as she sings about what appears to be a murderer or stalker on the prowl.

**"What Do I Get" b/w "Nobody Knows" 45 January 19, 1980 (Cherry Red CHERRY 9) (UK)**

This remarkable single, which merges Asheton's Stooges-influenced guitar riffs that drive the songs along, Niagara's distinctive vocals, and chaos that's interjected at times, verges on noise rock or no wave. This time instead of a kind of horror about outside events, there's a focus on internal pain.

**Genre:** Punk

## Deutsch Amerikanische Freundschaft

***Ein Produkt der Deutsch-Amerikanischen Freundschaft* LP June 1979 (Warning Records WR 001) (Germany)**

The term electro-punk is used sometimes for albums like this. But this is really music that uses post-punk as a foundation blending industrial and electronica with post-punk's distinctive jagged guitars. This debut album by this German band utilizes an urgent and unsettling atmosphere that many other German electronica bands in this era didn't have. There is an uneasiness to this music that reflects this time period. It's dark, sometimes plodding, sometimes discordant, sometimes almost violent-sounding.

The album consists of 22 untitled instrumentals. All but three are under two minutes long. While the songs generally don't go on long enough to become full-fledged songs in a conventional sense, the album is important for its blending of industrial and electronica into post-punk. Some may view some of these short instrumentals more like riffs than complete songs, but you can hear how post-punk would borrow from these experiments.

**Genre:** Post-punk

## Devo

***Mechanical Man* 7" EP August 28, 1978 (Elevator Records NICE 1) (UK)**

Long thought to be a bootleg, these early Devo recordings are apparently a legitimate release by a Virgin Records subsidiary reportedly included in some initial copies of their first album.

The music was recorded in 1975 and 1976 and is astounding in its innovation for the time period. It includes the corporate worker satire "Blockhead" as well as "Blackout" (both later rerecorded on Devo's second album) and "Auto-Modown," with its experimental rhythms and slow funk groove. More Devo songs from this era were later released on the albums *Hardcore Devo Vol. 1* (1990) and *Hardcore Devo Vol. 2* (1991), but these four tracks are deservedly legendary.

### Q: Are We Not Men? A: We Are Devo LP August 28, 1978 (Warner Bros. BSK 3239) (USA)

Devo had two phases. Most people associate them with their second phase, which was when they were a subversive synth-pop band after the massive success of their self-help satire song, "Whip It," in 1980. But for the first phase of their career they were a pioneering American post-punk band.

If Joy Division's music partly incorporated rhythms of the industrial sounds of Manchester, England, Devo's tempos at times sound like the equivalent of the mechanism of American Midwest factories. But Devo's lyrics are not about inner pain or emotions as with other post-punk bands. Devo is more philosophical and centered on the band's ideology of de-evolution, that humans are not evolving but de-evolving.

The concept of de-evolution gets a now iconic chant in "Jocko Homo" with its call-and-response of "Are we not men? We are devo." "Uncontrollable Urge" highlights the primal impulses of humans. The band brilliantly subverts the Rolling Stones' "Satisfaction" to emphasize those unhealthy impulses. The band also satirizes aspects of contemporary culture that exploit those desires, such as "Too Many Paranoias," about fast food culture, and "Come Back Jonee," which sabotages the cliché of the ambitious young man who wants to be a rock star but meets with tragedy instead of success.

### B Stiff 12" EP October 1978 (ODD 1) (UK)

Compiles their first three indie singles. Brian Eno would rerecord several of these songs for Devo's first album. While these original versions of "Jocko Homo," "Mongoloid," "Sloppy," and "Satisfaction" are perhaps not as punchy as the album versions, there's a rawness and purity that make these original versions superior. Contains the delightfully subversive "Be Stiff" as well as "Social Fools," a warning to those who conform.

### Duty Now for the Future LP June 1, 1979 (Warner Bros. BSK-3337) (USA)

Positioned between their first album, which received much attention from critics, and their third album, *Freedom of Choice*, which was a commercial success, this album is often overlooked and underrated. It's a midpoint between the two stages of the band's career: the Brian Eno–produced post-punk first album and the subversive synth-pop band that would achieve chart success. And in many ways it seems the most honest and authentic Devo album because they are free of the conventions of both post-punk and synth-pop. But it also may be Devo's most cynical worldview.

The songs are largely almost surreal interpretations of modern life that mock the impulses people have toward achievement, conformity, material possessions, pleasure, and sexual relationships. A consistent theme is ridiculing the urges toward romantic relationships, which is summed up in the title of the song "Strange Pursuit." This theme is also in "Triumph of the Will," named after a Nazi propaganda film, suggesting that the motivations toward pursuing romantic relationships may be the same. "Pink Pussycat" focuses on a relentless pursuit of a sex object, while "Smart Patrol/Mr. DNA" is an attack on the motives toward sex and procreation. Other songs portray other impulses, including conformity ("Blockhead") and achievement through pleasure and material security ("Clockout"), while the album-ending "Red Eye" appears to be about a restlessness toward impulses that never stop.

**"Penetration in the Centrefold" (B-side of "The Day My Baby Gave Me a Surprise") 45 June 1, 1979 (Virgin VS 265) (UK)**

The last of the Brian Eno–produced songs released from their milestone first album sessions. And it's one of their most energetic punk-influenced songs. It features one of the band's main themes, which is the baser aspects of consumerism. In this case it's the commodification of pornography and the viler urges it produces.

**Genre:** Post-punk

## The Dickies

**"You Drive Me Ape (You Big Gorilla)" (B-side of "Paranoid") 10" EP June 23, 1978 (A&M SP-12008) (USA)**

The first Dickies album, *The Incredible Shrinking Dickies*, is a grab bag of different approaches with too many cover songs with an overall feel of being too disparate. They would do much better on their second album. The best song on the album ended up on the B-side to their version of Black Sabbath's "Paranoid." It's fun wordplay pop punk. And it shows another direction in pop punk: songs that aren't about relationships but instead an almost innocent fun.

***Dawn of the Dickies* LP October 24, 1979 (A&M SP-04796) (USA)**

On their second album, the California pop punk group slowed things just down a little from their first album. And the enhanced production also helped shape them into well-crafted pop punk songs. The result is a classic pop punk album that has a fun, adolescent quality to it. That's different from the angry, adolescent, angst-filled pop punk that the Descendents would later largely create with their *Milo Goes to College* album in 1982.

Instead of songs about relationships as in many pop punk songs, the songs are often a playful celebration of popular culture. "(I'm Stuck in a Pagoda with) Tricia Toyota" is a tribute to a local TV newscaster. "Manny, Moe and Jack" is about the founders of an auto repair chain whose caricatures are on the company logo. Other songs have lyrics that sound like they could be based on low-budget horror movies ("Infidel Zombie" and "Attack of the Mole Men"). But the shortcomings of pop culture are here too. One of the best songs, "Fan Mail," focuses on overzealous fans who seem to only care about the trivial aspects of fame.

**"Gigantor" 45 June 28, 1980 (A&M AMS 7544) (USA)**

The Dickies had a bigger hit with their frenzied version of the theme from the children's TV show *The Banana Splits*. But it seemed too much like a rushed novelty song. This pop punk take on the animated Japanese TV show about a flying robot, however, is fun and a full-fledged pop punk song. It's even kind of righteous-sounding with its conviction that he's "ready to fight for right against wrong."

**Genre:** Pop Punk

## The Dicks

**"Hate the Police" b/w "Lifetime Problems" 45 May 19, 1980 (Radical Records NR 12142) (USA)**

Punk or early hardcore? Whatever you call it, it's one of American punk's great singles. The A-side from this Austin, Texas, band is about a policeman having a bad day

who just might take it out on minorities. "Lifetime Problems" features a chorus with a maniacal laugh by vocalist Gary Floyd.
   **Genre:** Punk/Hardcore Punk

## The Dils

### "I Hate the Rich" b/w "You're Not Blank" 45 September 20, 1977 (What Records WHAT-02) (USA)

Early Southern California punk band recalls British punk bands like the Clash, the Jam, and Northern Ireland's Stiff Little Fingers. "I Hate the Rich" is a straightforward indictment of the wealthy. The B-side is even better. It's an anti-hippie song that reminds people that the Summer of Love is 10 years gone.

### *198 Seconds of The Dils* 45 December 29, 1977 (Dangerhouse SLA-268) (USA)

Along with the Avengers, the Dils for a short time were America's answer to British punk and its social class consciousness. The A-side, "Class War," is a direct address about income inequality and the tension it creates. The B-side, "Mr. Big," is a warning to powerful people about what will come from the underclass. A worthy follow-up to their first single.
   **Genre:** Punk

## Discharge

### *Realities of War* 7" EP March 26, 1980 (Clay Records CLAY 1) (UK)

Are they hardcore? Or are they thrash? Or a combination of both? On the first four-song EP from this British band, it's a combination. By 1982 on their first album, *Hear Nothing See Nothing Say Nothing*, they essentially crossed over into a full-fledged crossover thrash band, more punk-influenced heavy metal than a form of hardcore punk.

The key to what makes Discharge different from hardcore punk is the heavier guitar, the use of guitar solos, a more guttural vocal, and an almost tribal drumbeat at times. There are hardcore punk conventions, however, because the songs are at breakneck speed and emphasize social commentary, something that almost all conventional heavy metal did not do. "Realities of War" and "They Declare It" are both anti-war songs. "But After the Gig" seems to be a critique of the band Crass, or perhaps fans of anarchistic punk, while "Society's Victim" shows the painful realization of being victimized by society.

### *Fight Back* 7" EP June 27, 1980 (Clay Records CLAY 3) (UK)

More compressed production and ultrafast songs makes this more hardcore punk–sounding than *Realities of War*. The vocal delivery still has a deep British raspy gritty quality that sounds at times more like a rabid Goth-like doom than the frustration and anger of most punk. The songs cover war, anarchy, the evils of the political and economic system, and organized religion.

### *Decontrol* 7" EP November 19, 1980 (Clay Records CLAY 5) (UK)

This EP leans even more toward hardcore punk than their first two EPs, particularly on the last track, "Tomorrow Belongs to Us," which features a call-and-response in the choruses that sounds most like a hardcore song. Like their first two EPs, there's a heavy emphasis on the horrors of war in "Decontrol" and "It's No TV Sketch." But once again the songs don't vary much in tempo. There's one speed. And that's fast. Discharge even had their own genre or subgenre named after them called D-beat (also Discore) after the distinctive drum pounding.

**Genre:** Hardcore Punk/Crossover Thrash Hybrid

## Disorder

### *Complete Disorder* 7" EP May 23, 1981 (Disorder Order 1) (UK)

One of the greatest and hardest rocking debut records of this period. How did they get the production sound? However that was accomplished, it's a riveting sound this band or anyone else during this time was never able to quite duplicate. DJ John Peel famously compared it to the roar of a Triumph motorcycle.

Part hardcore, part street punk, part noise punk, part crossover thrash, there's a compressed distortion in the guitar with just enough high notes and short solos at critical moments to keep things punky simple. All four songs are a similar tempo: fast! From the opening song, "Complete Disorder," where it sounds like chaos is ensuing with the cries of "disorder!" to the album-ending "Insane Youth," it sounds both like a manic soundtrack to an apocalypse and an exuberant cathartic energetic release.

**Genre:** Street Punk/Hardcore Punk

## DNA

### "You and You" b/w "Little Ants" 45 1978 (Medical Records 11-CAN 234) (USA)

This is no wave at its most deconstructionist. On "You and You" there's very little that fits together into anything resembling a traditional song. The piano thumps along at its own tempo while a guitar sounds like it's either being strangled or is shredding into pieces. A voice comes in with gravely shouting almost like a hardcore punk vocalist over expressionistic lyrics. The B-side is more subdued but no less deconstructionist. It uses percussion and rhythms like a slowed-down version of bebop and free-form jazz.

### *A Taste of DNA* 12" EP August 1981 (American Clave AMCL 1003 EP) (USA)

The production is less primitive than their single (the only other songs the band released during their time together was on the compilation *No Wave* LP). But the band still is perhaps the most experimental of all the no wave bands. The vocals almost seem like they come from the subconscious rather than real words, as if the voice itself is an instrument. Their best-known song is probably "Blonde Redhead," with its march-like drums leading into a post-punk rhythm with the band's trademark shredding guitar sound.

**Genre:** No Wave

## D.O.A.

### *Something Better Change* LP September 13, 1980 (Friends Records FR003) (Canada)

Canadian punk band's first album is mostly pre-hardcore. Before hardcore's dominance of American punk demanded a specific song structure, the punk bands remaining in the early 1980s fired off a range of punk approaches. And at its best, this album sounds pretty righteous. Like on "The Enemy," with its catchy chorus about recognizing who the enemy is: oppressive employers, the media, and the police. The culmination of the album is the ferocious "World War 3" with its Generation Jones–inspired Cold War fear of an apocalyptic ending battle.

Some songs still sound like early hardcore, however, such as "Get Out of My Life" and "The Prisoner," which are both fast paced. But the band experiments with different structures, such as in "Woke Up Screaming," which slows the pace down; the somewhat funky and near post-punk "Whatcha Gonna Do?"; and the almost pop punk "Last Night."

*Hardcore '81* **LP March 11, 1981 (Friends Records FR010) (Canada)**

Legend has it that this album's title is how the hardcore punk genre got its name. And while it isn't consistently hardcore punk, the songs are faster than on their first album. Covering 13 songs in less than 20 minutes, it's more of a grab bag of songs without the range of their first album. But at its best it sounds more forceful. The album starts off with an energetic trilogy of songs. "D.O.A." is an ominous song about recognizing a dark and possibly deadly part of one's condition, "Unknown" decries the commercialization that hardcore punk was so suspicious of, and "Slumlord" compares landlords to overlords.

From there the album takes some twists and turns. Some songs are very short, one features burping on the chorus, and there's an unneeded cover of Led Zeppelin's "Communication Breakdown." The most political song is "Smash the State," which calls life under oppression a "fascist rape." It ends with the breakneck "Waiting for You" at full-fledged hardcore speed for a total of 45 seconds.

**Genre:** Punk/Hardcore Punk

# Durutti Column

*Return of Durutti Column* **LP January 9, 1980 (Factory FACT 14) (UK)**

This guitar-centered instrumental post-punk is all about minimalism. The sparseness evokes a certain beauty different from the agitation often associated with post-punk. Yet there's sometimes a tension between the guitar and the percussion, as if Vini Reilly's guitar is working to transcend all limitations and constraints. Perhaps because the band is from Manchester, there is a melancholy and sometimes withdrawn aspect to the music. In some ways it's like a stripped-down post-punk movie soundtrack that alternates between contemplation and tension.

The album is a haunting and explorative showcase for Reilly's guitar, which at times integrates non-rock influences including jazz and classical styles into a post-punk guitar sound. All of this helped eventually expand the post-punk sound away from jagged guitars into more eclectic and melodic variations.

*LC* **LP November 15, 1981 (Factory FACT 44) (UK)**

The band expands on their sparse and somewhat muted debut album into a more complex and stronger sound. Added instrumentation intensifies the mood of these songs into an even more reflective and melancholy atmosphere. This album expanded the range of post-punk, particularly the use of guitar. The interplay between the percussion and Vini Reilly's guitar in songs like "The Act Committed" shows how to create tension without using what was coming to be a cliché in post-punk: the nervous, jagged guitar sound.

*LC* shows there were other ways to create a feeling of uneasiness. But there could also be a range of emotion, such as in "Jacqueline," which feels more optimistic and active, and "Messidor," which is both reflective and apprehensive. A few tracks feature some vocals that sometimes sound like a distant voice in distress. One of them is "Missing Boy," a compelling lament about Joy Division vocalist Ian Curtis.

**Genre:** Post-punk

## Ian Dury

*New Boots and Panties!!* **LP September 23, 1977 (Stiff SEEZ 4) (UK)**

Punk rock quickly made the retro pub rock movement in England obsolete. But two major things survived from it: Wilko Johnson's nervous jagged guitar from Dr. Feelgood and Ian Dury's songwriting and persona. Dury made it cool to have a regional accent. And he wrote about everyday British life in a poetic way that fit into the realism of punk rock. Most of this album is a bridge between pub rock and punk rock with songs that are slices of English life, such as "My Old Man" about Dury's bus driver father.

The last three songs on the album, however, are full-fledged punk songs. In the future, Dury would embrace a funk-based version of post-punk with an English dance hall influence. But this trilogy of songs is urgent and direct and shows a much darker side of life than he usually presents. "Blockheads" is almost a horror-like depiction of crude people who defy social conventions, "Plaistow Patricia" is about a woman living in the underside of life, and "Blackmail" uses ethnic stereotypes to portray an angry underclass.

**Genre:** Punk

## Ian Dury and the Blockheads

**"Hit Me with Your Rhythm Stick" 45 November 23, 1978 (Stiff BUY 38) (UK)**

A subversive post-punk funk experiment that somehow became a big hit in the United Kingdom. On the surface, a dance song peppered by a phrase James Brown and other R&B singers often used ("hit me!"). But underneath there's an interplay of tempos over Dury's regional accent and a saxophone explosion and middle break that recalls both free-form jazz and no wave experimentation.

**"Spasticus Artisticus" 45 July 24, 1981 (Polydor POSP × 285) (UK)**

Reworking the famous line "I am Spartacus" from the movie *Spartacus*, Dury comes up with a phrase to describe his disability (he was affected by polio, which left him partially paralyzed). It shows his anger at his limitations and his pride at maneuvering through it, also hinting that, by making it all a joke, by taunting it, he has more of a sense of control.

**Genre:** Post-punk

## Eater

**"Thinkin' of the USA" 45 May 27, 1977 (The Label TLR 003) (UK)**

The London lads wonder about the United States. It's the land of both the CIA and the SLA. And of Lou Reed and Richard Nixon. Is it a place to escape to? Maybe not after all.

*The Album* **LP October 11, 1977 (The Label TLR LP 001) (UK)**

Eater was the youngest of the early British punk bands. They were so young they changed their cover of Alice Cooper's "Eighteen" to "Fifteen." Influenced by glam and pop punk as well as straight-ahead punk, the album is more melodic than many other bands in 1977 who often just went for sheer energy.

The guitars sound just as influenced by the Velvet Underground as the Ramones. Many bands have covered the Velvet Underground, but few have made their covers as good as Eater's versions of "Sweet Jane" and "Waiting for the Man." They're both faster than the original but not the breakneck pace of many covers in the early days of punk. They also do a punky cover of David Bowie's "Queen Bitch."

The songs are short and pithy. Some with a teen perspective. "I Don't Need It" is about the hypocrisy and decadence of adulthood. The singer is trying to avoid growing up to be like them ("everybody knows that you're just a bunch of fakes"). The band isn't as good at the teen version of relationship songs. Although they may be teen anger fantasies, "No Brains" and "Get Raped" are disturbing. But, overall, this is 1977 punk that sounds spontaneous, youthful, and free of artifice.

**Genre:** Punk/Pop Punk

## Echo and the Bunnymen

### "Simple Stuff" (B-side of "Rescue") 45 April 19, 1980 (Korova KOW 1) (UK)

This may be the closest to straight punk this band ever recorded. Or perhaps it's one of the greatest mergers of punk and post-punk in this era. "We just pick out the simple stuff, we don't need all those complications," singer Ian McCulloch declares with a punk-like confidence.

### *Crocodiles* LP July 18, 1980 (Korova KODE 1) (UK)

Debut album from Liverpool band showed yet another new direction for post-punk. Jagged and sometimes discordant guitars were increasingly associated with post-punk. But this album had a less experimental sound where the guitars merge into the overall sound rather than dominating. Most of the time the band conveys moodiness, darkness, and a sense of isolation. But at times there are pop elements with a dark edge to the lyrics, such as in "Rescue," which pleads for help from conflict.

Overall, the album combines the moodiness with a strong sense of melody, such as in "Monkeys," which shifts from a gloomy feeling to a melodic chorus. The title track is the most driving song with the album's most aggressive guitars. "All That Jazz" (with its memorable line "see you at the barricades") is another standout track with its apocalyptic-like imagery. An innovative album with strong vocals by Ian McCulloch, whose voice soars with a more punk-like strength than the nervous vocals of many post-punk bands.

### "The Puppet" b/w "Do It Clean" 45 October 2, 1980 (Korova KOW 11) (UK)

Continues the pop and post-punk blend of songs from their first album. "The Puppet" could be about a personal crisis that is paralyzing the singer. Or it could be a political song about being controlled. "Do It Clean" contains an element of lostness to it with the declaration "I've been here there, everywhere; here there, nowhere."

### *Heaven Up Here* LP May 29, 1981 (Korova Kode 3) (UK)

It's less eclectic than their first album *Crocodiles*, but the consistency helps the band create a more definitive sound with fuller production. The more overt pop on some of their previous songs is pretty much gone. It's fixed in its steadiness and vision. As a result, it's probably the band's most powerful album.

The band continues the sense of melancholy and sometimes desperation and confusion from the first album. But the music complements these feelings more. The album starts more confidently with "Show of Strength" with its command that "all those things you think might count you can never set them down, don't ever set them down." That continues with the forceful "With a Hip," and then, starting with the ominous "Over the Wall," it proceeds through a sometimes deepening range of emotions, reflections, and anxieties. That includes the single "A Promise," about the disappointment of an unfulfilled promise, and "Dark Things," about the hope of exposing what was once hidden. But the album ends with "All I Want," which begins optimistically but then turns more ambivalent.

### "Way Out and Up We Go" (B-side of "The Cutter") 45 January 14, 1983 (Korova KOW 26) (UK)

A desperate vocal from singer Ian McCulloch propels this song that at times out-intensifies almost any song that would appear on their next album, *Porcupine*. McCulloch really sounds on the edge here. The imagery of alcohol, grieving, fear, and cryptic messages make this one of the band's most compelling and angsty songs.

### *Porcupine* LP February 4, 1983 (Korova Kode 6) (UK)

Echo's third album, *Porcupine*, shows how they could take post-punk in different directions. They add pop overtones and an almost orchestral feel at times. The musical experimentation starts with the album's first track, "The Cutter," introduced by an Indian instrument, giving it the feel of world music.

The sound of the Indian raga violin gives the song a spiritual quality that continues thematically throughout the album. Both introspection and a search for meaning dominate the album. "The Cutter" is about an identity crisis, and in "Clay" singer Ian McCulloch adopts the point of view of someone with somewhat of a split personality. "Higher Hell" also contains a contradictory nature within someone that forces the singer into self-examination. Other songs, such as "Ripeness," are a search for overall meaning, while other songs have religious and philosophical references. The album ends with "In Bluer Skies," a quiet plea and hope that somehow salvation awaits.

**Genre:** Post-punk

## Effigies

### *Haunted Town* 12" EP December 1981 (Autumn Records AU-3) (USA)

From Chicago's late punk era before hardcore punk took over the punk scenes in many U.S. cities. If this band were from Southern California, this EP would likely be regarded as one of the best records of this period. But Midwestern punk didn't receive the media attention that California punk did.

The entire EP is a depiction of defiance against oppression. In "Below the Box" the singer concludes that "when things fall short of expectations it's time to redefine." It may reach its peak in the title track, an ominous song about repressive conditions where "they've left me with the burden of a haunted town." That song concludes with the working-class anguish of "I can hear Monday coming!" "Mob Crash" sounds almost apocalyptic. The EP ends with "We'll Be Here Tomorrow," which asks, "Where do we go once we've seen the edge?"

**Genre:** Punk

# English Beat

### "Tears of a Clown" b/w "Ranking Full Stop" 45 December 8, 1979 (2 Tone CHS TT6) (UK)

This version of the Smokey Robinson song "Tears of a Clown" is the first of several successful covers this band would do. And it's another example how a second wave ska band can take a song that's a relic from another era and make it their own. The B-side is a jubilant ska scorcher with vocalist Ranking Roger toasting over an infectious beat.

### *I Just Can't Stop It* LP May 16, 1980 (Go-Feet Records BEAT 1) (UK)

Along with the debut albums by the Specials, Madness, and the Selector, this album defined second wave ska. Those debut albums not only were landmarks in the genre but also outlined what ska would be for decades to come. And *I Just Can't Stop It* is probably the most varied of those four major albums.

There's high-energy, fast ska in "Noise in This World," the slinky "Twist and Crawl," the almost reggae-paced "Big Shot," and some pop elements in "Best Friend" and "Hands Off... She's Mine." The band also recorded successful covers of the Andy Williams song "Can't Stand Losing You," the ska classic "Jackpot," and Prince Buster's "Rough Rider" and "Whine and Grine." Rather than the novelty of turning pop songs into ska such as some third wave ska bands would do in the 1990s, they make these songs their own.

The album's lyrics are also varied. There's a mixture of relationship songs like "Hands Off... She's Mine" and more socially conscious songs such as "Stand Down Margaret," a call for British Prime Thatcher to resign. Other politically charged songs include "Two Swords," about conflict with young neofascists; "Big Shot," a class-conscious examination of someone who represents oppressive forces; and "Mirror in the Bathroom," about a narcissist.

### "Too Nice to Talk To" 45 December 5, 1980 (Go-Feet Records FEET 4) (UK)

A successful example of how ska can be somewhat revamped but not watered down. This infectious combination of funk, pop, and ska really works over lyrics about a guy too shy to talk to a girl he sees dancing that he admires.

### "Save It for Later" 45 April 1, 1982 (Go-Feet Records FEET 333) (UK)

By the time of the band's third album, *Special Beat Service*, the English Beat went in a more eclectic and pop-centered direction. But this song stands out as an attempt to merge ska overtones into a pop song slower than ska. The lyrics are somewhat oblique but still haunting, which could be about someone trying to find their way in the world amid trouble and confusion. "Just hold my hand while I come to a decision on it," Dave Wakeling sings.

### "March of the Swivel Heads" (B-side of "Jeanette") 45 September 2, 1982 (Go-Feet Records FEET 15) (UK)

This is an instrumental variation of the song "Swivel Heads" from *Special Beat Service*. Many may recognize it from the movie *Ferris Bueller's Day Off* (it's used in the scene near the end when Ferris is running home). But it's a notable example of what can be called post-punk ska with its mixture of reggae, dub, jazz, and experimental music.

**Genre**: Ska

# ESG

### *ESG* 12" EP June 1981 (99 Records 99–04) (USA)

Integrating funk with post-punk was an integral part of the downtown New York City scene in the late 1970s and early 1980s. Some English bands did the same during this time period. But ESG from the South Bronx executed a different approach. Instead of the jagged guitars and post-punk tempo changes, they offered funk removed from its commercial and overproduced conventions into a new kind of funk minimalism. It's funk reduced to its essential core of bass, percussion, and vocals and eliminated other instruments and the overproduction associated with the funk genre.

This record was produced by Martin Hannett, who produced Joy Division, New Order, and Magazine, and it has a moody feeling and atmosphere consistent with those bands. "You're No Good" features a slow groove with a haunting chorus. "Moody" is funkier and has a repeated, almost torturous feeling in the lyrics that contrasts with the very danceable music. "UFO," with its discordant guitar riff, remains one of the most sampled songs of all time.

### *Come Away with ESG* LP September 23, 1983 (99 Records 003 LP) (USA)

Expands on the post-punk funk minimalism of their first EP. This debut album features all three songs from their previous EP, *ESG Says Dance to the Beat of Moody*, including the infectious "Dance." The album starts with the call-and-response of "Come Away with Me," which is like an invitation to follow the band with their combination of minimalist funk blended with post-punk. While some punk fans loathed the dominance of funk in the 1970s, ESG shows how funk can be modified by stripping it of its overproduction and banality and infusing it with a punk and post-punk spirit.

Although it's firmly post-punk in song structure, songs like "You Make No Sense," "About You" and "My Love for You" repeat a few direct sentences that give them a punk feel. And the album's instrumentals aren't filler. They're some of the best songs. "Chistelle" has an eerie but infectious reworking of a surf guitar riff combined with an intoxicating bass-led dance track, while "Tiny Steps" features a Latin rhythm.

**Genre**: Post-punk

# Essential Logic

### "Aerosol Burns" 45 May 21, 1978 (Cells Records Sell One) (UK)

After leaving the punk band X-Ray Spex, saxophonist Lora Logic started her own group. Their debut single is Essential Logic at their most frenetic. It's wonderfully anarchistic. Essential Logic went on to be a full-fledged post-punk band with their *Beat Rhythm News* album, but this single is a combination of punk energy and post-punk.

### *Beat Rhythm News Waddle Ya Play?* LP (Rough Trade ROUGH 5) October 25, 1979 (UK)

On their only album, Essential Logic did their own take on the post-punk sound. Although it's more controlled than their punk-influenced first single, "Aerosol

Burns," some of the songs sound almost like a jam. Their combination of jazz, funk, and post-punk with a prominent saxophone is a unique element to their variation on post-punk, as are Logic's yelpy vocals, which sometimes contain a disturbing affected dramatic quality. The vocals don't easily fit into the song, but almost work against the music, as if Logic's voice is another instrument that challenges the music.

The songs are so unpredictable it's almost unsettling to listen to. In "World Friction" there are tempo changes that make it defy categorization. Is it an experimental song or a punk-influenced song? It alternates between the two. Other songs, such as "Wake Up" and "Shabby Abbott," don't settle into a predictable groove. They alternate between tempos, as if the band is defying expectations of what to expect from a song. The most consistently melodic song, "Collecting Dust," makes the music ironic because it's a song of how apathy turns into a kind of detached despair.

**Genre:** Post-punk

## The Exploited

### "Dogs of War" 45 March 28, 1981 (Secret SHH 110) (UK)

Disturbing single from Scottish hardcore punk band. It's from the point of view of a solider who acts out his psychopathic tendencies by killing in war. He's so deranged and disconnected that he doesn't attach any meaning to killing others. And if there is any meaning, he doesn't care.

### *Dead Cities* 7" EP September 30, 1981 (Secret SHH 120) (UK)

Their first album, *Punk's Not Dead*, was, at its worst, hooligan rock. But here they show some progression toward more than just macho boasting and their definition of anarchistic living. "Dead Cities" is probably their best song. It depicts the oppression and boredom of working-class life. On the B-side is "Class Warfare," an ultrafast dystopian worldview of the working class under siege.

### "Attack" b/w "Alternative" 45 April 29, 1982 (Secret SHH 130) (UK)

Continues the theme from the *Dead Cities* EP of the working class being tormented and oppressed. In "Attack," the singer wants to do something to fight back, but it's "an enemy you can't find." "Alternative" is a harrowing song of a desperate working-class person who doesn't want to join the military but is told there is no alternative to liberate himself from his oppressive life.

### "Computers Don't Blunder" b/w "Addiction" 45 October 5, 1982 (Secret SHH 140) (UK)

Death on both sides of this record. On the A-side, computers are the technology that could lead to nuclear war. The song depicts the Generation Jones fear about the military in general. "Addiction" is a chilling account of the effects of addiction that ultimately lead to death.

### *Troops of Tomorrow* LP May 15, 1982 (Secret SEC 8) (UK)

The song "UK 82" from this album became the name for a movement of British bands that went beyond punk into something faster and more intense. This album was the dividing line for this band. They crossed over with this record into a new sound. The music became even faster. And the production became less raw and more polished to create what later came to be called crossover thrash with a combination of street punk, Oi!, and hardcore punk fused with heavy metal. The Exploited, along with GBH and Discharge, were all part of this new movement of punk. For some punk fans, this may be just a bridge too far with just too much heavy metal influence.

To hear the difference, listen to the song "Alternative" on the 45 and then listen to the remixed version on this album. Also, the title track blatantly uses heavy metal riffs. This band had always been aggressive. But the production and mix make this even more aggressive. There are dark anti-war songs such as "War" and songs (for example, "So Tragic") bashing what they consider phony music like the rockabilly revivalists and new wave bands.

### *Rival Leaders* 7" EP October 1, 1983 (Pax Records PAX 15) (UK)

A return to full-fledged punk. In a genre with many songs about the fear of nuclear war, "Rival Leaders" is one of the best. It's desperate, ferocious, and angry. Most people will die while leaders will survive in a bunker. "Army Style" is about firing squads who believe in "duty first" and will shoot when ordered. The EP ends with "Singalongbushell" with its simple chorus of "wankers" directed at those who believe punk is dead.

**Genre:** Hardcore Punk

## Eyes

### "TAQN" 45 February 1979 (Dangerhouse IZE-45) (USA)

The title comes from the chorus of "take a quaalude now." This Southern California pop punk song is a piercing satire of conforming to hippie drug culture, all with a chaotic keyboard and a mysterious and ferocious guitar solo.

**Genre:** Pop Punk

## The Faith

### *The Faith* split LP September 20, 1982 (Dischord No. 8) (USA)

Washington, D.C., hardcore band's album with vocalist Alec MacKaye (brother of Minor Threat's Ian MacKaye) is fast and full of insight and righteous anger. The songs are mainly about trying to find a way through confusion and oppression into self-empowerment and action. This is an album about trying to find a solution. But that requires taking action against oppressive forces. Like people who will limit you in "Trapped," hypocrites in "You're X'd," the need for self-examination leading to self-knowledge in "In Control," and rising above being misunderstood in "What You Think." The strength of this album is the intensity of internal emotion mixing with one's observations of the world rather than overt political songs that focus solely on the external.

For all of the progress, the album ends in an inability to figure things out with "Into the Black." It's not clear whether it's an ending confession of an inability to understand or whether it's a lament from the viewpoint of someone else who has descended into darkness. But it's a chilling view of what can happen if one doesn't feel empowered. All in all, it's all a journey that makes up one of hardcore's most powerful albums. The other side of the split album features songs by the Void.

### *Subject to Change* 12" EP December 1983 (Dischord No. 11) (USA)

A mini-masterpiece in the hardcore punk genre. Like Minor Threat's 1983 *Out of Step* album, *Subject to Change* shows how hardcore punk can expand beyond its limitations without losing its energy. The fuller and more realized production enhances this. The EP also features songs with various tempos to show how hardcore can vary its pace while still retaining its power and energy. The title track is slower than many hardcore songs, while "Say No More" features some pop elements.

But it's also important for its lyrics, which are some of the best in all of straight edge. Sometimes there's a cry for liberation from the oppression that substance abuse can cause. Other times there's a deadness that comes from conforming, compromising, and withdrawing, which the call-to-arms opening song "Aware" confronts. In "Limitations," MacKaye effectively assesses the kind of oppression that means "limit your options, limit your mind."

**Genre:** Hardcore Punk

## The Fakes

*Production* 7" EP September 28, 1979 (Deep Cuts Records DEEP TWO) (UK)

Overlooked post-punk from Scotland. The standout song is the title track featuring industrial-like sounds, pounding drums, and nearly spoken-word vocals. With its call to "keep the company moving with production," it's one of this era's great critiques of depersonalizing work. "Look Away" and "Sylvia Clarke" feature the kind of jangle guitars that would come to later help define the Scottish post-punk of Postcard Records.

**Genre:** Post-punk

## The Fall

*Bingo Master's Breakout* 7" EP August 11, 1978 (Step-Forward SF 7) (UK)

This Manchester post-punk band is built around the uncompromising Mark E. Smith, one of the most enduring and eccentric figures in post-punk. Despite numerous personnel changes, the Fall were also one of the most prolific bands over the years. And over the long haul, most of their material holds up. Pick any record by the Fall and there's something interesting on it, including this, the first record they released. Who else would write a song about a bingo card reader? Or "Repetition," which dismisses the predictability of punk music with a brief parody of Richard Hell's "Blank Generation" at the end.

One of post-punk's most consistent and important bands was the Fall. Over the long haul, singer and songwriter Mark E. Smith never compromised his vision and was one of the genre's most distinctive lyricists (Phil Crean Archival/Alamy).

### "It's the New Thing" b/w "Various Times" 45 November 17, 1978 (Step-Forward SF 9) (UK)

Smith follows up his critique of the music scene in "Repetition" on their first record with "It's The New Thing," which ridicules trendiness in pop music through the eras. "Various Times" divides itself into eras as well. The past, the present, and the future all show how flawed the human race is.

### *Live at the Witch Trials* LP May 16, 1979 (Step-Forward SFLP 1) (UK)

Recorded in just one day, the Fall's debut album is DIY spontaneous post-punk. At times Smith sounds like a poet spontaneously spouting his words out over the jagged post-punk music. Because of the speedy recording of the songs, some of them aren't as complete as they could be. But they have an appealing unconstrained quality.

Some of the songs are profiles of the downtrodden, the misplaced, and the forgotten, such as the drug users in "No Xmas for John Quays" and in "Futures and Pasts," a compelling song about lost childhood innocence. Other songs seem more from Smith's point of view of being an outsider, such as "Frightened," about a teenager who feels out of place, and "Two Steps Back," about a lost soul who can't progress. It features critiques of the music business, including "Music Scene"; "Crap Rap 2/Like to Blow," which condemns following trends; and "Rebellious Jukebox," which details the struggle to remain authentic. "Industrial Estate" is a warning about how the entire culture encourages compromising in order to succeed.

### "Rowche Rumble" 45 July 30, 1979 (Step-Forward SF 11) (UK)

The song's title is a variation of the company that manufactures the sedative Valium. The song is anything but calming. It has a frenetic—almost manic—pace and points out that while society decries the use of illegal drugs, there are people addicted to legal prescription drugs.

### *Dragnet* LP October 26, 1979 (Step-Forward SFLP 4) (UK)

A muddy, lo-fi production makes this album sound much darker and rawer than their first album. This reflects the subjects of the songs, such as "A Figure Walks," which focuses on a shadow self that torments the singer. At times there's a Goth-like depiction of ghosts, the occult, and the supernatural, such as in "Psykick Dancehall" and "Spectre vs. Rector."

This establishes some consistent song subjects that would continue into future albums. There are character profiles, usually of a criminal, mentally ill, or tormented person, such as in "Flat of Angles." Other songs use Mark E. Smith's spontaneous-sounding lyrics over jangle punk guitars, as in "Before the Moon Falls." Another ongoing theme is commentary on the music business, such as "Printhead," which critiques music journalists, and "Choc-Stock," which attacks the pop music industry and the devotion surrounding it. In songs like "Dice Man," Smith sounds like a reluctant prophet speaking out against the shortcomings of an entertainment industry he is nevertheless committed to. He dedicates himself to taking chances and experimenting with music, something Smith would do through his whole career.

### "Fiery Jack" 45 January 28, 1980 (Step-Forward SF 13) (UK)

One of Smith's great profiles of ordinary people. An alcoholic 45-year-old working-class man who spends too much time both thinking and drinking is angry and withdrawn. There seems to be no salvation at the end of the song, where he will only "eat this grenade" of booze that will seem to ultimately kill him.

### "Totally Wired" 45 August 30, 1980 (Rough Trade RT 056) (UK)

After some pills and coffee, the singer is "totally wired," but underneath it by the end of the song he admits he's in a "bad state" and is "always worried." The stimulants are apparently used to conceal grueling emotional states.

### *Grotesque* LP November 17, 1980 (Rough Trade ROUGH 18) (UK)

Their sound expands on their third album, which includes a batch of songs that are rockabilly-fueled post-punk. "Pay Your Rates" focuses on people who can't afford to pay their bills living in estate housing. "The Container Drivers" chronicles truck drivers, and "In the Park" is about someone who confesses, "I'm becoming everything I used to hate." There's a slower rockabilly-like riff that's part of the groove on "The NWRA," the album's ending opus. The title stands for The North Will Rise Again, and the lyrics are a lengthy poetic piece about how the North of England may one day have better conditions.

Some other unorthodox instruments are used on the album, including a harpsichord-sounding keyboard in "English Scheme" and a kazoo(!) in "New Face in Hell." Smith returns to speaking out against the music business in "C 'n' C-S Mithering" over an acoustic guitar and simple drumbeat. As usual, the entire album is all Mark E. Smith's show. The music is a backdrop to his words. It's all straightforward and spontaneous-sounding and simple with none of the musical complexity some other post-punk bands employed.

### *Slates* 10" mini-LP April 21, 1981 (Rough Trade RT 071) (UK)

Two of the six songs are ordinary for Fall mastermind Mark E. Smith. But four songs make this essential. They are all observations of a society in turmoil with a lyrical complexity that makes it sometimes difficult to discern a solid viewpoint about characters in a song. In "Prole Art Threat" there's some risk satirical or otherwise from people perceived as leftist or socialist, "Fit and Working Again" is about a worker who rallies himself to work, while "Slates, Slags, Etc." is about people condemned as outcasts. The last track, "Leave the Capital," is more direct and one of the best songs in the band's entire catalog. It's a triumphant call to leave the moral depravity behind, which in this song is represented by getting out of London.

### "Lie Dream of Casino Soul" b/w "Fantastic Life" 45 November 13, 1981 (Kamera ERA 001) (UK)

The catchiest single they made during this era of their career, with both sides about lies that trick people. "Lie Dream" is about the false promises of a casino, which may be a metaphor for the economic system. "Fantastic Life" is even better, with some added keyboard over an infectious beat about all the lies that promise a fantastic life throughout the ages.

### *Hex Enduction Hour* LP March 8, 1982 (Kamera KAM 005) (UK)

The Fall's finest album during this period works best because there's so much punk-fueled energy. Smith's sometimes abrasive lyrics are mixed down lower than other albums, which makes the music more prominent. There are background vocals on

"Jawbone and the Air Rifle," which make it almost sound like more of a complete song rather than the music always being a backdrop to Smith's vocals. "Just Step S'ways" is a danceable examination of so-called futurism in the culture. "Deer Park" and "Mere Pseud Mag. Ed." are so chaotic they almost sound like noise punk.

"The Classical" starts the album off with one of Smith's most frequent targets, which is the music industry itself. The almost Goth-like "Hip Priest" is another song about the music business, or perhaps perceptions about Smith himself, or anyone who is an artist. The song later achieved notoriety for being featured in the movie *The Silence of the Lambs* (1991). There's some sense of melancholy in parts of the album, such as "Winter" and "Iceland." The album ends with their longest song to date, "And This Day," which is more than 10 minutes long.

### "The Man Whose Head Expanded" b/w "Ludd Gang" 45 June 27, 1983 (Rough Trade RT 133) (UK)

The A-side is about a man who believes his knowledge is being ripped off by soap opera writers. "Ludd Gang" is short for Luddites, the group of nineteenth-century textile workers who fought against technology to preserve their jobs.

### "Kicker Conspiracy" b/w "Wings" 45 September 19, 1983 (Rough Trade RT 143) (UK)

A single featuring Smith's poet-like improvisational lyrics over driving contagious guitar parts. "Kicker Conspiracy" is a kind of shuffle with some words alluding to contemporary issues surrounding the hype and violence surrounding football. The B-side is even better, with an infectious guitar part over lyrics about wings that make it possible to time travel back to the 1860s U.S. Civil War era. When the time traveler returns, things have been altered because of what he did when he returned to the past.

### *Perverted by Language* LP December 5, 1983 (Rough Trade ROUGH 62) (UK)

This album marks a turning point in the band, and a prelude of what was to come. American guitarist Brix Smith joins the band. She sings on "Hotel Bloedel" (the first person to sing on a song by the Fall other than Mark E. Smith). Her voice contrasts with Smith's, as if juxtaposing innocence against jaded experience. And it's fascinating to hear a melodic voice over the instrumentation of the Fall rather than Smith's pointed vocals.

*Perverted by Language* is the best-sounding album in the Fall's career to that point. On songs like "I Feel Voxish," they sound like they're ready for the future rather than clinging to an established sound and approach. "Neighborhood of Infinity" is another highlight, with its processed vocals and tense guitar parts and prominent drums. The drums also drive the opening track, "Eat Y'self Fitter," and "Smile," with its story of a nightclub filled with people driven by superficial impulses.

**Genre:** Post-punk

# Fancy Rosy

### "Punk Police" 45 1977 (Mamicha Music MMS 2003) (Netherlands)

How's this for as story? A Puerto Rican–born singer from a German group called Pretty Maid Company records what is supposed to be a parody of punk. But either the creators made what they thought was a bad punk song and it turned out to be the opposite, or they actually tried to make a song that wasn't a parody disguised as a parody.

Whatever the case, over the years it has become a legendary cult classic. In a kind of strange version of dub, the song is repeated, creating a reverb effect making it sound like a police siren that gives it an overtone of a horror punk song. Another version was released on a compilation with the reverb toned down. But we'll take this unique sound. This was changed to an A-side from the original German 45, where it was a B-side.

**Genre:** Punk/Post-punk

## Fang

### *Landshark!* LP February 1983 (Boner Records FANG 1) (USA)

This album is a mixed bag. At its worst this San Francisco–area band records juvenile songs that may or may not be satires. But at its best it's exciting punk music with a thicker guitar sound that would influence grunge. And there are two memorable songs that express outrage at society's standards. "The Money Will Roll Right In" (which Nirvana later covered) ridicules defining success as possessing money and fame. It's another reminder of how different the Generation Jones perspective on success is from current definitions. "Law and Order" is a powerful song about the inadequacy of the legal system to solve societal problems.

"Diary of a Mad Werrwoulf" shows the emerging combination of punk and heavy metal that often uses horror imagery. But the best song on the album may be the most fun song. "Landshark," about a car that can leave others in the dust, is the band's own version of punk rock meets rockabilly. The singer is liberated and free from the oppression that dominates the rest of the album.

**Genre:** Punk

## Mick Farren and the Deviants

### "Let's Loot the Supermarket Again Like We Did Last Summer" from *Screwed Up* 7" EP December 1977 (Stiff LAST 4) (UK)

Along with Plastic Bertrand's "Ça Plane Pour Moi," one of punk's great one-hit wonders. A journalist and musician since the early 1970s, Farren released this single with an anarchist message that perhaps influenced Crass and the anarcho-punk movement. But the lyrics are kind of obscure. Who knows what it all means for sure?

**Genre:** Punk

## Fatal Microbes

### "Violence Grows" 45 May 17, 1979 (Small Wonder small 20) (UK)

Minimalist dirge-like song with contemporary stories of violence and its effects. The band was short-lived, but singer Honey Bane went on to have a career as a solo singer. Previously released on a split EP with the Poison Girls.

**Genre:** Post-punk

## Fear

### *The Record* LP February 21, 1982 (Slash SR-111) (USA)

This album changes the attitude of hardcore punk. No longer righteous punk rock or speaking for outsiders, the tone of this album is what came to be called bully rock:

obnoxious, homophobic, sexist, and more. It might be reassuring if there were a feeling of satire to it, but there's not a sense of that on most of the album.

Yet instead of canceling it because of some of its lyrical content, it must still be recognized that the music and the album's production were an important evolution in hardcore punk. By 1982, heavy metal elements started to be added to hardcore. And for better or worse, this album was among the first to do so. And it's not all bully rock. Some songs depict the hellish conditions of city living. And they're not without a political perspective. "Let's Have a War" and "Foreign Policy" are effective anti-war songs.

**Genre:** Hardcore Punk

## The Feelies

### *Crazy Rhythms* LP February 29, 1980 (Stiff SEEZ 20) (UK)

This New Jersey band over time earned a reputation as one of the best alternative bands. But their first album is also one of the most influential post-punk albums. It's tempting to call them part jangle punk and part Velvet Underground–influenced with their driving and intoxicating rhythms. Whatever it is, they put together a sound that influenced many indie American bands. Throughout the 1980s some alternative bands lifted the guitar style and de–post-punked it by slowing down the pace and varying rhythms into what was sometimes called alternative rock.

Thematically, in many ways the album is about the difficulty of trying to navigate modern life, particularly in relationships where there are often misunderstandings and miscommunication. Everything culminates in the ending song, "Crazy Rhythms," where the singer feels people are not being heard and suppress their real feelings and desires to please someone else (or because it won't make any difference no matter what is said). The music serves as a dramatic undercurrent to that conflict.

**Genre:** Post-punk

## Fire Engines

### *Lubricate Your Living Room* LP January 3, 1981 (Pop Aural ACC 001) (UK)

The Scottish bands Josef K and Orange Juice integrated pop and post-punk on the legendary Postcard record label. However, the Edinburgh band Fire Engines made more angular and jagged music that was solidly post-punk on the Fast Product label. Like the Gang of Four, they're both funky and frantic. And this is one of the best examples of post-punk guitar, particularly since about half of this album is instrumental.

The guitars are basically free-form instruments on songs like "Sympathetic Anesthetic." And that's coupled with what sometimes sounds like tribal beats because there appears to be no hi-hat or cymbal. And on songs like "Discord" there's an almost primal vocal with words so rushed that they're almost indecipherable. Sometimes the effect is closer to avant-garde or noise punk. The songs defy pop song conventions and traditional expectations of what even a post-punk band should sound like.

### "Candyskin" b/w "Meat Whiplash" 45 April 2, 1981 (Pop Aural POP 10)

The A-side is probably the band's most accessible song. The somewhat discordant guitar is kept more in the background. And the song features a solid melody with a memorable chorus that even utilizes strings. The B-side has a more driving rhythm but is also infectious. A single that shows how post-punk can contain pop elements without losing its edge.

### "Big Gold Dream" 45 December 14, 1981 (Pop Aural POP 13) (UK)

The verses and the instrumental sections surrounding them sound like a musical assault. The choruses are catchy, however, and even feature a synthesizer and female backing vocals. This combination could have been a whole new exciting direction for this band. Too bad this was their last recording during this period.

**Genre:** Post-punk

## Flesh Eaters

### *A Minute to Pray, A Second to Die* LP April 21, 1981 (Ruby Records JRR-101) (USA)

Southern California band led by singer Chris Desjardins, known as Chris D. The band's second album features punk and Southern California musicians from X, the Blasters, and Los Lobos. It mixes punk, post-punk, Goth, and even some theatrical-sounding music. Maybe the best way to describe it as a Goth-laced punk album with almost ironic theatrical qualities. Or maybe even a form of horror punk. Or perhaps an American variation of the Birthday Party.

At times there's post-punk stylizations, particularly a Captain Beefheart–like shrill saxophone on songs like "Digging My Grave" and "Satan's Stomp." Other times the songs almost sound like they could be a soundtrack to a movie or stage show. One of the most interesting is "Cyrano de Berger's Back," written by John Doe of X and which X released years later on their *See How We Are* album. The album ends with the apocalyptic "Divine Horseman," which falls somewhere between horror punk, Goth, and what could be a soundtrack to a B horror movie.

**Genre:** Post-punk

## Fleshtones

### "American Beat" 45 June 1979 (Red Star RSS-1) (USA)

Is it punk-influenced pop? Or another variation of punk pop? We're going to give this band the benefit of the doubt and call it a form of punk pop. Although many of the band's other music is in the alternative category with a combination of 1960s garage rock, rockabilly, R&B, or what came to be called American roots music, this song is bona fide pop punk in spirit. A slick and inferior rerecording was released in 1984.

**Genre:** Pop Punk

## Flipper

### *Generic Flipper* LP April 16, 1982 (Subterranean SUB 25) (USA)

A landmark album both lyrically and musically. The most enduring legacy of this San Francisco band may be how they slowed down punk. Before this album, punk was associated with being fast. But this album changed that. The album's second song, "Life is Cheap," sounds with its double-tracked vocals almost like a punk version of a Gregorian chant. "(I Saw You) Shine" is even slower and borders on a sluggish heavy metal song. Historically, the album may be best known for being one of the main influences on grunge, which slowed down punk and added other influences from hard rock, traditional rock, and heavy metal.

Lyrically, the album was important for its sense of lament and a near spiritual sense of despair and disillusionment. This starts ironically with the first song, "Ever," which, though it features handclaps associated with cheerful pop songs, has lyrics that convey an existential crisis about the purpose of life. "That's the Way of the World" is about unrealized dreams in a fallen world. On "Life" there is some resolution to the crisis of faith that runs throughout the album. And in "Living for the Depression" there is an angry resolution not to live like the masses pursuing consumerism and success. It ends with "Sex Bomb": just a few words repeated in what sounds like an ironic ending to an album that tries to make its way through the despair of modern life.
**Genre:** Punk

## The Flowers

### "After Dark" from *Earcom 1* compilation LP May 1979 (Fast Product Fast 9A) (UK)

The Scottish post-punk movement featured this overlooked band with a limited recording output. This is their finest moment. After a tense and angular instrumental build up, vocalist Hilary Morrison sings about a jumpy and disturbing hookup at a disco.
**Genre:** Post-punk

## Gang of Four

### *Damaged Goods* 7" EP October 19, 1978 (Fast Product FAST 5) (UK)

One of the foundational post-punk records of 1978, the year post-punk broke. "Damaged Goods" mixes a funky, danceable sound with jagged guitars. It was a major breaking point from the power chord fueled punk rock sound, that would become one of the major approaches in post-punk.

Also in "Damaged Goods," there's a mixture of the political and the personal that helped define the post-punk worldview. The language of consumerism is used to define an exploitative transactional relationship. It emphasizes how all is reduced to transactions, which can make any kind of relationship disingenuous. There is a double narration in "Love Like Anthrax" about the nature of love songs. "Armalite Rifle" is about the violence in Northern Ireland and features Andy Gill's searing razor guitar.

### *Entertainment!* LP October 8, 1979 (EMI EMC 3313) (UK)

Gang of Four's commentary on the political and economic system created one of the most biting and intelligent albums in post-punk. There's a piercing critique of both the roots of economic injustice and the practical reality of it. Like "Damaged Goods" (rerecorded for this album), "Natural's Not in It" is about how relationships are damaged by the transactional nature inherent in capitalism. "We all have good intentions but all with strings attached," singer Jon King sings. "Not Great Man" is about how history isn't made by great men, while "Guns Before Butter" uses some phrases by Nazi leaders to illustrate an oppressive society where there's pressure to be compliant.

"I Found That Essence Rare" is the futile search for whatever commodity leads someone to believe will make them happy. "At Home He's a Tourist" is about how capitalism makes one so restless that consumption of goods and culture becomes another futile search for something better. "Glass" shows how alienation in capitalism generates boredom. "5:45" focuses on the commodification of violence on television, where "guerrilla war struggle is a new entertainment."

### *Solid Gold* LP March 9, 1981 (EMI EMC 3364) (UK)

Less experimental but a still worthy follow-up to *Entertainment!* With the guitars mixed down, the band's sound becomes more blended. The lyrics often focus on the personal effects of the oppressive economic and social structure on the individual.

The album starts with "Paralyzed" about someone disillusioned with life because "what [he] wanted now just seems like a waste of time." "What We All Want" features an infectious funk groove and is about someone who can't understand why he's unhappy and is trapped in a yearning for fulfillment. "Why Theory" addresses where people's opinions of life come from. The grinding satire "Cheeseburger" tackles the band's consistent themes of the emptiness of consumerism and meaningless work. The song's narrator concludes: "Sometimes I think money is my only goal, it makes me sad."

"Outside the Trains Don't Run on Time" comes from a phrase associated with the dictator Benito. It's a song about fascist control of a household and by extension all of society run by an exacting patriarch: "discipline is his passion" and "order is his obsession." "He'd Send in the Army" also uses symbolism of a patriarchal homeowner coupled with military symbolism and points out the oppression of women under patriarchy. Over the course of the album, the hope for realization at the beginning of the album only leads to disintegration. There seems to be no real escape from the oppression.

### "To Hell with Poverty" b/w "Capital" 45 July 3, 1981 (EMI 5193) (UK)

"To Hell with Poverty" is about avoiding the pain of being poor. What else is there to do but get out the cheap wine? The B-side, "Capital," is a slower funk groove with some scratchy guitar in a song about the trap of consumerism and living in debt.

### *Songs of the Free* LP May 10, 1982 (EMI EMC 3412) (UK)

With bassist Sara Lee replacing the outgoing Dave Allen, the band changes their sound and goes even more in the direction of funk without some of the harder guitar-based post-punk edges. And the production gets more compressed with Andy Gill's guitar getting mixed down even more.

So even though the catchy first track, "Call Me Up," sounds like it might become popular on the radio (it still wasn't), the lyrics adhere to their consistent themes of the afflictions of consumerism and capitalism. "I Love a Man in a Uniform" did actually get radio airplay, perhaps because of people who did not understand the irony in it. It's a subversive song about the hypermasculine reasons for wanting to fight in a war.

"We Live as We Dream, Alone" depicts other consistent themes from this band, including meaningless work creating a feeling of alienation. The album ends with the thoughtful meditation "Of the Instant," in which someone is struggling with questions about the existing social and economic structure. *Songs of the Free* doesn't let guitarist Andy Gill loose like the first two albums, but it's the third of a trilogy of three important Gang of Four albums.

**Category**: Post-punk

## The Gangsters

**"We Are the Gangsters" (B-side of "Wooly Bully") 45 July 1980 (Big Bear BB 26) (UK)**

Excellent indie ska song from Birmingham band that unfortunately buried this gem on a B-side. It didn't get the attention it should have, and the band seems to have vanished into obscurity. Too bad. Danceable with a sense of danger throughout.
**Genre:** Ska

## GBH

**"No Survivors" 45 January 14, 1982 (Clay Records CLAY 8) (UK)**

Ferocious anti-war single from English punk band. Resist joining the military and live instead, the song advises. Over time the band—initially known as Charged GBH—would become known as one of the best crossover thrash bands. But here the band is all hardcore punk.

**"Sick Boy" 45 June 1, 1982 (Clay Records CLAY 11) (UK)**

Frenetic guitar sound takes hardcore about as far as it can go. It's a disturbing song about a mentally ill man (and criminal?) with a fixation on underage girls. This is a superior version compared to the rerecording on their *City Baby* album.

***City Baby Attacked by Rats* LP July 6, 1982 (Clay Records CLAY LP 4) (UK)**

We're not in hardcore punk, street punk, or Oi! territory anymore. There's a sped-up heavy metal guitar sound that, along with the polished production, makes this very different from their "No Survivors" single. The rerecording of "Sick Boy," with its heavy metal guitar opening, shows how much the band has changed. This album helped lay down a blueprint for the crossover thrash genre.

There is at times a near apocalyptic worldview of a dark society. That includes "Wardogs," about war bringing out the worst in people; "Maniac," depicting a psychopathic criminal; and "Passenger on the Menu," which shows how people will turn to cannibalism out of survival. These songs are a mixture of the macabre and the political that would become a staple of the crossover thrash genre.

**"Catch 23" b/w "Hellhole" 45 April 15, 1983 (Clay Records CLAY 22) (UK)**

More punk than crossover thrash but still with a heavy metal thrash guitar rather than Johnny Ramone punk style guitar, "Catch 23" is a defiant song about survival. "Hellhole" is better because it's punkier and faster. It's about a vigilante whose actions improve the conditions of the oppressed.

***City Baby's Revenge* LP November 1983 (Clay Records CLAY LP 8)**

After making an album that largely helped create the crossover thrash genre, the band pulls back from the heavy metal overtones of *City Baby Attacked by Rats*. They drop the heavy metal style guitar sound, have a rawer production, and shift to more realistic songs about the outsiders in life. As if to re-acknowledge their punk origins, they do a garage punk cover of the Stooges song "1970," which they title "I Feel All Right."

There's less of the apocalyptic almost horror movie imagery of their previous record. But it's there at times, such as in the harrowing "Valley of Death" with its depiction of "hell on earth" as well as the fear of destruction by technology in "High Octane Fuel." There's a frightening sense of inner torment in songs like "Faster Faster" and "Vietnamese Blues," the latter about a veteran returning home suffering from PTSD.

But most of this album depicts the underside of life that is grimly realistic and not containing the macabre imagery so prevalent in heavy metal. Addiction and drugs aren't romanticized. They're shown as agents of paralysis and a kind of slavery and mind alteration. By the ending, Louis Armstrong meets the Stooges of "Skanga," and the singer is wasted, feeling mean, and seemingly unable to do anything about it. He's too far gone.

**Genre:** Punk/Street Punk

## Generation X

### "Your Generation" b/w "Day by Day" 45 September 1, 1977 (Chrysalis CHS 2165) (UK)

Energetic debut single from band led by singer Billy Idol. The A-side is a take-off on the Who's 1960s anthem "My Generation" that daringly puts down the older boomer generation. The B-side is a critique of life in downtrodden, inflation-ridden, working-class England with depersonalizing factory jobs.

**Genre:** Punk

## The Germs

### *GI* LP October 15, 1979 (Slash SR-103) (USA)

Influential L.A. band's only album produced by Joan Jett is very fast punk, at the edge of hardcore punk. Or is it one of hardcore punk's first albums? No matter what it's called, it's rip-roaring fast for 1979.

But what may be most significant about this album is singer Darby Crash's lyrics. Underneath the growl and snarling voice is real poetry. There's a philosophical and literary quality to many of these songs. And a dark existential angst. The first song on the album is "What We Do Is Secret," a song about how oppression comes from keeping things concealed. It sets the tone for an album that will bring to light what is wrong.

The songs depict an underworld of lost characters tyrannized by a world that creates psychic pain. Perhaps the best song aimed at that painful world is "Land of Treason," an almost postapocalyptic mini-masterpiece. "Lexicon Devil" is about a tyrannical figure who uses words to mold both thoughts and actions. "Media Blitz" is another song about how people can be controlled by malicious institutional forces. Other songs seem autobiographical, as if Darby is trying to work out the demons of his past. "Manimal," for instance, is a song of inner warfare and trying to rise above baser animal instincts. Unfortunately, the band never got the chance to build on this album due to Darby's death in 1980.

**Genre:** Punk/Hardcore Punk

## Girls at Our Best!

### "Getting Nowhere Fast" b/w "Warm Girls" 45 April 12, 1980 (Record Records RR1) (UK)

Band from Leeds, England, featuring singer Judy Evans self-finances a single and comes up with a two-minute punk classic. "Getting Nowhere Fast" shows how

consumerism fails to satisfy. The name of the band comes from the B-side, a more post-punk leaning song about glamorous girls who "love mental children."
**Genre:** Punk/Pop Punk

## The Gordons

### *Future Shock* 7" EP October 1980 (GORDON-1) (New Zealand)

Before Sonic Youth, the Swans, or Big Black put out their initial records, this New Zealand band was steering post-punk in the direction of noise punk or noise rock. But it's more consistent with driving post-punk than the experimental or avant-garde parts of what came to be called noise punk. Not being part of the punk centers of New York, California, and the United Kingdom, this band wasn't adhering to any regional trends. Out there on their own, they created a bold and unique sound for the time period. If may not be full-fledged noise punk. But it's on the edge.

The ferocious "Future Shock," with its agitated drone guitar and desperate vocal, is one of the lost post-punk masterpieces of this time period. The pace slows down with the brooding "Machine Song" and ends with "Adults and Children," featuring a ferocious driving bass and shredding guitar.
**Genre:** Post-punk

## Government Issue

### *Legless Bull* 7" EP August 25, 1981 (Dischord No. 4) (USA)

Washington, D.C., band's recording debut blends punk and hardcore. For some of the album they slice through some of the oppressive pop culture of the time. That includes bands like Van Halen and Supertramp ("Rock & Roll Bullshit"); the band Crass, which they call preachy ("Anarchy is Dead"); the resurgence of cowboy clothes and gear because of the movie *Urban Cowboy* ("Cowboy Fashion"); and preppy dressers ("Fashionite"). And there are critiques of the punk scene itself, like the drugged-up violent thugs who come to hardcore punk shows ("Asshole"). And there's a song about the paralysis of boredom, the malaise of the Generation Jones era ("Bored to Death").

All in all, short and to the point, not holding back on feelings and observations. All the catharsis that hardcore punk should be. Essential hardcore on the reliable Dischord label.

### *Boycott Stabb* LP May 1983 (Fountain of Youth FOY 002/Dischord 10¾) (USA)

There's still the critique of mainstream culture that was the dominant theme on *Legless Bull*, such as "Plain to See," in which people shout at the singer, "Punk rock is dead, new wave is in." However, world-weariness and despair are setting in compared to the raw energy and anger of their debut.

"I've got no energy to fight," says singer John Stabb, as if the world is just too overwhelming in its demands and injustices. The world leaves the singer indecisive and paralyzed in "Lost in Limbo." "Happy People" mocks others who aren't angry at the way things are and are instead in a kind of state of denial and numbness about the conditions of life. "Sheer Terror" shows anger at those who criticize his punk persona. The song mixes in some heavy metal riffs. But whether it's a spoof of the heavy metal genre or an experiment with that musical form is unclear.

By the ending three songs, however, it's more about despair, darkness, and anxiety. Or perhaps it's an ending trilogy of songs flashing back to worse times in high school. "Partyline" is about gossiping but on a deeper level about betrayal and an inability to trust others. "Here's the Rope" goes from considering life as a "cheap soap opera" to a "life of misery." The album ends with "Insomniac," in which the singer is unable to sleep because of all he's worrying about. He can only "try to change [his] thoughts but it's getting hard."

**Genre:** Hardcore Punk

## The Gun Club

### *Fire of Love* LP August 31, 1981 (Ruby Records JRR 102) (USA)

Singer Jeffrey Lee Pierce builds on what the Los Angeles band X did: fusing punk with roots rock, rockabilly, and country. As punk was splintering after its initial explosion, this album was a groundbreaking incorporation of the punk spirit into rockabilly, county, and the blues. It's a sincere, exciting combination of the genres, not anything like the revivalist rockabilly acts that popped up during this era. Pierce can update the Robert Johnson "Preachin' Blues" and still have it sound like punk around the edges.

Like the blues, on *Fire of Love* there's a world-weariness with a theme of looking for salvation in a fallen world. There are allusions to God, hell, souls, and death—and even possibly Native American spirituality—in "Fire Spirit." There's something that feels like spiritual warfare throughout the album. Some of it is about worldly desire that fails to satisfy, such as on the lead track "Sex Beat." The singer seems to realize that there's something within him that's deeper than physical passion that he must discover. And much of the album is exploring what that might be.

Pierce goes back to other American music genres and adds a punk-like sensibility to them, but always with a dark, searching quality. "For the Love of Ivy" is frantic punk rockabilly. "Ghost on the Highway" sounds like something as old as the blues and country music. By the ending track, "Goodbye Johnny," Pierce is worn down by all of the searching. He's in the desert, that place of spiritual searches. This is the voice of an old soul, and it's riveting.

**Genre:** Post-punk

## Nina Hagen Band

### *Unbehagen* LP February 20, 1980 (CBS 84104) (Germany)

Whether it was with her band or as a solo artist, this German singer was all over the place. Sometimes she sounded like a cabaret singer, sometimes a demented opera singer; later she sang new wave pop or deconstructionist satirical pop. But she's at her true post-punk best here in the last album she made with her band before becoming a solo artist.

She sings in her native German, and her voice is a revelation. Hagen never confines herself to anything resembling convention. And the album is essential for redefining what a female voice can sound like in the post-punk era. The album starts with "African Reggae," where there's a layer of reggae music as a foundation to do her vocal acrobatics over. She enunciates her German in a combination of seduction and fear in "Alptraum." "Wau Wau" is perhaps her punkiest song from this era, with some Yoko Ono

yelps, animal-like sounds, and some guttural vocals. It's great fun. Also includes a German language version of Lene Lovich's "Lucky Number."
**Genre:** Post-punk

## Heartbreakers

### "Chinese Rocks" b/w "Born to Lose" 45 May 20, 1977 (Track 2094 135) (UK)

New York Dolls guitarist Johnny Thunders and drummer Jerry Nolan formed a band that seemed to be more proto-punk than fully part of the new punk movement. This single is their finest moment. The A-side (cowritten by Dee Dee Ramone and later recorded by the Ramones) depicts the ravaging effects of heroin addiction. The B-side is about being destined for failure and trouble amid bleak urban living.
**Genre:** Punk

## Richard Hell and the Voidoids

### *Blank Generation* LP October 8, 1977 (Sire SR 6037) (USA)

New York City 1970s punk icon (member for a while of both Television and Johnny Thunder's Heartbreakers) releases an album that is no straight-up, full-on punk album but instead a mixture of pop, punk, traditional rock, and even some Television-like pre–post-punk experimentation. The center of the album is the title track, which demarcated a generation that separated themselves from the baby boomers. The feeling in the song is emptiness, not belonging, and the media and money only providing false identities. These ideas would help shape the ideology of punk.

Legend has it that Sex Pistols manager Malcolm McLaren on a trip to New York was so impressed by the ideas behind the song "Blank Generation" and Hell's trademark look (spiky hair, ripped clothes, and safety pins used to hold clothes together) that he took it back to England, where he integrated it into the English punk scene.
**Genre:** Punk

## Hüsker Dü

### "Statues" b/w "Amusement" 45 November 24, 1980 (Reflex Records A REFLEX) (USA)

Debut single from Minneapolis trio that would go on to be one of the most important bands of the 1980s. The A-side is an explosive rant against an older woman who is so much of a poser she might as well be a statue. The B-side is a stirring call to arms against inaction.

### "In a Free Land" 45 January 26, 1982 (New Alliance NAR 010) (USA)

The band's sound is already shifting into a faster punk on the verge of hardcore. "In a Free Land" is powerful, melodic, political punk with terrific call-and-response vocals between singer Bob Mould and drummer Grant Hart. Their target here is an education system that enforces conformity and compliance and is not true freedom.

### *Everything Falls Apart* LP January 27, 1983 (Reflex REFLEX D) (USA)

Like the Wipers in Portland, Oregon, who were outside of major cities like New York, Los Angeles, and London and created their own unique variation of punk, Hüsker

Dü in Minneapolis made their own version of hardcore punk. And that's what makes this album so exciting. Hüsker Dü doesn't follow conventions or rules about what punk is supposed to be.

That means they can do a jokey version of the hippie song "Sunshine Superman." It's as if they took the "dare" choice in a contest to cover the most unlikely song they could think of. The title track sounds most like their later material with its melodic sense of hardcore punk. There's an irony to it, however, because it's a recitation of things going wrong.

The pain of being an outsider so consistent with punk is in "Afraid of Being Wrong," a harrowing song about being silenced out of fear. Other songs have almost Oi!-like choruses, such as "Target," which includes a chant of "don't participate, be lethargic!" And don't think this band can't still be ultrafast. "Signals from Above" is pretty much a crossover thrash song. And don't think they can't be contemplative. The ending song, "Gravity," wonders about the dark side of human nature.

**Genre:** Punk/Hardcore Punk

## Inflatable Boy Clams

### "Skeletons" from double 45 1981 (Subterranean SUB 20) (USA)

All-female San Francisco band is minimalist, avant-garde, and overlooked. Like the Raincoats, they defy pop music conventions. No guitars here. The song is largely driven by a bass line supplemented by a carnival-like keyboard and some interspersed percussion and a saxophone.

**Genre:** Post-punk

## Joe Jackson

### "I'm the Man" 45 September 25, 1979 (A&M AMS 7479) (UK)

Like Elvis Costello, Jackson is a musical chameleon. In just his first five years of recording, Jackson explored swing music, R&B, pop, ska, reggae, and other genres. On his best punk-inspired song, "I'm the Man," he points out that a greedy and manipulative force lies behind the merchandising of fads including kung fu, skateboards, and punk clothing. How does "the man" get his power? "I'll speak to the masses through the media," Jackson sings.

**Genre:** Punk/Pop Punk

## Joe Jackson Band

### "Beat Crazy" 45 January 2, 1981 (A&M AMS 8100) (UK)

During the two tone ska craze, Jackson's single from this third album (and attributed to his band) is a ska-inspired song that alternates between vocalists. The band's bass player, Graham Maby, sings a verse in a more conventional style, and then Jackson responds with his own verses that are potent variations of reggae's form of rapping called toasting. A fascinating modification of ska music.

**Genre:** Ska (variation)

# The Jam

***In the City*** **LP May 6, 1977 (Polydor 2383 447) (UK)**

The opening track, "Art School," from the debut album by this Woking trio creates a statement of purpose for the band and is a manifesto of the DIY punk movement. In England there was a cliché that misfits went to an art school if they couldn't fit into conventions. But "Art School" says you don't even need to do that. The message is that DIY punk is the new version of the British art school.

A similar message is in other songs. "In the City" conveys the energy and passion of being young in a city with much to express despite resistance from the older generation and danger from the police. It's a "My Generation" for the new punk movement. "Away

Unafraid to blend in musical influences outside of punk, the Jam—(left to right) Paul Weller, Bruce Foxton, and Rick Buckler—consistently spoke from the viewpoint of the working class or misunderstood youth. Their commentary on living in England during the Generation Jones era makes them one of the most enduring bands from this period (Peter Mazel/Photoshot/Everett Collection).

from Numbers" honors being an outsider and rejecting mainstream culture, an important emerging theme in punk. There's a youthful wisdom here of having courage to be what you really are in both "Away from Numbers" and "Time for Truth." The best half of this album lays down the foundation for the Jam's career that connected punk with social commentary and the voice of the everyman.

### "All Around the World" 45 July 8, 1977 (Polydor 2058 903) (UK)

Another rousing early Jam track that's a stirring call to arms for change. The call-and-response between Paul Weller and Bruce Foxton demands a "youth explosion": "We want a new direction." The optimism about change would dissipate as the band progressed.

### "This is the Modern World" 45 October 21, 1977 (Polydor 2058 945 ) (UK)

A song of emancipation from the limitations of the older generation and all of its oppression. Like some of their earlier songs, there's a contempt for elders who create oppressive rules.

### *All Mod Cons* LP October 28, 1978 (Polydor POLD 5008) (UK)

The Jam's third album solidifies their identity, and from here onward they became one of the most consistent bands to portray modern English life and Paul Weller becomes one of the era's best songwriters.

The album's first two tracks focus on the entertainment business with "All Mod Cons" about the fickleness of the music business and "To Be Someone" about the excesses of fame and the hedonistic lifestyle. Other songs include the escapist fantasies of an oppressed worker ("Billy Hunt"), an arrogant commuter businessman with a seedy underside ("Mr. Clean"), and the dangers of conformity ("In the Crowd"). The album ends with a pair of songs that show just how vital of a songwriter Weller is. "A Bomb on Waldorf Street" is an apocalyptic view of a violent society he describes as "a philistine nation of degradation." "Down in the Tube Station at Midnight" is a dystopian view of London subways where a man is robbed and assaulted by a gang of thugs.

### "Strange Town" b/w "Butterfly Collector" 45 March 2, 1979 (Polydor POSP 34) (UK)

One of the most enduring things about the Jam is that they present the perspective of outsiders and analyze the culture as outsiders. In "Strange Town," the singer is in an affluent area of London feeling alienated from the surroundings and ignored by the masses of people. And he fears being further ostracized in a place where "you'll be betrayed by your accent and manners." "Butterfly Collector" is a slower, haunting, angry song directed at the moral hollowness of a groupie-type figure.

### "When You're Young" b/w "Smithers-Jones" 45 August 29, 1979 (Polydor POSP 69)

Another brilliant non-album single. The A-side is a warning that the exuberance of youth gives way to an oppressive society that will beat out the hopes and passion of youth. The B-side shows the effect of a cruel culture on an older man who diligently works at an office for years. He's called in for what he hopes is a promotion and then finds he's laid off. And like some other punk songs, the message is a call to resist meaningless work. A version of "Smithers-Jones" with strings later appeared on their next album, *Setting Sons*, but this is the superior, guitar-driven version.

***Setting Sons* LP November 16, 1979 (Polydor POLD 5028) (UK)**

Reportedly this started as a concept album about three friends who reunite after a war and realize how much they've grown apart. Although that idea was scrapped, some songs on the album seem to relate to that idea. This all extends Weller's theme in the single "When You're Young" that the idealism of youth can vanish when growing older and trying to fit into the world.

"Burning Sky" perhaps hits the hardest with that topic. The song's narrator crosses the line into the compromises of adulthood, saying, "The values that we had once upon a time seem stupid now 'cause the rent must be paid." "Thick as Thieves" mourns a friendship that was close but yet lasted only for a while. The horrors of war come up in "Little Boy Soldiers" about young people joining the military. But contemporary conditions are depicted in two of the album's real triumphs. One is "Saturday's Kids," a harrowing and emphatic view of British working-class life. The other is "Eton Rifles," depicting a clash with students at an elite private school that becomes a metaphor for a clash with oppressive power.

**"Going Underground" b/w "Dreams of Children" 45 March 7, 1980 (Polydor POSP 113) (UK)**

A few years after the idealism of "All Around the World," the band takes a different approach to injustice in "Going Underground." There is no more of a call for change. Instead, it's about rejecting society altogether. It shows the frustration about the election of Prime Minister Margaret Thatcher. But the singer directs his anger at the public for electing her. "Dreams of Children" revisits a theme Weller also wrote about in "When You're Young" and "Burning Sky": is losing youthful idealism in an adult world that demands submission and conformity.

***Sound Affects* LP November 28, 1980 (Polydor POLD 5035) (UK)**

The band continues to grow and expand their sound by combining punk, post-punk, and pop. Sometimes there's a funk groove, other times the rhythms of post-punk, and sometimes there's a 1960s pop influence. Even though there's a change in sound, the Jam's major themes of economic inequality and the class system remain. "Pretty Green" shows the power of money itself to shape destiny. "Man in the Corner Shop" depicts the envy of people with more economic status. "Scrape Away" is about power itself and the hardness and mean-spiritedness that it produces.

Perhaps the most well-known song on the album is "That's Entertainment," which depicts working-class life using the most un-punk of all instruments: the acoustic guitar. The song contains harrowing images showing the bleakness, hopelessness, and violence entrenched in working-class life. In a kind of post-punk spirit, the song shows how punk-like social observations can be implanted into any genre of music, even the dreaded acoustic-guitar based song.

***The Gift* LP March 12, 1982 (Polydor POLD 5055) (UK)**

The band incorporates Northern Soul and R&B influences while still maintaining their punk roots. "Town Called Malice" is a piercing depiction of English working-class life with its ominous opening line: "Better stop dreaming of the quiet life 'cause it's the one we'll never know." Despite an upbeat Motown-style bass line, there's misery in this town. In "Ghosts," before encouraging others to try to rise above limitations, life is summarized by this question: "How do you feel at the end of the day? Just like you've walked over your own grave."

Other songs fall into the structure of the punk genre, including "Just Who Is the 5 O'Clock Hero?" where life is "a constant struggle just to exist." In "Running on the Spot," things are so challenging that it's enough to make one lose faith and hope.

**Genre:** Punk

## Joan Jett

### "Bad Reputation" 45 May 17, 1980 (Ariola 102 106) (Germany)

Jett was always the punkiest part of the all-female band the Runaways. Early in her solo career, however, she was more influenced by glam rock, 1960s garage bands, and traditional rock. But the title track to her debut album jumps out as a blistering punk anthem. It's fast, brash, and defiant.

**Genre:** Punk

## JFA

### *Blatant Localism* 7" EP July 18, 1981 (Placebo PLA-102) (USA)

The full name of this Phoenix-based band is Jodie Foster's Army, which connects to the attempted assassination of Ronald Reagan. Reagan's shooter, John Hinckley Jr., was obsessed with Jodie Foster and wanted to impress her by trying to kill the president. That's the subject of the song "JFA."

But most of the songs on the band's debut EP are not political, and the band eventually became more associated with skate punk than political punk. *Blatant Localism* is more about the confusion and exuberance of very early adulthood. "The easy life is in the past," the band says about being out of high school. But they find fun on the beach in "Beach Blanket Bongout," in which they declare they're skateboard punks, not surf punks.

**Genre:** Hardcore Punk

## JJ All Stars

### "Dambusters March" (from *Carry on Oi!* compilation LP) December 11, 1981 (UK)

The Oi! band 4 Skins used an alias on this version of the British warhorse movie theme. Could have fooled us. This sounds like a real ska band. A perfect intro or outro to just about anything.

**Genre:** Ska

## Johnny Moped

### "No One" 45 July 8, 1977 (Chiswick S15) (UK)

This band's later album *Cycledelic* is more pub rock with some punk blended in here and there. But this single is all 1977 punk with Brit sneer. There seems to be both pain and defiance in the singer's declaration that he's got no one.

**Genre:** Punk

## The Jolt

### "You're Cold" 45 September 30, 1977 (Polydor 2058 936) (UK)

When this Scottish band recorded their debut album the following year, they went more for mod-inspired power pop–inspired music. But their first single is catchy

and jubilant pop punk. They're just on the edge of power pop here but keep it in Buzzcocks-like pop punk terrain.
**Genre:** Pop Punk

## Josef K

### "Romance" (B-side of "Chance Meeting") 45 November 3, 1979 (Absolute ABS 1) (UK)

Named after the protagonist in Frank Kafka's novel *The Trial*, this short-lived Scottish band expanded post-punk. Instead of the jagged guitars associated with post-punk, they integrated a more varied guitar sound by Malcolm Ross that still provides a post-punk tension. That comes through in this B-side to their first single released independently. This single caught the attention of influential Postcard Records, a Scottish label that signed the band.

### "Final Request" (B-side of "It's Kinda Funny") 45 November 12, 1980 (Postcard 80 5) (UK)

Reflecting the lyrics, there's a sense of urgency and desperation in the music. Whether it's someone at the end of their life or someone at an end of a situation, it's a frightening glimpse of a calamitous conclusion to a crisis. Features a harrowing guitar solo that sounds like what someone in psychic pain would feel like.

### "Chance Meeting" b/w "Pictures of Cindy" 45 March 20, 1981 (Postcard 81 5) (UK)

The A-side is a reworked version of a song originally recorded in 1979. It remains one of the best blends of post-punk and pop. The song is about a chance encounter with someone with whom the singer has a past. The brass adds to the sense of drama. The B-side is more post-punk, with layers of guitars that both jangle and slice.

### "Sorry for Laughing" b/w "Revelation" 45 April 1981 (Les Disques Du Crépuscule TWI 023) (Belgium)

Josef K had a troubled recording career when it came to albums. They pulled their first album, *Sorry for Laughing*, and the second recorded album, *The Only Fun in Time*, had a mix that strangled the band's power. The band's best moments are on their singles, such as this one. The post-punk meets pop of "Sorry for Laughing" features a driving jangle guitar sound played with a punk-like fury. On "Revelation," Ross also plays fast but this time with a more urgent and sinister tone in a song about someone facing trouble on a ship. Whether the ship is metaphorical or not, this sounds like a journey into a realization.

### "The Missionary" b/w "Second Angle" 45 March 6, 1982 (Les Disques Du Crépuscule TWI 053) (Belgium)

Known as the Farewell Single, "The Missionary" on the A-side was originally recorded as a radio session with British DJ John Peel. It's about a near-religious missionary figure and features one of Malcolm Ross's most churning and intoxicating guitar parts. The second B-side is an instrumental version of "The Angle" from their *The Only Fun in Town* album where Ross's guitar is much more out front than the album version.
**Genre:** Post-punk

## Joy Division

*An Ideal for Living* 7" EP June 3, 1978 (Enigma PSS 139) (UK)

The ironically titled debut record of what could be post-punk's most revered band shows them with one foot in punk mode. All four songs were superior

Post-punk often focused on how an oppressive culture affected the individual internally. Ian Curtis of Joy Division powerfully expressed that inner conflict with some of the most influential music of the post-punk era (Retna Pictures/Avalon/Everett Collection).

recordings of punk-based tracks the band recorded earlier that remained unreleased for years.

This EP is musically and thematically different from what the band would later release. Also, the lyrics are all politically driven. "Warsaw" (the band's former name) is about Nazi leader Rudolf Hess's disenchantment with Adolf Hitler. "No Love Lost" continues the Nazi condemnation by talking about the atrocities the Nazis inflicted on Jewish women kept for the pleasure of Nazi soldiers (the band took its name from those units, which were called joy divisions). "Leaders of Men" criticizes manipulative politicians. The album's final track, "Failures of the Modern Man," may be the fastest song they ever recorded and summarizes the shortcomings of human nature.

### *Unknown Pleasures* LP June 15, 1979 (Factory FACT 10) (UK)

Is this post-punk's best album? It could be. Martin Hannett's production created a distinctive post-punk sound. Compared to on their first EP, Ian Curtis's voice is lower, more pronounced, and at times seems as if he's removed on a plane of his own. It's a new kind of post-punk with Goth around the edges and elements of industrial music. Some of it could be an attempt to create an industrial sound to replicate the sounds and aura of the band's hometown, the manufacturing city of Manchester.

Every song has a sense of urgency. Highlights include "Disorder," which seems to be a yearning for a transcendental experience to rise above modern living, which seems to provide no answers. The "Day of the Lords" has war imagery but could be about life in general as a battle with its haunting refrain of "when will it end?" "She's Lost Control" is based on someone singer Ian Curtis knew who had epilepsy (a disease Curtis was also diagnosed with). But the theme can be broadened out to whatever in life makes one feel out of control. "Shadowplay" is another highlight, which, like other Joy Division songs, is a search for something transcendental juxtaposed with worldly sensations that produce loneliness.

*Unknown Pleasures* is one of those albums that have such a new perspective and energy that it feels like it changes everything. It's one of a handful of post-punk albums that ignited the genre and did for post-punk what the Ramones and the Sex Pistols accomplished in starting the punk revolution.

### "Transmission" b/w "Novelty" 45 October 7, 1979 (Factory FACT 13) (UK)

Although *Unknown Pleasures* is now one of the most revered albums from this era, the band didn't release any singles from it. This is their first single. On one level it's thematically about the music scene at the end of the punk era with disillusionment setting in as the genre seems to be fading. But on another level it's about more universal topics. "Transmission" could be about the media ultimately being disappointing and just creating escapism. "Novelty" is about disenchantment when something runs its course and comes to an end, leaving an emptiness.

### "Atmosphere" b/w "Dead Souls" 45 March 18, 1980 (Sordide Sentimental SS 3002) (France)

In some ways this ominous song is similar to "Love Will Tear Us Apart" about a relationship ending with a lament in the chorus of "don't walk away." But as always with Curtis's lyrics it also could be a universal statement about the loss of any relationship and its impact. The layers of sound and production make this almost like a funeral march but with a dark beauty to it. "Dead Souls" is about feeling the pull toward something, with its menacing chorus of "they keep calling me."

**"Love Will Tear Us Apart" b/w "These Days" 45 June 20, 1980 (Factory FACT 23) (UK)**

Released after Ian Curtis's death, "Love Will Tear Us Apart" became the band's best-known song and is a kind of elegy for Curtis. On one level it's a breakup song chronicling Curtis's failing marriage. But like many of Curtis's songs there are universal implications and questions. Why does love not last sometimes? Do all human relationships have this element? What does one do with the hurt and disillusionment?

The song also features a soaring synthesizer and a distinctive drive bass line what would become two of the signature components of New Order, the band the surviving band members would form. The B-side is more upbeat musically and tells the strategies it takes to survive in the modern era.

***Closer* LP July 17, 1980 (Factory FACT 25) (UK)**

The band's second album is another landmark in the post-punk genre. It's darker and at times more experimental and Gothic-like than their first album. And Curtis's tone is gloomier. That's apparent from the leadoff track, "Atrocity Exhibition," with agitated, piercing guitars over a tribal-like drumbeat. The song is about exhibitions of entertainment through the ages that are almost like circus exhibits that exploit the entertainers. Perhaps Curtis was commenting on the idea that being in a modern rock band was somehow part of this tradition. In songs like "Isolation," Curtis's voice sounds even more remote, with a more dominant use of synthesizer. There's an existential kind of loneliness to the song.

Although the quality is at times quite desolate and dark, there's a spiritual depth to the sometimes almost relentless anguish. That's shown on the album cover, which depicts a graveyard sculpture of grieving women around the dead Christ. It's the grieving before a resurrection. And there are spiritual allusions within all the darkness of the album. In "Passover," Curtis compares the wilderness of the desert in the Book of Exodus to his own condition between two states of being. He is uncertain about what's ahead. In "Colony," after verses of lament comes the chant "God in his wisdom took you by the hand, God in his wisdom made you understand."

**"Komakino" b/w "Incubation" flexi disc 45 July 18, 1980 (Factory FAC 28) (UK)**

Quirky rhythms, nervous guitar, and a tribal type of beat give this a direct post-punk sound. The song is about something that provokes a conflict where "the questions arise and the answers don't fit." The B-side is a Velvet Underground–like instrumental.

**"She's Lost Control" 12" October 4, 1980 (Factory FACUS 2) (USA)**

After singer Ian Curtis's death, this version was released to the U.S. market with mixed up drums and guitar with an even more somber-sounding vocal than the *Unknown Pleasures* version. This was recorded shortly before Curtis's death, and it may be even more powerful than the original version.

**Genre:** Post-punk

# Judge Dread

**"Ska Fever" (B-side of "Lover's Rock") 45 October 1979 (Sire/Korova SIR 4028) (UK)**

This English singer released a string of infantile, double entendre reggae and ska songs. That problem is solved in this song because it's mostly instrumental with

some shouts interjected here and there. There is an authentic and infectious ska groove here.
**Genre:** Ska

# Killing Joke

### *Turn to Red* 10" EP October 26, 1979 (Malicious Damage MD 410) (UK)

English band's four-song debut EP is a post-punk blend of slowed-down punk, funk, experimental keyboard music, reggae, and industrial music. "Nervous System" is the highlight. It's a broad, sweeping song about the futility of working a 9-to-5 job and pursuing materialism, escapism, and success. This cycle is called a nervous system that the singer wants to escape. "Turn to Red" is a cross between an industrial and a dance song about the Cold War–era fear of nuclear annihilation. "Are You Receiving" is the angriest and most punk-inspired song, about life in a fallen society with surveillance, oppression, and detention of people who rebel.

### "Wardance" b/w "Pssyche" 45 March 6, 1980 (Malicious Damage MD5 40) (UK)

A transitional single between the post-punk of their EP and the variations on post-punk the band would introduce on the first album. Both sides of this single depict a dark dystopian view of contemporary culture. "Wardance" depicts a fascist society leading people to their demise, while the B-side, with its title that's a variation on the Greek goddess of the soul, is a terrifying view of a society where institutions are violent and corrupt.

### *Killing Joke* LP October 13, 1980 (Malicious Damage EGMD 5 45) (UK)

The band makes a major change by integrating industrial music and heavy metal into their sound. They take some of the slower riffs and musical conventions of heavy metal while maintaining a punk and post-punk lyrical perspective. The songs are generally slower, more like the plodding pace of heavy metal songs than the fast pace of punk. Comparing the rerecording of "Wardance" to the original 45 version makes it clear how much they changed.

*Killing Joke* is almost a concept album about a dystopian society. There's the social and political commentary of punk and impressionist lyrics associated with post-punk. But all of this is done largely with heavy metal riffs as a foundation. The anti-military "Tomorrow's World" and "S.O. 36" about environmental catastrophe feature grinding heavy metal guitar sounds. "The Wait," which appears to be an apocalyptic view of the effects of pollution, takes a similar guitar riff but with a faster pace. "Primitive" is somewhere in between. "Complications," a song about the perspective of an aristocrat dismissing the lower class, is perhaps the closest to their post-punk roots.
**Genre:** Post-punk

# Kleenex

### *Kleenex* 7" EP October 22, 1978 (Sunrise 078-S-064) (Switzerland)

This all-female Swiss band had the name Kleenex until threatened with a lawsuit from the company that owned the Kleenex trademark. After that they changed their name to LiLiPUT. This EP features their own version of punk that's slowed down enough to sound like post-punk at times. What's probably most punk about it are the simple riffs and repetitive vocal phrases. The lyrics on the opening track, "Beri-Beri," are simply "give it out, do it better and each day you'll feel nicer." The other songs also have sparse words in English. But they sing the EP's last track, "Nice," in Swiss German.

### "U" b/w "You" 45 May 12, 1979 (Rough Trade RT 014) (UK)

The band's last release as Kleenex splits the single into an "angry side" and a "friendly side." This is harder-sounding than their first EP. "U" features background vocal shrieks after each phrase culminating in a chorus of "it's a hard world, it's a bad world." The rest of the song are phrases about what's hard and bad, some understandable, some not. "You" features yelps of "you" between phrases, the most prevalent of which is "this is your life."
**Genre:** Punk/Post-punk

## Kraut

### "Unemployed" 45 November 1981 (Cabbage K-0002) (USA)

This New York City band is transitioning into hardcore on the B-sides. But the real gem here is the A-side. There's a rousing and righteous revolution-in-the-air spirit of first wave Brit punk with a hardcore punk-like urgency in the vocals.
**Genre:** Punk/Hardcore Punk

## LiLiPUT

### "Split" b/w "Die Matrosen" 45 January 6, 1980 (Rough Trade RT 047) (UK)

The band goes through some personnel changes after changing their name from Kleenex, including the introduction of a saxophone player. "Split" features a double vocal with exuberant harmonies and whooping. Lots of fun. The B-side, "Die Matrosen," is even better, with whistling between verses and an infectious melody. It seems to be about someone who can't handle being stood up for a date.

### "Eisiger Wind" 45 February 27, 1981 (Rough Trade RT 062) (UK)

This Swiss band delivers what's probably their best song. It's their punkiest, with fewer post-punk nuances. But just to show they're still lighthearted, there's some "la la la" between verses.

### *LiLiPUT* LP August 11, 1982 (Rough Trade ROUGH 43) (UK)

For their first album, LiLiPUT resists duplicating the sound of their two previous singles or mimicking what they did as Kleenex. Instead, like the second albums by the Raincoats and the Slits, they break down the post-punk genre not by deconstructing it but by integrating so many other types of music. They create a mini-masterpiece as the Raincoats did with their second album. These albums often remain overlooked, however, because they sound so different from how these bands started. At the time, the media and many of their fans couldn't follow them into the brave new world of daring albums.

On *LiLiPUT*, each song sounds very different from the others. It starts with the garage rock of "Do You Mind My Dream?" and ends with the catchy "Tong-Tong," with an array of percussion with the only vocals the words "tong-tong" repeated. About half the songs—like "In a Mess," "Outburst," and "Might Is Right"—have a rock or pop structure as a base. But the other half is bold experimentation. "Umamm" mixes a tribal beat

with shrieks in the background, "Tschik-Mo" features a chant over Asian-influenced music, and "Ichor" features a clarinet and mournful violin.
**Genre:** Punk/Post-punk

## Liquid Liquid

### *Liquid Liquid* 12" EP May 1981 (99 Records 99–07 EP) (USA)

This New York City funk-fueled experiment in post-punk adds world music, and particularly African and Latin percussion. The songs are instrumentals with improvised scat vocals, yowls, and other sounds. There's some no wave around the edges that makes it sound unconventional, such as on the ending track, "Rubbermiro." It's experimental because it doesn't contain conventional song structures, just an improvised experimental jazz-like jam.

### *Optimo* 12" EP March 12, 1983 (99 Records 99–11EP) (USA)

This is the band's best-known record because of the song "Cavern," which was used beyond what can be called sampling in Grandmaster Flash's "White Lines." The rap pioneers used instrumentation from "Cavern" not just for a few bars but for the entire song. After some legal battles, both bands suffered financially. The controversy overshadowed the rest of the EP. Too bad. It continues their post-punk and funk synthesis in glorious form, particularly on the infectious title track and "Scraper." And they add vocals at times, which provides an appealing complexity.
**Genre:** Post-punk

## Ludus

### *The Visit* 12" EP March 13, 1980 (New Hormones ORG 4) (UK)

Singer Linder Sterling was an artist and influencer in the British punk scene. She designed record covers for the Buzzcocks and Magazine. And she was friends from a young age with Morrissey. Rumor has it that Sterling was the inspiration for the Smiths song "Cemetery Gates." And she was the singer of this Manchester post-punk band. Their debut EP features a free-form/bebop jazz influence at times, particularly in "I Can't Swim I Have Nightmares." The jazz influence is also in Sterling's vocal phrasing, where her voice alternates between sarcasm, anger, delight, and insight, sometimes in a kind of scat.

The EP has one of the strongest feminist perspectives in this era of music. In "Unveil," she criticizes being a commodity: "I am your property, use me to sell my made machine masculine dreams." Within the punk with jangle guitars and tempo shifts of "Sightseeing" she sings, "You can't feel what I feel." It's not only a feminist statement. It's an overall feeling of how punk and post-punk bands felt misunderstood.

### *Pickpocket* cassette EP April 15, 1981 (New Hormones 1 CAT 1) (UK)

Ludus continues their jazz/post-punk fusion in what might be their most accessible album. But possibly their best release was only available as a six-song cassette album (it has since been released on CD). Every song is a winner. "Mutilate" is probably the closest the band got to punk rock. Perhaps the standout track is "Box," a kind of anthem for introverts about enjoying being alone. But like "See the Keyhole" on their album *The Seduction*, she's curious about interaction ("I am open to ideas, I am open and inviting"). Throughout this band's music there's a sense of how to navigate being a sensitive outsider.

***The Seduction*** **double 12" EP December 14, 1981 (New Hormones ORG 16) (UK)**

Manchester post-punk band's first album continues the feminism of their EP *The Visit*. In "Unveiled," singer Linder Sterling speaks out more about how women are commodified, while in "Mirror Mirror" she declares, "I'm the one who will not play your game."

With the exception of the very experimental "Herstory" and the instrumental "The Dynasty," the album is generally less jazz influenced. The songs and vocals are tighter, more controlled, more self-assured. The single, "My Cherry Is in Sherry," is perhaps the most accessible track. "See the Keyhole" is about an introvert who wants to be out in the world more. The final song, "The Escape Artist," is one of the most melodic and hopeful, but it ends with a frightening scream. Underneath the playfulness, confidence, sarcasm, observation, and declarations of independence there's still that threat of fear to be a woman in this era. Throughout the album Sterling seems vulnerable yet observant, sometimes sarcastic yet fearful.

**Genre:** Post-punk

## The Lurkers

### *Fulham Fallout* LP June 1, 1978 (Beggar's Banquet BAG 2) (UK)

Overlooked Brit punk album with a diverse approach that's one of the highlights of the first few years of punk. They showed where punk could go after its initial blast of energy by adding some pop elements while not fully going over into pop punk.

However, even the songs with more of a pop punk sound have dark lyrics to give it tension. "Ain't Got a Clue" is the story of a parolee with nowhere to go. "Shadow" is about jealousy of someone wealthy but with a threat of violence underneath. Even "Jenny," which on the surface sounds like a love song, is about being in a love with a woman jailed for murder.

Other songs sound outright desperate. "Total War" is a Clash-like song about the feeling of oppression. "Self-Destruct" and "It's Quiet Here" are about internal pain. The more exhilarating song is "Go Go Go," one of the great punk instrumentals with a combination of punk, surf guitar, and garage rock. It'll get you up and moving.

**Genre:** Punk/Pop Punk

## Madness

### "The Prince" b/w "Madness" 45 September 1, 1979 (2 Tone CHS TT3) (UK)

The band's only record on the 2 Tone label. Both songs were rerecorded for their first album, and fans still debate which versions are the best. But they're both worth having. The album versions are fuller and better arranged. But there's a rawness and stripped-down quality to the 2 Tone single. "The Prince" is a tribute to the Jamaican singer Prince Buster, a major influence on second wave ska, while the B-side is one of his songs, which the band reportedly named themselves after.

### *One Step Beyond* LP October 19, 1979 (Stiff SEEZ 17) (UK)

Great fun that expands the ska genre because of its range of styles and integration of pop. Unlike the other significant ska bands, Madness isn't usually overtly political ("Land of Hope and Glory" being an exception on this album). But there's something subversive about the high energy here. It's almost like a defiant party to overcome the

**Although based in ska, Madness—(clockwise from bottom left) Mike Barson, Mark Bedford, Daniel Woodgate, Chris Foreman, Cathal "Chas Smash" Smyth, and Graham "Suggs" McPherson—incorporated other influences as well. This helped enable the band to endure long after the British ska craze of the late 1970s and early 1980s subsided (Mirrorpix/Everett Collection).**

late 1970s doldrums. It's clear from the start that Madness is a pop band as well as a ska band, although this album is their most ska oriented. This combination of ska and pop may come from what are probably the band's two biggest influences, the spirited ska of Prince Buster and the pub rock pop of Ian Dury with its deeply British subject matter and regional vocal phrasing.

Ian Dury's singing style, which borders on a British version of rap, would continue to be an influence throughout Madness's career. But it starts here with "In the Middle of the Night," about a newspaper shop worker who steals underwear at night, and "Mummy's Boy," about someone "hiding something dirty." There's also the ska-influenced pop that would also define them, with songs like "My Girl" and "Bed and Breakfast Man." "Rockin' in A Flat" mixes some rockabilly with ska.

But the straight-ahead ska on this album is some of the most recognizable in all of second wave ska, starting with their scorching version of Prince Buster's "One Step Beyond," a song that instantly means "this is a party." "Night Boat to Cairo," about a trip down the Nile River, would become one of their most popular songs. "Tarzan's Nuts" and "Swan Lake" are ska instrumentals that also blend in pop elements, particularly through the use of piano.

### "Mistakes" (B-side of "One Step Beyond") 45 October 26, 1979 (Stiff BUY 56) (UK)

Underneath the burst of fun recorded for their first album is this world-weary B-side that pointed ahead to later songs like "Grey Day" and "Cardiac Arrest." But perhaps there is no Madness song as dark as this one. This is a unique song in this band's career that's difficult to categorize. But with its syncopation, it sounds reggae-inspired. It's filled with a weighty sense of the unfairness in life.

### *Work, Rest, & Play* 7" EP March 21, 1980 (Stiff BUY 71) (UK)

EP released between their first two albums includes three essential non–LP tracks. "Deceives the Eye" is an Ian Dury–influenced song about a shoplifter from a broken home. "The Young and the Old" is about an old man who lives a double life and won't grow up. But the best is "Don't Quote Me on That," which is an autobiographical account of being misquoted and misunderstood by the media. These three songs are danceable and meaningful and together comprise an interesting musical midpoint between their first two albums.

### *Absolutely* LP September 26, 1980 (Stiff SEEZ 29) (UK)

The Ian Dury influence gets even more pronounced. That starts with the album's first track, "Baggy Trousers," about nostalgia for the chaos and clamor of school days with such rapid-fire lyrics that it's almost like an early rap song. Other songs, including "E.R.N.I.E.," "Close Escape," and "On the Beat Pete" have the Dury influence in vocal style but are uniquely Madness both musically and lyrically.

Despite the glorious pop ska combination, "Embarrassment" is the story of a young woman being ostracized because she is pregnant. This juxtaposition of upbeat music with more downhearted or unsettling lyrics would add a depth to this band that would take them far beyond their image as a party band. Some songs on side two would go in that complex direction, like "In the Rain," which has an irresistible pop sound but features a story about someone lost in ambivalence. To show how far the band would go in exploring where to expand ska, the album ends with an instrumental very different from "One Step Beyond," which opened their previous album. "Return of the Los Palmas 7" is a ska/cha cha/cocktail music combination that shows this band is taking a step beyond into other territory.

### "In the City" (B-side of "Cardiac Arrest") 45 February 12, 1982 (Stiff BUY 140) (UK)

This is the band's last blast of bona fide ska before Madness largely reinvented themselves with a blend of influences and became a great pop band. As good as most of the songs are on their third album, *Seven*, and their fourth album, *Rise & Fall*, they can't be completely defined as ska albums. Because "In the City" is more ska-based, that must have been why the band relegated this catchy fun song to a B-side when it easily could have been an A-side and probably a hit.

**"House of Fun" 45 May 10, 1982 (Stiff BUY 146) (UK)**

Just before the magnificent pop album *Rise & Fall*, which covered all kinds of musical territory, Madness dips back into their more ska-oriented past with this combination of ska and pop. It's a rollicking song about a 16-year-old coming of age but with a hint that trouble may be on its way.
**Genre:** Ska

## Magazine

**"My Mind Ain't So Open" (B-side of "Shot by Both Sides") 45 January 16, 1978 (Virgin VS 200) (UK)**

The fastest song this band recorded outpaces pretty much anything by the Buzzcocks, the band Howard Devoto left to form Magazine. There's a frenzied saxophone solo to add some chaos. This is Magazine at their punkiest. It's the flip side to their seminal "Shot by Both Sides" single, which would later appear on their debut album, *Real Life*.

**"Touch and Go" 45 April 15, 1978 (Virgin VS 207) (UK)**

The second Magazine single is nearly pop punk. There's a punk-like sneer in the singer's disapproval of a woman who promises "instant intimacy." Unlike their first single, "Shot by Both Sides," it didn't make it on to their first album, *Real Life*.

***Real Life* LP June 9, 1978 (Virgin V 2100) (UK)**

The band's first single, "Shot by Both Sides," included on this album, transformed the music world. It opened the door for what came to be called post-punk. It was released not long after the Sex Pistols breakup, which in some ways felt like the end of not just a band but the initial punk era. "Shot by Both Sides" offered a new direction. It contained the energy of punk but was more complex musically. At first punk was a movement toward simplicity. But "Shot by Both Sides" showed it was possible to maintain the energy of punk while being more musically daring.

*Real Life* wasn't an expansive blueprint for post-punk. Public Image Ltd., Gang of Four, Wire, and Siouxsie and the Banshees would release records the same year that would show more possibilities of where post-punk could go. However, this album was a significant turning point into post-punk. And the album isn't just variations of "Shot by Both Sides." "Definitive Gaze" assimilates layers of keyboards, while "My Tulpa" sounds like a punk song that's modified by slowing down the pace.

To break the stereotypical tempo of punk songs, "Recoil" is fast but uses some quirky rhythms, while "Motorcade" has two distinct tempos. "The Light Pours Out of Me," with its creeping bass line and guitar parts, features somewhat of a funk feel with a triumphant, dramatic chorus. "Parade" is slower and somber, almost like a music hall song, yet the lyrics and vocals show a perspective that there's just something wrong. Devoto's voice at times has an ominous, Gothic-like quality to it that also was influential.

**"I Love You, You Big Dummy" (B-side of "Give Me Everything") 45 November 28, 1978 (Virgin VS 237) (UK)**

Remake of an avant-garde blues song by Captain Beefheart turns it into a lot of punk fun with some of legendary post-punk guitarist John McGeoch's distinctive guitar parts. This is Magazine's last blast of a hybrid of flat-out punk with post-punk around the edges.

*The Correct Use of Soap* **LP May 2, 1980 (Virgin V 2156) (UK)**

After their largely plodding and monotonous second album, *Secondhand Daylight*, Magazine reconfigures their sound and returns reinvigorated. They create a new sound that moves beyond their first album. Devoto integrates post-punk into the keyboard-dominant sound becoming more prevalent on the charts.

With its combination of keyboards and John McGeoch's guitar, the opening track, "Because You're Frightened," creates a formula that many synth-oriented bands would water down and commercialize. "A Song from Under the Floorboards" and "Sweetheart Contract" are both catchy, post-punk pop songs. But the album has a variety of ways to create keyboard-driven post-punk songs. One of the best is "Model Worker," about an obedient worker who considers himself to be an example of what the state wants. With its allusions to Dostoevsky's *Crime and Punishment*, "Philadelphia" concludes with a kind of post-punk jam. Guitarist John McGeoch would leave the band after this album and join Siouxsie and the Banshees.

**Genre:** Post-punk

## Marie et les Garçons

### *Marie et les Garçons* 7" EP 1977 (Rebel Records RB 7701) (France)

Adventurous post-punk from French band that later became associated with the New York no wave movement. The biting, jagged guitars and throbbing bass that became associated with post-punk drive this one. "Rien à Dire" shifts halfway through from a Television-like meditation into a full-fledged urgent post-punk song. "A Bout De Souffle" is more driving from the beginning and ends in a glorious screeching guitar.

### "Attitudes" b/w "Re-Bop" 45 March 1978 (Spy Records SPY 305) (France)

Rather than the post-punk of their debut record, this takes a turn into a more discordant and quirky variation on no wave. "Attitudes" features a more plodding rhythm than the energy of their first record, although it is much more melodic than the work of other bands associated with no wave. The more pop-oriented "Re-Bop" has a surf guitar meets jangle guitar with a Modern Lovers influence.

**Genre:** Post-punk/No Wave

## Mars

### "3-E" b/w "11,000 Volts" 12" 1978 (Rebel Records RB 7802) (France)

The no wave movement was so brief and so largely ignored that some bands didn't get to develop. Like this band, who came and went all too quickly. This is one of no wave's best moments. And it came from a band that supposedly had no musical knowledge or background before making a record.

"3-E" deconstructs the structure and expectations of a rock song. But there's still a Velvet Underground–like drive to it. And the lyrics are a nightmarish vision of life in the city. "11,000 Volts" is slower, sung by China Burg in a slurred tonality that makes her voice an instrument.

**Genre:** No Wave

## Maximum Joy

### "Stretch" 45 September 5, 1981 (Y Records Y 11) (UK)

This blend of world music, post-punk, and funk seems like a satire of self-improvement. There's something that sounds subversive about the almost disturbing screams of "stretch." It sounds more imperialistic than self-empowering.

**Genre:** Post-punk

## MDC

### *Millions of Dead Cops* LP February 1982 (R Radical MDC 1) (USA)

Like the Dead Kennedys and Jodie Foster's Army, this is another hardcore band with a controversial name. Although the Austin, Texas, band would say MDC stood for different things, one of them was Millions of Dead Cops, the title of their debut album. In 14 songs in a little over 20 minutes, they confront many of the targets for anger and anxiety of the Generation Jones era.

It starts with "Business on Parade," which aims at the entire political and economic system where there's "government by the rich, poor man's life a bitch." Life also looks bleak in "Born to Die," a dystopian view of the American life run by fascists and racists. The feeling of everything being rigged and working against ordinary people perhaps comes together best in "I Remember," about the false promises of America and the reality of poverty, lack of opportunity, and police brutality. The album ends with "American Achievements," an ironically titled song about the downside of America. Other subjects include homophobia in "America's So Straight," a movie icon in "John Wayne Was a Nazi," landlords in "Greedy and Pathetic," and dysfunctional families in "My Family's a Little Weird."

**Genre:** Hardcore Punk

## The Mekons

### "Where Were You?" b/w "I'll Have to Dance Then" 45 November 29, 1978 (Fast Product FAST 7) (UK)

The Leeds band makes their own version of a punk/post-punk hybrid before they went all in on post-punk with their debut album. On "Where Were You?" some guitar strums lead into an ominous, long drumroll. Then a series of observations followed by questions such as, "I want to find out about your life, do you like me?" The B-side continues the theme of loneliness over a march-like beat.

### *The Quality of Mercy Is Not Strnen* LP November 26, 1979 (Virgin V 2143) (UK)

What's most distinctive about this album is that it sounds raggedy and almost improvised, which gives this a fresh sound. They sound like songs that aren't quite formed yet. It's a DIY version of post-punk. The strange title of the album has to do with the photograph on the cover of the monkey with a typewriter. It's based on the infinite monkey theorem, the idea that a monkey at a typewriter randomly typing keys would eventually type a book or even the works of William Shakespeare. Perhaps this is a metaphor for what this band attempts on this album, which is to play in their DIY way to make something more substantial.

The band would go on to experiment with many different instruments, but this album is more minimalist with the emphasis on guitars and drums. There's something consistently subversive about songs that aren't really parodies but a kind of deconstruction and ridicule of song conventions. "After 6" and "What" both sound like parodies of a pop song, while "What Are We Going to Do Tonight?" sounds like a satire of a punk song. "Trevira Trousers" ends with a repetitive chant over nervous-sounding post-punk guitars—almost a parody of post-punk.

### "Teeth" 45 March 3, 1980 (Virgin SV 101) (UK)

Driving, punk-like song with synthesizer and instead of the jagged guitar of post-punk, a jagged violin. In the song, the problems just keep on coming. This produces a kind of apprehension, but the only outlet is talking in pubs about "war and money, oppression and more."

### *The Mekons* LP January 7, 1981 (Red Rhino RED MEK 1) (UK)

The band adds other instrumentation to go beyond the DIY guitar-driven song structures of their debut album. This makes the songs more complex and varied. It's a significant shift that almost makes them sound like a different band.

That's clear from the first track, "Snow," which uses a swirling synthesizer with the guitars that were so prominent on their first album are buried in the mix. The song also features a monotone narration. This voice represents the bourgeoisie observing trouble outside from inside a privileged home. Several other songs on the album, including "Business," use narration over a keyboard-driven sound. As on the band's first album, some of the songs subvert musical genres more than they parody them. The violin-driven "Institution" comes across as subversion of a folk song, while "I'm So Happy" is an ironic title for what appears to be a parody of a post-punk song.

### "Fight the Cuts" (B-side of "This Sporting Life") 45 October 4, 1982 (CNT Productions CNT 008) (UK)

The band returns to their punkier origins. This jangle punk song shows the 1980s outrage against government cuts to social programs. It happened in the early 1980s in both Britain and America and contributed to the Generation Jones disillusionment with politics.

**Genre:** Post-punk

## The Members

### "Solitary Confinement" 45 March 26, 1978 (Stiff/Off Records OFF 3) (UK)

A convincing portrayal of someone moving to the city hoping for something better. But it only leads to working an oppressive job during the day and isolation at night eating TV dinners watching television alone. The singer's "I really don't know if I'm dead or alive" captures the reality of disillusionment and deprivation of urban working life for the young.

### "Sounds of the Suburbs" 45 January 23, 1979 (Virgin VS 242) (UK)

This could be the backstory of the singer of the band's first single, "Solitary Confinement." It details the boredom and unfulfillment of suburban living. Clamor is all around. Loneliness, boredom, and isolation are everywhere.

**Genre:** Punk

## The Membranes

***Muscles*** **12" EP May 23, 1982 (Rondelet 12 ROUND) (UK)**

The title track somewhat resembles Feelies-like jangle punk. But the Membranes put their own British stamp on it with a song about the hypermasculine qualities of the military and the people it attracts. The catchy "All Roads Lead to Norway" is a combination of jangle punk and funk. "Entertaining Friends," with its refrain of "why are you watching me?" with a whistle blown at points, is a subversive dance song. Don't overlook the instrumental "Great Mistake," which is infectious.

**Genre:** Punk/Post-punk

## Lizzy Mercier Descloux

***Press Color*** **LP February 1979 (ZE ZEA 33004) (USA)**

After one record with the no wave band Rosa Yemen, French singer Mercier Descloux releases a solo album that's in the post-punk category but incorporates jazz, European pop, no wave, and funk. She doesn't deconstruct music the same way she did in Rosa Yemen by dismantling musical forms. Instead, she's subversive by inhabiting musical conventions and subverting them. Like reworking Peggy Lee's "Fever" into her own version called "Tumor" and a funk-and-disco blend in a cover of the 1960s psychedelic song "Fire."

What holds it all together is that, like that of a jazz singer, Mercier Descloux's voice works like an instrument itself, gliding over songs like "Jim on the Move," where she twists and bends, reciting "Jim on the Move" over and over again. In "No Golden Throat" she scats and stretches her voice over a blend of a reggae and funk slow groove.

**Genre:** Post-punk

## Method Actors

**"Do the Method" from *This Is It* 7" EP November 1, 1980 (Armageddon AS 006) (UK)**

If there's a connection between the jangle punk of the Feelies and R.E.M.'s *Chronic Town* EP, it's in this song by this Athens, Georgia, band. The Method Actors later took a severe change of musical direction into a funk-influenced post-punk band. But they really hit their groove here.

**Genre:** Post-punk

## The Middle Class

***Out of Vogue*** **7" EP September 1978 (Joke Records 09831) (USA)**

At just over a minute long, the title track changed music. It's likely that this is the first full-fledged hardcore punk song. That's somewhat up for debate, however, because both Black Flag and the Bad Brains formed earlier but didn't release records until after this one. And while there were some songs by punk bands that were fast, this has some important traits of hardcore punk. Like the shouted-rather-than-sung lyrics, the response vocals in the chorus, and the fast pace, particularly with the drum and bass tempos. The songs "You Belong" and "Insurgent" are also fast and hard. But at the time there was no hardcore punk scene for them to latch onto. So they grew in a post-punk direction.

**Genre:** Hardcore Punk

# Minor Threat

### *Minor Threat* 7" EP June 14, 1981 (Dischord 3) (USA)

After the Teen Idles broke up, Ian MacKaye formed Minor Threat, one of the greatest and most influential hardcore bands. MacKaye sings in a voice of an everyman with lyrics that are universal, such as "I Don't Want to Hear It" about shutting down lies and hypocrisy. It has broad appeal because it can apply to so many situations. Another somewhat universal feeling is feeling like an outcast and threatened in "Seeing Red," while "Minor Threat" resists the values and priorities of the adult establishment.

Perhaps the best-known song is "Straight Edge," which is about not using alcohol and drugs. MacKaye didn't intend to start a whole movement with this song. But it spread into a whole subgenre of hardcore punk. At the time drugs were associated with hippies and superstar bands with drug-soaked concerts in large arenas and stadiums. But it was also about the punk ethos of being engaged and active, not numbing oneself from life, and the ability to make one's own decisions about how to live. That also is expressed in "Bottled Anger," in which MacKaye makes a further connection between excessive drinking and violence.

### *In My Eyes* 7" EP December 10, 1981 (Dischord 5) (USA)

Half of this four-song EP includes two songs that continue the straight edge themes from their first EP. "In My Eyes" outlines the reasons that people use drugs, including peer pressure and wanting to create a false image of being cool. In "Out of Step with the World" there's an acceptance that being straight edge will make someone feel out of place and rejected. The sometimes-misunderstood song "Guilty of Being White" expresses frustration about being perceived as racist when one is not. The album ends with a cover of the Monkees' "Steppin' Stone" that starts out sounding like it's coming out of a transistor radio as if from another time period but builds into a more full-fledged punky version with MacKaye reinventing the song as defiant resistance.

### *Out of Step* LP March 1983 (Dischord 10) (USA)

At a point when hardcore punk was showing its musical and lyrical limitations, this album provided a way out of those constraints. During an era when short hardcore songs were becoming a cliché, this album featured longer and more developed songs. Well-produced without being overproduced, the songs maintain the energy of hardcore while showing how to vary the musical styles enough to make the genre more experimental and relevant.

At this point Minor Threat was somewhat like the Clash of hardcore punk, with lyrics that represented an everyman sense of morality and integrity. And musically *Out of Step* in some ways did for hardcore punk what the Clash's *London Calling* accomplished for the initial era of punk, which is to lead it out of the stereotypes of the genre. But here, the band does more subtle experimentations within the hardcore genre. "Betray" uses a different tempo for the last part of the song, "Think Again" features a bass solo, and the first half of "Look Back and Laugh" is more slowly paced before breaking into the hardcore punk pace. The ending song, "Cashing In," sounds like a traditional punk song at times and at other times like a parody of a rock song.

The lyrics also turn away from the clichés of hardcore punk's overtly political subject matter. The songs are more personal, about betrayal in friendships and also the dangers of selling out. It seems like it's on the edge of young adulthood weighing what's truly important in life. "Cashing In" shows the punk suspicion of posers masquerading as punks and criticizes bands who are in it for money. "Out of Step" is an updated version of "Out of Step with the World" from their *In My Eyes* EP that again reiterates how following a punk ideology, particularly the straight edge mindset, will make one an outsider.

**Genre:** Hardcore Punk

## The Minutemen

### *Paranoid Time* 7" EP December 13, 1980 (SST-002) (USA)

They would go on to innovatively experiment with combining punk, hardcore, and post-punk. In the long run, that would make them one of the most influential American bands of the Generation Jones period. But there's something pure, concise, and direct about their first record that they never quite matched.

There are just seven short songs, every song conveying feelings and observations succinctly and effectively. They're like punk rock telegrams from a war zone. Many songs are about societal oppression that brings confusion, anger, and alienation. This perhaps comes together best in the ending three songs, with "Fascist," about living under tyranny of the ruling class; "Joe McCarthy's Ghost," comparing contemporary society to the communist witch trials of the 1950s; and "Paranoid Time," showing how the fear of nuclear annihilation is so strong the singer can't focus on much else.

### *The Punch Line* LP November 1, 1981 (SST-004) (USA)

California band's first album is 18 songs over two sides of an album that totals just over 15 minutes. Although the Minutemen were known as a punk band, they utilized post-punk approaches. The rapid-fire bass playing by Mike Watt usually drives the songs more than the guitars. At times it sounds funk-influenced, and at times it has some early rap-like vocal deliveries. There are tempo changes and shifts consistent with post-punk music. But unlike post-punk bands, the songs are ultrashort.

The musical eclecticism confused some people when this album was released in a more tribal era of different genres with music fans in different camps. But that changed further on in the 1980s and into the 1990s, when this musical diversity was more accepted. The lyrics in the songs are also varied. Some are impressionistic post-punk lyrics. Others are about racial tension ("Boiling" and "Disguises"), economic inequality ("The Struggle"), the proliferation of violence through the ages ("History Lesson"), and the fear of war ("Parade").

### *Bean-Spill* 7" EP July 4, 1982 (Thermidor T8) (USA)

In some ways it's a continuation of their first album. The guitar is more dominant here, however. And the songs are generally punkier. With just five songs in a little over six minutes, there isn't time for the musical eclecticism of their first album. Highlights include "If Reagan Played Disco," about how the then president is a fascist-like leader who manipulates the public, and the first version released of one of their best-known songs, "Split Red," about imperialism gone wrong.

***What Makes a Man Start Fires?*** **LP January 1983 (SST-0140) (USA)**

The Minutemen go beyond the short songs of their initial records and formulate fuller and more complete songs. While other post-punk bands employed the funk genre, the Minutemen used a less polished and more raggedy and punkier integration of funk. This made it different from the more polished post-punk funk that New York bands played. While the lyrics contain poetic and somewhat fragmented short lines consistent with some of post-punk, there's a rawness that made the band acceptable to punk audiences.

There are straight-ahead punk songs such as "Bob Dylan Wrote Propaganda Songs," "One Chapter in the Book," and "'99." But the center of this album is their experimentation combining funk, post-punk, and punk. There's a range of approaches from the slow funk of "Fake Contest" to the frantic post-punk of "East Wind/Faith."

***Buzz or Howl Under the Influence of Heat*** **12" EP November 1, 1983 (SST-016) (USA)**

Known for most of the album being recorded live in the studio without overdubs reportedly for $50. The quickness of recording makes many of the songs sound spontaneous and somewhat more dangerous. The no-frills production gives D. Boon's guitar a cutting, upfront rawness. And Boon's guitar playing is a revelation on this album. The tension Boon creates with the guitar in songs like "Little Man with a Gun in His Hand" and "Self-Referenced" makes for some of the best Minutemen songs.

There's no pigeonholing the band. There's everything from the garage funk of "Cut" to the almost Captain Beefheart–like experimentation of "The Product." The most fully realized song is "I Feel Like a Gringo," about a visit to Mexico.

**Genre:** Post-punk

# The Misfits

***Static Age*** **LP (recorded 1978, released February 27, 1996) (Caroline Records CAR 7520–1) (USA)**

New Jersey band that came to be associated with the subgenre of horror punk initially couldn't get a record label to release their first album. So this album wasn't put out until almost two decades later. Some of the songs were released on the "Bullet" 45 (1978), *Horror Business* EP (1979), and *Beware* EP (1980). However, hearing the entire intended album and not just the songs released at the time shows how groundbreaking the band was. They combined punk, pop punk, and horror punk, and there's even elements of what would become hardcore punk and crossover thrash. In New Jersey this band was separated from the New York City punk scene, and their sound was different, influenced by heavy metal music, horror movies, and comic books.

*Static Age* starts with two songs about the media—"Static Age" and "TV Casualty"—that sound like late 1970s full-fledged punk but with a key difference that ended up putting them into another whole category or punk called horror punk. Like the Goth subgenre of post-punk would do, they inserted a sense of the macabre. But horror punk was much more overtly disturbing than Goth would be. So "Bullet," about the assassination of President John F. Kennedy, focuses on the horror of the moment with explicit violent imagery.

Other songs sound like straight-ahead punk, like "Attitude" and "She," the latter based on Patty Hearst, an heiress-turned-bank-robber after she was kidnapped by an underground radical group. It was one of the major news stories of the 1970s. Other songs borrow from pop culture and movies. "We Are 138" reportedly alludes to George Lucas's sci-fi movie *THX 1138*. But there's also a tribute to the spirit of B movies in "Teenagers from Mars," with its ending "we don't care" recalling the Sex Pistols song "Pretty Vacant." The Misfits never made their songs sound like novelty songs even if they were inspired by B horror movies. They played them with the same seriousness they played their other songs. And they had hooks. Really good hooks. So even a disturbing song such as "Last Caress" features a catchy melody over the lyrics about a brutal criminal.

### *Night of the Living Dead* 45 October 31, 1979 (Plan 9 PL1011) (USA)

"Night of the Living Dead" features one of those trademark hooky choruses with just the word "no." It's one of several tributes to classic horror movies. This one is about the 1968 zombie film directed by George Romero. There's the same approach in "Where Eagles Dare," with its catchy chorus of "I ain't no goddamn son of a bitch." "Rat Fink" is a Ramones-like song written by novelty song writer Allan Sherman. The production here is more compressed than *Static Age*. That almost makes it sound like its from a distant time period, even for the time it was released.

### *Horror Business* 45 June 26, 1979 (Plan 9 PL 1009) (USA)

If you want to collect all of the Misfits songs from this era, "Teenagers from Mars" is on the *Static Age* album. But two songs on this EP aren't, including the B-side, "Children in Heat." But the real gem is the A-side. "Horror Business." It's mostly about the movie *Psycho*, but the 1978 reference reportedly is about the death of Sid Vicious's girlfriend, Nancy Spungen. Also notable for the picture sleeve, which was the first appearance of the Crimson Ghost, a character from a film serial that became the band's mascot and logo.

### *3 Hits from Hell* 7" EP April 17, 1981 (Plan 9 PL1013) (USA)

The A-side "London Dungeon" slows the pace down from most of their songs and is based on their experience being jailed after a skinhead attack outside a concert in London. Like some of their other songs, "Horror Hotel" is based on a classic horror film. In this case, a 1960 movie starring Christopher Lee. "Ghouls Night Out" features their trademark melodic punk, this time with lyrics about cannibalism.

### "Halloween" 45 October 31, 1981 (Plan 9 PL 1017) (USA)

The compressed production gets even more extreme, so this song is primitive-sounding, almost as if it's a mono recording from another time period. (To hear an alternative to this mix, check out the version from the unreleased *12 Hits from Hell* album widely available on the internet.) Consistent with the band's approach, the song is almost pop punk but with violent imagery in some of the lyrics. Here, Halloween becomes a night of anarchy and violence.

### *Walk Among Us* LP March 13, 1982 (Ruby Records JRR 804) (USA)

After years of just putting out singles and EPs, this is the band's first full-fledged album released during the initial era of the Misfits. Most of the song titles sound like they could be the names of classic B horror movies ("I Turned into a Martian," "Devil's Whorehouse," "Braineaters"). And there's one song about an actual horror film ("Astro Zombies"). The songs from their singles and EPs inserted horror into real situations, but with a few exceptions this sounds like punk horror movies. This album may be responsible more than anything else for the horror punk genre.

But this isn't novelty-type horror punk. There's a sense of danger. While "I Turned into a Martian" sounds like a B movie, it's played with the sense that it's an urgent identity crisis. But they do deliver their own horror version of the Cold War–era fear of nuclear war in "Nike-A-Go-Go." "Violent World" continues the theme of a horror-like feeling about the nature of society. And the ending song, "Braineaters," while a parody of Oi! music, also sounds like a condemnation of skinhead ideology.

And there's some variety of genres here. "All Hell Breaks Loose" and "Mommy Can I Go Out and Kill Tonight?" sound almost like hardcore punk songs. "Vampira" is a rockabilly-like tribute to the actress from *Plan 9 from Outer Space*. And they still can do subversive pop punk such as "Skulls."

**Genre:** Punk/Horror Punk

## Mission of Burma

### "Academy Fight Song" b/w "Max Ernst" 45 June 14, 1980 (Ace of Hearts AHS 104) (USA)

Boston trio became one of the most significant American post-punk bands. Instead of venturing into experimentation with jagged guitars, quirky vocals, and a funk undercurrent that was becoming increasingly associated with post-punk, they merged punk and post-punk. They retained the energy of punk perhaps more than any other American post-punk band. This fusion made them a legendary band over the years and was an enormous influence on both 1980s alternative music and grunge.

This debut single is a gem. "Academy Fight Song" is about a student feeling alienated at a prep school. Once again, the punk ethos is as outsider who declares, "Stay just as far from me as me from you." "Max Ernst," about the avant-garde artist, features some ominous, heavy guitar and an ending playful chant of "dada," one of the artistic movements Ernst was associated with.

### *Signals, Calls, and Marches* 12" EP July 11, 1981 (Ace of Hearts AHS 1006) (USA)

The six-song EP begins with its best-known song, "That's When I Reach for My Revolver," with its subversive, semi-pop punk chorus. It reflects disillusionment, perhaps the album's most prominent theme. "Fame and Fortune" is directly about that. There is the intoxicating allure of seeking success even though it seems nearly impossible, ending with the contradictory chant "fame and fortune is a stupid game and fame and fortune is the game I play." This breakdown takes other forms with the deconstructionism of "This Is Not a Photograph," while "Red" and "Outlaw" contain surreal and almost horror movie elements.

### *Vs.* LP September 16, 1982 (Ace of Hearts 10010) (USA)

The band's only full-length album during this era is adventurous. Each song utilizes a different approach for their take on post-punk. Generally, the songs are energetic, with more dominance by Roger Miller's guitars. By 1982, hardcore punk ascended to the dominant form in the American subculture of punk. This forced punk-centered bands to generally be faster.

But there are some slower songs that focus on what appears to be epiphanies or realizations about the present moment. "Trem Two" and "Einstein's Day" are ponderous and nearly mystical in tone. But most of the album is energetic. "Secrets" is faster paced but also calls for understanding of something beneath the surface, of what's "underneath the gaze." "The Ballad of Johnny Burma" contains hardcore-punk fastness and an almost subversive rockabilly-influenced vocal. The most straight-ahead punk song is "That's How I Escaped My Certain Fate," which sounds like a breakup with his partner moving away. The song produces conflicting emotions of what's honest and what isn't, what's good and what isn't, what's regretful and what isn't.

Perhaps the best song is the ironically titled "Fun World," a kind of art rock presentation with menacing guitar sounds about disillusionment in both childhood and adulthood. In the present day, the singer feels a desperate attempt to try to smash through the disillusionment.

**Genre:** Post-punk

**"Okay/No Way" (B-side of "Trem Two") 45 July 25, 1982 (Ace of Hearts AHS 106) (USA)**

This song has such a breakneck pace that it's essentially part hardcore punk and part post-punk. The incongruous song title is reflected in the uncertainty in the lyrics. The song itself seems to be about the dread of ambivalence and the pain of going back and forth between belief and nonbelief.

**Genre:** Post-punk

## Modern English

**"Swans on Glass" 45 January 19, 1980 (4AD AD6) (UK)**

The band had a big hit two years later with the pop song "I Melt with You." But their second single, all glorious post-punk, is the band's best song. The lyrics are almost a surreal series of images and feelings. This all swells to a chorus of "I'm turning around" with some spoken background words. There's also some mighty punk-meets–post-punk guitar.

**Genre:** Post-punk

## Mo-dettes

**"White Mice" 45 December 14, 1979 (Mode 1) (UK)**

This all-female British band created a more pop-oriented version of post-punk. This song is nothing like the nervous rhythms and vocals of some post-punk. It's basically an unconventional pop song that at times seems on the verge of ska. Lead singer Ramona Carlier has somewhat of an unconventional delivery, with words rushed together, sometimes sounding like it's a mixture of languages. When you can make out the words, the lyrics focus on a desire for an attractive masculine man. Is this a satire or do they mean it?

**"Dark Park Creeping" 45 October 17, 1980 (DERAM DET 2) (UK)**

This is more conventional post-punk and very different from their pop-oriented first single, "White Mice." There's some dirty guitar that's all post-punk that drives the song.

**Genre:** Post-punk

## Mofungo

***End of the World*** **cassette album October 10, 1981 (Mofungo Music none) (USA)**

Out of the ashes of late 1970s no wave came this eccentric album featuring avant-garde legendary musician Elliott Sharp. It remains an underrated gem, and every song has a different quality. But overall, we'll call it a combination of post-punk, no wave, and jangle punk. Whatever you want to label it, it's a compressed lo-fi mini-masterpiece from a band that defied trends to create a unique vision of life after no wave. It's intentionally compressed sound almost makes it sound like it comes from another age.

It starts with the reggae-meets–post-punk–meets-funk of the title track. "Scratch House" is propelled by a tribal beat that is the band's own version of the New York downtown dance sound without conventional funk influences. "El Salvador" is a cross between cutting post-punk guitar and a Velvet Underground–like drone. "Just the Way," with its swirling keyboard, is somewhat of a subversive pop song. "Why Do You Say" sounds improvisational in the tone of no wave, while "Boss Alligator" has the eccentricity of Captain Beefheart.

**Genre**: No Wave/Post-punk

## Monochrome Set

**"Eine Symphonie Des Grauens" b/w "Lester Leaps In" 45 July 10, 1979 (Rough Trade RT 019) (UK)**

The title of the A-side translates as "Symphony of Horror." Although the song is a mixture of post-punk and pop, the lyrics are Goth-influenced. The contrast between the music and the lyrics is part of what makes this song so interesting. Perhaps to lift the gloomy overtones of the A-side, "Lester Leaps In" is a cheery, energetic instrumental that sounds like it could be part of a soundtrack to a movie or TV show from the Generation Jones period. There's a place in the world for this kind of jubilation.

**Genre**: Post-punk

## Naked Raygun

***Basement Screams*** **12" EP August 1983 (Ruthless RRNR03) (UK)**

A varied record, somewhere between punk and post-punk. And that makes it somewhere between the Effigies and Big Black within the Chicago punk sound of this era. This is another album from 1983 that still uses post-punk sensibilities but features a variety of different styles and approaches that point to the eclectic quality of 1980s alternative music.

"Bombshelter" and "Tojo" sound post-punk, with tribal-like drumming. "Potential Rapist," about a woman walking alone at night who fears being raped, is more in the style of a punk song. "I Lie" is the band's take on a pop punk song. The biggest surprise is "Swingo," a blend of ska, post-punk, and punk. "Mofo" is a parody of dance music with its declaration that "in America you got to do more than singing and dancing on the floor."

**Genre**: Punk/Post-punk

## Necros

### *IQ32* 7" EP October 17, 1981 (Touch & Go 3/Dischord 4½) (USA)

Right away this Ohio band lets it be known what they think about where they came from: "Midwest fuck you!" is what is said at the end of the title track, the first song on the album. What else don't they like? Interracial fighting, the threat of war, and high school. They were teenagers when they first formed their band two years earlier. So there's a youthful perspective and honesty to the songs about high school ("I Hate My School," "Public High School," and "Peer Pressure"). And it's all direct with nine songs in a little over nine minutes. Produced by Ian MacKaye of Minor Threat.

**Genre:** Hardcore Punk

## Negative Approach

### *Negative Approach* 7" EP July 1982 (Touch & Go T&G 7) (USA)

Landmark punk record from Detroit band. Within 10 songs in about nine minutes, they pack in many styles and approaches to punk with a hardcore edge. The consistent theme is someone under attack from so many different directions but is defiant enough to somehow survive.

The best-known song is "Nothing," a masterpiece in the punk genre. There's pain in the vocal about the brutality of life creating a deadly sense of emptiness and self-loathing. This is the sound of someone facing the abyss. There's a fierce bass guitar solo and a searing guitar sound like Stooges meets the future of Sonic Youth. Vocalist John Brannon has one of the most emotional voices and fastest deliveries in all of hardcore punk. Just check out the ending of "Why Be Something That You're Not."

**Genre:** Punk/Hardcore Punk

## Negative Trend

### *Negative Trend* 7" EP September 1978 (Heavy Manners HM-1) (USA)

Along with the Avengers, this San Francisco punk took the spirit of the first wave of British punk to address current social conditions. "Mercenaries" is about mercenaries who "kill for pay" in places like Rhodesia. "Meat House" uses some surreal butcher house imagery to describe a place of debauchery, and perhaps it's extended as a metaphor for all of society. The desperate "Black and Red" is a bleak churning song, but the energy is recaptured with "How Ya Feeling," a harrowing account of down-and-out characters who are at "the top of the bottom."

**Genre:** Punk

## New Order

### "Ceremony" b/w "In a Lonely Place" 45 January 22, 1981 (Factory FAC 33) (UK)

After the death of singer Ian Curtis, the surviving members of Joy Division carry on under the name New Order. Both songs on their first single were unreleased Joy Division songs rerecorded with Bernard Sumner taking over as vocalist. "Ceremony" was Joy Division's attempt to write a more uplifting, potentially commercial song, and it's a midpoint between the sounds of Joy Division and New Order. "In a Lonely Place" is a haunting and somber B-side, as close to a Joy Division sound as this band has ever been. The versions of these songs on the 12-inch version were rerecorded and don't have the atmospheric sound of this single.

### *Movement* LP November 14, 1981 (Factory FACT 50) (UK)

*Movement* succeeds as a transitional album out of Joy Division. The band sounds different without the gravitas of Ian Curtis's voice and lyrics. But New Order begin to establish their own sound. They do that partly by relying more on the use of synthesizer. Both Bernard Sumner and Peter Hook take turns singing to fill in for Ian Curtis. The weight of vocalist Ian Curtis's tragic death hangs over many of the songs, however. It is the darkest and gloomiest of New Order albums. *Movement* essentially grieves Curtis's death and the end of Joy Division.

Band members have said that "IBC" stands for "Ian Curtis buried." Even in the album's most accessible track, the opening "Dreams Never End," there's a sense of mourning. Of all the songs, the Joy Division–like "Doubts Even Here" sounds the most like Curtis's vocals with its line "memories are all that's left" preceding part of Psalm 77 ("Has God forgotten to be gracious? Has he in anger withheld his mercies?"). There's a sense throughout the album of trying to understand Curtis's death but not being able to do it, such as in "Senses," the chorus of which states, "No reason was ever given." The album ends with "Denial" with its declaration that "the answer's not there." There isn't a sense of resolution about the darkness that has descended.

### *Power, Corruption, and Lies* LP May 2, 1983 (Factory FACT 75) (UK)

Some will say this isn't a post-punk album and is instead part of the synthesizer-based era of 1980s music. That's definitely the case with "Blue Monday," released after New Order's first album and before this album. But "Blue Monday" was not included on this album because the full-fledged move into keyboard-dominated music in that song wasn't consistent with this album.

*Power, Corruption, and Lies* is in many ways the end of the post-punk era of this band, which started as Joy Division. As *Movement* provided a transition out of Joy Division into New Order, this album is a transition out of post-punk into more mature, synth-based music. But there still is enough of a post-punk sensibility to make it post-punk.

There's a sense of grief at times that continues from New Order's *Movement* album about the death of Joy Division's singer, Ian Curtis. "We All Stand" contains foreboding about "the end of the road where all futures go," while "Your Silent Face" contains the same sense of confusion and loss that is on *Movement*. And the album ends with "Leave Me Alone" conveying a "deep sense of universal loneliness." "Age of Consent" and "The Village," however, show some feeling of at least having the desire to move past something painful and start something new and better.

**Genre:** Post-punk

## The Nips

### "Happy Song" b/w "Nobody to Love" 45 October 17, 1981 (Test Pressings TP5) (UK)

The best single from Shane MacGowan's first band. MacGowan would later go on to be the lead singer of the Pogues. Originally called the Nipple Erectors, the Nips started as a combination of power pop, rockabilly, and pop punk. Their third and last single produced by Paul Weller of the Jam are their best two songs. The A-side shows MacGowan at his punkiest: "I want to burn everything to the ground." The B-side is more pop punk.

**Genre:** Punk/Pop Punk

## The Offs

### "Zero Degrees" (B-side of "Everyone's A Bigot") 45 1978 (415 Records 911–39) (USA)

An American version of ska punk fusion from this San Francisco band. Two tone British ska got all the attention, but this was undoubtedly a later influence on West Coast ska and third wave ska. A great ska lost treasure.

**Genre:** Ska

## Oh-OK

### *Wow Mini Album* 7" EP August 16, 1982 (DB Records DB 63) (USA)

Debut record by Athens, Georgia, band with Lynda Stipe on vocals (sister of R.E.M.'s Michael Stipe). This trio has no guitarist. The songs are propelled by the bass, which gives them a distinctive sound. And this is a more pop-oriented post-punk that points to the coming genres of alternative and indie music.

There's almost a childlike perspective but with a post-punk tension underneath. "Playtime" captures the happiness of a child's play, but there's something more ominous about the desire to "run until the blood pounds." Other times there's a sense of wonder in the lyrics, which, like some other post-punk, contains short literary-like words. There's a dance-like groove in "Brother" about someone who "is for an expanding whole," and there's something defiant in "Person," which concludes, "I am a person and that is enough!"

**Genre:** Post-punk

## Opus

### "Good Procedures" b/w "The Atrocity" 45 1979 (Catatonic OPUS 1) (USA)

This Southern California punk band released an indie single and then disappeared. Over time it has become one of punk's rarest and most valuable 45s. Part of the reason may be the A-side, "Good Procedures," which slows the pace down from the usual punk tempo and adds some post-punk elements and a catchy chorus, which stands out from most punk at the time. "The Atrocity" is straight-ahead punk driven by a gnarly garage rock guitar.

**Genre:** Punk

## Orange Juice

### "Blue Boy" 45 August 11, 1980 (Postcard 80–2) (UK)

Orange Juice was the most successful of the bands on the Scottish label Postcard Records. They leaned more toward pop than post-punk. But on this single they integrated post-punk and pop using guitars that are both driving and melodic. Orange Juice and their labelmates Josef K influenced alternative music by creating this cross between post-punk and pop that progressed way past 1960s-soaked power pop.

### "Simply Thrilled Honey" 45 October 12, 1980 (Postcard 80–6) (UK)

More complex than "Blue Boy" with shifting rhythms and an almost tribal drum part at times, this is the midpoint between the Velvet Underground and the Smiths. It includes a soaring guitar that is kind of a melodic jagged guitar. Two years later, Orange Juice would record "Rip It Up," which would become their most popular song. It was a pop song with funk-influenced post-punk around the edges. But that song would be on the other side of post-punk. It was more 1980s new pop looking back at post-punk.
**Genre:** Post-punk

## Penetration

### "Don't Dictate" b/w "Money Talks" 45 November 5, 1977 (Virgin VS 192) (UK)

Fiery debut single from British band with singer Pauline Murray, one of the first female punk singers. "Don't Dictate" is about resisting conformity and obedience. It could be a feminist declaration, a political statement, or anything else that leads to taking a more independent anti-authoritative stand. The B-side is straight-ahead righteous Brit punk.
**Genre:** Punk

## Pere Ubu

### "Final Solution" 45 March 18, 1976 (Hearthan HR 102) (USA)

While bands in New York City and England were making the first punk records and receiving media attention, in Ohio, Pere Ubu had post-punk tendencies before the genre was solidified. The lyrics about feeling like an outsider are all Generation Jones punk. The singer is too physically inadequate to be attractive to girls; his parents think he's weird and ostracize him. The only salvation comes in being part of a music community of misfits who understand his feelings.

### "The Modern Dance" 45 August 25, 1977 (Hearthan HR 104) (USA)

This version of "The Modern Dance" is superior to the version released on their album *The Modern Dance*. While the band in their early singles was somewhat of an underground-sounding avant-garde band, this creates the spirit of post-punk. But like their "Final Solution" single and other punk records, it's immersed in the punk persona of being an outsider. The song's character is someone who can't understand the current culture and who will "never get the modern dance."

### *The Modern Dance* LP March 9, 1978 (Blank Records 01) (USA)

Debut album with one foot in punk/proto-punk and the other one in the avant-garde. Vocalist David Thomas immediately makes this sound like something unorthodox. The vocals don't contain any of the rock star cliches about what a singer should sound like. There's something of a high-pitched, nervous tension in his voice, like someone who is in a state of agitation, desperation, or alarm.

The album begins with its punkiest sing-along song, "Non-Alignment Pact," and ends with the ironic and fascinating "Humor Me," with Thomas saying that, if the world is a joke, "well then humor me." In between those two songs, to show how the band refuses to be easily categorized, the songs sometimes alternate between a more traditional rock structure and the experimental. "Laughing" switches between free jazz, the avant-garde, and garage-band based punk. "Chinese Radiation" goes sometimes off into a jazz song. "Life Stinks" alternates between the album's most overt Stooges riff and what sounds like an avant-garde band jamming. It's early punk and proto-punk at the center but avant-garde elements around the edges. They cross over into full-fledged experimentation in "Over My Head" and "Sentimental Journey."

### *Dub Housing* LP November 3, 1978 (Chrysalis CHR 1207) (USA)

Avant-garage. That's what Pere Ubu's combination of garage band punk and the avant-garde is sometimes called. And it's easy to see why. Like their first album, *Dub Housing* consists of both Stooges-like proto-punk garage rock and the avant-garde influenced by musicians like Captain Beefheart.

A few songs on *Dub Housing* are more accessible than their first album. That's partly because of an addition of simple synthesizer parts. This gives them a kind of faux pop ironic feel as in the first two songs, "Navvy" and "On the Surface," which with its mock 1960s organ sounds is almost a parody of a beach song.

"I, Will Wait" is a garage band funk song, while "(Pa) Ubu Dance Party" is an ironic dance song. Experimentation is still there, however, in "Blow Daddy-O," "Codex," and "Thriller," which are full-fledged avant-garde pieces. But whatever the song, vocalist David Thomas's voice always has a high-pitched uneasy quality. This is a band that refuses to bend to commercial considerations. They would go on to have a fascinating, uncompromising career.

**Genre:** Post-punk

## Pigbag

### "Papa's Got a Brand New Pigbag" 12" May 6, 1981 (Y Records Y 10) (UK)

One of post-punk's great instrumentals. Part of the song's irresistible percussion is somewhat of a variation of the Burundi style drumming that bands like Bow Wow Wow used. And there's a prominent horn section. It's not solely a ska- or R&B-inspired brass section, however. There are parts where the horns go off into bebop-like riffs that recall the more discordant traits of no wave. The 12-inch version is superior to the 45 because there's more time for the fun to go on.

### "Sunny Day" 45 October 28, 1981 (Y Records Y 12) (UK)

Another memorable instrumental from this band. But it's more funk-oriented and smoother than "Papa's Got a Brand New Pigbag." Instead of percussion, it relies more on a funk groove.

**Genre:** Post-punk

## Pink Military

### *Blood & Lipstick* 12" EP September 20, 1979 (ERIC's 002) (UK)

EP from Liverpool post-punk band with singer Jayne Casey covers a lot of ground. "Spellbound" is a fusion of punk and post-punk, while the title track is a post-punk version of a dance song with jagged guitars, percussion rhythms, simplistic keyboard, and

Casey's ethereal vocals. Side two gets more experimental with "Clown Town" and "I Cry."

**Genre:** Punk/Post-punk

## Plastic Bertrand

### "Ça Plane Pour Moi" 45 December 1, 1977 (Vogue 45 × 140316) (France)

Who cares if almost all of it is sung in French? Even if you don't understand a word of it, the youthful and carefree punk energy of 1977 is infectious. That's why it's become one of the most enduring songs of that year. The title translates to something like "everything's working out for me." The rest is somewhat incoherent, pretty much a pastiche of images and phrases. But whatever. It doesn't matter. The exuberance of punk is there.

**Genre:** Punk

## Poison Girls

### *Hex* 12" EP September 5, 1979 (Small Wonder WEENY 4) (UK)

Punk was a vehicle for the underrepresented and the unconventional. This anarcho-punk band was led by Vi Subversa, a woman in her mid–40s with two children. Her voice is more world-weary and strained than those of other punk bands' much younger singers. This gives gravitas to songs like "Ideologically Unsound," which declares, "I'm so lost, so are you, we all don't know what the hell to do." The song that may be the most autobiographical is "Jump Mama Jump," which details how she's unappreciated as a wife and mother.

### "Persons Unknown" 45 split single May 19, 1980 (Crass Records 421984/1) (UK)

At first, the song encourages people to speak out. Then for several minutes singer Vi Subversa lists the different people who shouldn't withdraw into anonymity. That includes housewives as well as "plumbers in boiler suits, truants in coffee bars who think you're alone" and ends with "cleaners of lavatories, the old with their memories." Sometimes anarcho-punk groups can come off as somewhat clinical and sarcastic. But this song shows sincerity and empathy.

### "Bully Boys" b/w "Pretty Polly" flexi disc 45 July 1980 (In the City none) (UK)

Supposedly inspired by groups of far-right gangs that disrupted punk rock concerts, "Bully Boys" lashes out against the "pornography of violence." "Pretty Polly" is about a suburban girl who believes she is being liberated by moving to the city and being sexually promiscuous. But she is only "anxious to please" and still a victim of sexism and exploitation.

**Genre:** Punk

## Iggy Pop

### *The Idiot* LP March 7, 1977 (RCA APL 1–2275) (USA)

After three raucous albums with the Stooges, Iggy Pop radically changed musical direction for his first solo album. After he befriended David Bowie, they both went to Germany to record. Perhaps overcontrolled by Bowie, Iggy Pop created an album that was nothing like the Stooges. And it puzzled some of his longtime fans because it changed in tone from garage rock to art rock. But Iggy Pop's voice (altered into something almost mechanical and ironic-sounding) over music that at times sounds almost like early industrial music makes for one of the more interesting albums of this era.

Given that Iggy Pop was recovering from substance abuse at the time, there's an irony to some songs that sound like slowed-down and ironic depictions of partying, such as "Nightclubbing" with is plodding beat. If there were a soundtrack to zombies going to a nightclub, this would be it. "Funtime" also features an ironic call to partying with its cry of "we want some." "Dum Dum Boys" chronicles casualties of excess and is one of several songs that show a downside to the drugs so associated with the 1970s. But the album has other tones, like the near pop of "China Girl" (which Bowie later recorded), a variation on a crooner ballad in "Tiny Girls," and an ending song, "Mass Production," that has an almost industrial sound to match the view of life working in a factory.

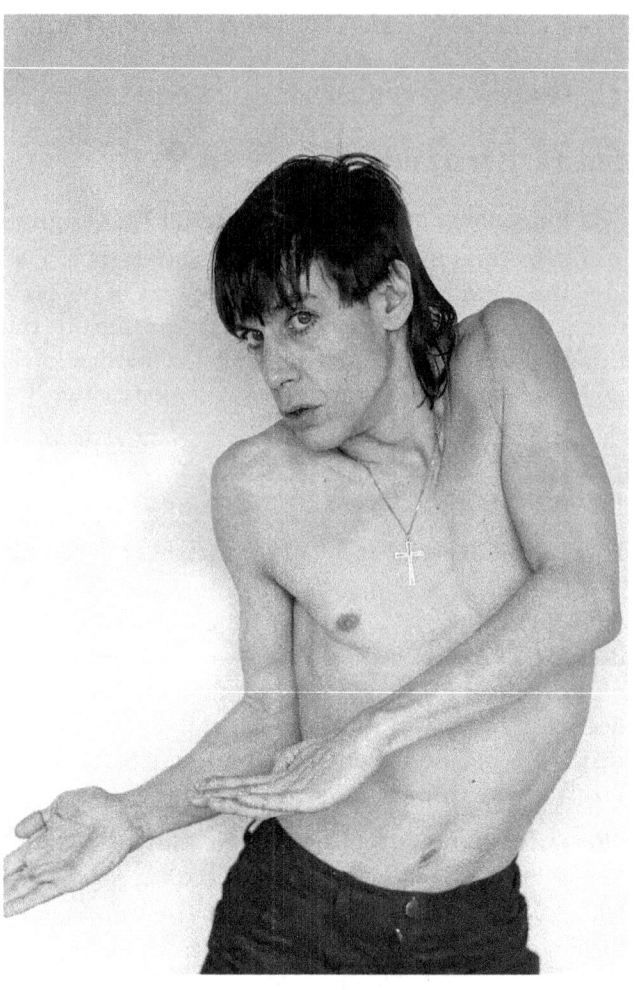

Iggy Pop helped shape both punk and post-punk. After he served as one of the major forces in proto-punk with the Stooges, his album *The Idiot* was one of the biggest influences on the emerging post-punk genre (Mirrorpix/Everett Collection).

### *Lust for Life* LP September 9, 1977 (RCA AFL 1–2488) (USA)

After the fascinating dark experimentation of *The Idiot*, this is more of Pop's trademark garage band–inspired punk music. The album is a remarkable cross between this new production that seems more post-punk and the raw energy of Iggy's punk roots. The title track, with its tribal-like drumbeat, is the best-known song. Does the lust of life here mean clarity of living without addictions? Or does it refer to his excessive past? The other well-known song is "The Passenger," about being in a state of transcendence and living in the moment. A passenger submits to control and just enjoys the ride of life.

Most of the album sounds much lighter and more spontaneous than *The Idiot*, as if it's an attempt to get away from the darkness of that album. However, the struggles of fighting addiction and hedonism are in "Some Weird Sin." And despite its beautiful melody, "Tonight" is about a woman dying, possibly from an overdose. More irony comes in "Success," with its R&B-like call-and-response. The ending "Fall in Love with Me" is like a Stooges jam with improvised lyrics over a dance beat.

### *New Values* LP April 20, 1979 (Arista AB 4237) (USA)

After recording *The Idiot* and *Lust for Life* with David Bowie, Iggy returns with former Stooges guitarist James Williamson producing. The result is one of Iggy's most eclectic and satisfying albums. Sure, he can turn on the Stooges–like garage band sound easily and effectively in songs like "I'm Bored," "Five Foot One," and "Billy Is a Runaway." But he seemed to know that this could become a cliché. So he wants to be more adventurous. By the time punk appeared in 1976 he was on to an early form of post-punk. And he was a master at adapting the punk spirit, attitude, and perspective into different musical variations.

The first three songs reintroduce a Stooges-influenced layering of guitars but in controlled, tight songs. The title track contains the kind of search that Pop had been on in his initial solo albums, which is a longing for something of value. There's a kind of spiritual search that continues from his first two solo albums. "Don't Look Down" and "Angel" are heartfelt, gospel-influenced songs, while "The Endless Sea" is such a haunting song that one wonders if it expresses a desire for transcendence or self-destruction.

### "Bang Bang" 45 May 7, 1981 (Arista ARIST 407) (UK)

Starting with the opening line "this isn't the right thing to do, so let's go!" it's somewhat of an update thematically of "Funtime" from *The Idiot*. It's a faux party song with ironic vocals about hedonism and escapism ("My problems can't follow me!").

### "Run Like a Villain" 45 August 31, 1982 (Animal Records CH FLY 2634) (UK)

Features the energy of the Stooges in a mature voice with some of his best poetic lyrics and a solid contemporary sound. Once again Iggy fights the affliction of boredom in this era. He makes a case to flee limitations, oppression, and malaise.

**Genre:** Punk/Post-punk

## The Pop Group

### "She Is Beyond Good and Evil" 45 March 6, 1979 (Radar ADA 29) (UK)

Like punk music, post-punk pretty much avoided love songs. But England's the Pop Group makes a single about what on the surface seems like the ideal woman but may be a metaphor for something mystical. She's "the one thing that you cannot buy" and "Western values mean nothing to her." Is it the spirit of a force of love or generosity? Or does a woman embody these ideals? The song starts with a dub-meets–post-punk guitar part that leads into a song that combines reggae, world music, post-punk, funk, jazz, and the avant-garde.

### *Y* LP April 21, 1979 (Radar RAD 20) (UK)

A courageous debut album that makes no attempt at commercial acceptance. Some of it can be described as funk meets the avant-garde. That comes through in "Thief of

Fire," which is mostly funk-oriented but contains an extended section of a jazz-like improvisation with a screeching saxophone. "Words Disobey Me" begins as a funk-like song but then goes into a combination of experimental music, dub, avant-garde jazz, and no wave. It's as if the band was determined not to create anything that sounded conventional. This occurs also in "We Are Time," which has a surf-guitar riff but then changes into a feedback and a dub fueled almost jazz piece. These are all songs that subvert the expectations of pop music structures.

It's post-punk stripped to its core. And what's left is the more experimental undercurrent. So there's a lot of that. "Snowgirl" is a cross between experimental jazz and the avant-garde. "Savage Sea" and "Don't Sell Your Dreams" are experimental pieces with elements of no wave–like deconstruction. Bands for decades would incorporate the styles here into more conventional formats. But the band is all in on this album at being unpredictable, experimental, and uncompromising.

### "We Are All Prostitutes" 45 November 6, 1979 (Rough Trade RT 023) (UK)

Funk-heavy song that says that everybody's up for sale and that "capitalism is the most barbaric of all religions" where consumerism is a form of fascism. Things will get so bad that future generations will rise up, Stewart hopes in one of his most anguished voices.

**Genre:** Post-punk

## The Pretenders

### *The Pretenders* LP January 11, 1980 (Real Records RAL 3) (UK)

Singer/guitarist Chrissie Hynde was an integral part of the early London punk scene and has a punky, I'm-not-going-to-take-any-shit attitude. But the band was a mixture of punk and 1960s-inspired rock and pop. The most influential punk they made was the first side of this album and the final track, "Mystery Achievement," on side two. Between that were songs that became hits, like the Phil Spector–inspired remake of the Kinks song "Stop Your Sobbing," the pop of "Kid," and a slightly reggae-tinted "Brass in Pocket."

But the sound and the fury of the punk songs are a revelation. "Precious" starts the album with, among other things, leaving limitations in her hometown. "Tattooed Love Boys" is a frightening song about a rape by a motorcycle gang with James Honeyman-Scott's guitar sounding like a chain saw cutting through flesh. "Up the Neck" is about a woman being beat up during sex. The album ends with "Mystery Achievement," which expresses a kind of yearning for some accomplishment. It accompanies the ideas in the lead song, "Precious," about wanting something more and wondering just when fulfillment will occur.

**Genre:** Punk

## Psychedelic Furs

### *Psychedelic Furs* LP March 3, 1980 (CBS 84084) (UK)

For this album, the Psychedelic Furs were moody, unorthodox, and post-punk. From there they would go on to join other bands that started in this era who would integrate elements of post-punk into a more new pop sound. But here there's a Goth-like examination of underground and mainstream institutions and the ideas inherent in them.

"We Love You" mocks idol worship of anything, whether it's film stars, cars, or what's on TV. "Wedding Song" is a bleak view of a wedding, while "Fall" ridicules conventional lifestyles including marriage. The most introspective song is "Sister Europe," a haunting Velvet Underground–meets–torch song with a pervasive sense of loneliness and isolation. The entire album, however, features a dark worldview with a sarcastic tone at times to all singer Richard Butler sees. Even what is perhaps the album's most musically jubilant track, "India," contains the sarcastic perspective: "We will dance alone and live our useless lives."

### "Soap Commercial" (B-side of "Pretty in Pink") 12" June 4, 1981 (CBS A 13 1327) (UK)

Joy Division producer Martin Hannett recorded an EP with the Psychedelic Furs that was never released. But songs from the sessions showed up on B-sides, including this sarcastic song using the idea of a soap commercial as a symbol of oppressive commercialism.

**Genre:** Post-punk

## Public Image Ltd.

### *Public Image: First Issue* LP December 8, 1978 (Virgin V 2114) (UK)

What do you do after you start one revolution? You start another one. After giving punk the voice of social commentary in the Sex Pistols, in Public Image Ltd., Lydon helps ignite the post-punk genre.

Perhaps the most important song on Public Image's first album is the initial single, "Public Image," which reportedly is an angry rebuke at the other members of the Sex Pistols and former manager Malcolm McLaren. It's a fierce declaration of independence from being misunderstood and unappreciated. Anger also comes through in "Low Life," about an "egomaniac traitor" and a "bourgeois anarchist." "Attack" appears to be a broader condemnation on those who profited from the Sex Pistols. Other songs point to different directions post-punk would have, such as the funk dance groove of "Fodderstompf"; the Goth-like "Annalisa," about a teenage girl who people believe is possessed by the devil; and "Theme," which is a more experimental slow groove.

### *Metal Box* LP November 14, 1979 (Virgin METAL 1) (UK)

In an exciting era of the early years of post-punk, Public Image's second album explores where the genre can go in a deeper way than almost any other post-punk album. Because of its variety and the experimentation, it remains one of the most important post-punk albums. Although Lydon's vocals are a critical part of this, what makes this especially innovative is the music. It's as if this band threw out all the rules of punk, post-punk, and music in general and started from scratch. Instead of dismantling song structure as no wave would do (and as Public Image would somewhat do on their next album, *Flowers of Romance*), the intent here is to go as deep as possible into possibilities. There's sometimes a spontaneous quality, with Lydon's vocals sounding improvisational.

Jah Wobble's bass guitar and Keith Levene's guitar playing chart new territory in the genre. Wobble's playing is simple and reggae-like sometimes. Levene's guitar is slicing at times, accenting the songs and giving them tension. This innovative instrumentation is apparent from the beginning with the infectious groove of the 10-minute "Albatross." As Lydon did on the first album, he makes this a song of liberation against oppressive forces trying to control him. Other highlights include "Memories," with Levene's guitar being run through a processor, and "Swan Lake" (previously known as "Death Disco"), a song about death over a dance beat giving the whole song a disconcerting aura. "Poptones" is about a kidnapped girl, "Careering" features a synthesizer and is about someone leading a double life, "Socialist" is an instrumental with Wobble's bass propelling it, while "Chant" features a repeating line of "mob, war, kill, hate" over what sounds like improvised vocals by Lydon.

The album originally was packaged in metal containers with three 45 RPM records. The album was later rereleased without the canisters as *Second Edition* with a conventional album package.

### *Flowers of Romance* LP April 10, 1981 (Virgin V2189) (UK)

With bassist Jah Wobble no longer in Public Image, Lydon responds by minimizing the sound. He makes a radical decision to not include any bass on the album. The result is a bold album that's very experimental using a sparse set of instruments, some of them unconventional. The dominant instrument is the drums, which often provides either a tribal-like world music–inspired beat or serves as a background for experimentation occurring around it. It's a daring record and is considered one of the most anti-commercial albums ever made.

Free of the bass guitar and pretty much all conventions of even punk or post-punk, this is a unique album in this era of many unconventional records. The album's first song, "Four Enclosed Walls," features just drums, Lydon's voice, and some sound effects. "Track 8," with its somewhat sarcastic semi-narration, uses percussion; swirling, tension-filled keyboards; and Levene's eerie plucking guitar. Levene's guitar also adds some atmosphere to the march-like beat in "Go Back." In "Flowers of Romance," Lydon, as on Public Image's first album, anticipates carrying on after troubles in a band ("I'll take the furniture, start all over again").

"Banging the Door," a song about being harassed by people outside Lydon's home, is the one song that sounds the most like other Public Image songs. But the rest of the album is daring and unconventional. By the album's last track, "Francis Massacre," it all sounds something like no wave with nothing resembling a traditional song structure.

### "This Is Not a Love Song" 45 September 5, 1983 (Virgin 529) (UK)

After the experimentation of *Flowers of Romance*, Lydon's record company reportedly tells him to write a hit for the next album. He releases a subversive attempt at a commercial song, which ironically becomes Public Image's biggest hit. "Big business is very wise, I'm inside free enterprise," Lydon sings about playing along with the farce of writing a hit song over a semi-dance beat.

**Genre:** Post-punk

## Purple Hearts

### "Frustration" 45 November 1, 1979 (Fiction FICS 007) (UK)

Out-of-character song from a band usually regarded as a revivalist mod power pop

band. Here, they switch into convincing pop punk. But unlike some pop punk, the lyrics are filled with an angst and frustration that consumes and paralyzes.
**Genre:** Pop Punk

# Pylon

### "Cool" b/w "Dub" 45 November 28, 1979 (DB Recs DB 53) (USA)

Singer Vanessa Briscoe shows why she's one's of the most powerful forces in post-punk. On Pylon's debut single she sings about having a transcendental experience. But as with everything she sang, there's an enormous sense of urgency, as if she's at an emotional peak having to shout from some deep inner place about what she's discovering. The B-side has that intensity too. She's listening to music that's "the sound of sorrow" yet finding something cathartic in it.

### *Gyrate* LP October 31, 1980 (DB Recs DB 54) (USA)

Two well-known bands during this period from Athens, Georgia—the B-52s and R.E.M.—are the ones that get all the attention. But what about some love for this band from the same Southern college town? Pylon is one of the handful of great American post-punk bands. If America wasn't ready for the energy and anger of punk a few years earlier, then it really wasn't ready for the more experimental and unorthodox post-punk of American bands like Pere Ubu, Mission of Burma, the Bush Tetras, and Pylon.

Although there are funk elements associated with Pylon's post-punk such as "Volume," much of the album is a successful synthesis of punk and post-punk. There's a lot of energy here. And Briscoe's vocals are one of the reasons why. Although some of the lyrics are simple and childlike, her growling voice, which seems to come from some deep place in the psyche, makes for a compelling juxtaposition with the words.

Often the lyrics seem to be improvised, as in "Danger," a ferocious warning. The closing track, "Stop It," is a kind a post-punk anthem of what's legitimate music and what isn't. "Read a Book" is an anti-media song that suggests turning off the TV to read instead. Other songs are about navigating the perils of modern life such as mindless jobs in "Working Is No Problem" and learning how to drive (which means navigating the imposing modern world) in "Driving School."

### *Chomp* LP April 12, 1983 (DB Recs DB 65) (USA)

The image of a dinosaur on the cover could be a symbol of how this band was perceived at the time of this album's release. It was the same day as R.E.M. released *Murmur*, which helped usher in an era of more eclectic and accessible college rock/alternative music. Although Pylon's second album was another standout album in American post-punk, the band's passionate and powerful style was increasingly becoming perceived by the music establishment as anachronistic. Radio-friendly new wave and college rock was dismantling the punk and post-punk revolution. But over time things get reevaluated. Pylon are revered as an important band from this era while many new wave and college rock bands are largely forgotten.

*Chomp* isn't as groundbreaking or as raw as *Gyrate*, but it offers more possibilities for where post-punk can evolve. It starts with the magnificent "K," which recalls the sound of *Gyrate* but with a more controlled vocal. "Yo-Yo" and "M-Train" are funk-inspired, and perhaps the album's best track, "Beep," is a funk and post-punk fusion with lyrics that seem to be about trying to capture something artistically despite all the limitations. *Chomp* also includes perhaps their best-known song, "Crazy" (later covered by R.E.M.). The second side of the album contains some of their ambitious music, with some songs that are somewhat vignettes on modern life, including "No Clocks," about transcending the demands of life; the wandering and searching in "Gyrate"; and "Altitude," about watching the familiar fade away.

**Genre:** Post-punk

## Radiators from Space

### "Television Screen" 45 April 25, 1977 (Chiswick NS 10) (UK)

As punk spread around the globe, this Irish punk band scored chart success in their native country with this early punk single. "Television Screen" is a punk/rockabilly hybrid spilling out anger at not only the media but also the music aristocracy with rock stars spouting "rich man's blues" while others have to steal guitars because they can't afford them. It ends with a defiant resistance to Richard Hell's punk song, saying, "Don't call me blank generation, I'm doin' the best that I can." The song was rerecorded for the band's first album, *TV Tube Heart*, but was slowed down and overproduced.

### "Enemies" 45 September 10, 1977 (Chiswick NS 19) (UK)

The best song on their first album *TV Tube Hearts*, "Enemies" retains the bite of their first single. This pop punk/punk hybrid is about betrayal, feeling like an outsider, and being under attack. But could the references to enemies also have political overtones? Features a rousing ending punky tirade ("this guitar is a gun!").

### *Ghostown* LP July 25, 1979 (Chiswick SWK 3003) (UK)

The band by this point shortens their name to the Radiators. Although they don't entirely eliminate it, they tone down the pub rock and 1960s-influenced power pop from their first album *TV Tube Heart*.

The centerpiece of the album is "Song for the Faithful Departed," an epic commentary on contemporary Irish life. With allusions to Catholicism and Irish writers, this song depicts oppressive conditions where "an underdog's wounds aren't so easy to mend." This is a band determined not to be pigeonholed, and there are many different musical styles here. "Johnny Jukebox" is one of the great rockabilly-influenced punk songs of this era. "Ballad of Kitty Ricketts" is almost like a punk variation on a dance hall song. "Million Dollar Hero" and "Let's Talk About the Weather" have power pop influences but with meaningful lyrics about Irish life.

What holds it all together is the piercing social observations. As Stiff Little Fingers in *Inflammable Material* depicted Belfast, this album reveals contemporary life in Dublin. Lead singer Philip Chevron later became lead guitarist of the Pogues. *Ghostown* was rereleased in 1989 with songs rearranged in a different order and some songs substituted. Stick with the original.

**Genre:** Punk

## Radio Birdman

### *Radios Appear* LP July 1977 (Trafalgar TRL 1001) (Australia)

Although they have one foot still in proto-punk, this is still a landmark album, particularly for Australian punk. The album's first song, a cover of the Stooges song "T.V.

Eye," is faster than the original but still retains some garage band sound. Overall, this is more controlled with traditional rock lyrics of the boomer generation rather than the angst-ridden punk of the Generation Jones bands.

The album is best when Radio Birdman plays faster, as in "Hand of Law" and "Do the Pop," which have pop punk choruses. The album ends with the punkiest song, "New Race," the best song on the album. Although there's a too-long guitar solo, the anthem-like song possesses a defiant tone about youth discontent that's more penetrating than the rest of the album. The album was reconfigured for release overseas. Get the original Australian version.

**Genre:** Punk

## The Raincoats

### "Fairytale in the Supermarket" 45 May 1, 1979 (Rough Trade RT 013) (UK)

The song has both the social observations of punk and the experimentation of post-punk. "No one teaches you how to live," laments singer Ana da Silva. What follows is a series of impressions of what people do in modern life to try to make sense of things.

### *The Raincoats* LP December 5, 1979 (Rough Trade ROUGH 3) (UK)

The Raincoats could have made an album continuing the punk and post-punk hybrid of "Fairytale in the Supermarket." Instead, they progress in an entirely different direction and produce one of post-punk's best albums. It's experimental and melodic at the same time, both delightfully amateurish and tight-knit, unpolished and yet perfectly in control. Some of this comes from the unconventional drumming of ex–Slits drummer Palmolive, who somehow holds everything together, keeping up with the violin of Vicky Aspinall, the Velvet Underground–influenced guitar, and the harmonies between the two singers.

Many songs are about the inability of men to understand women. "Off Duty Trip" is about a soldier who defines women by the pinup pictures he keeps near him in the military and as a result can only exploit women. Lora Logic adds some chaos with her saxophone to "Black and White," in which the singer asks, "Is it love when I don't know who you are?"

"The Void" is probably the bleakest song, about a kind of existential crisis of hopelessness and emptiness. "Life on the Line" is about not being able to find a safe place, while "In Love" romance leads to such a roller coaster of emotions that it isn't enjoyable. It ends in a tone of misunderstanding and solitude as a man gets up and leaves without looking at the singer in "No Looking." This inability to see is a metaphor for the entire album, which focuses on the loneliness and miscommunication of life, particularly in romantic relationships.

### *Odyshape* LP May 21, 1981 (Rough Trade ROUGH 13) (UK)

For their second album, the Raincoats go beyond post-punk to a kind of post-post-punk. With drummer Palmolive no longer in the band, the band turns to more sparse and experimental percussion as well as widening the range of instruments used. And the violin is even more prominent, integrating a classical music influence.

The album's tone is generally more subdued than their first album. At times there's a gentle kind of beauty, such as in the ending instrumental section in the opening song "Shouting Out Loud." At times it even has a mystical feeling, such as

"Dancing in My Head," which is sung in a higher pitch: "Physically feeling tired but my spirit is dancing, dancing in my head and in my heart." Other times there's a fragile sense of tragedy as in the oppressed woman in "Family Treet." The feminist perspective continues from their first album in the title track about a woman with body image insecurities. The last three songs are more experimental, with the album's final track, "Go Away," most recalling the band's first album. But overall, *Odyshape* remains underrated because it's so different from their first album. This band was too bold and adventurous to repeat itself.

### "Running Away" b/w "No One's Little Girl" 45 May 27, 1982 (Rough Trade RT093) (UK)

One can imagine record executives looking at the lack of sales and the largely savage reviews of the Raincoats albums after they came out (music critics often couldn't understand the music of Generation Jones). "Write a pop song," they might have said to the Raincoat ladies. And so they did, with "Running Away." But they couldn't release anything that wasn't great. And it's complex. Despite its beautiful melody and background vocals and prominent trumpet, the running away described in the song is restless escape that isn't fulfilled. "No One's Little Girl" is also melodic but staunchly defiant, about someone who resists being entrapped.

**Genre:** Post-punk

## The Ramones

### *The Ramones* LP April 23, 1976 (Sire SASD-7520) (USA)

The album that started it all. "Blitzkrieg Bop," with its chant of "hey ho, let's go," is for Generation Jones what the Beatles' "I Want to Hold Your Hand" was to the boomers. Basically, time to throw out what came before and start all over. Form your own band. Make your own sound. But unlike with the Beatles, American radio and TV was having nothing to do with the Ramones. So the revolution went underground.

And this album was the starting point for that revolution. The short songs, the subject matter of the songs, the buzz saw guitar, the gritty lyrics, even the album cover of the band shot in a New York City alley was the complete punk package. Everything before this was proto-punk. This was the new day. The word "punk" is even mentioned in "Judy Is a Punk."

"I Wanna Be Your Boyfriend," "Blitzkrieg Bop," and "Listen to My Heart" invented pop punk. "I Don't Wanna Go Down to the Basement" and "Chain Saw," with its allusion to *The Texas Chain Saw Massacre*, jump-started the idea of horror punk. "Havana Affair" is punk's version of a political song. "53rd and 3rd" is about a male prostitute showing how gritty punk can be. "Loudmouth" and "Beat on the Brat" showed anger at oppressors, and the album ends with "Today Your Love, Tomorrow the World," which could be a satire of fascist ideology.

### *Leave Home* LP January 25, 1977 (Sire SA 7528) (USA)

The follow-up to their explosive and influential first album expands the band's vision. And the production gives them a somewhat fuller and less raw sound. But they do this without compromising their energy. They retain their command of the pop punk genre, which they basically created, with the uplifting "Oh, Oh, I Love Her So." But

The Ramones—(left to right) Johnny Ramone, Joey Ramone, and Dee Dee Ramone—solidified the punk sound that inspired numerous punk bands over the decades. Johnny Ramone's so-called buzz saw guitar helped shape the punk sound (Directphoto Collection/Alamy).

there's also a dark side to the pop punk genre in the haunting "I Remember You," about being tormented in a relationship. This adds an irony to pop punk that would be influential on the genre. The band's fascination with horror punk also continues, with "You're Gonna Kill That Girl" and "You Should Never Have Opened That Door."

On some songs they tackle more subjects but often with a darker twist, like severe mental illness in "Gimme Gimme Shock Treatment" and militarism in "Commando." The high point of the album is "Pinhead," with its declaration inspired by the classic horror movie *Freaks*: "We accept you, one of us." It is a celebration of being different and an outsider. The song's chant of "D.U.M.B. everyone's accusing me" may have been a response to the music industry and media at the time the Ramones were accused of being dumb. But this album proves this band is here to stay.

### *Rocket to Russia* LP November 4, 1977 (Sire SRK 6042) (USA)

The Ramones would have earned its place in history if all they released was their first album. But the band is at the height of its powers on their third album. It's basically a perfect punk album—and a balance between euphoric pop punk songs and those with a darker side despite the always energetic music. This juxtaposition doesn't seem calculated and is almost a philosophical statement about how life is somehow a mixture of both modes of being.

The horror and the jubilant are there right in the beginning track of "Cretin Hop." The DDT-induced medical treatment in "Teenage Lobotomy" leads directly into the high-powered pop punk of "Do You Wanna Dance?" The album concludes with the infectious "Why Is It Always This Way?" which despite its upbeat music asks for answers to unfair tragedies.

But the elation is there too. Most notably "Sheena Is a Punk Rocker," one of the very best punk songs. It celebrates an independent female punk rocker who rejects beach culture and disco and moves to New York City. If hippie culture encouraged people to return to nature, this is doing the opposite by uplifting the excitement of urban living. "Rockaway Beach" and "Locket Love" are exuberant pop punk masterpieces. And in "Ramona" the band makes a shout-out to their fans with the line "hey you kids in the crowd, you know you like it when the music's loud."

### *Road to Ruin* LP September 15, 1978 (Sire SRK 6063)

After three brilliant albums, the Ramones failed to catch on in America past a limited punk fan base. So the band went in another direction of mixing in different sounds to try to gain a wider audience. About half of *Road to Ruin* is consistent with the driving punk from their first three albums. "I'm Against It," "She's the One," and "Bad Brain" all feature the winning Ramones sound. "I Wanna Be Sedated," which tackles the ever-present problem of boredom that plagued the late 1970s, is one of the band's best songs. "I Just Want to Have Something to Do" is also about boredom but is slowed down with more of a chant sing-along style of "wait! now!"

In a precursor to their next album, the misguided, Phil Spector–produced *End of the Century*, there are un–Ramones like sounds and songs such as the acoustic guitar dominated "Questioningly," a bland cover version of "Needles and Pins," and folk-rock pop in "Don't Come Close." Play the half of the album or so that's in the classic Ramones style and skip over the rest.

### "Rock N' Roll High School" 45 June 1, 1979 (Sire SRE 1051) (USA)

Pop punk paradise here. The title track from their B movie classic directed by Roger Corman is classic straight-up pop punk. No angst, no mental illness, no gritty street scenes—just "fun." That means muscle cars, romance, and teenage kicks. Once again the Ramones release a song that should have been a hit.

### *Pleasant Dreams* LP July 24, 1981 (Sire SRK 3571) (USA)

In an apparent attempt to reach a broader audience, the band hired 1960s "Wall of Sound" creator Phil Spector to produce the band's fifth album, *End of the Century*. Unfocused and scattered, the album lacked continuity and energy (and had one song with strings!) and left this once mighty group sounding like a lost and destroyed band. The experience apparently took its toll but expanded their perspective. The band reinvented itself with a new phase that might be called a more mature and world-weary punk perspective. The band would essentially grow up while struggling to hold on ideals despite being besieged by outside forces from an oppressive world.

The guitars could have been mixed higher, but Marky Ramone's drums sound like gunshots at times, and that's clear on the album's first track, "We Want the Airwaves," which, like the work of many frustrated bands from this period, condemns the limitations of radio airplay. The album's most popular song, "The KKK Took My Baby Away" is an ominous song about racist kidnappers. Although there's still a sense of fun on "C'mon Now," "All Quiet on the Eastern Front," and "She's a Sensation," the car crash death in "7-11" seems like a metaphor for death of youthful dreams. "9 to 5 World" shows an almost permanent sense of being an outsider in the culture.

But it's the last two tracks that sum up this more mature perspective of not understanding the world in "This Business Is Killing Me" and "Sitting in My Room," the latter with its declaration of "it's us against them." In 2023, they released a vinyl remix of the album with Johnny Ramone's guitar still not mixed high enough but the drums mixed down and the vocals up. Not the ideal remix but an interesting one.

**Genre:** Punk

## Red Crayola

### "Born in Flames" 45 August 23, 1980 (Rough Trade RT 054) (UK)

Longtime American experimental collective band from Texas redefined themselves after a move to England. In the post-punk era they collaborated with musicians from Essential Logic, the Raincoats, and Swell Maps. Lora Logic from Essential Logic sings on this song, which imagines rebels conquering tyrannical forces. A 1983 dystopian indie film would take its title from this song and feature the song in the film.

**Genre:** Post-punk

## Red Cross

### *Red Cross* 12" EP March 28, 1981 (Posh Boy PBS-1010) (USA)

Like other California punk bands from this era before hardcore punk hit its peak, this is an eclectic mix of punk, pop punk, surf punk, and some elements of the coming hardcore punk phenomenon. "Cover Band" disses bands who play Top 40 songs. "Annette's Got the Hits" features a surf-guitar–meets–heavy-metal guitar riff. "I Hate My School" is an early teen angst pop punk song where cliques become a vehicle for social commentary. The band at this time included future Circle Jerks guitarist Greg Hetson and Ron Reyes, one of Black Flag's singers, on drums. The band later changed their name to Red Kross.

**Genre:** Punk

## Redskins

### "Lev Bronstein" 45 July 17, 1982 (CNT Productions CNT 007) (UK)

The title of the song is the real name of Russian revolutionary Leon Trotsky. The song is a tribute to Trotsky and to the growing solidarity movement in Poland. A fascinating cross between post-punk funk and a near hardcore punk sound.

Genre: Punk/Post-punk

## R.E.M.

### "Radio Free Europe" 45 July 8, 1981 (Hib-Tone HT 0001) (USA)

The band's debut single, released on the Hib-Tone label, is faster than the version rerecorded on their first album, *Murmur*. Peter Buck's guitar would reintroduce the 1960s-style jangly guitar without it being the power pop sound most people associate with that sound. And likely influenced by punk, it would be faster than most anything from the 1960s, perhaps influenced by the Feelies, who a year earlier released their influential first album, *Crazy Rhythms*. The lyrics by singer Michael Stipe are sometimes oblique (and notorious for the difficulty of deciphering them) and add to the post-punk atmosphere.

***Chronic Town* 12" EP August 10, 1982 (I.R.S. SP 70502) (USA)**

The band's first EP expands on the jangle post-punk of their "Radio Free Europe" single. "Gardening at Night," with its driving guitars, contains a falsetto-like vocal by Michael Stipe that gives the song a mysteriousness, delicacy, and sense of empathy. "Gardening at night just didn't grow," Stipe sings with a lament that somewhat contrasts with the warmness of the guitars. "Carnival of Sorts" seems to be an escape from a circus-like life in a "chronic town." "1,000,000" is a mysterious song that could be about a transcendental moment of immortality, but it's to its credit that the song is open to many interpretations. "Stumble" adds some percussion and some tempo changes that perhaps make it musically the most unorthodox song on the album.

**Genre:** Post-punk

# The Replacements

***Sorry Ma, Forgot to Take Out the Trash* LP August 24, 1981 (Twin/Tone TTR 8123) (USA)**

Perhaps because the band is from Minneapolis and not from the hardcore punk capitals of Southern California and Washington, D.C., the Replacements created their own variation of punk. The songs are a cross between garage band rock, punk, and hardcore punk. Although the album is fast and furious, there's a sense of melody that became part of the band's signature sound.

The production is primitive. And some songs are energetic throwaways. Yet this is the beginning of what will become one of the very best bands of the 1980s. There are some gems here, such as "Don't Ask Why," which rips along in ragged punk glory. "Somethin' to Dü" is about Hüsker Dü, the other Minneapolis band that would become well known in this era. In "Shutup" singer Paul Westerberg sums up criticism of the band: "Tommy's too young, Bobby's too drunk, I can only shout one note, Chris needs a watch to keep time." A grab bag of garage band punk styles, some that work and some that don't. But at its best it shows the seeds of what this band would grow into.

***Stink* 12" EP June 24, 1982 (Twin/Tone TTR 8228) (USA)**

This eight-song EP is more aggressive, punkier, and much better produced than their debut album. The band is on fire here. Bob Stinson really lets loose on the guitar, which helps drive these songs. Only "Dope Smokin' Moron" is hardcore punk fast. The rest of the album is driving punk rock. Perhaps the best song is "Stuck in the Middle," about their plight in the middle of the country in Minnesota. "Go" is the slowest song they'd done to this point and has a mournful, yearning, urgent tone that songwriter Paul Westerberg explored further in later albums.

***Hootenanny* LP April 29, 1983 (Twin/Tone TTR 8332) (USA)**

The band breaks out of their punk limitations with an album with one foot in their punk roots and the other in the eclectic qualities of alternative and college rock. It's not only a transitional album for the Replacements but also for the punk genre. While "Run It" and "You Lose" wouldn't sound of place on their first two albums, the album's standout track is "Color Me Impressed," which almost seems to open up a new category of punk. It's slowed down from their initial punk songs in a pop-influenced punk that's far different from British pop punk. The words reflect a theme that would reoccupy songwriter Paul Westerberg, which is the dark side of drinking and partying. In "Color Me Impressed" the partyers dress up to impress, but underneath it all they are depressed. "Hayday" reflects this theme somewhat too with its declaration that "it ain't gonna last" emphasizing how fleeting good times are.

Other songs go into more experimental territory, showing how the band would take different musical directions during the rest of the 1980s. "Take Me to the Hospital" is rockabilly-inspired, while "Buck Hill" is an early roots-influenced instrumental. "Lovelines" is a blues-based riff over Westerberg reading from personal ads from newspapers. "Willpower" is a dark and haunting ballad about an internal warfare about wanting to stop what appears to be a bad habit.

**Genre:** Punk

## Rezillos

### *Can't Stand the Rezillos* LP July 21, 1978 (Sire 56530/SRK 6057) (UK)

The only album by this Scottish punk band hasn't aged as well as other albums from the heyday of the original punk era. That's because the Rezillos come off too much like a novelty band at times. The songs sometimes have a rockabilly-meets-punk sound that seems less genuine. There are also cover songs from Gerry and the Pacemakers, the Dave Clark Five, and Fleetwood Mac that seem gimmicky and almost like parody punk.

Still, the album features the power from the initial blast of punk. This era is like a coming of age for punk that remains exciting years later. "My Baby Does Good Sculptures" and "Flying Saucer Attack" are fun despite the campiness. We'll forgive them for their shortcomings and give in to the raw energy, at least on this album. Most of the band soon after this album renamed themselves the Revillos and released albums that were a cross between an homage and a parody of 1960s surf-based music and pop.

### "Top of the Pops" b/w "20,000 Rezillos Under the Sea" 45 July 26, 1978 (Sire SIR 4001) (UK)

This version of "Top of the Pops" is better than the one on their debut album. It's more controlled, which makes it even more of a subversive pop punk song. It's one of their only songs with any of the social observation that was the center of the punk era. The target here is the popular British TV show *Top of the Pops*, which presented bands lip-synching to Top 40 hits. The song calls the show out as just a "stock market for your hi-fi." The critique of the show is also a symbol for the superficiality of television in general as well as commercialism. The B-side may be their most fun song. It's their version of "The William Tell Overture," featuring a saxophone and a kazoo.

**Genre:** Punk/Pop Punk

## Ritual

### "Mind Disease" 45 October 6, 1982 (Red Flame RF712) (UK)

Goth-influenced post-punk with drumming that's a cross between very fast tribal drumming and D-beat. The Goth-inspired imagery appears to be about someone with a disease of the mind that's so terrible it feels like death is coming. Two of the members went on to join the Death Cult, which later became the Cult.

**Genre:** Post-punk

## Tom Robinson Band

### *Rising Free* 7" EP February 8, 1978 (EMI 2749) (UK)

This four-song live EP is bookended with two blistering, anthem-like songs. "Don't Take No for an Answer" offers a persistent sense of defiant resistance with a sing-along chorus, while "Right On Sister" supports feminism. Between those two songs is "Glad to Be Gay," which continues Robinson's technique of outlining problems in the verses before featuring a jubilant chorus. The verses are about the oppression of gays and the pressure to stay in the closet about it. In 1978, this was a daring thing to do. And despite the BBC banning it, this is perhaps Robinson's best-known song.

### *Power in the Darkness* LP May 5, 1978 (EMC 3226) (UK)

Robinson's first hit was the non-album single "2-4-6-8 Motorway," which leaned more toward power pop than pop punk. For his debut album, Robinson took the sense of melody from "Motorway" and combined it with politically charged punk to make an album full of basically sing-along social commentary. The beginning track, "Up Against the Wall," is an example of that, with verses depicting the late 1970s social problems in England and the choruses becoming a rousing sing-along. "Ain't Gonna Take It" is similar, with the verses about prejudice and then a defiant but catchy chorus. This duality between the problems outlined in the verses and the optimism of the sing-along choruses was Robinson's defining structure for some if his most popular songs. And the first part of this album focuses on that.

The second side of the album is more about a battle between opposing forces of right and wrong. "Man You Never Saw" is a present-day battle of oppression, while "The Winter of '79" looks ahead to an apocalyptic-like confrontation. "You Better Decide What Side You're On" insists on picking a side. "Power in the Darkness" ends the album by outlining what both sides think they must do to destroy the other.

**Genre:** Punk/Pop Punk

## Rosa Yemen

### *Rosa Yemen* 12" EP July 1978 (ZE Records 12003) (UK)

Before she recorded solo albums, French singer Lizzy Mercier Descloux was in this short-lived no wave duo. One lead guitar and one rhythm guitar accompany Mercier's voice. It's a minimalist version of no wave. Each song is like a short, intense deliberation, more recited than sang, sometimes phrased with a sense of terror, desperation, or almost a primal kind of catharsis.

Although it's not as musically frenetic as most no wave, there's still something unsettling about these songs. Often the guitars have a disturbing quality to them. They churn and drone in a sound that produces tension and a feeling of things being off-kilter. Mercier Descloux's voice is an instrument of its own, seemingly working at its own pace over the music as if she's sometimes at odds with it.

**Genre:** No Wave

## Rubella Ballet

### *Ballet Dance* 7" EP September 12, 1982 (XNTRIX XN 2005) (UK)

Two members are the children of Poison Girls singer Vi Subversa. And they sound like a new generation that won't conform to anarcho-punk clichés. "Ballet Dance" is pop punk, and, because it's so lo-fi, "Something to Give" sounds avant-garde. It's the two B-sides that are the standouts. "Unemployed" is straight-ahead punk, while "Krak Trak" is a celebratory combination of punk and post-punk.

**Genre:** Punk/Post-punk

## Rudi

### "Big Time" 45 May 10, 1978 (Good Vibrations GOT 1) (UK)

Belfast band's debut single leans more pop punk than power pop. This song was notable for its melodic chorus and the guitar riffs. Another Northern Ireland band the Undertones would craft the pop punk sound into something more definitive.

**Genre:** Pop Punk

## Ruefrex

### "One by One" 45 November 1979 (Good Vibrations GOT8) (UK)

Band from Belfast, Northern Ireland, starts with a slowed-down observation from a hillside looking down at a city during sunset. There's either a real or imagining of a conversation with a woman with views about eternal life and judgment. Then about a minute and a half in, the song becomes faster and shifts into an apocalyptic-like scene of a city in peril. Is it the imagination of the observer? The point of view of the woman about an apocalypse? Or an observation of the actual city using apocalyptic imagery? A compelling and important record in Northern Irish punk.

### "Capital Letters" 45 April 1983 (Kabuki KAR7) (UK)

After a long absence, the Belfast band returns for their best straight-ahead punk song. In a year when punk was splitting, fragmenting, or fading, this song still shows that righteous, driving punk is never dated. There's some nuclear war imagery, religious references, and a sense that things are out of control. "I've canceled all appointments because the world's gone insane," is singer Alan Clarke's response to all the chaos.

**Genre:** Punk

## The Runaways

### "School Days" b/w "Wasted" 45 October 14, 1977 (Mercury 6167 587) (UK)

The punk attitude and persona in the teenage all-female band the Runaways was most pronounced in guitarist Joan Jett. After singer Cherie Currie left the band and Jett took over lead vocals, the band adopted for at least this single a punkier sound. "School Days" is a punk pop–flavored song about being 18 and feeling liberated from the limitations of high school. The B-side about drug excesses is probably the band's best song.

**Genre:** Punk

## The Ruts

### "In a Rut" b/w "H-Eyes" 45 January 24, 1979 (People Unite RUT 1) (UK)

The catchy sing-along chorus is almost ironic because it's about the trap of a deadening limbo. It joins other 1970s punk singing about boredom and malaise as if it's disease. The singer is so much in a rut that even his feelings are shut off. The midsection of the song, with its eerie, contemplative, scratchy guitar, is a fascinating emotional variation in a punk song. The B-side, "H-Eyes," is about the dangers of heroin. The drug would later claim the life of the band's singer, Malcolm Owen.

### "Society" (B-side of "Babylon's Burning") 45 (Virgin VS 271) June 5, 1979

High-powered song with suspicions about both government surveillance and the media. Propaganda is the main purpose of the media, which is both out of touch with reality and exploitative. One of several significant songs during this period that condemns the media for propagandizing and ignoring real problems.

### *The Crack* LP September 29, 1979 (Virgin V 2132) (UK)

By 1979, punk was three years past its inception, and in England post-punk was the emerging trend. So who would hold up punk's energy? *The Crack* was one of the great later punk statements that took the energy of Year Zero punk, updating the sound while at the same time retaining its energy. This remains an important album because it outlined a possible new pathway for punk. But because singer Malcolm Owen died the next year, it will always leave punk fans wondering how the band could have built on this if Owen had lived.

The leadoff track, "Babylon's Burning," is a punk song with imagery and lyrics influenced by reggae and a Rastafarian perspective. "Babylon" matches the theme of tribulation in some reggae songs with apocalyptic imagery. They directly combine reggae and ska in "Jah War." The album also shows that thematically punk still has much in common with reggae songs about feeling like an oppressed outsider, such as on "S.U.S.," about a law that allowed people to be arrested for looking or acting suspiciously. "Something That I Said" and "Backbiter" have pop punk–like choruses; "Out of Order," "Criminal Mind," and "You're Just A…" are straight-ahead punk, while "Savage Circle" is also fast but contains almost post-punk embellishments.

### "I Ain't Sophisticated" (B-side of "Jah War") 45 October 31, 1979 (Virgin VS 298) (UK)

It takes just two minutes for the Ruts to ridicule the privileged. They even use a football chant chorus in what could be an homage/parody of Sham 69. Whatever the case, the Ruts unleash their working-class perspective to chastise private school elitist students with "high-fog brain-wash" who are "pseudo-high-brow."

### "Staring at the Rude Boys" 45 March 27, 1980 (Virgin VS 327) (UK)

Captures the tension in England between skinhead racists and the multiracial phenomenon of two tone ska. In the song, a group of skinheads attack ska devotees (rude boys) dancing in a nightclub to ska music. It shows how tribal music was in this era and how much of a clash there was between political and music subcultures.

### "West One (Shine on Me)" 45 August 22, 1980 (Virgin VS 370) (UK)

The final single by this band is their biggest attempt at a commercial hit with more conventional compressed production. Can they take this step without losing their punk foundation and attitude? They do, even when a saxophone solo is added. There's something almost cinematic about the imagery of the singer being on a city street with streetlights shining on him. Singer Malcolm Owen died just before this single was released, and the surviving band members continued on as the Ruts D.C.

**Genre:** Punk

## Saccharine Trust

### *Paganicons* LP December 10, 1981 (SST 006) (USA)

A unique and influential album because it adds a dramatic, somewhat experimental, and emotionally vulnerable quality to the hybrid of punk and post-punk. Some of what's so different is because of vocalist and lyricist Jack Brewer, who sometimes sings in a theatrical-like sneer but also at times sounds like someone driven to a near emotional breakdown. "Pain is real as real is pain," Brewer sings in "Effort to Waste." And the album reinforces that feeling.

There's also some religious imagery adding to the gravitas, such as on "Community Lie," which sounds like an updating of the woman threatened to be stoned to death in the gospels. The spiritual imagery continues in "A Human Certainty," where Brewer's voice at one point snarls and growls, followed by an ironic "I'm OK now" and then a monologue about a dream that at times sounds like someone who has perhaps lost touch with reality. Although most of the album is beyond basic punk, this band can also play more straight-ahead punk, as in "Mad at the Co.," a short and fast blast of energy about exploitative and meaningless jobs; the sarcastic "We Don't Need Freedom"; and "I Am Right," a somewhat tragic song of bad consequences.

Genre: Punk/Post-punk

## Sado-Nation

### *Sado-Nation* 7" EP May 1980 (Trap Records T-006) (USA)

One of the era's most overlooked gems. This Portland, Oregon, band uses a distinctive Pacific Northwest driving guitar sound with urgent vocals that would eventually influence the grunge sound of Seattle. The vocals are split between the band's two singers. David Corboy sings on the menacing "I'm Trouble" and "On Whom They Beat," the latter about being attacked by oppressive forces. Leesa Anderson sings on the more pop punk "Gimme You" and "Mom and Pop Democracy," with its haunting chorus of "in America we're supposed to be free." Produced by Greg Sage of the Wipers.

Genre: Punk

## The Saints

### "I'm Stranded" b/w "No Time" 45 September 28, 1976 (Fatal none) (Australia)

The original Australian punk band. This is the first punk recording released outside the United States. It came out less than six months after the first Ramones album and before the Damned, the Sex Pistols, or the Clash released records. "I'm Stranded" is one of punk's great moments. Despite the raw energy, there's a loneliness, alienation, and ostracization that fits a major punk theme of being an outsider. The B-side is a scorcher, with layers of driving guitars and one of early punk's most forceful guitar riffs.

### *Eternally Yours* LP March 13, 1978 (Harvest SHSP 4078) (Australia)

The first Saints album seemed rushed, somewhat repetitious, and failed to live up their stunning debut single, "I'm Stranded." But on their second album they got it together with one of punk's most varied albums from this period but with a solid social perspective. It starts with "Know Your Product," about the manipulations of the advertising industry. The song introduces horns into the punk sound, perhaps as an ironic touch to the lyrics. "Lost and Found" is a condemnation of an oppressive and manipulative political system, while "Private Affair" condemns conformity. These songs rival the social statements that British bands were making in the late 1970s.

"The Perfect Day" is a ferocious song about internal pain caused by oppression. "Ostralia" covers apathy in their native country as well as American dominance. "I'm Misunderstood" is almost a follow-up to "I'm Stranded" with the same theme of alienation. It ends with two minutes of pop punk fun in "International Robots," which almost sounds like a parody of what they think will be a hit song. One of the best albums during the short time between the initial explosion of punk and the introduction of post-punk.

**Genre:** Punk

## Savage Republic

### "Film Noir" b/w "O Andonis" 45 September 1983 (Independent Project IP 009) (USA)

Moody and intoxicating post-punk from California band with a cinematic theme on both sides of the single. In "Film Noir" the confessional lyrics depict an emotional crisis that is a post-punk version of a film noir narration. The B-side is more upbeat, with a marching beat of an instrumental song by Greek composer Mikis Theodorakis from the Costa-Gavras movie Z.

**Genre:** Post-punk

## The Scars

### "Adultery" b/w "Horror Show" 45 March 20, 1979 (Fast Product FAST 8) (UK)

Paul Research's nervous guitars drive the ominous "Adultery," about the consequences of an extramarital affair. On the B-side, the Scottish post-punk band's "Horror Show" summarizes *A Clockwork Orange*'s violent disturbing story. Is it because they're comparing that dystopian nightmare to contemporary times?

### *Author! Author!* LP April 10, 1981 (Pre PREX 5) (UK)

Although there is some pop influence, *Author! Author!* is moodier than what many of their Scottish contemporary post-punk bands were doing. The Scars can create melodic songs when they want to, but here they are determined not to inject too much pop. It's just another indication of how post-punk bands rejected commerciality.

Only in "All About You" do they seem to capitulate to pop. Attached to the end like an afterthought after the menacing "Your Attention Please," it still has a moody quality to it. Songs like "Everywhere I Go" and "The Lady in the Car with Sunglasses on and a Gun" are slower but with an interesting undercurrent of tension. There also is an element of fear and loss in songs like "Leave Me in Autumn" and "Fear of the Dark," That angst comes across most in "Your Attention Please," which features no singing but is a terrifying Cold War–era narration about an impending nuclear attack. Of all the fear-of-nuclear-war songs released during this period, this is one of the most disturbing.

**Genre**: Post-punk

## Scream

***Still Screaming*** **LP January 1983 (Dischord 9) (USA)**

Another seminal hardcore punk record from the Dischord label. This is part of a trilogy of Dischord releases, including Minor Threat's *Out of Step* and the Faith's *Subject to Change*, that redefine hardcore punk as more varied and able to incorporate other influences while still maintaining the cathartic energy. While some hardcore punk bands sounded hard-and-fast formulaic, those three records went beyond the clichés and rigid format of hardcore punk. This is an album from a band that does not want to be pigeonholed as strictly hardcore.

Scream also has a sense of melody and some variance in the songs missing from some other hardcore bands including reggae, traditional rock, and traditional punk influences. And their songs aren't just prophetic views of things going wrong. They call for unity and fight in songs like "Solidarity," "Stand," "Fight/American Justice," "Amerarockers," and the triumphant "U. Suck A./We're Fed Up." There's a sense of hope at times that isn't on some other hardcore punk records. But the album also points out societal problems. The album starts with "Came Without Warning," about the suddenness of nuclear war. The song also can be seen as a metaphor for anything that obliterates one's worldview into disorder, which is also conveyed on songs like "Bedlam" and "Your Wars/Killer."

**Genre:** Hardcore Punk/Punk

## The Screamers

***Demo Hollywood*** **12" EP (recorded 1977, released May 14, 2021) (Superior Viaduct SV177) (USA)**

The Screamers were the most legendary punk band never to release an album when there were together. Fans for years knew them from a few videos of their raucous live performances, members of California punk bands praising them, and the band's iconic logo of singer Tomata du Plenty with his spiky hair. Although demos surfaced on bootlegs for years, it was decades later that some early recordings were officially released. And the songs live up to their mythical status.

The band's lineup featured two keyboard players rather than guitars. Sometimes their music is called techno punk or synth punk. "Magazine Love" criticizes the unrealistic depictions of life in the media. "Master Dolores" and "Punish or Be Damned" feature religious imagery, while "Peer Pressure" condemns conformity.

**Genre:** Punk

## Scritti Politti

***Skank Bloc Bologna*** **7" EP November 18, 1978 (St. Pancreas SCRIT 1) (UK)**

For anyone who remembers this band from the MTV synth-pop days of "Perfect Way," it may be a surprise that this band started as an art collective post-punk band. Along with the Human League, Scritti Politti is probably the most radical example of a band's digression from the avant-garde to a commercial synth-pop band. Scritti's debut record is one of the earliest examples of indie post-punk. The title track features a reggae beat meeting the jarring guitars of post-punk. The B-side "Is and Ought the Western

World," critiques Western institutions, and the second B-side, "28/8/78," ends with a news broadcast over music. Renowned for its DIY picture sleeve with an itemized list of what it cost to make the record.

**Genre:** Post-punk

# The Selecter

### "On My Radio" b/w "Too Much Pressure" 45 October 13, 1979 (2 Tone CHS TT4) (UK)

Two tone band's bouncy debut single about how bad mainstream radio is. "It's just the same old show on my radio," singer Pauline Black laments. At a time when there were few alternative outlets for punk and ska bands to be heard, the Selecter joins the punk bands who blasted the blandness of radio. The B-side was rerecorded for their album, but the slightly slower version from this single is less rushed and more pronounced. The chants of "too much pressure" sum up the anxiety of the times.

### *The Selecter* LP February 23, 1980 (2 Tone CDL TT 5002) (UK)

One of the four classic debut albums of second wave ska (the others are by the Specials, Madness, and the English Beat). Like the Specials and the English Beat, these are mostly songs that reflect the economic and cultural issues of late 1970s England but also balanced out by songs about relationships or just flat-out dance songs. Of the mighty four ska albums, this was the only one with a female singer. And of the four albums, this one is generally and consistently the fastest. And while the beat is up-tempo and danceable, it may be the most politically charged lyrics of all the ska bands.

The album starts by expanding on the subject of their first single, "On the Radio," by mocking the radio with "Three Minute Hero," in which someone who is miserable at their job listens to the radio for escapist pop songs. Another standout track is the infectious "Out on the Streets," in which the singer wants some excitement to overcome boredom but knows trouble will probably come from it. The covers of reggae songs—such as "Everyday," "Murder," and "Carry Go Bring Come"—are all so taken over by the band's sound that they sound like they could be the band's own material. The band can also have fun, however, as "James Bond" shows.

### "The Whisper" b/w "Train to Skaville" 45 August 8, 1980 (Chrysalis CHS S1) (UK)

Single released between the band's two albums is a gem. Despite the upbeat music, "The Whisper" is about trying to escape the betrayal of a lover by going out on the town "looking for some bad action." The B-side is an excellent version of the first wave ska classic "Train to Skaville." They make the ska classic their own with a groove that makes its both moody and danceable.

### *Celebrate the Bullet* LP February 6, 1981 (Chrysalis CHR 1306) (UK)

Ska faced the same problem punk did after its initial explosion. Both are limited musical forms. This album answers what ska bands faced: how do you retain the energy and social statements of ska while musically growing? Like punk, the fickle mainstream media wanted to write off the often politically charged second wave ska phenomenon as a fad. To counteract that, this misunderstood album by the Selecter, along with the Specials' second album, *More Specials*, and their *Ghost Town* EP, was an attempt to redefine ska.

The immediate reaction by audiences used to the two tone dance energy of the Selecter's first album may be confusion, because *Celebrate the Bullet* tones down the danceable energy. And the band had the bad luck of releasing "Celebrate the Bullet" as the album's first single between the shootings of John Lennon and Ronald Reagan. Although the song was about not taking revenge, radio wouldn't touch it. So the album didn't get the attention it should have.

But this was a brave and innovative record with meaningful social statements and was innovative musically. Standouts include "Deep Water," about the personal effects of economic deprivation; "Washed Up and Left for Dead," showing a tragic ending for the oppressed; and "Bristol and Miami," which, despite being probably the most upbeat ska music on the album, is about riots in cities separated by an ocean but both with similar racial and economic problems.

**Genre:** Ska

# Sex Pistols

*Never Mind the Bollocks, Here's the Sex Pistols* **LP October 28, 1977 (Virgin V 2086) (UK)**

The Ramones' first album solidified the punk sound and image. But this album gave punk its connection to social and political commentary. It's impossible to imagine that punk could ever have taken off without this album. This album gave punk its purpose, its attitude, its vision. This album changed everything. Perhaps most importantly because of the lyrics and persona of lead singer Johnny Rotten.

**Johnny Rotten (Lydon) of the Sex Pistols went beyond the outsider stance of punk and proto-punk to make punk a political and social force. He later became one of the most important figures in post-punk with Public Image Ltd. (Mirrorpix/Everett Collection).**

It starts with the Cold War–era view of "Holidays in the Sun" at the symbolic epicenter of it: the Berlin Wall. "Bodies" is from the point of view of an aborted child, or perhaps it's a metaphor for the underclass who are being oppressed. "No Feelings" and "Pretty Vacant" are about the superficiality and selfishness in humans.

"God Save the Queen" is one of the most important punk songs. Notorious because it was released to coincide with the Queen's Silver Jubilee, it not only targeted a specific authority figure, but also was a sweeping indictment of the entire idea of aristocracy and the class system it creates. "Anarchy in the U.K." calls for upheaval in a society where "your future dreaming is a shopping scheme." It ends with "New York," in which Rotten denies the Sex Pistols are influenced by New York City bands and openly condemns the New York Dolls. The final song is the mighty "EMI," which denounces their former record label (which dropped them) but also is a statement about commodification of punk bands in the music industry.

### "My Way" (B-side of "No One is Innocent") 45 June 30, 1978 (Virgin VS 220) (UK)

After the separation of John Rotten/Lydon from the Sex Pistols, manager Malcolm McLaren released the movie *The Great Rock and Roll Swindle*, which included Sex Pistols bassist Sid Vicious singing the crooner classic "My Way." Later released as a single under the Sex Pistols name, it starts off sounding like kind of train wreck parody. But as it goes along it becomes a defiant sneer of a revision and one of this period's great relics.

**Genre:** Punk

## Sham 69

### "Borstal Breakout" b/w "Hey Little Rich Boy" 45 January 6, 1978 (Polydor 2058 966) (UK)

Sham 69's punk was deeply working-class with trademark sing-along choruses that were the inspiration for the football chant-like choruses of Oi! music. Sham 69 never released an album that was solidly consistent. They were a singles band; the four singles they released in 1978 are of particular note. "Borstal Breakout" is the first of these, about an escape from a youth detention center. The B-side, "Hey Little Rich Boy," shows the disdain the working class feel for the affluent.

### "Angels with Dirty Faces" 45 April 28, 1978 (Polydor 2059 023) (UK)

The song title comes from a 1938 gangster movie starring James Cagney about growing up in the poverty-stricken slums of New York City. Like the movie, the song is about being downtrodden outsiders living amid violence and poverty. In the midst of the economic downturn of the late 1970s, the song is about having potential to do good but being marginalized, abandoned, and resented.

### "If the Kids Are United" 45 July 14, 1978 (Polydor 2059 050) (UK)

The band's best song is one of punk's most infectious anthems. It also has elements of a glam rock song with its guitar part and a sing-along football chant-like chorus and handclaps. It's an idealistic and a spiritual-like call for empathy and unity.

### "Hurry Up Harry" b/w "No Entry" 45 October 5, 1978 (Polydor 2059 065) (UK)

The A-side of the final single of the band's run of 1978 singles shows the working-class escape of "going down the pub." The B-side outlines the band being rejected by the embassy for entry into the United States ("they didn't want us in the USA, we didn't wanna go there anyway"). Someone suggested they go to what the band renames "New York shitty." But they'd rather stay in their own country and not have to Americanize their approach.

**Genre:** Punk

## Shonen Knife

### *Burning Farm* 8" LP July 20, 1983 (Zero 0–0783) (Japan)

Delightful quirky pop punk/post-punk hybrid from Japanese band. Only one of the album's eight songs is in English. That's the Ramones-like "Twist Barbie," which satirizes wanting to be like a "sexy girl" and is the most punk-like song on the album. (This album's CD reissue included a delightful studio outtake of the Ramones' "I Wanna Be Sedated," and in 2011 the band released *Osaka Ramones*, a full album of Ramones covers.)

Like Plastic Bertrand's "Ça Plane Pour Moi" and Kleenex/LiLiPUT, it doesn't matter that the songs aren't in English. Instead, it shows the universality of punk and gives punk an international quality. What also makes this album different is that it's often more post-punk than punk with unusual rhythms and tempo changes. This is less Ramones or Buzzcocks buzz saw guitar than a lighter, jerky, jangly guitar. But, like punk guitar, it sounds simple and DIY.

There's also a sense of innocence at times, such as on "Animal Song," which almost sounds like a children's song or a nursery rhyme. "A Day of the Factory" uses some unusual percussion effects as if throwing the sounds in just for fun. "Burning Farm" is probably the most post-punk, with more complicated percussion, a more aggressive guitar, and an almost ironic-sounding chorus from the R&B song "Land of 1,000 Dances."

**Genre:** Punk/Post-punk

## Simple Minds

### *Empires and Dance* LP September 12, 1980 (UK)

This Scottish band's first two albums were largely meandering and inconsistent, as if they were trying to find their musical identity. From the first track, "I Travel," it's clear there's something more striking and forceful and post-punk on this record. There's an intoxicating but subversive dance beat. The lyrics are not about the wonders of travel, however, but about the oppression and disparity of what was seen while traveling stark, Cold War–era Europe.

The title *Empires and Dance* summed up two major elements of the album. It's a reflection on the effects of empires set to music that's club-friendly. "Celebrate" has a Gothic-like feel, almost an ironic dance song. "This Fear of Gods" features screeches and an almost no wave or experimental jazz sound to offset the dance beat. Some songs are experimental, like "Twist/Run/Repulsion," which features an excerpt of Gogol read in French interspersed with impressionist lyrics and layered vocals. The album is important for showing how to merge post-punk and electronic music.

### *Sister Feelings Call* LP October 16, 1981 (Virgin OVED 2) (UK)

Initially released as a part of double album paired with *Sons and Fascination* but later released separately. That's likely because the music is so different on the two records. *Sons and Fascination* was a precursor to the more pop synth–oriented songs that would lead this band to commercial success.

*Sister Feelings Call* isn't the groundbreaking album that *Empires and Dance* was. It's less daring, less experimental, but it still contains some of the ideas that made that album so great. *Sister Feelings Call* starts the way their previous album *Empires and Dance* did, with an intoxicating dance song. This time it's "Theme for Great Cities," one of post-punk's great instrumentals. In "20th Century Promised Land" there's an interplay of keyboards, post-punk tribal-like drumbeat, and Jim Kerr's vocals that are strong but with a sense of melancholy observation. The experimentation from *Empires and Cities* continues in "League of Nations," sounding almost like one of the dark songs by the duo Suicide.

**Genre:** Post-punk

## SIN 34

### *Die Laughing* 7" EP June 22, 1982 (Spinhead Records SP-001) (USA)

It's somewhat rare for a hardcore punk band to have a female singer. And not only is Julie Lanfeld the standout hardcore punk singer of the Generation Jones era; this EP is one of the best in the hardcore genre.

The opening track, "American America," demystifies the image of America, saying it's the product of propaganda. Lanfeld wants to know the truth about her country, not the false images. "Children Shall Not Be Heard" features Lanfeld's vocals at first over a bass line leading to a climactic declaration: "You don't know what I'm about!" Then she unleashes some tempo changes that make this song a harrowing account of growing up feeling invisible and lost but determined to transcend the oppression. The EP concludes with the ultrafast "Join the Race," about soul-crushing 9-to-5 jobs: "We'll all die eventually without being who we wanted to be."

**Genre:** Hardcore Punk

## Siouxsie and the Banshees

### "Hong Kong Garden" 45 August 8, 1978 (Polydor 2059 052) (UK)

Magnificent first single from what will be one of post-punk's greatest bands. This song is more pop-oriented than what will come, but John McKay's guitar made for one of post-punk's defining moments. This was a new sound that would be emulated by other bands for decades to come. The song also shows the deep romantic qualities of the Goth-like perspective. The song describes a Chinese food restaurant with reverence and wonder.

### *The Scream* LP November 14, 1978 (Polydor POLD 5009) (UK)

After the introduction of the atmospheric, Goth-like short song "Pure," with haunting distant chants, guitar plucking, and occasional drumbeats, comes the mighty fast, jagged guitar in "Jigsaw Feeling," followed by Siouxsie's commanding vocals. And we're into a seismic shift in the music scene.

A year after the Sex Pistols inspired a generation of punks, *The Scream* influenced a generation of post-punk musicians. Guitarist John MacKay kicked off a generation of post-punk guitar players as Johnny Ramone's buzz saw guitar launched so many punk bands. But the album is also important for its lyrics. There's not only a Goth-like perspective at times that would become a subgenre of the post-punk movement but also an emphasis on personal internal struggles with a punk-like simplicity to the words. And at times, like on "Overground" and "Metal Postcard," the pace slows down, showing how not everything has to played at breakneck speed. Although "Overground" is slower, it conveys tension and defiance in its fear of conformity.

Other songs, like "Mirage" and "Switch," have social commentary about major institutions in society from the media to psychiatry. "Carcass" is a surreal, Goth-like story about a butcher with affection for animal carcasses. Is this a bizarre, Goth-like perspective or some kind of social commentary? It's to the band's credit that it could be either. There's also a feeling sometimes of instability on this album, like something is off-kilter, as in "Jigsaw Feeling."

At the forefront of post-punk and its subgenre of Goth was Siouxsie and the Banshees. With her Egyptian-inspired makeup, jet black hair, and commanding vocals, singer Siouxsie Sioux conveyed mystery, wonder, and pathos with a sense of punk anarchy under the surface (Polydor/Alamy).

### "The Staircase (Mystery)" 45 March 23, 1979 (Polydor POSP 9/2059 089) (UK)

A throbbing bass line, tribal-like drumming, jagged swirling guitars, and some mysterious-sounding keyboards give this song a Goth vibe. It's almost surreal in its imagery. There's apparently a mystery of some kind to solve here that causes things to be off-balance.

### "Love in a Void" (B-side of "Mittageisen") 45 June 30, 1979 (Polydor 2059 151) (UK)

After they started a musical revolution with *The Scream* LP and its post-punk sound, they go back to their punk roots. There's righteous anger delivered here against phony celebrities, ignorant music critics, greedy musicians, and other people in the morally bankrupt music business.

### *Join Hands* LP August 31, 1979 (Polydor POLD 5024) (UK)

The band's second album takes a turn in a darker and more Goth direction. Much of the album are songs that courageously confront the darkness of life, mostly caused by people who oppress others. The punk ethos is to speak out against tyranny. *Join Hands* does something similar but with a prophetic, Goth-like view of a world full of shadowy oppression.

The album starts with "Poppy Day," sung from the point of view of dead soldiers, followed by "Regal Zone," about leaders who oppress, perhaps the same rulers who caused the deaths of the soldiers, while "Icons" is about religious fanaticism. "Premature Burial" is based on an Edgar Allan Poe story about someone being buried before they die, but perhaps it's a metaphor for suffering before one's death. "Playground Twist" is about children who are bullied and left to fend for themselves, ending with the hope the tormentors will be punished.

The album ends with a 14-minute, punky version of "The Lord's Prayer" that alternates between phrases from pop songs ranging from "Twist and Shout" to "Knocking on Heaven's Door" to Blondie's "One Way or Another." It's a riveting, desperate plea to understand the divine. On one level, it seems to end in doubt, but yet, Siouxsie sings, "The prayer goes on." The entire album is not an easy one to listen to, but it's a powerful statement about trying to understand the sources of the darkness in life.

### "Eve White/Eve Black" (B-side of "Christine") 45 May 30, 1980 (Polydor 2059 249) (UK)

Continues the theme of "Christine," which is the fragmentation of a woman's personality into different parts. The musical tempos shift halfway through to illustrate the divided states, led by the ominous cry of "Let me out of here." Ending with wailing shrieks of agony, it's one of their most disturbing songs.

### *Kaleidoscope* LP August 1, 1980 (Polydor 2442 177) (UK)

For the band's third album, John McGeoch takes over on guitar and Budgie is the band's new drummer. And the Banshees record their most varied album to date. After the groundbreaking post-punk of *The Scream* and the Goth-oriented *Join Hands*, *Kaleidoscope* goes into new territory.

On the first track, "Happy House," it almost sounds like a new band. McGeoch's guitar at times is run through a processor to sound eerie, at other times he picks his guitar in a kind of jangle post-punk. Budgie creates a tribal-like beat with jazz-like embellishments at times, generating an underlying tension to the song. Over this are Siouxsie's vocals, with a sense of irony but also repressed pain at keeping up a facade. There's also keyboard embellishments as well as acoustic guitar runs on "Christine," a song about a woman with a divided personality.

"Christine," like other songs on the album, is not Gothic in a stereotypical way featuring horror movie imagery, vampires, and other clichés the mainstream media associates with the genre. Instead, it's in the tradition of Goth in literature, which injects a sense of uneasiness and something disturbing and irrational underneath the surface, such as the fragmentation in "Christine." Other songs also feature this quality, including "Trophy," about the futility of achievement, where what looks attractive on the surface isn't what is there underneath. The same theme is in "Paradise Place," about women altering their appearances. And on *Kaleidoscope*, there's a freedom to explore different musical forms such as the addition of keyboards on the ethereal "Lunar Camel"; the drum machine–laden "Red Light"; and "Skin," a percussion-driven song that anticipates Siouxsie and Budgie's side project, the Creatures.

### "Israel" b/w "Red Over White" 45 November 28, 1980 (Polydor POSP 205/2059 3052) (UK)

Released between the band's third and fourth albums, "Israel" is a complex song about the longing for a home, the awareness of ancient tradition, and contemporary tensions. It features haunting chants and a choir to emphasize the spiritual component to the story of Israel. "Red Over White" is another complex song with fairy-tale imagery, including a reference to Hans Christian Andersen's fairy tale *The Snow Queen* and a disturbing buildup to what seems like a violent event that could possibly make the title mean blood on snow.

### *Juju* LP June 19, 1981 (Polydor POLS 1034) (UK)

Just when the band seemed to be going in a direction of more keyboard-based music with *Kaleidoscope*, they return to a guitar-based driving sound. And just as John McKay's playing on *The Scream* influenced a generation of post-punk guitarists, John McGeoch's guitar parts on *Juju* shaped post-punk and alternative music guitarists for years to come. His guitar playing features both the raw power and force of punk yet varies it with different tones and approaches.

On the Orwell-like depiction of surveillance, "Monitor," there's a driving guitar with a punk-like sense of energy. On "Head Out" and "Halloween" there is a jarring, slicing guitar run through a processor. Anything is possible with the guitar playing, and that's apparent right from the beginning with "Spellbound," where McGeoch uses an acoustic guitar played at a furious, punk-like pace.

The lyrics to "Spellbound" are about being entranced in what appears to be a transcendental state, or at least about feeling as if being taken over by something. Like all of their albums during this period, there's spiritual imagery at times, including on "Into the Light" and "Sin in My Heart." There are songs that focus on fear, like the horror movie–like "Night Shift," while "Voodoo Dolly" is a flat-out avant-garde assault and perhaps the most experimental they would get during this era. In a career full of daring and innovative albums, this might be the band's peak.

### "Congo Conga" (B-side of "Arabian Knights") 12" July 24, 1981 (Polydor POSPX 309) (UK)

Innovative song with keyboards and guitars leading to a triumphant tribal dance beat coupled by McGeoch's guitar that alternates between post-punk and funk. It's a blend of the modern and something more Indigenous. Siouxsie and Budgie would later explore percussion-driven world music further in their side project, the Creatures.

### "Fireworks" 45 May 21, 1982 (Polydor POSP 450) (UK)

Effective use of strings in this stand-alone single. It's a precursor to the diversity of instruments that would be used on the *A Kiss in the Dreamhouse* album. Perhaps the fireworks imagery is erotic, perhaps it's defiant empowerment.

### *A Kiss in the Dreamhouse* LP November 5, 1982 (Polydor POLD 5064) (UK)

As always, the Banshees progress with every album. John McGeoch's guitar was the center of their previous album, *Juju*, but on this album they use a variety of instruments, including a recorder, chimes, and strings. The songs are mixed together in a kind of post-punk Wall of Sound. In some ways it's similar to *Kaleidoscope* because every song explores a different musical approach. But here the songs have multiple layers of instruments and soundscapes that is more expansive than *Kaleidoscope*. Part of the album's excitement is this multiplicity. One never knows what's coming next.

Some songs—such as "Green Fingers," "She's a Carnival," and "Painted Bird"—are a kind of post-punk with sophisticated pop touches. But as is often the case for this band, there's a darkness underneath. What looks attractive on the surface features something treacherous and dangerous underneath. All three of these songs are complex.

"Melt" and "Cocoon" are post-punk torch songs with lots of tension underneath the melodies. "Circle" is a portrait of a cycle of oppression that goes from generation to generation, with music that features a repetitive sound emphasizing the song's sense of entrapment. The album ends with the intoxicating "Slow Dive," a violin-accented, funk-like dance song. Another landmark album from perhaps the most influential post-punk band.

**Genre:** Post-punk

## Sisters of Mercy

### "Body Electric" 45 January 26, 1982 (CNT 002) (UK)

On their second single, this British band from Leeds creates their trademark sound and finds their niche in the Goth-influenced post-punk genre. It uses an ironic dance drum machine beat with jagged guitars in the right places and a voice filled with a gravitas that comes from both too much experience and too much fragility. The song ends in a kind of horror movie cry of terror and paranoia: "This place is death with walls."

### "Alice" b/w "Floorshow" 45 November 21, 1982 (Merciful Release MR 015) (UK)

Like "Body Electric," the song is about a journey through a disturbing environment. It's an *Alice in Wonderland* homage with a woman named Alice going through a series of encounters in a kind of underground filled with drugs and tarot cards. And like "Body Electric," it ends in urgency. This time the vocalist shouts, "Alice don't give it away!" "Floorshow" is even better, with an infectious, industrial Goth sound and imagery of the underside of life.

### "Anaconda" b/w "Phantom" 45 March 1983 (Merciful Release MR 019) (UK)

"Anaconda" uses a drum machine and some compressed production to create a more accessible sound during a time when drum machine–fueled, synth-based music grows in popularity. But the lyrics are anything but accessible. The song is about a woman apparently self-destructing from drug addiction, which is compared to being strangled by a dangerous snake. The instrumental "Phantom" continues the drum-machine-meets-Goth textures in an expansion of post-punk. It's so atmospheric it sounds like the soundtrack to a Goth movie.

### "Temple of Love" 45 October 7, 1983 (Merciful Release MR 027) (UK)

The imagery is cryptic. But it appears to be someone searching for transcendence in what appears to be a sacred kind of love but ends up falling apart. It's all a swirling, Goth-like, spiritual battle that in the end may not be about romantic love at all.

**Genre:** Post-punk

## Ska-Dows

### "Apache" 45 June 13, 1980 (CHEAP 1) (UK)

Fun remake of classic instrumental. Integrates a Madness-style saxophone, spaghetti-Western guitar riffs, and a frantic vocal. Captures the energy of the second wave ska era.
**Genre:** Ska

## The Skids

### "Sweet Suburbia" b/w "Open Sound" 45 September 1, 1978 (Virgin VS227) (UK)

This Scottish group is one of the best bands of this era because they're a combination of late punk and early post-punk and because Stuart Adamson is one of the most distinctive guitarists of this period. He can easily combine or alternate between driving punk and more experimental post-punk.

"Sweet Suburbia" is a critique of suburban living that's summed up as be born, live, mate, and die. The way singer Richard Jobson phrases the lyrics makes them almost incomprehensible, making one wonder if they're even being sung in English. The B-side, "Open Sound," celebrates their unique sound ("don't look for the easy tone, one way just restricts our view").

### "Night and Day" (B-side of "The Saints Are Coming") 45 October 25, 1978 (Virgin VS232) (UK)

Seems to be a story of a woman injured in a car crash perhaps connected to some sort of crime. To accent this, Adamson's guitar sounds at times like police sirens.

### *Scared to Dance* LP February 23, 1979 (Virgin V2116) (UK)

The band's first album leads off with probably the band's most popular song, "Into the Valley." It's one of several songs the band would record about war and the military. War was a large theme in their songs, reflecting the Generation Jones preoccupation with the Cold War and its psychological effects. Singer Richard Jobson's phrasing of lyrics became, along with Adamson's guitar sound, a distinctive part of their sound. On "Into the Valley" they are notoriously difficult to understand, particularly the first line of the chorus, which actually is "Ahoy! Ahoy! Land, sea and sky."

Another one of their best-known songs is "The Saints Are Coming," about a relationship between a father and a son. But the religious symbolism means it could have all kinds of potential meanings. A rerecording of "Charles" from the band's first single is a superior version, with surreal lyrics about a factory worker turning into part of the machinery. Some songs are energetic, like "Of One Skin" and "Scale," with punk-like fury, while others experiment with post-punk variations of tempos and song structures, as in "Dossier," with its waltz-like pace, and "Six Times."

### "Masquerade" double 45 May 17, 1979 (Virgin VS 262) (UK)

"Masquerade" points to the deviation the band made on their upcoming second album, *Days of Europa*. It features a synthesizer, which takes away some of the band's power. But nonetheless it's a solid song with war imagery. "Out of Town" and "Another Emotion" have the drive of their first album.

**"Charade" 45 September 7, 1979 (Virgin VS 288) (UK)**

The Skids went in a different direction with their second album, *Days of Europa*, that featured awkward keyboards that seemed to strangle the band's sound. But on this song the synthesizer is kept to a minimum and Adamson's guitar carries the song along.

**"Working for the Yankee Dollar" b/w "Vanguard's Crusade" 45 November 16, 1979 (Virgin VS 306) (UK)**

A bit of an XTC groove on "Working for the Yankee Dollar" with a slight pop feel to the post-punk sound. It's about the American war machine, with references to both the Vietnam War and World War II. The B-side features a majestic spaghetti-Western riff from Adamson's guitar.

**The Absolute Game LP September 5, 1980 (Virgin V 2174) (UK)**

For their third album the Skids go in a more solidly post-punk direction than their second album. One of the standout tracks is "Hurry on Boys," which musically sounds like it's laying the groundwork for Adamson's next band, Big Country. Like Big Country, there's a feel of traditional Scottish music integrated with post-punk. "Out of Town" is the song that sounds like the Skids' older sound. It was originally the B-side to the single "Masquerade" and seems to be about some kind of transcendental experience when removed from familiar surroundings. But who knows?

Figuring out what the songs mean is part of the fun of listening to the Skids. Perhaps "Circus Games" and "Arena" compare modern times to the Roman days. Or maybe not. "Circus Games" features background vocals by children, so it could be about the effects on children. Easier to decipher is "The Devil's Decade," which is about poverty and despair in a working-class town.

**"Monkey McGuire Meets Specky Potter Behind Lochore Institute" (B-side of "Goodbye Civilian") 45 October 18, 1980 (Virgin VS 373) (UK)**

This instrumental really lets guitarist Stuart Adamson shine. It's part surf guitar, part punk-meets–post-punk hybrid. It's all to a steady marching drumbeat.

**Genre:** Punk/Post-punk

## The Slits

***Double Peel Sessions* LP (recorded September 19, 1977 and April 17, 1978, released February 11, 1987) (Strange Fruit SFPMA207) (UK)**

Enormously important and influential band started as an all-female group. They were brilliant. But for whatever reasons (it may have to do with personnel changes or wanting to leap into post-punk and not record a punk album), the band sabotaged themselves by not releasing their early songs at the time. So what we have of their first material are the songs recorded for DJ John Peel released years later.

The main reason to get this album is the 1977 Peel session of four songs. "Vindictive" is an absolute anthem with a chorus featuring singer Ari Up alternating between "I'll spit on it" and "I'll shit on it." "Shoplifting" is a frantic call to "do a runner" and shoplift out of economic necessity. "New Town" is a portrait of an unsatisfying town where they are "sniffing televisena or taking footballina." "Love and Romance" is a sarcastic view of a romantic relationship. The last three songs were rerecorded for their *Cut* album. Those very different versions are good. But they don't match the energy here.

*Cut* LP September 5, 1979 (Island ILPS 9573) (UK)

After recording their punkiest versions of their songs for radio DJ John Peel, they release their debut album two years after they started performing live. Over that time they moved out of punk into post-punk. And *Cut* is a landmark album for how it integrates reggae influences with post-punk. The reggae influence is all over the album, starting with "Instant Hit," a cautionary tale about the self-destruction of drug addiction. However, this isn't an album that's just reggae variations. The band skillfully incorporates reggae influences into a sound of their own.

And like reggae and punk, there's a critique of conformity and the mainstream culture. The anti-consumer song "Spend Spend Spend" is about someone who went shopping because "[she] went to satisfy this empty feeling." The band's critique of radio is in "FM," which in the song stands for "frequent mutilation." The version of "Shoplifting" with Ari's shrieks recalls some of the energy of the 1977 Peel session version. "Typical Girls" calls out conformity, while "Adventures Close to Home" was written by their former drummer Palmolive and later recorded by the Raincoats, the new band she joined. In the spirit of the band being independent and outspoken, the album was notorious and controversial for its cover image of the band nude with mud smeared on them.

"In the Beginning There Was Rhythm" split 45 March 14, 1980 (Y Records/Rough Trade Y1/RT 039A) (UK)

Released as part of a split single with the Pop Group, the Slits go beyond reggae-influenced music of the album *Cut* into a mixture of funk, world music, and reggae. This is an even more adventurous move into the experimentation of post-punk with some of singer Ari Up's most passionate and best vocals. There's also a combination of rap, reggae toasting, and jazz improvisational singing. The whole song is a celebration of rhythm.

"Earthbeat" 45 August 17, 1981 (CBS A 1498) (UK)

There are some good moments on the band's second album, *Return of the Giant Slits*, but not enough. Perhaps being so misunderstood and unappreciated, they just ran out of energy. However, this single has a fascinating integration of more subdued rhythm over ethereal lyrics.

**Genre:** Punk/Post-punk

# Patti Smith Group

"Pumping (My Heart)" b/w "Ask the Angels" 45 January 1977 (Arista 10 C 006–98.834) (Spain)

After the monumental *Horses* album in 1975, Smith's second album, *Radio Ethiopia*, was a disappointment. But this features the two best songs on the album. They're both driving punk spiritual anthems. "Pumping" is a jubilant leap into courage and transcendence when she feels "total abandon." "Ask the Angels" is, in the words of the song, a "battle cry." It's an apocalyptic-like scenario with Smith declaring herself a rock-and-roll fighter as she summons angels for what she calls a war.

*Easter* LP March 3, 1978 (Arista AB 4171) (USA)

While Smith's first album, *Horses* (released during the pre-punk period), was so groundbreaking for its mostly expansive songs with Smith's poetic lyrics, this is a succinct album that is perhaps Smith's most eclectic. It's a leap forward from her second album, *Radio Ethiopia*, with a fascinating integration of spiritual and religious imagery. That starts with the opening track, the idealistic call to arms "Till Victory," where she pleads, "God, do not seize me please till victory." "Ghost Dance" is about a sacred dance by Native Americans but also contains imagery from the Book of Exodus of receiving "manna from heaven from the most high." She recites part of Psalm 23 in "Privilege (Set Me Free)." The title track explores suffering and resurrection.

It also includes some of Smith's hardest rocking songs, such as "25th Floor" segueing into "High on Rebellion." The fastest of all is "Rock N Roll N****r," which includes people she admires, from Jesus to painter Jackson Pollock. These are outsiders, she says, but "outside of society is where I wanna be." This just reinforces the idea of artists, spiritual people, and punk rockers as outsiders. The album also includes her biggest hit, "Because the Night."

### *Wave* LP April 27, 1979 (Arista AB 4221) (USA)

What a journey Smith took in the original incarnation of her career. She seemed to go through all the phases of this era. She made the great proto-punk and early no wave influence "Piss Factory," was the conduit between proto-punk and punk in the album *Horses*, explored full-fledged punk rock on *Easter*, and *Wave* is her own variation of post-punk fitting that spirit into styles that range from near no wave to ballads.

The best-known song on this album is "Dancing Barefoot," which may be the most mystical song in her career for an artist who often sang about the transcendental and the spiritual. The sparse "Hymn" sounds like it could be either a love song or a devotional religious song. "Seven Ways of Going" recalls both no wave and the experimentation of "Radio Ethiopia." "Broken Flag" is one of the most beautiful songs she has ever written about a march toward Algiers.

Punks doing covers of 1960s songs often was a novelty or an attempt at commercial success. But in Smith's version of the Byrds song "So You Want to Be a Rock 'N' Roll Star," she completely steals this song. She takes it out of psychedelic pop and into full-fledged punk. Her spoken segment emphasizes the suspicion of stardom and commercialization.

**Genre:** Punk/Post-punk

## The Smiths

### "Hand in Glove" 45 May 13, 1983 (Rough Trade RT 131) (UK)

Punk and post-punk were genres initiated by misfits. The punks could be angry and the post-punks bold. But what about the sensitive souls ravaged by working-class life and years of being outsiders? Singer Morrissey gave them a voice. He was a stalwart of the initial punk scene in Manchester who formed a band years after the initial punk explosion.

Johnny Marr's guitar playing may have been influenced by Scottish post-punk pop bands like Josef K. But it's not sunny pop. That's because there's sometimes a contrast between the brightness of the guitars and Morrissey's voice. There's also an eclectic quality to the guitar playing that helped make them popular during the more musically diverse 1980s alternative music era.

On this debut single there's a defiance to "Hand in Glove," which may be about a same-sex relationship where the singer is so devoted he doesn't care about what others think. That's because love is something he values that others won't understand.

**"Jeane" (B-side of "This Charming Man") 45 October 28, 1983 (Rough Trade RT 136) (UK)**

One of the best early Smiths songs is a dark portrayal of working-class life. "The low life has lost its appeal," Morrissey sings. An existence of deprivation has ruined a relationship and left the singer disillusioned and hopeless.

**"This Charming Man" 12" December 3, 1983 (Rough Trade RTT 136) (UK)**

The A-side contains two versions of "This Charming Man" (the Manchester version is better than the London version). Morrissey is at his most playful in this song, which appears to be about an encounter between two men, one of whom is poor, which makes him feel inadequate. "Accept Yourself" is a firsthand account of a sensitive young person battered by feelings of inferiority, while "Wonderful Woman" has almost a Goth-like atmosphere to it about a woman with sinister propensities but who is nonetheless alluring and enticing.

**Genre**: Post-punk

# Snatch

### "I.R.T." 45 February 1977 (Bomp! 108) (USA)

The duo of Judy Nylon and Patti Palladin release an unconventional punk song, one with just vocals and guitars. For just 35 cents, riding the New York City subway can entertain with its depravity, the singers tell us.

### "All I Want" b/w "When I'm Bored" 45 January 27, 1978 (Lightning LIG 505) (UK)

The duo goes beyond the stripped-down sound of their debut single and release a full-fledged punk song. Great attitude and harmonies with a layered sound make "All I Want" one of the outstanding overlooked songs of this time period. The B-side is part garage rock, part punk theatrical rock, which says there's entertainment everywhere in life because "when I'm bored, everything's my scene."

**Genre:** Punk

# Social Distortion

### "Mainliner" (B-side of "Playpen") 45 October 14, 1981 (Posh Boy PBS 11) (USA)

Social Distortion was part of the Southern California hardcore punk scene. But right from their debut single, they were different. They had one foot in traditional rock, blues, and even country music. They had an appreciation for other genres of music and didn't want to be pigeonholed in the hardcore punk genre. This is a cautionary tale about the dangers of heroin.

### "1945" 45 December 17, 1982 (13th Floor SD 4501) (USA)

A song about the atomic bombing at Hiroshima with horrific imagery. Many bands from the Generation Jones era wrote about the fear of nuclear war. But this song reminds people that it isn't ungrounded fear. It already happened.

### *Mommy's Little Monster* LP June 1983 (13th Floor SD 1301) (USA)

The band's debut album doesn't follow the conventions of either punk or hardcore. That's because there's a profound sense of sadness to the characters in most of these songs. Even early in his career, singer Mike Ness sounds like an old soul. The feeling of melancholy is perhaps rooted in the band's affection for blues and country music with tales of outsiders, ramblers, losers, and people consumed by regret and loss. These weighty themes of the downtrodden propelled by energetic punk music would become the band's trademark sound.

"No one said life would be easy" is all Ness can say when describing poverty and misery in "It Wasn't a Pretty Picture." "Hour of Darkness" is about a person who experienced being close to death, while the title track details the lives of both a boy and a girl rejected by their mothers. "Another State of Mind" is an almost postapocalyptic search for the only person the singer realizes understands his life. By the end of the album there are songs about feeling like an outcast for being a punk in "All the Answers" and in "Moral Threat," where he is beaten up for being a punk.

Through it all, Ness sounds world-weary for someone in his early twenties. But this is Generation Jones speaking. And world-weariness came early for them.

**Genre:** Punk

## Sonic Youth

### *Sonic Youth* 12" EP March 1, 1982 (Neutral Records n. 1) (USA)

This debut EP doesn't feature the New York band's trademark unconventional guitar tunings. That became such a characteristic of Sonic Youth that this EP sounds different from anything they would do later. Still, it shows Sonic Youth formulating what will make them one of the most significant bands to emerge from this era.

The first side leans more toward a more low-key version of post-punk, such as the hypnotic "She Is Not Alone" and the spoken word interplay in "I Dreamed I Dream." The second side goes more toward a no wave–influenced sound, particularly in the last track "The Good and the Bad." It isn't as radical as no wave. But it shows how a band can integrate a no wave sensibility into something new.

### *Confusion Is Sex* LP February 11, 1983 (Neutral Records n. 9) (USA)

Sonic Youth's mission at this point in their career seems to be salvaging no wave by infusing it into a new sound often called noise punk or noise rock. The songs here generally do not entirely settle into a conventional song structure. But the songs are more conventional than experimental no wave. This experimentation would be an enormous influence on alternative music of the 1980s and 1990s, which would integrate some of this sound although few bands would be as bold or adventurous.

Kim Gordon is featured prominently, singing on about half the album. "Protect Me You" recalls the drama, beauty, and eeriness of the Velvet Underground, which aside from no wave is a big influence on this band. Garage rock and the Stooges are an influence, too, so that's why there's a lo-fi version of "I Wanna Be Your Dog" featuring some of the guitar anarchy of no wave. On "Shaking Hell" Gordon repeats some phrases that sometimes sound like an erotic song, other times like a horror movie. "Making That Nature Scene" uses the backdrop of the city's decay to serve as a depiction of prostitutes. Other songs show a band trying out different musical forms with their unconventional tunings, including "Lee Is Free," a no wave–like instrumental experimental piece.

### *Kill Yr Idols* 12" EP October 1983 (Zensor Zensor 10) (Germany)

There's a live song and a song from their first album, but also three other songs that are the reason to get this EP. "Kill Yr Idols" features Thurston Moore's blistering vocals attacking a rock critic. But it also can be viewed as a punk-inspired song about an establishment that doesn't understand. "Brother James" is an apparent tribute to James Brown but more about how music offers salvation. It features swirling guitars that sound like a swarm of insects. "Early American" is an elegy-like song with a tribal-like beat at the beginning instrumental section before a chime-like background and guitar picking over Kim Gordon's beautiful, eerie vocals.

**Genre:** Post-punk

## The Sound

### "Brute Force" (B-side of "Heyday") 45 September 6, 1980 (Korova KOW 10) (UK)

An ominous keyboard riff, a shredding-like guitar sound during the verses, and a scorching lead guitar propel this antiauthoritarian song. States something chilling about authority: the only way to get power is to trample on the weak.

### *Jeopardy* LP October 27, 1980 (Korova KODE 2) (UK)

*Jeopardy* contains both direct punk-like angst as well as the more musically adventurous and personally oriented pain consistent with post-punk. "Heyday" is the punkiest song, with a soaring chorus. It expresses Generation Jones angst about oppressive forces keeping people from being their best. "Heartland" is a defiant song with confidence there is something good out there to rise above desperation and injustice. "Resistance" is a rousing song about fighting subjugation with a chorus with just the word "resist!"

But *Jeopardy* also features songs with a more post-punk perspective about the weight of personalized pain. The album starts with "I Can't Escape Myself," where oppression and imprisonment are self-inflicted. The haunting "Hour of Need" is about the darkness of isolation. Sometimes punk and post-punk themes are combined, as in "Words Fail Me," which features a punk-like drive and phrasing and with lyrics about a lack of self-understanding and inability to communicate rather than oppression from the external.

### *From the Lion's Mouth* LP October 22, 1981 (Korova KODE 5) (UK)

More contemplative and reflective than their first album, *From the Lion's Mouth* doesn't have an overt punk influence. Instead, there's a focus on the introspective accentuated by gloomier music than almost anything on *Jeopardy*. The album starts off optimistically with "Winning," about transcending difficult circumstances, and is followed by "Sense of Purpose," which is lyrically similar to the punkier songs from *Jeopardy*. It summons a call to arms to have the brains and heart "to have a sense of purpose again."

But the album from there is mostly about facing internal demons with a trilogy of songs demonstrating a spiritual crisis. First there is "Judgment," which asks, "Can there really be, someone up above me who judges me when my time is up?" It's followed by "Fatal Flaw," about the pain of "growing away from the light," and then "Possession," about a spiritual warfare between opposing forces that the singer calls God and the devil. It ends with the ominous "New Dark Age" about the discouragement and world-weariness that comes from struggling with the weight of so many spiritual and personal battles. The album ends much darker than where it began. But in the process the Sound created one of post-punk's most memorable albums about fighting to overcome the struggles of life.

**Genre:** Post-punk

## Soundtracks & Head

### "Rain Rain Rain" b/w "Ghost Train" 12" June 1982 (Rough Trade RT 104) (USA)

After the British post-punk band Swell Maps broke up, drummer Epic Soundtracks and guitarist Jowe Head released these two songs as a duo. The A-side has an infectious almost jazz-like groove with female vocals. "Ghost Train" features a tribal beat with guitar picking. Supposedly this was from a planned forthcoming album that was never released.

**Genre:** Post-punk

## The Specials

### "Gangsters" split 45 July 28, 1978 (2 Tone TT1) (UK)

The song that kicked off second wave ska was a split single with the Selecter. Based on Prince Buster's "Al Capone," this song was danceable music about corruption that induces fear. "I dread to think what the future will bring when we're living in gangster times," Terry Hall sings.

### The Specials LP October 26, 1979 (2 Tone CDL TT 5001) (UK)

Perhaps the definitive second wave ska album. It pays homage to the first wave ska movement with some covers, including Prince Buster's "Too Hot" and Toots and the Maytals' "Monkey Man." But they are not only relevant to the times but also so inhabited by the sound of the Specials that they become their own songs. The album starts with "A Message to

The Specials—(clockwise from bottom left) Jerry Dammers, Lynval Golding, Neville Staple, Terry Hall, John Bradbury, Roddy Radiation, and Horace Panter—were on the indie 2 Tone label, which laid the foundation for the second wave ska movement. This era of ska merged the energy of punk with the rhythms of Jamaican ska music (LFI/Photoshot/Everett Collection).

You Rudi," warning a young man on the verge of going into a life of crime to stop from going astray. It ends with a remake of the 1960s ska song "You're Wondering Now," with its ominous uncertainty about what's ahead when things are dismantled and in disarray.

Among these songs are originals chronicling what's going on currently. "Nite Klub" demystifies the culture of working-class escapism by going to clubs where they spend their money drinking, while "Too Much Too Young" is about an early pregnancy that ultimately oppresses a young woman. "Doesn't Make It Alright" denounces prejudice and calls out how the instigators are oppressed themselves. "Concrete Jungle" is about the fear of violence and crime in the city. "Do the Dog" outlines the deep divisions of the era, both in politics and youth culture. It all adds up to not just a great ska album but one of the best albums of this entire era of music.

**"Rat Race" b/w "Rude Boys Outta Jail" 45 May 24, 1980 (2 Tone CHS TT11) (UK)**

"Rat Race" contains innovative percussion, keyboards, and a guitar part over lyrics about the futility of mainstream work culture. But the main target is college students grooming themselves for corporate culture. The sing-along B-side celebrates reformed criminals ("they used to be tough, but now they're keeping cool").

***Too Much Too Young* 7" EP January 26, 1980 (2 Tone CHS TT7) (UK)**

EP with live songs that captures the energy of one of the best live acts of this era. After a version of "Too Much Too Young," the band goes through raucous and spirited covers of first wave ska classics. The first is "Guns of Navarone," followed by what's called the "Skinhead Symphony" of "Long Shot Kick the Bucket," "Liquidator," and "Skinhead Moonstomp." Just try sitting still through this.

***More Specials* LP October 4, 1980 (2 Tone CHR TT 5003) (UK)**

Because it wasn't as fast-paced and danceable as the most popular songs on their debut album, at the time the album wasn't met with as much enthusiasm as it should have been. But this is a daring, creative attempt to build on, advance, and rework the second wave ska sound the band basically created with the "Gangsters" single and their debut album.

There are all kinds of expressions, tempos, and variations of ska here. That comes after the album's opening track, their cover of "Enjoy Yourself," which sounds most like it could have been on their debut album. It's an ironic party song with melancholy lyrics ("The years go back as quickly as you wink/Enjoy yourself, it's later than you think"). Some of the best songs include "Man at C&A," a reggae-tinged Cold War–era fear-of-nuclear-war song, and "Hey, Little Rich Girl," a mid-tempo tragic story of a wealthy young girl who descends into making porno movies. "Do Nothing" is a melodic song about the effects of both boredom and oppression. "Sock It to 'em J.B." is more soul than ska, while "I Can't Stand It" is a duet between singers Terry Hall and Rhoda Dakar.

**"Ghost Town" 7" EP June 20, 1981 (2 Tone CHS TT17) (UK)**

There are so many words you can use to describe the massively important song "Ghost Town." Haunting. Piercing. Prophetic. Written during an era of economic downturn, riots, and social upheaval in England, it shows an almost dystopian atmosphere of unemployment, poverty, violence, and closed businesses. The song is slower in an almost mournful tone with disturbing sounds after the chorus that make it sound like a soundtrack from a horror movie. The two B-sides also have a melancholy aura reflecting the era. "Why" is a firsthand account of racism and repeats the question, "Tell me why?" "Friday Night, Saturday Morning" is a futile and disappointing attempt to escape working-class oppression by going out to nightclubs.

### "Racist Friend" 45 September 3, 1983 (2 Tone CHS TT25) (UK)

After the departure of three key members of the Specials to form Fun Boy Three, the band carries on as Special AKA. Rhoda Dakar and Stan Campbell trade off on lead vocals on this song advising to cut yourself off from any friend or family member who is racist.

**Genre:** Ska

## SS Decontrol (SSD)

### *The Kids Will Have Their Say* LP July 1982 (XClaim! no. 1/Dischord no. 7½) (USA)

The most influential and important Boston hardcore band. Their debut album features 18 songs in 20 minutes. So they're fast fast fast with their combination of punk and hardcore with some heavy metal around the edges. Singer Springa's phrasing is one of the most distinctive in all of hardcore. Not only does he spit out the words so quickly, his tone is so anguished that even when you can't understand what he's saying it doesn't matter. Just the sound of his voice gets the point across.

That this band has something urgent to say is there right from the beginning with "Boiling Point," about repressed feelings that must be unleashed. And they do. The album is a profound portrayal of being besieged on so many different levels. "Do You Even Care" is about being harassed for being a punk, while "Police Beat" is about violence against punks. Other songs, such as "Fight Them" and "Not Normal," are about being hassled for being part of the straight edge movement. "Wasted Youth" points out the connection between drug culture and apathy.

But oppression also comes from the political and social system itself, including "Teach My Violence," which emphasizes the inherent violence embedded in society. The entire album almost sounds like it's apocalyptic because it's so urgent. It makes sense that it concludes with the doomsday scenario of "The End."

### *Get It Away* 12" EP March 1983 (XClaim! X3) (USA)

Ferocious hardcore EP with a garage thrash edge to it with Al Barile's guitar that contains some of the most powerful straight edge–themed songs in hardcore punk. "Forced Down Your Throat" condemns both drinking and drugs, while "Get It Away" is an anti-smoking song. "Under the Influence" poses a question to people who drink and use drugs: "Can't you see you'll never be free?" "X-Claim" declares: "We can rock together without getting high."

And it's a landmark album musically. The vocals sometimes sound primal, and it's difficult to discern the words as if they come from a deep place of agony. While there are some songs that are at breakneck speed, there's sometimes a more dramatic heavy metal influence that gives these songs complexity. "No Reply" concludes the album in an almost desperate and terrifying dread of no response from someone. It seems symbolic of the lack of answers to the problems presented on the album. It's a harrowing ending to one of the most compelling records in all of hardcore.

**Genre:** Hardcore Punk

## State of Alert (S.O.A.)

### *No Policy* 7" EP May 16, 1981 (Dischord 2) (USA)

Short-lived Washington, D.C., band fronted by Henry Rollins. Rollins would help define and expand the possibilities of the hardcore punk genre when he joined Black Flag for their *Damaged* album. And at times there are the seeds of what he would go on to do. The highlight of this record is "Blackout," which portrays internal pain that would be a central theme on *Damaged*.

It's all about energy here, running through a range of topics. "Lost in Space" features a straight edge theme, and other songs are about the contemporary punk scene and the violence of the era. But overall this EP is notable for Rollins's phrasing. Like rappers, hardcore punk singers have a specific tone and phrasing that makes them distinctive. And there's enough here to show that Rollins would be one of hardcore's heavyweights.

**Genre:** Hardcore Punk

## Stiff Little Fingers

### "Suspect Device" b/w "Wasted Life" 45 March 17, 1978 (Rigid Digits SRD-1) (UK)

This debut record from this Northern Ireland band about the Troubles in Belfast is one of the fiercest in the punk genre. While other bands talked of riots and potential wars, Stiff Little Fingers wrote from firsthand knowledge about an actual ravaged, war-torn city. And they were defiant about the oppression ("I'm a suspect device the Army can't defuse"). The B-side continues the anti-war and anti-imperialist themes with a call for young people to not waste their lives joining the military. The rerecorded versions of both songs on their first album are good, but the rawness and urgency of this indie single make it superior.

### "78 RPM" (B-side of "Alternative Ulster") 45 October 16, 1978 (Rough Trade/Rigid Digits RT 004) (UK)

A summary of the 1970s with a call for revolution in 1978. There's a count off of all the years in the 1970s with most years producing either oppression or boredom. Things got better with punk exploding in 1977, and now there's a desire that things might really change in 1978. Captures the hopes of the early punk movement.

### *Inflammable Material* LP February 3, 1979 (Rough Trade ROUGH 1) (UK)

One of the great debut albums in the punk genre. It's like hearing dispatches from a war zone. And Belfast in the late 1970s was essentially a war zone. The songs are a personalized view of living under those conditions. Rather than making political statements, the songs are from the point of view of the people living under these conditions.

"Law and Order" is about the injustice of authority; "Here We Are Nowhere" shows the paralysis that both boredom and fear cause. Even a love affair is told through war imagery in "Barbed Wire Love." The cover version of "Johnny Was" is the band's first foray into reggae, something they would explore more on their next two albums. "Breakout" is a more universal song about getting out of limitations, which would be a major theme on their second album. The album's culmination and best song, however, is "Alternative Ulster." It's a desire to change the conditions of Northern Ireland. The songs asks a series of questions before declaring a call to action: "Grab it and change it, it's yours!"

### "Straw Dogs" b/w "You Can't Say Crap on the Radio" 45 September 19, 1979 (Chrysalis CHR 2368) (UK)

"Straw Dogs" is another compelling anti-war and anti-imperialist song. The B-side is anti-censorship but also symbolizes how limiting and tyrannizing mainstream radio is. At the time there were few or no alternatives to it. A musical revolution was in full force, but it largely wasn't on the radio. The song ends with an homage to the Clash's "Capital Radio."

### *Nobody's Heroes* LP March 14, 1980 (Chrysalis CHR 1270) (UK)

The band's first album, *Inflammable Material*, was dominated by songs about the Troubles in Northern Ireland. Their second album makes broader statements about overcoming limitations and barriers. The overall message is that without determination to overcome naysayers and society's oppression, you'll drown in inner and outer oppression.

That theme starts with the first song, "Gotta Gettaway," about leaving the restrictions of a hometown and being misunderstood and ostracized. "Wait and See" is about rising above the frequent criticism of punk bands that they are musically limited. "Nobody's Hero" warns the audience not to think of the band as heroes and to be the heroes of their own lives: "Be what you are." "At the Edge" also is about following one's chosen path and not listening to people who define what you believe in as "stupid hopes and dreams." "Tin Soldiers" also encourages young people to stay true to themselves or they will regret it and lose their youth by signing up for the military.

### "Back to Front" 45 July 11, 1980 (Chrysalis CHS 2447) (UK)

Non-album single that appears to be about hooligans who torment people at the beach on vacation and harass Blacks. The references in the song to "front" could refer to the National Front, a far-right, neofascist political party that gained more prominence during the economic downturn of the era in England.

### *Go for It* LP April 20, 1981 (Chrysalis CHR 1339) (UK)

Like the transition the Clash made with their third album, *London Calling*, on their third album Stiff Little Fingers make a leap beyond a consistent punk sound. They expand the punk spirit into songs that go beyond the basic punk musical structure. Like the Clash's *London Calling*, this is a successful expansion of the punk vision and sound.

"Roots Radicals Rockers and Reggae," "The Only One," and "Safe as Houses" blend punk and reggae in different approaches with different tempos. "Go for It" is an instrumental that defies characterization. There's even an uncharacteristic love song (although focusing on conflict) with "Just Fade Away." The album ends with the chilling "Piccadilly Circus," about a man being stabbed while walking outside his London hotel. "Silver Living" successfully incorporates a horn section and is in some ways an extension of the song "Breakout" from their first album and "Gotta Gettaway" from their second album. The song encourages people to rise beyond their limitations by overcoming the clichés people say to keep people in their place. The message is: Don't think about how things can be worse, think of how they can be better.

### *Now Then....* LP October 3, 1982 (Chrysalis CHR 1400) (UK)

Yes, this album is overproduced. If you play "Suspect Advice" and "Alternative Ulster" and then play this album it almost doesn't sound like the same band. This album was an attempt to adapt to changing musical trends with the production going at times toward a power pop sound. But while the production drags the energy down and there are a few real misfires, most of the songs are strong.

There's an interesting turn toward outlining the personalized effects of oppression, such as on the album's first track, "Falling Down," about a runaway girl. Another standout track is "Won't Be Told," about learning life's lessons firsthand. The final track "Is That What You Fought the War For?" is about the World War II generation and how their idealism didn't last. The best track on the album may be "Bits and Pieces," about younger people lost and oppressed living in crime-ridden places while parents work and aren't there for them.

**Genre:** Punk

## The Stimulators

### "Loud Fast Rules!" b/w "Run Run Run" 45 1980 (No Label CB-570) (USA)

The title of this A-side from this pre-hardcore New York City punk band became a kind of punk call to arms slogan. Instead of the standard buzzsaw guitar there's Denise Mercedes's innovative blistering lead guitar through much of the song as well as tribal-like drums from 12-year-old Harley Flanagan who would later go on to form the Cro-Mags. The B-side is more pop punk but with the same winning formula.

**Genre:** Punk

## The Stranglers

### *Rattus Norvegicus* LP April 16, 1977 (United Artists UAG 30045) (UK)

Like XTC, the Stranglers are an eclectic band difficult to categorize. Some will argue (as with XTC) that they are a pop band, not punk or post-punk. But *Rattus Norvegicus* (also known as *Stranglers IV*, even though it's their first album) is mostly a pop punk album but far different from guitar pop punk. Perhaps musically their most distinctive quality is that keyboards are overlaid on top of a guitar and sometimes they have unconventional song structures that point to the coming of post-punk.

That all combines in the opening track, "Sometimes," which features their own version of pop punk and an unusual drumbeat that is like a primitive version of post-punk. On the pop punk side there is "London Lady" and "Get a Grip on Yourself." The Stranglers often use keyboards as a substitute for a lead guitar. But this isn't the slick keyboard sound that would dominate new wave pop music. There seems to always be chaos within the keyboard sound. That culminates in the ending track, "Down in the Sewer," a punk mini-rock opera consisting of four songs and an epic-sounding interplay at the end between keyboards and guitar.

### *No More Heroes* LP September 23, 1977 (United Artists UP 36277) (UK)

With punk in full force, the Stranglers speed up the pace with an album that's less varied but overall more consistently punk than their first album. It's not overtly political, but there still is the feeling that the songs are from the point of view of the underclass, like the assessment of British life in "English Towns."

Two singles from the album show where the punk culture was during this magical musical year. "Something Better Change" appears to be about the punk scene itself, with the singer asking why he is so resented and so much of an outsider. But he knows that some people just aren't going to understand: "No More Heroes" is about everyone from Leon Trotsky to the fictional character Sancho Panza from the novel *Don Quixote*. The song indicates the feeling that there was no one to look up to when there was so much distrust and disillusionment with political and social institutions.

### "5 Minutes" 45 January 27, 1978 (United Artists UP 36350) (UK)

Probably the band's most straight-up punk song. It's a true story about a woman raped in band member Jean-Jacques Burnel's apartment in London while he was playing a gig. Apparently the five minutes mentioned in the song is all it takes to go from a safe part of London to a dangerous part of London.

### *Black and White* LP May 12, 1978 (United Artists UAK 30222) (UK)

For their third album, the band retains the energy of their first two albums. But they branch out to be more controlled, more confident, more visionary. And even philosophical. All of this makes this their definitive album.

*Black and White* presents a theme of things going wrong told from the point of view of working-class characters. But it also shows a philosophical view of how time is used. The album opens with "Tank," about someone with no future who sees the military as a way out. And he can show some violence and hypermasculinity there. "Outside Tokyo" is about a factory that makes watches but seems to have a more overall statement about time itself. "Sweden" continues an examination of time by describing a place that is so boring that there's "too much time to think, too little to do." "Hey! (Rise of the Robots)" is about industrial robots replacing human workers. "Toiler on the Sea" is a ferocious song about someone working on a boat encountering all kinds of troubles. And the album ends by going back to the theme of time in "Enough Time," with the haunting ending refrain of "have you got enough time?"

### "Shut Up" (B-side of "Nice N' Sleazy") 45 April 26, 1978 (United Artists UP 36379) (UK)

Just over a minute long, this is probably the fastest song they did during this period. With its shouted chorus, it could also be a proto-hardcore song. The singer wants an argumentative, talkative person to just shut up.

### "Bear Cage" 12" March 7, 1980 (United Artists 12-BP 344) (UK)

A plodding, almost post-punk drumbeat with post-punk jagged guitar and cascading keyboards is one of their most unique songs. The extended 12-inch contains a chant and post-punk guitar flourishes not on the 45 version. It's about living under oppression, reportedly written about Cold War–era East Germany.

**Genre:** Punk/Pop Punk

## Subhumans

### *Demolition War* 7" EP November 1981 (Spiderleg SPIDLE THREE) (UK)

An important record because it combined anarcho-punk and the growing hardcore punk sound. It's a dynamic midpoint between these two punk subgenres that likely was an influence on another punk subgenre: the UK 82 movement.

The leadoff track, "Parasites," is a ferocious blast of energy that uses horror imagery and fear of government violence and war. The same spirit is in "Society," a frenetic dystopian view of present conditions. The band also has initial Brit punk as a foundation, however, with songs like "Drugs of Youth," about excessive drug use, and "Animal," which condemns the pretensions of elite college students. "Who's Gonna Fight in the Third World War?" is perhaps the fastest song and recalls the rage, fear, and directness of American hardcore. But best of all may be the closing track, "Human Error," a raw, reggae-influenced song about nuclear war.

*The Day the Country Died* LP January 1983 (Spiderleg SDL 9) (UK)

The band's debut album is somewhat of a concept album about a dystopian society. There are several references to George Orwell's *1984*, such as in the opening track, "All Gone Dead," as well as "Big Brother," which depicts a surveillance state. The lyrical themes suit the Cold War–era fear of both nuclear war and a rising totalitarian government, but it isn't just a science fiction–like glimpse into what could be. The album is powerful because much of it is a tour through an already dystopian-like society such as in "Dying World," which shows a society in decay.

Some songs contain a theme of society manipulating people into their own self-destruction, such as tobacco causing disease and death in "Ashtray Dirt." "No" and "I Don't' Want to Die" show a defiant rebelliousness against oppression. However, it ends with the call to arms of "Black and White," which implies there's so much injustice that it must be met with resistance.

**Genre:** Punk/Hardcore Punk

## Suburban Lawns

### "Janitor" 45 November 12, 1980 (Suburban International 91680) (USA)

Over the years this California band's singer, Su Tissue, has attained legendary status. This indie single shows why. This song contains one of the most fascinating unconventional vocal deliveries in post-punk. During the verses she uses a kind of bewildered semi-narration and then switches in the choruses to a mini-shriek, yelps, and a hiccup-like vocal. But there's no way to really describe the way she sings. But there's nothing affected about it. Her voice is truly an instrument.

### *Baby* 45 12" EP May 3, 1983 (I.R.S. SP7053) (USA)

What's essential are the three songs Su Tissue sings (although her vocals should be mixed up higher, c'mon!). "Flavor Crystals" shows off Tissue's ability to uniquely phrase words, and "Cowboy" features Tissue's voice scatting over a slow, pseudo-funk beat. The best song is "Baby," with its pulsating rhythm and World Beat–meets–post-punk sound. Their only album released in 1981 was an overproduced mess with not enough Su Tissue featured. They regained their footing here, but the band broke up after this release.

**Genre:** Post-punk

## Subway Sect

### "Nobody's Scared" 45 March 23, 1978 (Braik BRS 01) (UK)

Raw but melodic song that captures a dystopian atmosphere of late 1970s England. There's a feeling that it's challenging to truly know yourself in such an oppressive society where "everybody is a prostitute." There's a blend of guitars and drums, including an ominous shredding guitar solo, that takes this beyond the standard punk sound.

**Genre:** Punk

## Suicide

### *Suicide* LP December 28, 1977 (Red Star RS 1) (USA)

Milestone album that influenced no wave and created what came to be called synth punk or electronic punk. On the West Coast, the Screamers substituted keyboards for guitars. But Suicide was not punk with synthesizers. This was something entirely different. It was minimalist music with keyboardist Martin Rev creating an array of sounds as a compelling backdrop to Alan Vega's vocals. They have an improvisational quality to them with echo and reverb that recall both rockabilly and dub reggae.

The album also is a reflection of its time period with a dark view of 1970s American life. "Ghost Rider," based on a comic book hero, has the superhero assessing contemporary America, where "America is killing its youth." In "Rocket USA," the TV star and his girlfriend about to crash seem to be a metaphor for the country itself. "Johnny" is about a man "cruising the night looking for love, he's looking so mean, he's feeling so tough." The minimalist lyrics and the sparse music make the song frightening. What's going to happen? The ambiguity adds to the terror.

The centerpiece of the album is the frightening "Frankie Teardrop," about a desperate and financially struggling factory worker who kills his wife, six-month-old son, and then himself. The screams Vega makes over a steady keyboard drone are terrifying. The whole effect is like the soundtrack to a blue-collar horror film. And at the end of the song Vega says, "We're all Frankies, we're all lying in hell." The album ends with the dirge-like "Che," another 1970s song of disillusionment. This time the revolutionary Che Guevara is the false hero. This album defies characterization, but we'll call it minimalist punk.

**"Dream Baby Dream" b/w "Radiation" 45 November 9, 1979 (Island/ZE WIP 6543) (UK)**

"Dream Baby Dream" features a vocal repeating many of the same words in a reverie over a sweeping keyboard. This is a technique Vega did in the first album, particularly in a song like "Cheree." But here there's a more conventional keyboard sound that is much more dominant and mixed up higher. But the plea to always dream is an antidote to all of the darkness and limitations they described on their first album. It's a hypnotic, intoxicating song and an almost transcendental meditation on hope. The B-side is much more like the tone of the first album musically over Vega's lyrics about a fear of an apocalyptic nuclear war.

**Genre:** Punk (minimalist version)

# The Swans

### *The Swans* 12" EP August 1982 (Labor LAB-17) (USA)

A dark, even somewhat sinister EP that's a combination of no wave, post-punk, and Goth. Although this came to be known as noise punk or noise rock, there's even a case to be made that it's slowed-down horror punk. The no wave guitar riffs and horn-like shrieks are around the edges in "Laugh," a surreal song about everyday experiences that transform into horror-like incidents. "Speak" appears to be about someone who can't speak, with urgent music emphasizing the pain of the suppression. The most disturbing song is "Sensitive Skin," about horrors inflicted on someone in a basement. This is one of the darkest records of this period.

### *Filth* LP May 27, 1983 (Neutral N11) (USA)

Along with Sonic Youth and Big Black, the Swans developed and defined noise punk. Their first album is a blend of no wave, industrial music, and very experimental post-punk. They use two drummers and two bass players, which emphasizes the percussion and the song's repetitive and churning rhythms. Vocalist Michael Gira also sounds tormented, almost with a Goth-like horror at the world he sees.

However, some songs are punk-spirited underneath with a sense of outsider outrage. In several songs the anger is directed at hypermasculine powerful figures, such as in "Power for Power" and "Freak," with its fears about how "strong men win at violence and abuse," and the authoritative figure of "Big Strong Boss." But like Big Black, there's a sense of something primal in human nature that leads to baser impulses and actions, such as in "Right Wrong" and "Blackout," where people get so drunk that they pass out. This is one of the most challenging albums of the era, but over the years it has come to be regarded as an important and influential one.

**Genre:** Post-punk

## Swell Maps

### "Read About Seymour" 45 January 30, 1978 (Rather GEAR ONE) (UK)

British band's debut single features brothers who renamed themselves Nikki Sudden and Epic Soundtracks. It's a combination of punk, proto-punk style garage rock, and early post-punk. It's a minute and a half of herky-jerky fun.

### *A Trip to Marineville* LP June 27, 1979 (Rather/Rough Troy One/Rough Two) (UK)

The album starts with the spoken words "say, that's a swell map." And this album is a type of map. What territory doesn't this band cover? Garage rock, pop punk, punk, jangle punk, post-punk, no wave, early noise rock. It's all here. The album's first track, "H.S. Art," asks the question: "Do you believe in art?" Let's throw it all together and see what happens, the band seems to believe. And the band is even subversive about its own songs. The most pop punk song on the album, "Another Song," ends with the line "this is just another song and now it's going to stop." And then the song stops.

Songs like "Full Moon in My Pocket" and "Blam!!" fuse punk and post-punk together. Those songs were a kind of map for alternative bands in the future about how to construct a driving, post-punk song. But the album is also at times very experimental. That starts at the end of the first side with "Bridge Head, Pt. 9." Is it no wave or early noise punk? A bit of both. Toward the end of the second side it goes even further. "Gunboats" is an eerie, somewhat drony dirge, while "Adventures Into Basketry" is an instrumental no wave–like jam. It ends with the garage-band-meets-art-rock instrumental "Lion of the Surf." If there's a connection between Velvet Underground's *White Light White Heat* and Sonic Youth, this is it.

### "Let's Build a Car" 45 January 28, 1980 (Rather/Rough Trade Gear Seven/RT 036) (UK)

If the Stooges were a post-punk band, they would have sounded something like this. The infectious guitar part and double-tracked vocals propel a song praising DIY ideology. It's street philosophy with advice in the chorus: "Whatever you are saving for, at least know what you're waiting for."

### *Jane from Occupied Europe* LP August 16, 1980 (Rough Trade ROUGH 15/Rather Troy 2) (UK)

After the innovative and daring *A Trip to Marineville*, this is at least on the surface a much more controlled album. Songs like "Let's Buy a Bridge" and "Big Maz in 'The

Desert from the Trolley'" have a noisy chaos to them as songs on *Marineville* did. But the overall sound makes it sound less punchy. However, about half of the album are instrumentals with differing soundscapes, including the almost chill groove of "Big Empty Field," the disturbing "Mining Villages," and the surf-guitar-meets post-punk of "Collision with a Frogman vs. The Mangrove Delta Plan."

However, at times they construct a kind of cross between jangle punk and post-punk. "Border Country" features jangle punk as a starting point and adds some more experimental post-punk elements like a clanky piano, chant-like background vocals, and some sound effects. "The Helicopter Spies" and "Blenheim Shots" are also catchy jangle punk songs infused with post-punk touches to give it complexity and tension.

**Genre**: Punk/Post-punk

## Symbol Six

### Symbol Six 12" EP October 15, 1982 (Posh Boy PBS 1030) (USA)

Southern California band's debut record is straight-ahead punk that demystifies the California of the Generation Jones era. It kicks off with "Ego," which punctures pretensions that in the end only have surface appeal with nothing real or meaningful. "Taxation" is about how the tax system hurts the working class and benefits the wealthy, while "Beverlywood" is a tour through the seedy side of Hollywood.

**Genre**: Punk

## Talking Heads

### *Talking Heads: 77* LP September 16, 1977 (Sire SR 6036) (USA)

Initially in the Generation Jones punk era, funk was the enemy. That's because of the commerciality and superficiality associated with it. But this album was one of the first records to reconfigure it by fusing funk with what came to be called post-punk in songs like "Who Is It?" Something else that became associated with post-punk is a nervous guitar and vocal sound. The tense guitars at the beginning of "Psycho Killer" are coupled with David Byrne's vocals that helped to define the phrasing and persona of post-punk singers. There are also tempo changes that sometimes were associated with post-punk.

The lyrics are reductionist, simple, and almost childlike at times. They're sung almost like a confession from a diary or someone's inner thoughts, nothing like standard rock singing in the 1970s. But some songs point to an ironic detachment from altruistic feeling, such as "Don't Worry About the Government" and "No Compassion." The punkiest-sounding song is the ending "Pulled Up," in which Byrne sounds most self-assured. This is more restrained than what will come from this band but still a distinctive debut record.

### "Psycho Killer (Acoustic Version)" 45 December 8, 1977 (Sire 1013) (USA)

The B-side of the album version of "Psycho Killer" is edgier than the album version. That's because avant-garde cello player Arthur Russell added frightening and jarring cello parts, giving it a menacing feel, particularly in the outro. Perhaps his parts were taken out because it wasn't a radio-friendly sound. But once you've heard this version, you miss the piercing cello sounds when hearing the standard version.

The Talking Heads—(left to right) Chris Frantz, David Byrne, Jerry Harrison, and Tina Weymouth—were so groundbreaking and innovative that they were post-punk before post-punk was a genre. The band often conveyed the uneasiness and tension of trying to maneuver through modern life (John Shelley Collection/Photoshot/Everett Collection).

### *More Songs About Buildings and Food* LP July 14, 1978 (Sire SRK 6058) (USA)

Producer Brian Eno's layering of instruments and more sophisticated and intricate production helped the band expand their identity and deepen their sound. And while the energy of punk didn't show up much on their first album, it's here from the opening marching beat of "Thank You for Sending Me an Angel" to the driving, funk-fueled punk of "I'm Not in Love." The album is not only a leap for the band past their more minimal debut album but also an exciting expansion of post-punk. The slowed-down creeping bass-driven cover of Al Green's "Take Me to the River" even scored them a Top 40 U.S. hit, a rarity in America for any band with the punk or post-punk label. "Stay Hungry" features a funk-meets-post-punk sound with Eno's production that points ahead to the band's masterpiece *Remain in Light*.

Byrne's lyrics deepen from the first album. In "Artists Only" he celebrates artistry, and in "Found a Job" he encourages people to get in touch with their own creativity, even if it means making a sitcom (!). The album ends with "The Big Country," a country-tinged song that rejects Middle American living with Byrne declaring, "I wouldn't do the things those people do, I wouldn't live there if you paid me." If ever there was a band that had an urban perspective, sound, and persona, it's the Talking Heads.

### *Fear of Music* LP August 3, 1979 (Sire SRK 6076) (USA)

This album shifts into darker territory than their previous album. The album is almost like transmissions and posts from a dystopian city as in "Life During Wartime," an almost postapocalyptic glimpse of urban survival. Other songs are built around characters struggling with navigating the alienation, apprehension, or fear of modern life. Byrne's vocals also at times sound improvisational or even preacher-like. And they express an internal battle, as in "Mind," in which drugs, religion, and science can't change the singer. "Memories Can't Wait" is another song about mental struggle that portrays a feeling of near paranoia. "Animals" sounds like a song about the mental collapse of prejudice more than about literal animals. The album ends with "Drugs," a nightmarish vision of a mind disoriented by drugs.

As an antidote there's "Heaven," a hope for a utopia where the frenzy of modern life is replaced with a "place where nothing ever happens." And the album starts with the African rhythm–based "I Zimba," a precursor to the world music influence that would be explored even more on their next album, *Remain in Light*.

### *Remain in Light* LP October 8, 1980 (Sire SRK 6095) (USA)

The musical experimentation of Byrne and Eno's *My Life in the Bush of Ghosts* (recorded between the Talking Heads' third and fourth albums), with its world music and African rhythms, is an obvious influence on this record.

The lyrics expand a common theme in the Talking Heads' music: agitation about the demands and shortcomings of modern life. Some of their songs are about insights into a spiritual-like depravation people experience. In "Born Under Punches," it's someone who works in the government who realizes the effect he's having on others. Other songs are more about a personal crisis of conscience. "Crosseyed and Painless" is about waiting for some realization that will bring some direction. "Once in a Lifetime" features someone in a full-fledged midlife existential crisis.

Other songs are about characters in different stages of either crisis, epiphanies, or searches for meaning. "The Great Curve" is about hoping for a transcendental experience, while "Houses in Motion" is a frightening song because it's about someone who realizes he's just going through the motions of life. "Seen and Not Seen" is about someone trying to create an ideal self-image. The album ends with the dirge-like "The Overload," which shows the emotional weight of trying to maneuver through life.

### *Speaking in Tongues* LP June 1, 1983 (Sire 1–23883) (USA)

The funky lead track, "Burning Down the House," extends the theme from *Remain in Light*'s "Once in a Lifetime," showing an inability to navigate the demands of modern living. The singer tries to crush that oppression by annihilating what tyrannizes him. Other songs continue observations about society, such as "Making Flippy Floppy," about the dangers of conformity, which leads to spiritual deadness, while "Slippery People" depicts trying to sustain a direct spiritual experience. The eerie "Swamp" mentions a devil with a plan who misleads people and creates societal chaos.

There is a consistent theme of a clash between higher spiritual impulses and baser instincts. The album ends, however, with a song of gentle transcendence, "This Must Be the Place," which describes a feeling of bliss: "I love the passing of time, never for money, always for love." That feeling may come, however, from realizing that being at home may manifest from being more in the present moment no matter where you are.

**Genre:** Post-punk

## The Teardrops

***In and Out of Fashion*** **12" EP February 14, 1979 (Big Bent Records Big Bent Three) (UK)**

While former Buzzcocks member Howard Devoto went on to form the post-punk band Magazine, Buzzcocks bass player Steve Garvey takes on this side project with some members of the Fall to make his own version of post-punk. And like Devoto, he easily maneuvers into it.

Side A is the best, with "Leave Me No Choice," which sounds somewhat like a drunken sing-along at a bleak moment. "Pompous" is a part-condemnation-part-realization about an oppressive person who just "can't help being a creep." The second side is too much parody. "Teenage Vice" somewhat lampoons the post-punk sound but is still pretty listenable, while "Blueser Blue" is a satire of a plodding blues rock song where the joke gets old pretty quickly.

**Genre:** Post-punk

## Teen Idles

***Minor Disturbance*** **7" EP December 19, 1980 (Dischord 1) (USA)**

Singer Ian MacKaye's first band and the legendary Dischord label's first release. The iconic cover features Xs on the hands of Ian's younger brother Alec (singer in the Washington, D.C., bands the Untouchables and later the Faith). The X's were to show someone was under the legal drinking age but still able to attend punk concerts. In "Minor Disturbance" and "Teen Idles" the band criticizes not being able to attend concerts because they are underage.

This EP helped shape hardcore punk with eight songs in less than 10 minutes. It's also a fascinating time capsule of the major issues in the punk scene at the time. "Fleeting Fury" laments the decline of British punk and by doing so makes a statement of purpose for hardcore punk. "Fiorucci Nightmare" criticizes superficial fashion. "Get Up and Go" is a defiant song shredding a common disapproval of punks at the time, which is that they weren't good enough musicians. The anti-drug ideas that would make up the straight edge movement are in "Sneakers" and "Deadhead," the latter a condemnation of the Grateful Dead, perhaps the band most associated with drug use. After the band broke up, MacKaye took hardcore even further with Minor Threat, one of hardcore punk's greatest bands.

**Genre:** Hardcore Punk

## Teenage Film Stars

**"Odd Man Out" 45 April 17, 1980 (Wessex WEX 275) (UK)**

Members of Television Personalities release a Madness-like pop ska song. Features an infectious repetitious saxophone riff, and some driving percussion accents. Rereleased a few months later on the Blueprint label.

**Genre:** Ska

## Teenage Jesus and the Jerks

**"Orphans" b/w "Less of Me" 45 (Migraine CC-333) April 25, 1978 (USA)**

Along with Glenn Branca's records, Teenage Jesus probably made the most influential records of the no wave movement. This single laid the groundwork for going beyond post-punk guitar into something more dissonant and anti-rock that would later influence noise rock. As with other no wave music, it reduces songs to basic components. Here it's a guitar that at times sounds like it's shredding, a throbbing bass, tribal-like percussion, and Lydia Lunch's primal vocals. "Orphans," with its frightening imagery, is almost horror rock, while "Less of Me" is more literary-like in its lyrics. A colossal debut single in this band's all-too-short career.

**"Baby Doll" b/w "Freud in Flop" and "Race Mixing" 45 March 1979 (Migraine CC-334) (USA)**

Like their first single, "Orphans," "Baby Doll" is a horror-like disturbing song about something that sounds violent happening to someone vulnerable. The dirge-like beat makes this all sound ominous. The two instrumentals on the B-side are short bursts of energy that sound like what noise rock grew out of. Also check out the tracks by Teenage Jesus on the *No New York* compilation; these are the only other songs this band released during this era.

**Genre:** No Wave

## Television

*Marquee Moon* **LP February 8, 1977 (Elektra 7E-1098) (USA)**

At the time some critics thought Television was not a part of the punk movement because their songs were longer and sometimes improvisational. But the band was ahead of its time in showing how flexible the post-punk genre would be and how an album can be a kind of spiritual journey with self-examination and awareness of life's insights and mystical experiences.

From beginning to end the album shows different spiritual states, starting with "See No Evil," with its lack of consciousness the narrator has about what he is doing wrong. "Venus de Milo" is a kind of mystical adventure though urban life. "Marquee Moon" is a 10-minute opus with the narrator recalling different experiences that shifted his consciousness. Musically, the dueling guitars of Tom Verlaine and Richard Lloyd accentuate those changes that almost seem like mystical encounters.

"Guiding Light" shaped the style for their second album, *Adventure*, with its more subdued and melodic structure about some force leading him thorough the dark nights. "Prove It" is a plea for facts to solve his spiritual crisis and for something knowable to hang on to. It ends with "Torn Curtain," a metaphor for something being ripped to glimpse another state of being.

*Adventure* **LP April 7, 1978 (Elektra 6E-133) (USA)**

The jagged edges from the first album are largely gone, with the exception of "Foxhole." While not as innovative as *Marquee Moon*, the album takes a direction into a more melodic post-punk. This would have a tremendous influence on indie rock/alternative rock in the 1980s that also divorced itself from the more challenging and experimental forms of post-punk.

Like *Marquee Moon*'s "Guiding Light," there's a quality of mysticism and transcendentalism to some of the songs. Perhaps the influence is some of the Velvet Underground's music (particularly their third album), but Television creates their own melodic post-punk structure. The album starts with "Glory," with a hope for something transcendental. It's followed by "Days," which is perhaps the Television song with the loveliest melody. There's a beauty to "Days" and other songs on *Adventure* that shatters the idea that post-punk is angry or cold. A sense of quiet beauty and transcendence is also in "Carried Away." There's not the barrage of images there was in *Marquee Moon*, but there's still a mysteriousness on the concluding "The Dream's Dream."

**Genre:** Post-punk

## Television Personalities

### *Where's Bill Grundy Now?* 7" EP November 1978 (Kings Road none) (UK)

A genuine relic from the initial punk era with many contemporary references satirizing early punk culture. The title track seems to be sympathetic to the TV host Bill Grundy, who conducted the notorious Sex Pistols TV interview that resulted in obscenities being broadcast on live TV, one of the most notorious events in early punk history. "Happy Families" imagines punks as older parents living a more conventional life. The best-known song is "Part Time Punks," which, like "Posing at the Roundhouse," sees punk fashion as an ornament and costume and implies that punks may not be living out their ideals.

### *And Don't the Kids Just Love It* LP March 7, 1981 (Rough Trade ROUGH 24) (UK)

There's some 1960s imagery on the album cover, which features 1960s stars Twiggy and Patrick Macnee (the latter from the TV show *The Avengers*). But the band refuses to make their sound retro. There's some 1960s influence, such as the surf guitar of "Diary of a Young Man," which they blend with the post-punk affection for spoken word over music. Other songs take 1960s British pop and run it through a post-punk shredder while still maintaining a sense of melody. It's a cross between minimalist pop punk and minimalist post-punk. They use experimentation and unconventional post-punk structures such as a bass substituting for a lead guitar in "This Angry Silence" and "The Glittering Prizes."

There's a sense of melancholy to the album, of people not finding their place. "This Angry Silence" describes a dysfunctional household, unrequited love, and fear of crime. Other songs are character portraits, like the infectious "The Glittering Prizes," about a repressed office worker who hopes for something better, or "La Grand Illusion," about a sad-looking girl. It ends with "Look Back in Anger," where the singer is regretful and angry. It seems to sum up everything that came before it in this album. Something is wrong with the stories of characters in these songs, and anger is a proper response to inhuman conditions.

**Genre:** Post-punk

## Theatre of Hate

### "Do You Believe in the Westworld?" b/w "Propaganda" 45 December 9, 1981 (Burning Rome TOH 1) (UK)

Propelled by a marching drumbeat and produced by the Clash's Mick Jones, this is like a post-punk spaghetti Western with near dystopian imagery of a disillusioned cowboy. Could it all be a metaphor for the collapse of Western ideals? The flip side compares Nazi propaganda to current propaganda and is nearly more punk than post-punk.

**Genre:** Post-punk

## Theoretical Girls

### "U.S. Millie" b/w "You Got Me" 45 September 1978 (Theoretical Girls none) (USA)

The only record from the band featuring Glenn Branca, the seminal experimental guitarist known for alternative tunings and other guitar techniques that became central to no wave and noise rock. The A-side is a delightful experimental march. The B-side is as no wave as it gets, with dirty guitar, industrial lashing sounds, and tribal drums. The guitar parts are revelatory.

**Genre:** No Wave

## This Heat

### *Deceit* LP October 4, 1981 (Rough Trade ROUGH 26) (UK)

On their previous album, *This Heat*, this English band was much more experimental than post-punk. But the album is mostly filled with structured songs, not just avant-garde experiments of tones and sounds. This is a landmark album for showing how experimental music can be integrated into post-punk.

The vocals are sometimes more a religious-like chant than anything resembling standard rock vocals. The album starts with "Sleep," which sounds like an Eastern chant. "Triumph" blends no wave deconstruction, world music, and chant-like vocals. "Shrink Wrap" combines chant, world music, and dub. Everything is up for grabs, such as the opening of the U.S. Declaration of Independence set to a dirge-like beat in "Independence." It sounds like the music of a lost civilization.

"S.P.Q.R." (the title comes from a Latin abbreviation for the Roman Empire) is probably the closest to a standard post-punk song, with ferocious percussion and jittery guitars. "We're all Romans," the band sings, as if imperialism is the norm. It's followed on the album by "Cenotaph," which warns that "history will repeat itself" amid images of nuclear war. The album ends with the disturbing "Suffer Bomb Disease," which imagines the soundtrack to nuclear war.

**Genre:** Post-punk

## Throbbing Gristle

### *20 Jazz Funk Greats* LP December 10, 1979 (Industrial Records IR0008) (UK)

A deceiving title. This is anything but jazz funk. Like other British bands such as 23 Skidoo and This Heat, their first recordings were experimental albums. This album, however, crosses over from purely experimental music into post-punk. And it became one of the defining influences on industrial music. The use of electronic keyboards also had a post-punk sense of urgency and atmosphere, making it far different from how keyboards are used in synth-pop.

Nothing resembles a traditional song structure. It is more like somewhat disturbing ambient music. "Beachy Head" is eerie. "Still Walking" features a pulsating keyboard with spoken word and sound effects that is a precursor to industrial music. The band seems determined to make no song comfortable to listen to. Every song has an underlying tension. The only relief is "Walkabout," an instrumental that sounds like a more conventional krautrock song. When there are words in the songs, they are usually recorded to sound obscure and distant. One song with vocals is "Persuasion,"

which is one of the most disturbing songs of all on this album about a horrifying seduction.
**Genre:** Post-punk

## T.S.O.L.

### *T.S.O.L.* 12" EP March 26, 1981 (Posh Boy PBS-1013) (USA)

This Southern California band gets right to the point in the album's lead track, "Superficial Love," which ends with "Ronald Reagan can shove it." There's a lot of anxiety about the Cold War, the military draft, and American militarism in general. The standout track is "Abolish Government/Silent Majority," with its imperative: "Wake up silent majority!"

Had T.S.O.L. stuck with this sound, they likely would have become one of the great hardcore bands. After this EP, however, the band went in a radically different direction. They became a Goth-influenced horror punk band with a greatly different sound from this brave and energetic record.
**Genre:** Hardcore Punk

## Tuxedomoon

### "No Tears" from *No Tears* 7" EP 1978 (Not on Label none) (USA)

The first three songs on this EP are somewhat interesting, keyboard-driven experiments, but the ending title track goes in a whole other direction. It's a stunning combination of frantic electronic punk and experimental post-punk with a Goth-like feel.

The song is about someone who appears to be immune from his own humanity and emotions: "I feel so hollow I just don't understand, nothing turned out like I planned." To a variation of a march, keyboards, and grinding guitars, the singer sounds on the edge of hysterical despair, realizing that he can no longer cry. Is he emotionally drained? Or does he realize that to survive the misery he must cut himself off from his natural feelings?
**Genre:** Post-punk

## TV Smith's Explorers

### "The Perfect Life" 45 October 9, 1981 (Kaleidoscope KRLA 1590) (UK)

Former member of seminal Brit punk band the Adverts melodramatically combines pop punk and post-punk. Some may say the song's mix and dominant keyboard makes this a bridge too far into new wave. But the song is more consistent with the underrated Adverts' second album, *Cast of Thousands*. There's an immediate desperation and longing in Smith's voice that starts with the line "someday it'll all make sense." Is the song a sincere hope to find better things? Or is it all a satire about expectations? Or some of both?
**Genre:** Pop Punk/Post-punk

## U2

### "11 O'Clock Tick Tock" 45 May 23, 1980 (Island WIP 6601) (UK)

The Edge's guitar gives this song gravitas and is the center of this song. Lyrically the song starts a theme that would continue on the band's first album: a sense of vanishing youth.

### *Boy* LP October 20, 1980 (Island ILPS 9646) (UK)

The members of U2, who at this time were in their late teens or just barely 20, mourn a lost youth on this album. It's somewhat of a spiritual battle against a threat that lies on the other side of innocence when moving from adolescence into early adulthood.

"Out of Control" laments being born into a life filled with chaos where "there's blood at the garden gate" perhaps recalling the Fall in the Garden of Eden. There's a feeling that life itself is too out of control and tumultuous. "Twilight" also depicts the confusion in transitioning into early adulthood between light and dark, where "in the shadow boy meets man." "An Cat Dubh" is about a temptress trying to lure singer Bono further from a state of innocence, but in the end the singer realizes the danger. It segues into "Into the Heart," where it's possible to return to a childlike perspective to receive insight. And as a kind of antidote there's "Stories for Boys," in which the singer receives inspiration from art that provides direction.

At times the album offers some salvation or at least some comfort about reaching young adulthood. In "A Day Without Me" the singer starts to gain some insight by shedding his ego. "I Will Follow" is about an unconditional love that could be either a mother's love for her son or perhaps divine love.

### "Gloria" 45 October 1, 1981 (Island WIP 6733) (UK)

U2's second album, *October*, may be the first modern Christian rock album, long before Christian rock largely turned to praise music. The first track on the album, "Gloria," is a declaration about submitting to a higher power with a chorus in Latin and some tempo shifts that combined both punk and post-punk.

### "A Celebration" 45 March 22, 1982 (Island WIP 6770) (UK)

A single with an energy lacking on most of their second album. Once again it's the Edge's post-punk guitar that propels this song as well as the lyrics, which are almost a punk rock Christian anthem nearly apocalyptic in tone.

### *War* LP February 28, 1983 (Island ILPS 9733) (UK)

After a first album about a loss of innocence and a second album focused on Christian spirituality, for much of this album U2 blends punk and post-punk with an emphasis on the effects of war. It starts with the ominous marching beat of "Sunday Bloody Sunday," about violent strife in Northern Ireland; "Seconds" is about fear of nuclear war; "New Year's Day" was inspired by the Polish Solidarity movement; and "The Refugee" is about a woman apparently forsaken in war by an American soldier and left a refugee. These songs show the personal effect of war on individuals.

For a band that often creates an atmospheric sound, the music on this album is generally rawer to reflect the tension inherent in the song lyrics. "Drowning Man" and "40," however, recall the spiritual qualities of their previous album *October* as well as "Surrender," which is a depiction of fallen people facing spiritual battles. At its best moments, *War* stands out as U2's album with the most punk spirit.

**Genre:** Post-punk

## U.K. Subs

### *Another Kind of Blues* LP September 20, 1979 (GEMLP 100) (UK)

The title of the album is a clue. At times the music sounds like the work of a punk band with its roots in the pub rock of blues and rockabilly doing their own blend of punk and traditional rock genres. So in some ways the album is ahead of its time by integrating some traditional genres with punk as bands like X and the Gun Club later did.

But they explore other genres: traditional punk in "World War," pop punk in "Stranglehold," and even an early hardcore-like sound in "Disease" and an early Oi!-like chorus of "B.I.C." Thematically, despite the musical eclecticism, it's mostly held together by an emphasis on social conditions. A Generation Jones urgency about breaking out of oppression runs throughout. There's a fear of repressive authority in "Killer," "C.I.D.," and "Young Criminals." And as with so many bands in this era, in "World War," the fear of nuclear annihilation arises. "Crash Course" is a critique of the media aimed particularly at privileged journalists, while "I Live in a Car" is about not having a home. Even the pop punk "Tomorrow's Girls" is a story about a girl who isn't "pre-programmed" and wants more than oppressive 9-to-5 jobs.

### *Brand New Age* LP April 8, 1980 (GEMLP 106) (UK)

The production is tightened up from their eclectic first album into a more consistent but compressed sound. Singer Charlie Harper's vocals are mixed down, and the guitar turns into a gritty, Stooges-like garage band sound. Overall, the album is darker and bleaker than their first album. The album slides downhill quickly, though, when they go back to the more traditional rock lyrics in songs like "500 CC" and "Dirty Girls." But, fortunately, that's not much of the album.

The album was released in the early 1980s and, keeping with a Generation Jones perspective, the new decade didn't look much better than the desolate 1970s. "Brand New Age" foresees in the new decade only more surveillance, oppression, and "anonymous people going nowhere." One standout track is "Rat Race," about an oppressive, working-class lifestyle of work and excessive drinking: "If you're hungry you get in the race." The other is "Warhead," with a Joe Strummer–like vocal and some reggae guitar rhythms about several countries getting ready for war. "Bomb Factory" features a similar theme about war preparation around the world. Most of the album contains a coherent political message of social observations, including "Organized Crime," which compares politicians to gangsters.

### "Keep on Running" b/w "Perfect Girl" 45 April 3, 1981 (GEM GEMS 45) (UK)

This combination of punk and pop punk is accessible but still powerful. "Keep on Running" is an urgent declaration to leave limitations in the spirit of traditional punk. "Perfect Girl" shows how this band can write catchy pop punk when they want to.

### *Shake Up the City* 7" EP November 9, 1982 (Abstract Records ABS 012) (UK)

The band takes a turn into a harder-edged, raw, and fast sound in sync with the UK 82 movement. Whether it's called street punk, Oi!, hardcore, or punk, these are three explosive, anthem-like songs. "Self-Destruct" features the urgent chorus of "999 Self-Destruct," "Police State" is a dystopian-like vision of oppression, and "War of the Roses" sounds like the soundtrack to a civil war.

**Genre:** Punk

## The Undead

### "Verbal Abuse" b/w "Misfit" 45 1983 (Post Mortem PM 1002) (USA)

Band featuring former Misfits guitarist Bobby Steele. Both songs unleash anger and revenge against tormentors. "Verbal Abuse" targets a specific person but "Misfit" appears to be aimed at an outside world that views him as "some freak from a menagerie."
**Genre:** Punk

## The Undertones

### *Teenage Kicks* 7" EP September 23, 1978 (Good Vibrations GOT 4) (UK)

The debut EP from this Northern Ireland band takes pop punk in another direction. The title track is slower than the usual Ramones and Buzzcocks foundation that created pop punk. And throughout the EP, the Undertones often are celebratory and joyous without sounding vacuous. "Smarter Than U" is a put-down of an intellectual. "True Confessions" is about someone who puts on a facade, while "Emergency Cases," since it mentions the emergency number in the U.K., may be some kind of social commentary or political song. Or maybe not. It doesn't matter. All in all, a milestone pop punk record.

### "Get Over You" 45 January, 16, 1979 (Sire SIR 4010) (UK)

This goes even more in a pop punk direction with what seems like an unconventional girl with whom the singer is infatuated. The band incorporates a power pop–inspired chorus while still retaining their punk energy. Infectious and exciting punk pop.

### *The Undertones* LP May 5, 1979 (Sire SRK 6071) (UK)

Who says pop punk can't be an art form? Celebratory and subversive at the same time, the band's first album is irresistible. The Undertones take pop conventions and smuggle them into a pop punk structure. "Family Entertainment" features a melodic guitar riff, and there's a simple keyboard part on "Here Comes the Summer" that accents the song. These are small touches but effective ones. They make the songs innovative so they put their own stamp on the pop punk genre.

The Undertones show that pop punk can be subversive by putting lyrics about misfits and outsiders underneath cheerful-sounding pop punk. Both "Jimmy Jimmy" and "(She's a) Runaround" feature tormented and lost souls. There's the sad protagonist in "Jimmy Jimmy," who no one ever listened to and who is ultimately led away in an ambulance. "(She's a) Runaround" is about a woman who is yearning and searching and a hot mess at the same time. "Male Model" switches the gender stereotypes and has a boy wishing he could grow up to be a model. But it's because of a desire to rise above his working-class circumstances to have a job where he doesn't have to wear secondhand clothes. "I Gotta Getta" is the story of people who want more out of life than what their situations provide.

Sometimes people may think this band is dumber than they are and that they never sing about social situations in their Northern Ireland homeland. But pay closer attention and there is dissatisfaction and strife underneath those catchy pop punk melodies.

**"You've Got My Number" 45 September 28, 1979 (Sire SIR 4064) (UK)**

With its "Batman Theme"-like guitar riff leading into an infectious chorus, and a banging piano to end the song, another pop punk masterpiece. The Undertones continue to experiment within the pop punk structure to come up with innovative hooks and touches.

**Hypnotized LP April 18, 1980 (Sire SRK 6088) (UK)**

Somewhat more produced than their first album. But still more inspired pop punk. The lead track, "More Songs About Chocolate and Girls," is apparently a takeoff on the Talking Heads' *More Songs About Buildings and Food*. This shows that the band has an awareness and sense of humor about their pop punk sensibilities. "It's never too late to enjoy dumb entertainment," singer Feargal Sharkey sings.

More enjoyable pop punk is here, including "There Goes Norman," about a man who could have some sinister intentions. And within all the fun there's some class-based anger. "My Perfect Cousin" is a put-down of a college-educated family member who plays the synthesizer and hangs out with the "art school boys." "Whizz Kids" is about successful kids whose prosperous times won't last. But you gotta try to do something. The Undertones outline that in "Hard Luck," which criticizes the lazy who don't try to rise above their situation.

Generally, the songs are more sophisticated than on their first album. But on a few songs it feels like the fun is fading, particularly with "Wednesday Week," which is slower and sounds more like a 1960s-influenced song than punk or pop punk.

**Genre:** Pop Punk

## The Untouchables

**"Tropical Bird" b/w "The General" 45 1983 (Dance Beat DB-102) (USA)**

The A-side from this early American ska band is an instrumental that sounds like an expansion of the experimentation from the second Specials album into a sound that could be called post-ska. Great atmosphere and groove. The B-side is an upbeat, danceable song. And it's fascinating because while it sounds partly like two tone–inspired ska, there's also something different about it that seems to point ahead to 1990s third wave ska.

**Genre:** Ska

## Uproar

***Rebel Youth* 7" EP 1982 (Beat the System RAW1) (UK)**

1982 was an exciting time in British punk for the combination of street punk, Oi! chant choruses, hardcore, and traditional punk that was on the edge of crossover thrash. This reinvigorated punk before many bands crossed over into more polished heavy metal–oriented music. And this Uproar record is one of the best of the era, with the spirit of what the Clash might have sounded like if they started in the UK 82 era.

Side one is more defiant, with the title track and "No War No More," one of the most rousing anti-war songs of this era. Side two features two riveting songs about people trampled and defeated, with "Fallen Angel" and the ending "Victims." the latter with its harrowing realization that "nobody cares, you're all alone." Another overlooked great indie punk record of this era.

**Genre:** Street Punk/Hardcore Punk

## Urban Waste

### *Urban Waste* 7" EP 1982 (Mob-Style MSR2) (USA)

With the Bad Brains as a foundation, this band along with Agnostic Front and Antidote helped create the New York hardcore sound. Urban Waste's debut record brutally chronicles a decaying and early 1980s New York City ravaged with crime and corruption ("Wasted Life," "No Hope," "Police Brutality"). But power comes from the catharsis of embracing being a misunderstood outsider in "Public Opinion" and in the defiant "Reject."

**Genre:** Hardcore Punk

## Various Artists

### *Dance Craze Soundtrack* LP February 14, 1981 (2 Tone CHR TT 5004) (UK)

When the ska movement in England was at its peak in 1980, the most popular ska bands were captured on film for the *Dance Craze* movie. The film's soundtrack contained 15 of the 27 songs in the film. Rather than featuring several songs in a row from each band, there's a mixtape approach. The songs are put together in an order that, like a good mixtape, varies the pace with different styles and tempos. The songs of the six bands featured (the Specials, Madness, the Selecter, the English Beat, the Bodysnatchers, and Bad Manners) all flow together coherently.

And most of these songs are thrilling live. "Concrete Jungle" by the Specials is so fast that it's pretty much punk rock. "One Step Beyond" by Madness races along in almost a punk frenzy. The Bodysnatchers' "So Easy" come mores alive in concert, transcending the studio version, which was perhaps a little too timid and pop-oriented. Along with the Specials' live EP *Too Much Too Young*, this captures the live excitement of the ska craze.

**Genre:** Ska

### *Flex Your Head* LP February 17, 1982 (Dischord 7) (USA)

Collection of Washington, D.C.'s hardcore punk bands on the Dischord label. That includes Ian MacKaye's Teen Idles and Minor Threat, Henry Rollins's S.O.A., and some of Dischord's best bands, like Government Issue and the Void. But also notable for the songs by the Untouchables (Alec MacKaye's first band), Red C, and Deadline, three bands that broke up too soon.

The album transcends so many other sampler albums because it includes songs that are not available anywhere else and there doesn't seem to be any filler. The short, hardcore songs fit the sampler format where songs begin and end quickly. The double album comes across like a mixtape that someone diligently assembled.

The most underrated band may be the short-lived Deadline, who conclude the album with a trilogy of essential songs from this era. Sure, they can play fast and hard, like on "Hear the Cry," but there's also the haunting "Stolen Youth" and the drama and tempo changes of "Aftermath." Other highlights are Artificial Peace's suburban lament, "Wasteland"; Youth Brigade's ferocious "Last Word"; the Untouchables' cathartic sing-along "I Hate You"; and Red C's urgent "Pressure's On," which sounds like the singer's being pursued in a life-and-death battle. Includes some essential cover songs, including Minor Threat's version of Wire's "12xU," the Teen Idle's very fast version of the Stooges' "No Fun," and S.O.A.'s version of the Monkees' "I'm Not Your Steppin' Stone."

**Genre:** Hardcore Punk

***No New York*** **LP December 8, 1978 (Antilles AN-7067) (USA)**

While in New York City between producing albums for Devo and the Talking Heads, producer Brian Eno heard no wave music played live. He was fascinated by this more extreme artistic form of post-punk. So he documented the sound on a compilation album that over the years has come to represent no wave perhaps more than any other record. The album featured four songs each from four bands: the Contortions, Teenage Jesus and the Jerks, Mars, and DNA.

In "Dish It Out," the Contortions are at their fastest, with singer James Chance sounding more like a punk singer, while in "I Can't Stand Myself" he sounds like a no wave variation on James Brown. But the Contortions were an anomaly because they were less deconstructionist in their sound than the other bands on the album. Teenage Jesus and the Jerks, with singer Lydia Lunch on songs like "The Closet," sound more like what became defined as no wave. So does the band Mars on songs like "Helen Fordsdale," with its scat-like, surreal vocals, screechy guitars, and tribal-like drumming. But the most definitive no wave songs are by DNA, who close the album with the album's best song, "Size," with guitarist Arto Lindsay's shredding guitar.

**Genre:** No Wave

***This Is Boston, Not L.A.*** **LP May 1982 (Modern Method Records MM 012) (USA)**

The title track is a 30-second blast of energy that says hardcore punks shouldn't imitate Southern Californian punk. Although Los Angeles area bands earned a lot of attention during the height of hardcore punk, many major U.S. cities featured its own scene with distinct bands and variations on hardcore. *This Is Boston, Not L.A.* captures seven Boston hardcore bands during what may have been the height of hardcore in 1982.

The album starts with six songs from Jerry's Kids, one of Boston's best-known hardcore bands. Many of the songs are at a breakneck pace, featuring lots of angst, including "Desperate," with its ominous plea to "let me out," and the ultrafast "I Don't Wanna." Songs by the Proletariat are slower, with almost an English punk sensibility of Crass and the post-punk fury of the Gang of Four. There are seven songs by Gang Green, including songs, like "I Don't Know" and "Narrow Mind," that are about as frenzied fast as hardcore gets. The album concludes with eight songs by the Freeze, leading up to the ending "This Is Boston, Not L.A." Like the Proletariat, their songs are more varied. There's satire in "Idiots at Happy Hour," a spoken-word vocal in "It's Only Alcohol." In perhaps the best song, "Time Bomb," after being "bored of boredom" the singer is about to do his own variation on detonation.

**Genre:** Hardcore Punk

# Varukers

***I Don't Wanna Be a Victim*** **7" EP June 1982 (Inferno HELL 4) (UK)**

Like Discharge, this British band is linked with the D–Beat genre with its pounding drums and heavy metal influences. Although the Varukers use the dirty-sounding heavy metal guitar like Discharge, the chorus of "I Don't Wanna Be a Victim" is based on melodic punk. The lyrics are deeply political, although the resistance here is more of a call to arms and less dark than Discharge generally is. The compressed production makes this sound appealingly garage rock and raw.

**Genre:** Hardcore Punk

## Tom Verlaine

### *Tom Verlaine* LP August 30, 1979 (Elektra 6E-216) (USA)

Verlaine wrote some of these songs when he was in the band Television. In some ways, his debut solo album is a successful extension of Television. In other ways, it goes into other territory. Overall, it's a strong album, but he uses a variety of approaches, some of which work better than others.

The songs originally written for Television are some of the best, particularly the ending three songs, which form a kind of trilogy. "Red Leaves" features some of the jagged feel of Television coupled with lyrics about a mystical-like encounter. The melodic and beautiful "Last Night" sounds like it could be from Television's second album, *Adventure*. "Breakin' in My Heart" features Ricky Wilson of the B-52s with driving guitar rhythm and a searing emotional guitar solo.

Verlaine also tries to break into a new direction from Television. "Yonki Time" is spoken word over music with a kind of shuffling beat. "Mr. Bingo" reaches into both blues and funk. "Souvenir from a Dream" features a catchy piano riff. "Kingdom Come," which David Bowie later covered on *Scary Monsters*, is about a kind of imprisonment but hope for deliverance. Overall, the album shows how there can be a quieter kind of post-punk.

**Genre:** Post-punk

## Vice Squad

### *Last Rockers* 7" EP January 20, 1981 (Riot City Records RIOT 1) (UK)

Blistering debut EP from British punk band led by singer Beki Bondage. It starts with the disillusionment of "Living on Dreams," which is perhaps a condemnation of the hippie idealism about revolution and systemic change. There's sarcasm about perverse and disconnected sex in "Latex Love." It culminates in the epic title track. It's a grim and terrifying apocalyptic view of nuclear war in which "politicians do the thing no God can forgive." At points in the song there's an ominous Gregorian chant–like background over the driving beat.

**Genre:** Punk

## Virgin Prunes

### "Moments and Mine" 45 June 27, 1981 (Rough Trade RT 72) (UK)

A stream-of-consciousness narration that alternates between two different voices. In some ways it sounds like an identity crisis that ends in confusion and indecision. Like some of this band's other music, there's a near theatrical quality blending with post-punk.

### "Pagan Love Song" 45 May 3, 1982 (Rough Trade RT 106) (UK)

Sometimes this Irish band's music was experimental, sometimes in the direction of new wave, sometimes almost theatrical. But here, the band finds a groove that puts them into Goth-influenced post-punk. But no gloomy voice from singer Gavin Friday. It's a theatrical frightening vocal with horror elements.

**Genre:** Post-punk

## The Void

***The Void*** **split LP September 10, 1982 (Dischord 008) (USA)**

From the opening guitar sounds of "Who Are You?" we're not just in standard hardcore punk territory anymore. There's a thicker, sludgier, more heavy metal–sounding guitar with some hard rock screeches at times. But the Void's songs are often fast like hardcore punk with an anguished vocal. This is one of the seminal albums in the evolution of the merger of hardcore punk and heavy metal. The pace of the songs and the vocal delivery are similar to hardcore, but the heavy guitar injects a more hard rock sound. And at times the vocals have a strained sound that would later become associated with some crossover thrash.

The album starts with the frenzied "Who Are You?" which is an ominous introduction about being misunderstood and ignored. And the songs feature many themes that preoccupied Generation Jones and hardcore punk. "Ignorant People" is about someone who has sold out: "You ... prostituted your mind, now you don't control yourself." "Ask Them Why" and "My Rules" are both about questioning authority and finding an authentic self outside of what society dictates as the norm.

But there is some preoccupation with violence, horror, and death, which are heavy metal tropes that would become a staple in crossover thrash. "Time to Die" is essentially a horror punk song about a person who wants to be a serial killer. "War Hero" is an anti-military song but from the viewpoint of a soldier who wants to kill. "Condensed Flesh" is about the Holocaust and focuses on the brutal physical terrors of the victims. The other side of this split album features songs by the band the Faith.

**Genre:** Hardcore Punk

## The Waitresses

***Wasn't Tomorrow Wonderful?*** **LP January 13, 1982 (Polydor PD-1-6346) (USA)**

This Ohio band is usually written off as a quirky new wave band. But they were an offshoot of post-punk, albeit a more accessible one. But as catchy as their songs are, there's often something unsettling about the music, particularly the post-punk guitar and the screeching saxophone that was the antithesis of the 1980s smooth pop saxophone.

Aside from the near novelty song "I Know What Boys Like," their first album shows how to take some of the experimental elements of post-punk and put them into a more pop format. But what's distinctive about the Waitresses is singer Patty Donahue. Her vocal delivery alternates between playfulness, sarcasm, defiance, and self-empowerment in a singing style called sprechgesang, a cross between singing and speaking used by some post-punkers, including Fred Schneider of the B-52s, Mark E. Smith of the Fall, and Kim Gordon of Sonic Youth. Other bands used it occasionally or weaved it in with other vocals, but Donahue utilized it in a way that became the band's trademark.

Donahue also subverts clichés about topics that female singers used at the time. The album starts with "No Guilt," which subverts the breakup song genre so embedded in pop music. "I'm sorry but I didn't get suicidal, it wasn't the end of the world!" she gleefully says. In "Go On," Donahue outlines the neuroticism associated with romance and ends with Samuel Beckett's famous line "I can't go on, I'll go on." The album ends with the its most unconventional song, "Jimmy Tomorrow," which to the sound of eerie organ, scratching guitar, sound effects, and discordant saxophone features Donahue's stream-of-consciousness confessional monologue about trying to adjust to feeling disillusioned that climaxes in "I guess I set impossible goals and I don't know when to quit" before explosive choruses that ask her if she has found any solutions.

**Genre:** Post-punk

## The Wake

### *Harmony* LP December 21, 1982 (Factory FACT 60) (UK)

Factory Records created a distinctive industrial-laced post-punk sound that has become associated with Joy Division. Those production textures are on this album. But the Wake deserves better than being called a watered-down Joy Division. This Scottish band (containing one former member of Altered Images) expresses their own dark and inquisitive vision.

However, like Joy Division, the music is immersed in an existential and spiritual crisis. This starts with the ominous opening track, "Judas," about a disillusioning betrayal that carries through to the explosive "Testament," with its refrain of "every day we pray for lost and lonely souls." The rest of the album continues this journey of attempting to find epiphanies within uncertainty that culminates in "Immaculate Conception." Is it a rejection of the spiritual quest he's pursued through the album? Or is he withdrawing from the world so he can continue the journey?

**Genre:** Post-punk

## The Wall

### "Ghetto" 45 August 12, 1980 (Fresh Records FRESH 17) (UK)

Righteous Brit punk in the spirit of the Clash and Stiff Little Fingers. A driving, military-like marching beat propels this song. And then an ominous chorus with the words "ghetto, barbed wire!"

**Genre:** Punk

## The Weirdos

### "We Got the Neutron Bomb" b/w "Solitary Confinement" 45 March 17, 1978 (Dangerhouse SP-1063) (USA)

The punk generation grew up in the Cold War. That meant living with the fear of nuclear war. This Los Angeles band released this song about a bomb that reportedly killed humans but spared buildings. The B-side is a driving song about alienation.

### *Who? What? When? Where? Why?* 12" EP September 22, 1979 (Bomp W3 BLP-4007) (UK)

An influential EP because it moves beyond the basic punk sound into showing other possibilities for the punk genre. The highlight is probably the first track, "Happy People," a subversive punk pop song that conveys what punks felt: people who were too happy would just torment them for their realism. But those people aren't really happy because they're "ravaged by desire."

The band shows other variations for punk with the psychobilly of "Jungle Rock"; some horror punk riffs and even heavy metals riffs on "Hit Man"; the slowed-down punk in "Idle Life"; and the satire in "Fort USA," which sounds like a gateway to hardcore punk.

**Genre:** Punk

# The Wipers

### *Is This Real?* LP February 22, 1980 (Park Avenue Records P.A. 82801) (USA)

There are many underrated bands in this era, but the Wipers from Portland, Oregon, are perhaps the most overlooked band of all. Because they weren't from the punk centers of New York City, Southern California, or major U.K. cities, they came up with their own version of punk music. In many ways it was the link between punk and grunge, which would take off in another Pacific Northwest city, Seattle. The seeds of grunge are in the guitar sound, the song structures, and the vocal delivery. In an homage to the influence of the Wipers, Nirvana covered "D-7" and "Return of the Rat" from this album. But unfortunately, the association with Nirvana perhaps defines them too much as the major influence on grunge rather than a great band in their own right.

Their debut album is their most varied. There's even some garage band–influenced pop punk with "Mystery" and on the title track. But what would be this band's trademark would be the driving guitars on songs like "Tragedy" and "Don't Know Who I Am." Although the album starts with "Return of the Rat," which could be a song about the rising conservatism that came with the election of Ronald Reagan, a lot of the album is the pain of being an outsider and feeling alienated from society. "Invasion from the outside works its way inward," Greg Sage sings in "Window Shop for Love." "Don't Know Who I Am" is about an identity crisis. By the ending track, "Wait a Minute," there is a pause for reflection and questioning with a refrain of "wait a minute" but still a realization of the pain of being an outsider. This is a monumental debut that conveys a confidence that the band could do just about anything.

### *Youth of America* LP November 11, 1981 (Park Avenue Records PA 82802) (UK)

For their second album, the Wipers modify their sound to a punk/post-punk hybrid. There's a more compressed production. And the songs are longer. There are just six songs on the entire album. And there are sections in many of these songs with more complex structures consistent with post-punk. It's an even more penetrating worldview of contemporary conditions than their first album and an almost nightmarish view of living in contemporary America.

Frustration with social conditions is in the album's first track, "Taking So Long," with its repeated refrain "it's taking so long!" "Can This Be" features the driving guitar the band is best known for and sounds most like their first album. But it's similar in its frustration and confusion about life not changing for the better. The six-minute, mostly instrumental "When It's Over" is a ferocious, apocalyptic-like vision where life is like "living in the void but the void grows colder."

The idea of a broken contemporary America that oppresses young people concludes with the epic 10-minute title track. If there was a midpoint between the Velvet Underground and Sonic Youth, this song is it. The long instrumental passage in the song is a precursor of noise punk. The song is the band's magnum opus, a stunning post-punk epic about how life in America for young people is about "living in the jungle, fighting for survival."

### *Over the Edge* LP February 28, 1983 (Brain Eater EATER 2) (USA)

The Wipers' most musically consistent album is a portrayal of young American life. There's a sense of the dark side of America and of human nature in general. The album's opening song, "Over the Edge," sets a tone of being at the breaking point where "you take and never give, makes it so hard to live." What the singer sees triggers questions about the meaning of life itself in "What Is" and "Now Is the Time," where there is the repetition of "now is the time, where is the truth?" as if all of life comes down to this central question. There are songs about the limitations of living in oppressive circumstances, such as "Doom Town" and "Romeo," the latter with its driving beat about a film noir–like search through city streets on a futile search for love. The loneliness of feeling like an outsider is in "No One Wants an Alien," in which singer Greg Sage says he's "dreaming of a place far away" because he feels like a stray animal where he lives.

That sense of loneliness reaches its peak in the only slow song on the album, "The Lonely One." But the album ends with the most optimistic song, "This Time," which asks a haunting question: "Don't you feel the things you miss?" The album concludes with the energy to make things different and that somehow life will change. There's something that feels so monumental and important about this album. It feels like listening to it regularly could change your life—or at least change the way you view the world.

**Genre:** Punk/Post-punk

## Wire

### *Pink Flag* LP November 28, 1977 (Harvest SHSP 4076) (UK)

The variety of songs and song structures create a blueprint of the shape of punk, hardcore, and post-punk to come. Of all the major albums from 1977, *Pink Flag* perhaps looks most to future musical trends. The songs are largely bursts of energy, with only six of the 21 songs over two minutes long.

"Mr. Suit" may not be a full-fledged hardcore punk song, but it certainly contains the seeds of the genre with its vocal delivery, call-and-response, and syncopated structure. Some of the other shorter songs also sound like the future of hardcore, including "12XU," which Minor Threat later covered. "Reuters" and "Pink Flag" are slowed-down punk that predate the slower punk of Flipper. "Lowdown" and "Strange" point to post-punk, "106 Beats That" sounds like a synthesis of punk and coming post-punk, "Ex-Lion Tamer" is melodic punk, and "Fragile" and "Mannequin" show a pop sensibility that points beyond pop punk to indie pop.

For some of the album there's the social commentary consistent with British 1977 punk. As with other punk bands, one target is the media. "Reuters" is a narrative of a news correspondent who reports seeing atrocities, while "Ex-Lion Tamer" is about TV viewers being susceptible to TV heroes like the Lone Ranger. "Mannequin" is directed at what appears to be a model or perhaps someone fashionable. "Mr. Suit" is an angry song targeted at an establishment figure.

### "Dot Dash" b/w "Options R" 45 June 23, 1978 (Harvest HAR 5161) (UK)

The A-side is melodic pop punk paradise far superior to the pop of *Chairs Missing*'s "Outdoor Miner," a minor hit for the band in the U.K. that was all too psychedelic pop. The B-side, with its punk-meets–Velvet Underground guitars, is another gem. This could have been a whole other direction the band could have gone in. But they devoted their second and third albums largely to post-punk.

### *Chairs Missing* LP September 8, 1978 (Harvest SHSP 4093) (UK)

From the nervous, jerky guitars and primal percussion that starts the album, this is far different territory from their first album. The pace is generally slower with layers of complexity. There are no more ultrashort blasts of energy. Instead, there are more developed and experimental songs. And like other post-punk to come, there's a turn away from the overtly political and social commentary to the personal and the more artistic. Or more like anything goes. There's everything from the story of a shipwreck ("Marooned") to a song about the actress Sarah Bernhardt ("Practice Makes Perfect").

Even the songs that could be socially conscious are more open to interpretation, such as "I Am the Fly." What does the fly represent? This is the ambiguity that would often come from post-punk rather than the directness of punk lyrics. "Men 2nd" and the eerie "Marooned" also are complex, with both containing lyrics that could be symbolism for being lost. Similarly, the sea imagery of "Being Sucked in Again" can also not be taken literally and instead could represent the pain of being adrift. But it's followed by "Heartbeat," which is a feeling of transcendence with more sea imagery.

There are other songs that aren't so experimental. There's the punky "Sand in My Joints"; the melodic pop of "Outdoor Miner"; and the closing track, "Too Late," an explosive combination of Velvet Underground meets punk and post-punk that even points a little to noise punk. It shows this band could be ferocious if they wanted to be. But they were more interested in experimenting and seeing where they could take the post-punk genre.

### "A Question of Degree" 45 June 2, 1979 (Harvest HAR 5187) (UK)

Between *Chairs Missing* and *154*, the band releases a brilliant and catchy post-punk single. Despite its infectious melody, there's an ominous atmosphere concluding with the menacing chant of "Can I?" before collapsing into a driving guitar sound.

### *154* LP September 23, 1979 (Harvest SHSP 4105) (UK)

As *Chairs Missing* was so different from *Pink Flag*, *154* goes in even another direction. But not without a few exceptions. As with *Chairs Missing*, there are some tracks that recall the band's energetic first album. The ferocious "Two People in a Room" is nervous post-punk with a deep sense of foreboding driven by a simple but effective guitar line. "The 15th" and "Map Ref. 41N 93W" show how post-punk can merge with pop.

But the center of the album goes beyond *Chairs Missing* into even more experimentation, stretching the definition of post-punk and even adding keyboards at times, which provides a sense of disorientation and melancholy. "The Other Window" and "Indirect Enquiries" integrate narration into the post-punk sound. Both are disturbing songs, with the narrator in "The Other Window" seeing brutality from a train window while "Indirect Enquiries" features a chant of "you'd been defaced" with a cacophony of unsettling sounds at the end.

"I Should Have Known Better" has almost an industrial-like sound, while "On Returning" is an adventurous song that combines industrial, post-punk, and avant-garde keyboard music. "Once Is Enough" is a raw, industrial-influenced post-punk song, while "A Touching Display" and "40 Versions" point to synthesizer-driven, avant-garde post-punk.

### "Our Swimmer" 45 May 26, 1981 (Rough Trade RT 079) (UK)

Catchy post-punk with some pop elements propelled by a melodic bass line. The lyrics are about a swimmer who is graceful and feels like he was born to do it. But he's still not getting where he wants. A metaphor for those of us struggling to do what we feel like we're destined to do? Or is it about an unhealthy obsession? Or something else entirely? It's a strength of this band and post-punk that it's open to interpretation.

**Genre:** Punk/Post-punk

## Jah Wobble

### "Betrayal" 45 April 15, 1980 (Virgin VS 337) (UK)

Public Image Ltd. bassist solo song released after his departure from the band is essentially a rant about an unfaithful relationship. But it's all over a ferocious post-punk swirl of sounds. That includes a dramatic guitar accenting the chorus, a spooky synthesizer laced over top, Wobble's innovative bass playing, and a beat that combines funk and reggae.

**Genre:** Post-punk

## X

### *Los Angeles* LP April 26, 1980 (Slash SR-104) (USA)

One of punk's most important debuts depicts the dark side of Southern California. While there was so much attention at decaying New York City in this era, it's clear there's something wrong on the West Coast too. *Los Angeles* is a tour of the myth of California as a place of opportunity and peace. Instead, it shows the failure of the American Dream. Perhaps more than any other California punk album, *Los Angeles* redefined California music both musically and lyrically. We're no longer in the world of the Beach Boys and the Eagles.

The album redefines California as filled with crime, poverty, and drugs. Rather than call for revolution or change as some British punk did, it's about detailing the sordid life of the city. Side one starts with "Your Phone's Off the Hook, But You're Not," which outlines crime; "Johnny Hit and Run Pauline" is about a rapist; "Sugarlight" is about heroin; and "Nausea" is a gritty depiction of a hangover that comes from alcohol and not being able to escape poverty. It's all a grim view of urban life.

Side two starts with "Los Angeles," which is about someone who flees the city in what at the time was called "white flight" away from urban centers. There's the decadence of the upper class that uses the lowers classes for pleasure or exploitation in "Sex and Dying in High Society." "Unheard Music" is another Generation Jones–era song about the blandness and escapist quality to songs on mainstream radio. It ends with "The World's a Mess, It's in My Kiss" with a declaration that "nothing is united, and all things are untied." There is no resolution to the problems. There's a fatalism here that would be a part of California punk music.

### *Wild Gift* LP May 4, 1981 (Slash SR-107) (USA)

X is at their punkiest in the Generation Jones anthem-like "We're Desperate." It's about the tyranny of landlords and being so poor that it requires moving and feeling that home can be obliterated at any time. But it also captures a general feeling of the time of the desolation of downtrodden urban living. There are also some shorter songs that are fast-paced, punk-inspired songs, such as "I'm Coming Over" and "Back 2 the Base."

But for the majority of the album the band goes beyond the basic punk sound of *Los Angeles* into integrating other musical forms, particularly rockabilly and country. Billy Zoom's guitar and the harmonies of Exene Cervenka and John Doe are arguably the basis for what came to be called cowpunk or country punk. "Beyond and Back," with its train-like drum rhythm and twangy guitar, perhaps shows this best. "It's Who You Know" also innovatively blends punk and a rockabilly drum rhythm.

Most of the album also lyrically shifts from the gritty social observations of Los Angeles into songs about relationships. Their remake of their indie single "Adult Books" and songs like "When Our Love Passed Out on the Couch" and "White Girl" show people either fumbling through relationships, trying to figure them out, or discouraged by them.

### *Under the Big Black Sun* LP June 30, 1982 (Elektra 60150) (USA)

The album cover looks like it could be from a film noir movie. If film noir characters could have been in a punk band, they would likely have sounded like X. One of the album's major threads is a film noir–like journey through the dark side of American life. Also, singer Exene Cervenka's sister died in a car crash a couple of years earlier. The band decided to address that on this album. So there's a theme of death and loss. But within this darkness is probably their most emotional and strongest record.

The album starts with almost apocalyptic imagery of a deadly wolf on the prowl in "The Hungry Wolf," with an ominous guitar and tribal-like drumming. It sets the tone of the album as taking place in a vicious predatory world. On side two, "Real Child of Hell" depicts down-and-out struggling characters. The album ends with "The Have Nots," an ode to the proletariat in which "dawn comes soon enough for the working class." The song name-checks renowned working-class bars in Southern California and around the country: "Here we sit, a shot and a beer after another hard-earned day."

Exene wrote about her sister in several songs. In "Riding with Mary" there's the line "remember my sister was in a car," "Come Back to Me" is a torch-like song about missing someone, and "Dancing with Tears in My Eyes" is a countryish cover song also about the pain of missing someone. "Under the Big Black Sun" combines the two themes of film noir–like images of city life with death, including this ominous line: "Mary's dead, good morning midnight."

### *More Fun in the New World* LP September 30, 1983 (USA)

One of the great albums in the form of post-punk that incorporates other genres while keeping the punk spirit. On *More Fun*, punk blends with American roots music including blues, R&B, rockabilly, and country. X sometimes still effectively does their trademark combination of punk, hardcore punk, and a touch of rockabilly in songs like "Devil Doll," "Make the Music Go Bang," and "I See Red." And they do a punk rockabilly fusion in their cover of the Jerry Lee Lewis song "Breathless."

The rest of the album, however, contains variations on the punk sound. The march-like "The New World" is about Generation Jones disillusionment with the result of deindustrialization. The band calls out the ruin of cities such as Flint, Michigan; Gary, Indiana; and Mobile, Alabama. The contemplative "I Must Not Think Bad Thoughts" condemns the new wave played on the radio as "glitter disco synthesizer" music while name-checking bands that aren't played, including the Minutemen, Black Flag, and D.O.A. "True Love" is almost pop punk. "True Love Pt. 2" features an R&B groove with the band reciting lines from songs including folk songs, Elvis Presley, Tammy Wynette, and Curtis Mayfield. This shows that X sees themselves in the tradition of folk, rock, and R&B pioneers and not limited by the labels of punk. *More Fun in the New World* is their most accessible album while still maintaining their punk edge.

**Genre:** Punk/Post-punk

## Xmal Deutschland

### "Schwarze Welt" ("Black World") 45 July 21, 1981 (Zickzack 31) (Germany)

Although it's sung in German, the music helps convey what the lyrics mean. The combination of German electronica, industrial music, and post-punk angst reflect the song's emphasis on a black world filled with black fog and black hearts. It's both ominous and infectious.

### *Incubus Succubus* 12" EP May 26, 1982 (Zickzack ZZ 110) (Germany)

Seminal EP in the Goth subgenre of post-punk. On "Schwarze Welt," the band hit on a distinctive combination of electronica, industrial, and post-punk. Here, they intensify the industrial element with lots of Goth imagery (within the German lyrics) about demonic forces preying on sleeping women. Even if you don't understand the words, the music conveys the sinister content of the lyrics. "Zu Jung Zu Alt" is about a force granting death as a blessing because it alleviates earthly suffering. Death also is a theme in the fast-paced "Blut Ist Liebe."

### *Fetisch* LP April 11, 1983 (4AD CAD 302) (UK)

Intoxicating and danceable. It shows that not all Goth post-punk is slow-paced and gloomy. Singer Anja Huwe's vocal delivery sounds like someone in a trance who can lure you into that state too. There's a juxtaposition between the supernatural-fueled horror imagery in her German words and the music, which often combines post-punk, Goth, and early industrial music.

The opening track, "Qual" ("Agony"), became an international dance hit when released on a 12-inch. But the lyrics are sung from the point of view or either a vampire or death itself. "Geheimnis" ("Secret") is about some kind of person or force that takes pleasure in inflicting violence. Even when talking about the power of love in "Boomerang" it's described as both a wild adventure and something entrapping. "Danthem" slows down the pace into a kind of dirge for the fate of young people with some military-like music effects. But it's not necessary to understand the lyrics. This album is essential for the music.

**Genre:** Post-punk

## X-Ray Spex

### "Oh Bondage Up Yours" b/w "I Am a Cliché" 45 September 30, 1977 (Virgin VS 189) (UK)

Explosive debut single uses S&M imagery on the A-side to illustrate the idea of exploitation in general. Singer Poly Styrene was reportedly inspired to write it after seeing a pair of bondage trousers and saw it as a metaphor for other types of exploitation and entrapment. The flip side is not only about boredom but also how conformity makes people lose their identity.

Styrene, a mixed-race young woman just out of her teens who wore braces, defied conventions of what a lead singer of a band could be. And also defying expectations of bands with female singers, there were no songs about romantic relationships. The single also contained some innovative saxophone that made their sound at the time somewhat distinctive.

**"Age" (B-side of "Germfree Adolescents") 45 October 27, 1978 (EMI INT 573) (UK)**

A song about how women are not just commodified by their appearance but how aging destroys women's self-identity, at least by society's standards. "You know it's a million-dollar fear if lines creep in over here," singer Poly Styrene sings.

***Germfree Adolescents*** **LP November 16, 1978 (EMI INS 3023) (UK)**

Singer Poly Styrene confronts the oppression of consumer culture among other topics on X-Ray Spex's landmark 1978 album *Germfree Adolescents*. This made her one of the most important singers in the Generation Jones punk era (Mirrorpix/Everett Collection).

Like the Sex Pistols, this band came and went quickly with one album. It wasn't the cultural earthquake *Never Mind the Bollocks* was. But what an album. Many of these songs are about how identity and personality are damaged and altered by the oppression inherent in exploitative capitalism.

In "I Live Off of You," life is defined primarily by oppression and exploitation. Consumerism is a major theme in songs such as "Art-I-Ficial," in which the singer confesses she has been molded and fragmented by consumerism. "Identity" goes further, saying that people's self-identity is damaged by media images. "Plastic Bag" confronts not only the exploitation in advertising but also how it produces apathy about what really matters. In "I Can't Do Anything" a person is so oppressed they are rendered helpless.

"Germ Free Adolescents" slows down the pace with a song about a woman who tries to scrub away all that's unacceptable, while there's a warning of science going wrong in "Genetic Engineering."

As an antidote to the oppression, "Let's Submerge" is a call to go "down to the underground" of punk rock with Richard Hell name-checked. But "I Am a Poseur" condemns those who are into the fashion of punk and just want attention rather than being truly liberated. Image consciousness and fraud can invade anything, even the punk music scene.

**Genre:** Punk

# XTC

### 3D 12" EP October 7, 1977 (Virgin VS 18812) (UK)

Quirky debut record from a band that would go on to influence the future of both pop punk and post-punk. In the same spirit as other 1977 British bands, there's a declaration that this is a different age and the lingering 1960s cultural influence must go to make way for the new. "She's So Square" ridicules a girl who dresses like she's from the psychedelic era and listens to Vanilla Fudge and the Yardbirds. They also ridicule contemporary disco and funk in "Dance Band."

### *White Music* LP January 20, 1978 (Virgin V 2095) (UK)

XTC's first album is important because it's punk-influenced pop different from the pop punk of the Ramones, Buzzcocks, and Undertones. Because there's prominent use of keyboards without the guitars mixed high, XTC may have influenced the non-punk radio-friendly pop of new wave. But like Blondie, they go beyond the Ramones buzz saw guitar to create a kind of new pop influenced by the punk spirit.

But the band also has early post-punk qualities. The manic "Cross Wires" with its wild syncopation, "Do What You Do," and "Neon Shuffle" sound like demented rockabilly songs run through a post-punk pop shredder. "Spinning Top" features a funk groove with post-punk syncopation that would become a widespread technique in post-punk. But the album captures some of the major targets of punk. "Radios in Motion" is about the inertia of the radio, where "the songs are too slow." "Into the Atom Age" ridicules materialistic living, while "New Town Animal in a Furnished Cage" is about boredom, the Generation Jones–era virus.

And like the *3D* EP, they want to dismantle the worship of the 1960s to create something new. There's an absolute deconstruction of Bob Dylan's 1960s warhorse "All Along the Watchtower" with singer Andy Partridge imitating Dylan but also parodying his voice. In one song the band decomposes one of the icons of 1960s pop culture.

### "Are You Receiving Me?" 45 September 27, 1978 (Virgin VS 231) (UK)

On the surface it's about a betrayal in a relationship. But in the punk era it can be broadened to be about deception and disconnection from the larger culture. Features singer Andy Partridge's punk-like snarl in the chorus.

### *Drums and Wires* LP August 17, 1979 (Virgin V 2129) (UK)

After their second album, *Go2*, that didn't break any new ground and was too saturated with keyboards, a revamped XTC gets more adventurous. From the opening track, "Making Plans for Nigel," they go beyond the fast-paced, punk-inspired pop on their first album, *White Music*. The drum part and tempo in "Nigel," reportedly musically inspired by Devo's version of "Satisfaction," shows a shift into a form of post-punk that is more pop-based with more complex instrumentation.

The tempo changes, the intricacies of the songs, and the layering of instrumentation in songs like "When You're Near Me I Have Difficulty" and "Millions" also show this shift into post-punk. "Day In Day Out" and "Roads Girdle the Globe" feature a slow, funk-like groove blended with a post-punk sense of uneasiness. But they still build on the fast-tempo, punk-influenced pop of their first album, such as the blistering romp "Outside World" and the quirky pop-infused "Helicopter" and "Real by Reel." But this is more controlled than the herky-jerky frenzy of their first album.

XTC also takes a turn to more socially conscious lyrics. "Making Plans for Nigel" is about a young person being groomed for a job in a steel factory. Because he is silent about it, his parents feel he must be happy with factory life. The degradation of work also comes up in "Day In Day Out." The affluent shelter themselves from poverty and trouble in "Outside World," while the dirge-like and dark "Complicated Game" shreds the idea that effective political change can happen from any political party. "That Is the Way" details the dangers of conformity; "Real by Reel" sketches the dangers of government surveillance; and "Roads Girdle the Globe" mocks the progress of "the concrete robe" of a highway system, perhaps because progress in other areas in society appears so elusive.

## *Black Sea* LP September 12, 1980 (Virgin V 2173) (UK)

With a more aggressive production than *Drums and Wires* and overall less experimentation, this is their most important album. They build on the social commentary from *Drums and Wires* with a ferocious opening three songs. "Respectable Street" is a class-based song satirizing the elite, who, like the denizens of "Outside World" from *Drums and Wires*, want to be far away from the problems of the troubled masses. "Generals and Majors" is another Generation Jones Cold War–based song about fear of World War III. "Living Through Another Cuba" is a ska-influenced song about repeating the nuclear war scare of the Cuban Missile Crisis in the early 1960s. On side two, "Paper and Iron" continues the theme of unfulfilling work from "Day In Day Out" from *Drums and Wires*.

The album ends with the drum-driven "Travels in Nihilon," an eerie song that could be about how the promise of punk music burned out. And sprinkled through the album are catchy, post-punk pop songs in "Love at First Sight" and "Burning with Optimism's Flames."

## "Don't Lose Your Temper" (B-side of "Generals and Majors") 45 August 9, 1980 (Virgin VS 365) (UK)

Pop punk gem about a girl who takes an office job and is starting to lose her identity. She doesn't look the same or act the same. "Whatever happened to my fighting biting lightning lioness?" singer Andy Partridge asks.

## "Ball and Chain" 45 February 26, 1982 (Virgin VS 482) (UK)

With the steady eruption of drums, this sounds like it could have been from *Black Sea* instead of *English Settlement*. There's a football chant–like chorus and lyrics about the destruction of homes and communities for an illusion of progress. An early anti-gentrification song.

**"No Thugs in Our House" b/w "Chain of Command" and "Limelight" 45 May 14, 1982 (Virgin VS 490) (UK)**

"No Thugs in Our House" is the rowdiest moment from *English Settlement* about a boy whose parents can't believe their child would get into trouble with the police. Intricate blend of instrumentation that shows what direction the band could have gone in if they didn't pursue more acoustic-based music with *English Settlement*. If the human body is basically a military operation, then what is the hierarchy? That's what Andy Partridge wonders in "Chain of Command." "Limelight" shows the narcissism of being famous.

**Genre:** Post-punk

## Y Pants

***Beat It Down* LP April 1982 (Neutral Records N-Two) (USA)**

This band is associated with the short-lived no wave movement in New York. But this all-female band released this record after no wave's heyday. Y Pants uses some of the same percussion techniques and avant-garde approaches as no wave, but it's not as aggressively deconstructionist and jarring. It's more in the spirit of the Raincoats than Teenage Jesus and the Jerks. And it's keyboard-centered rather than guitar-based. And to add to the unorthodox but somewhat playful feeling, there's a toy piano used in some songs.

The songs are less based on the aesthetic lyrics of no wave and more about the confusion and disillusionment about romantic relationships. Most songs are about being pulled in and out of problematic relationships. The highlight of the album is "Barbara's Song," a haunting song with a narrative of a woman who has expectations in a relationship that are shattered after she is taken advantage of. "I didn't know what I was doing anymore" is the narrator's harrowing realization. "Beat It Down" is the most experimental song, in which the singer tries to suppress feeling attracted to someone, while "Love Is a Disease" goes further by portraying a relationship as a kind of illness.

**Genre:** No Wave/Post-punk

## Young Marble Giants

***Colossal Youth* LP February 3, 1980 (ROUGH 8) (UK)**

This Welsh trio created an album that's monumental because it's perhaps the first minimalist post-punk album. With its bare-bones, stripped-down sound, it signified a new direction in post-punk that also influenced 1980s alternative music. It showed how tension is created not just with loud guitars but with a subdued voice, a guitar, bass, and occasional keyboards. Post-punk is for thoughtful introverts too, this band seemed to say. There's a juxtaposition between Alison Statton's serene voice (singing as if she's trying to sing as quietly as possible) with the often nervous guitar indicating underlying agitation. The album is a journey of a loss of innocence and youth that brings alienation, restlessness, and a bewildered sense of acceptance but with an undercurrent of quiet defiance.

The opening track, "Search for Mr. Right," is a song less about seeking a person than an ideal. Then throughout the album there's a sense of things going wrong. In "Wurlitzer Jukebox," the singer asks a question, but she's not heard above the sound of the jukebox. The world is just too chaotic and loud. And ultimately there's a feeling of youth slipping away. In "Colossal Youth" the singer concludes the only way to defy it is youthful perspective. But later Statton sings just three lines in "Salad Days" that indicate there's been a painful loss of youth.

Then comes a concluding trilogy of songs showing a shift toward living in a compromised state. "Credit in the Straight World" conveys the painful realization that succeeding in the oppressive "straight world" requires conceding too much. "Brand New Life" goes further by stating that life is about adapting to conflict more than it is breaking out of it. But the singer makes a vow that she won't let people in if they ring at her door. Is she committed to a life of isolation? Whatever the case, the album concludes with the instrumental "Wind in the Rigging," which makes the album end with a feeling of a kind of contemplation more than a solid conclusion.

### *The Final Day* 7" EP June 7, 1980 (Rough Trade RT 043) (UK)

The title track is frightening because of the sparse instrumentation over descriptions of a vision of an apocalyptic end. In some ways it's the embodiment of a line from T.S. Eliot's "The Hollow Men" that the world will end "not with a bang but a wimper." It's yet another compelling song from a Generation Jones–era band about the fear of sudden nuclear war.

Two other non-album tracks, "Radio Silents" and "Cake Walking," were also just as good as anything from their *Colossal Youth* album, but the songs are more ambiguous. "Radio Silents" is a quiet plea for politeness on the surface at least, while "Cake Walking" seems to describe what makes something difficult or worthwhile.

**Genre:** Post-punk

## Youth Brigade

### *Sound & Fury* LP June 1983 (Better Youth Organization BYO 002-R) (USA)

Not to be confused with Washington, D.C., band with the same name. And this album shouldn't be confused with their 1982 album with the same title. After being disappointed in the results of their first album the previous year, they stopped pressing copies of it and went back into the studio to rerecord another album with the same title they released in 1983. This was a good decision. The songs are stronger and more varied. It joins albums like Minor Threat's *Out of Step* that redefine the hardcore genre in 1983 by differing the approach beyond what was beginning to become the rigid hardcore punk format. There's elements of punk, hardcore, Oi!, and traditional rock (and even some funk and rap in "Men in Blue"). But there's still a direct energy with a hardcore punk vision and perspective.

There's also a theatrical quality to the call-and-response and tempo changes in some songs. And there's the strange doo-wop of "Duke of Earl" and the satirical children's song "Jump Back." The message seems to be that they don't take themselves seriously, at least at times. Other songs, like "Modest Proposal" and "Blown Away," are more Generation Jones fear-of-nuclear-war songs. They also have some of the traits of positive hardcore in the anti-suicide song "Did You Wanna Die" and "Live Life," the latter reassuring: "There's meaning somewhere, you've just go to search." "What Will the Revolution Change" is an ending song about how things won't change, which concludes the album on a somewhat uncharacteristic cynical note.

**Genre:** Punk/Hardcore Punk

## Zero Boys

***Vicious Circle*** **LP July 1982 (Nimrod Records NIM-001) (USA)**

Indiana band combines punk, pop punk, and hardcore but leans more to hardcore overall. This is a ferocious album and generally overlooked, likely because they were from the Midwest instead of the East or West Coasts. The tone is set with the ominous opening song, "Vicious Circle," about the exhaustion, disillusionment, and futility of living in a brutal world. And some of the album is a topical tour of contemporary societal ills. "New Generation" ridicules hippies, disco, and the rockabilly revival. "Civilization's Dying" denounces gun violence by using examples of the president, the pope, and John Lennon being shot. The satirical shuffle of "Living in the '80s" condemns the radio continuing to play 1960s bands.

And there are songs about the punk scene. "Drug Free Youth" seems to be about straight edge, while "Hightime" ridicules the chaos of a drug-plagued lifestyle. The ferocious "Outta Style" shows the price for being a punk, which continues in "Trying Harder," which is in the tradition of the Clash's "All the Young Punks" and Stiff Little Fingers' "Wait and See." There's a determination to keep going despite opposition and ridicule about being in a punk band.

**Genre:** Hardcore Punk

## The Zounds

***You Can't Cheat Karma*** **7" EP August 29, 1980 (Crass Records 421984/3) (UK)**

This politically charged UK band is a fascinating mid-point between the punk idealism of the Clash and the gritty, post-punk realism of the Gang of Four. Released on the anarcho-punk band Crass's record label, it starts with the title track about someone who realizes there's something wrong but doesn't know what to do about it. The explosive "War" features a Joe Strummer–like call-to-arms vocal reciting places where there is violence in the world. "Subvert" advises oppressed workers about how to "work for revolution in your place of employment."

**Genre:** Punk/Post-punk

# Appendix
*Proto-Punk, Post-Punk and Second Wave Ska Influences*

## David Bowie

***The Rise and Fall of Ziggy Stardust and the Spiders from Mars* LP June 16, 1972 (RCA SF 8287) (UK)**

Although the *Ziggy Stardust* album is largely acoustic guitar–based with a theatrical quality at times, there's a more aggressive, Velvet Underground–style proto-punk sound in "Suffragette City" and particularly the driving guitar in "Hang on to Yourself." Bowie first tried this musical style in "Queen Bitch" from his *Hunky Dory* album. But he speeds up the pace here. Although it would be another leap to Johnny Ramone's buzz saw guitar, the guitar breaks in "Hang on to Yourself" may have been an inspiration for the Ramones' "Teenage Lobotomy."

Although the other songs don't have a similar proto-punk musical sound, there's a thematic quality in a few songs that make it thematically proto-punk. Like the opening "Five Years," with its descriptions of characters living in a world that seems to be on the verge of apocalyptic end. As if it's an antidote to the hopelessness in "Five Years" is "Soul Love," which like the Velvet Underground's third album strips humanity to its core spiritual need for love and goodness. There's a light and dark mood in these two songs that feels proto-punk underneath all the rock star and space imagery this album would be associated with.

**"Rebel Rebel" 45 February 15, 1974 (RCA LPBO 5009) (UK)**

A dirty-sounding, infectious guitar riff highlights lyrics about an androgynous, misunderstood outcast that points to the outsider persona of punk. There's something so jubilant, intriguing, and liberating in this maligned figure Bowie sings about. The outro, with Bowie seeming to improvise street poetry, is one of proto-punk's most exciting moments.
**Genre:** Proto-punk

## Can

**"Vitamin C" 45 February 26, 1973 (United Artists UA 35 472 A) (Germany)**

German experimental band that in this song went beyond the usual jam band formula popular in this era. With an almost desperate chorus of "hey you, you're losing," there's a pre-punk angst. The infectious drumming is a cross between a marching beat and jazz with some eerie organ around the edges.

**Genre:** Proto Post-punk

## Captain Beefheart

### *Trout Mask Replica* LP June 16, 1969 (Straight STS 1053) (USA)

When post-punk musicians wanted to throw out the rigidity of punk rock and no wave musicians were deconstructing music itself, some of them looked to this album for inspiration. And if there was an album that conveyed that anything goes, it's this one.

The first track, "Frownland," sets the tone for the album with its varying riffs and tempos from different instruments. This is what the Shaggs did with their *Philosophy of the World* album unintentionally. Here it was done intentionally, like a form of free jazz. Songs like "Wild Life" feature guitar parts that point to the jagged, nervous guitars of post-punk.

Generally, the experimental, more avant-garde songs work better than the blues subversions or Beefheart reciting his poetry over music. Sometimes the album focuses on the human condition, such as the Depression-era "The Dust Blows Forward and the Dust Blows Back," the pain of missing those killed in a war in "Veteran's Day Poppy," and the horror of the Holocaust of "Dachau Blues." There's also a satire of hippie culture in "Ella Guru" and of small-town conservatives in "Moonlight on Vermont."

**Genre:** Proto Post-punk/Proto No Wave

## Alice Cooper

### *Greatest Hits* LP August 1, 1974 (Warner Bros. W28030) (USA)

Because Cooper also influenced hard rock, heavy metal, and shock rock, and received mainstream success, Cooper is largely underrated as an influence on punk even though he was part of the Detroit proto-punk movement that also included the Stooges, MC5, and Death. Like other proto-punk music, his songs were so raw and real that they went against the more utopian hippie songs of the time. Cooper's concerts also could use disturbing imagery that accented the danger and edge in his songs, which in many ways made him the godfather of horror punk.

About half of the songs on Cooper's greatest hits album are essential proto-punk songs. They include Cooper's breakthrough hit, "I'm Eighteen," which describes both the angst and the exuberance of leaving adolescence behind for young adulthood: "I've got a baby's brain and an old man's heart," it "feels like I'm living in the middle of doubt." "Elected" is about the hypocrisy and dishonesty of political slogans, the ferocious "School's Out" is an anti-authoritative anthem, and "No More Mr. Nice Guy" contains something essential about modern living: the world does not respond well to kindness.

**Genre:** Proto-punk

## Death

### *For the Whole World to See* LP (recorded 1975, released February 17, 2009) (Drag City DC 387) (USA)

Virtually unknown at the time they were together, this Detroit-based band recorded songs that sound as close to punk and hardcore punk as any proto-punk music would come. If there's a connection between the Stooges and the Ramones, this is it.

The band only released one single when the band was together. So when an album of seven songs was finally released more than three decades later, it was a revelation to punk fans. But it raised questions about why this music was suppressed for so long. Why weren't they known during the 1970s? Did the name Death doom them to obscurity? Or were they not supported for racist reasons because they were an all-Black trio?

If there was a guitar god in the proto-punk era, it's David Hackney. The guitar parts during the ending instrumental part of "Politicians in My Eyes" makes for some of the gnarliest guitar playing of this era. "Rock N' Roll Victim," parts of "Politicians in My Eyes," and tempo changes in "Freaking Out" even point ahead past punk to hardcore punk. Perhaps all the confusion about how to fit in the music industry during this time is what led to the compelling "Where Do We Go from Here?" The album ends with the single they released during the original band's formation, which is the brilliant "Politicians in My Eyes," which condemns the corruption of the political system.

**Genre:** Proto-punk

## Dr. Feelgood

### *Down by the Jetty* LP January 1975 (United Artists UAS 29727) (UK)

The pub rock phenomenon in England was ultimately a retro movement. The songs were mostly revised rockabilly, blues, and R&B songs. But of all the pub rock bands, Dr. Feelgood stands out for one reason: guitarist Wilko Johnson. He played an aggressive choppy guitar style that influenced post-punk bands.

Johnson's guitar makes it sound like punk and post-punk are coming. It's there in "She Does It Right" with guitar parts that sound too gritty, too frenetic, too jagged for a pub rock band. And it's even there in the single "Roxette," a standard, blues-based song with harmonica but with constant tension in the guitar. "Cheque Book" features a funk-like guitar part that would influence post-punk, while "Keep It Out of Sight" may be the best song on the album because it features Johnson's fiercest guitar with unorthodox tempo changes.

**Genre:** Proto Post-punk

## Bob Marley

### *Live!* LP December 5, 1975 (Island ILPS 9376) (UK)

Musically, punk and second wave ska were influenced most by first wave ska. But the reggae singer Bob Marley was such a powerful songwriter and singer that his socially conscious lyrics influenced the punk era. He was also instrumental in introducing Rastafarianism to the world. This form of Christianity often referred to a fallen and corrupt Western world as Babylon. This worldview, with its idea that society may be in the time of tribulation, had apocalyptic-like language that appealed to punks.

This live recording captured Marley at a raucous London concert with an enthusiastic audience. The energy from the audience indicates the hunger for music with anger about social conditions. "How many rivers do we have to cross to talk to the boss?" Marley asks in "Burnin' and Lootin'," while in "Them Belly Full (But We Hungry)" he says, "A hungry mob is an angry mob." The album ends with the anthem "Get

Up Stand Up" with its ending chant of "don't give up the fight." After being introduced to punk, Marley embraced it. In 1977 Marley released "Punky Reggae Party," a celebration of the blending of punk and reggae that name-checks the Clash, the Damned, and the Jam.

**Genre:** Proto–Second Wave Ska

## MC5

*Kick Out the Jams* **LP February 22, 1969 (Elektra EKS-74042) (USA)**

This album by this Detroit band has one foot in what wouldn't have been unusual in the year of Woodstock. That means a blues-based sound with 1960s excesses. And it's recorded live with a somewhat muddy production. But there's another part of the album that makes it proto-punk. That's a heavier guitar sound that predates the later fusion of hard rock, heavy metal, and punk. And there are a few songs that are more blatantly political than most proto-punk that were an influence on British political punk and hardcore punk.

One of them is the notorious title track with its once-censored opening line. There has been some debate over the years about what the song title means. But we like the one that says it's about knocking down restrictions and limitations. Even though it's blues-based and slower, "Motor City Is Burning" is about riots in Detroit and the Black Panthers. But otherwise, there are too many songs that seem to be about the masculine thrill of sexual conquests. And it ends with the extended, trippy "Starship," which now sounds more dated than experimental. Overall, the album is a mixed bag. But there's enough here that's proto-punk and influential.

*Back in the USA* **LP January 15, 1970 (Atlantic SD 8247) (USA)**

In about half of *Back in the USA*, the songs are stripped down enough and the production altered to feature a simpler, punk-like guitar rather than the heavier guitar sound on their other two albums.

The best song is "The American Ruse," a song that expresses frustration about a false mythology about America. "High School," later used in the Ramones movie *Rock 'N' Roll High School*, is a catchy, proto–pop punk song. "Call Me Animal" has a Stooges-like primal energy, while "The Human Being Lawnmower" is an ominous song about destruction. We didn't need covers of 1950s warhorses "Tutti Frutti" and "Back in the USA," but the best of this album has a place in the development of laying the groundwork for punk music.

**Genre:** Proto-punk

## The Modern Lovers

*Modern Lovers* **LP (recorded in 1971 and 1972, released July 1976) (Home of the Hits BZ-0050) (USA)**

Although commercial success never came to the Velvet Underground, they inspired bands like the Modern Lovers. "Roadrunner" features driving guitars with an organ (played by Jerry Harrison, who would later join the Talking Heads). It's the kind of song the Velvet Underground's "What Goes On" set a template for. However, unlike the darkness of the Velvet Underground, "Roadrunner" is a celebration of the modern world and its distractions, like driving down the highway listening to music. "Someone I Care About" and "Modern World" also feature a Velvet Underground–influenced guitar sound.

Like Lou Reed, singer Jonathan Richman also writes songs about unorthodox subjects, but from an innocent perspective rather than the darkness of the Velvet Underground. "Pablo Picasso" is about how the famous painter was a magnet to women. In "Old World" he yearns for something better with its "arcane knowledge" from the past compared to conditions in the 1970s. Whether it's ironic or not, there's some pre–straight edge ideology in "She Cracked."

**Genre**: Proto-punk/Proto Post-punk

## Neu!

### *Neu! 75* LP June 1975 (United Artists UAG 29782) (Germany)

Neu! was formed by two former members of Kraftwerk. The first side of this album features some early forms of chill electronica and ambient music, including the very pleasant "Ibi." But side two is where proto-punk emerges. It goes into much darker territory with two songs that influenced both punk and post-punk.

"Hero" is the song that influenced punk. It blends guitars and a Velvet Underground–like sound with a vocal that may have Iggy Pop at its roots but with a more of a snarl that must have influenced punk singers. "You're just another hero running through the night trying to lose your mind" sings vocalist Klaus Dinger, as if it's a demented and more sinister variation of the theme later covered in Modern Lovers' "Road Runner." The other song on side two is the instrumental "E Musik," which sounds like krautrock-meets-the-Velvet-Underground. It points more to post-punk than the electronica that would influence synth-pop and new wave music. This driving drumbeat would come to be known as motorik.

**Genre**: Proto-punk/Proto Post-punk

## New York Dolls

### *New York Dolls* LP July 27, 1973 (Mercury SRM-1-675) (USA)

Along with the Stooges' *Raw Power*, this is the link between the end of the so-called glam rock era to the punk explosion that started in 1976. But the New York Dolls have a different sound and attitude than the Detroit garage guitar bands like the Stooges and MC5. The Dolls are all New York in attitude and stripped down with no jams or extended songs. Although they were cross-dressing onstage, they were different from the more posh English glam bands. An urban grittiness permeated their look, attitude, and music.

And while not overtly political, the songs conveyed at times the downtrodden condition of downtown 1970s New York City. In "Subway," singer David Johansen sings, "I can't ever understand why my life's been cursed, poisoned, condemned." Songs like "Trash" have the feel of the underside of city life. While not overtly political, "Vietnamese Baby" captures something about the fallout from the unpopular war that ended the year this album was released with its ominous ending line: "Now that it's over, what are you going to do?" But perhaps it's the first track, "Personality Crisis," that most points to the breakdown the era had on the individual where "frustration and heartache is what you got." While the Stooges were full of primal force and the power of the id, there's something vulnerable in the Dolls' version of proto-punk.

**Genre:** Proto-punk

**Too Much Too Soon LP May 10, 1974 (Mercury SRM-1-1001) (USA)**

Many of the songs use irony and humor to warn against 1970s excess such as "Babylon," a journey to a Long Island town into exploitation and decadence. "It's Too Late" condemns depravity while "Who Are the Mystery Girls" contains a pop influence but with the ominous question "what do you know about love?" "There's Gonna Be a Showdown" continues the combination of danger and fun sounding like it could be a soundtrack to either a party or an apocalypse. It all leads to the concluding "Human Being" near mystical in philosophical self-appraisal and assessment of the human condition.

## Nico

**The Marble Index LP November 29, 1968 (Elektra EKS-74029) (USA)**

Feeling constrained playing the blonde chanteuse as a solo artist and with the Velvet Underground, Nico dyed her hair dark, wrote her own songs, and shifted her sound to make what may be the first Goth album.

*The Marble Index* is a daring album with a haunting and eerie stark beauty. It's the Goth flip side of *Chelsea Girls*. It's a minimal album with sparse instruments. Most distinctive is the harmonium with a drony quality that would influence the Goth subgenre of post-punk.

"Can you follow me? Can you follow my distresses?" are the first lines of "Lawns of Dawns" after the opening one-minute "Prelude." And what follows is a striking, Goth-like minimalism that may reach its apex in the mesmerizing "Frozen Warnings." "It is as though you're getting closer to your soul," she sings in "Roses in the Snow." "Facing the Wind" sounds almost like a future no wave song with some discordant sounds and instruments that seem to work against each other rather than harmonizing.

**Genre:** Proto-Goth

## Yoko Ono

**Fly LP September 21, 1971 (Apple SVBB 3380) (USA)**

If Ono recorded during the late 1970s instead of the early 1970s, she would have been considered part of the no wave and post-punk movements. But in the early to mid-1970s she was an iconoclastic singer ahead of her time. It didn't help that she was married to John Lennon, a 1960s icon whose fans were largely unaccepting of his wife's music because it was so experimental.

Want to know what inspired the shrieks on the B-52s song "Rock Lobster"? They may have come from songs like "Mind Train" and "Hirake." On "Don't Worry Kyoko," Ono's pained, wailing vocals make her voice sound like an instrument with its roots in free-form jazz. "O' Wind" features a world music groove and a tribal-like beat combining the avant-garde with world music. There are also full-fledged avant-garde pieces such as "Airmale" that helped lay the foundation for noise punk, while "Don't Count the Wave" has a deconstructionist, no wave–like sound to it.

**Genre:** Proto Post-punk/No Wave/Noise Punk

## Iggy Pop and James Williamson
### "Kill City" 45 (recorded 1975, released March 17, 1978) (Radar ADA) (UK)
After the third Stooges album, Iggy Pop teamed up with guitarist James Williamson to make an album that was scrapped and then rereleased after the success of Pop's albums *The Idiot* and *Lust for Life*. The album was very uneven, but this single has a Stooges-like power.
**Genre:** Proto-punk

## Prince Buster
### *Fabulous Greatest Hits* LP 1968 (Fab MS1) (UK)
This Jamaican singer was perhaps the biggest inspiration on second wave ska. The Skatalites popularized the ska genre, but they were mostly an instrumental band. Prince Buster's songs exuded personality and attitude that musicians in the punk era latched on to. The Specials, Madness, and the English Beat covered his songs. The first Madness single, "The Prince," was a tribute to Prince Buster; it also mentions the song "Earthquake," which is on this album.

Prince Buster deserves a solid retrospective of his music. For now, this is the best we have. It features at least some of his groundbreaking songs. They include "Al Capone," the basis for the Specials song "Gangsters," the song that kicked off the two tone second wave ska craze. There's also the slower paced "Too Hot," about crime-ridden Jamaica, and the frenetic "Texas Hold Up." In a predecessor to rap, Buster toasts over some songs including "Judge Dread," where he takes the role of a judge accessing the crimes that rude boys have committed.
**Genre:** Proto–Second Wave Ska

## Lou Reed
### *Transformer* LP November 8, 1972 (RCA LSP 4807) (USA)
Lou Reed's second solo album continues the themes of some Velvet Underground songs about outsiders who won't live by the limitations of mainstream culture. That desire for liberation takes them to dark and decadent places but also to moments of clarity and peace. This spiritual tension between dark and light helped mold the punk persona, the outsider who is prophetic about the culture's shortcomings and unafraid to face life's seedy and dark places.

Some songs are characters going on a journey to find their identities, often through redefining their gender roles and seeking transcendence through drugs and sex. This comes through in "Walk on the Wild Side," which seems to celebrate the desire for liberation yet is cautionary and somewhat sarcastic about where that freedom leads. In "Hangin' Around" Reed rejects the phony mysticism and drug use with the observation that "you're still doing things that I gave up years ago." "Vicious" alternates between playfulness and danger.

In one of Reed's most beautiful songs, "Perfect Day," there is a desire for transcendence but with an ominous ending: "You're going to reap just what you sow." The tension between what is true transcendence comes through in "I'm So Free" where it's ultimately unclear whether it's true or false transcendence. What seems to matter to Reed is portraying the desire to transcend that is so fundamental to human existence.

**Genre:** Proto-punk

## Roxy Music

### "Virginia Plain" 45 August 4, 1972 (Island WIP-6144) (UK)

The band's debut single smashes the chanty power pop glam rock of T. Rex, Slade, and Gary Glitter and takes the genre in a more art-rock direction. This song is a complicated but energetic mini-masterpiece. It points to the power of punk in its energy and the experimentation of post-punk with its avant-garde flourishes.

### *For Your Pleasure* LP March 23, 1973 (Island ILPS 9232) (UK)

Because keyboardist Brian Eno was in Roxy Music for the band's first two albums, they were the band's most experimental. Their first album, *Roxy Music* (1972), has its moments, particularly in the opening track "Re-Make/Re-Model," but overall it's too experimental and meandering, a bit too trapped in the era's emphasis on longer songs. But *For Your Pleasure* is a much tighter series of songs but still with an avant-garde edge.

"Do the Strand" is a bouncy, almost subversive dance song with an Eastern European feel. The ballad "Beauty Queen" features an almost ironic longing for beauty with a ferocious instrumental passage that undercuts the song's structure. "Editions of You," with its vicious instrumental section, is a frantic proto-punk song with saxophone and keyboards emphasizing the dark side of passion. "In Every Dream Home a Heartache" is a disconcerting song about an inflatable doll, while "The Bogus Man" is nightmarish and creepy, almost like a demented dancehall song. The title track ends with a disturbing experimental pastiche of music.

### "Street Life" 45 November 1, 1973 (Island WIP 6173) (UK)

The singer longs for a break from the routine and goes outside to walk and take in the street scene. What follows is a glimpse of the world itself from the elite to the downtrodden. Captures the social observations that will be an important component in punk and post-punk.

**Genre:** Proto Post-punk

## The Shaggs

### *Philosophy of the World* LP June 15, 1969 (Third World TCLP 3001) (USA)

This album, recorded by three teenage Wiggins sisters from Fremont, New Hampshire, is a work of unintended genius. Reportedly a psychic told the girls' father that one day he would have daughters who would become a famous singing band. He bought them instruments and paid for an album to be recorded in a small studio even though they were not accomplished musicians. Rarely playing in sync with each other and often out of tune, somehow it all works, like free-form jazz or pre–no wave that somehow comes together. This is DIY long before the term was created.

Because of their innocence, they don't write many love songs. Instead, there are more childlike observations of the world. They write about automobiles ("That Little Sports Car"), a lost cat ("My Pal, Foot Foot"), the radio as a friend ("My Companion"), and the thrills of a holiday ("It's Halloween"). Yet there seems to be a sadness about their innocence ending in "Why Do We Feel?"

And what is the philosophy of the world the album is named after? People are never satisfied with what they have, according to the song. Sounding like the author of the Book of Ecclesiastes, the sisters conclude: "You can never please anybody in this world." They're also philosophical in "Things I Wonder": "The things I wonder most are the things I never find out."

**Genre:** Proto Post-punk

## Skatalites

### "Guns of Navarone" 45 March 1965 (Island WI 168) (UK)

At one time this Jamaican band were the biggest ska band in the world. They mostly played instrumentals with a driving dance beat. They were tight and structured, almost like a variation of the unity of a big band. This laid a foundation for the second wave ska movement. As in the case of Prince Buster, there's not a good compilation of the Skatalites' music. But this song that the Specials later covered is a good sample of their music.

**Genre:** Proto–Second Wave Ska

## Patti Smith

### "Piss Factory" (B-side of "Hey Joe") 45 November 1974 (Mer 601) (USA)

Smith's forceful poetry is recited over music that's a cross between jazz and proto post-punk. It's the beginning of one of modern music's greatest artist's careers and the sound of a new, rebellious generation. The autobiographical account of working in a factory is a metaphor for 1970s oppression and for any institution that is demoralizing. "It's the monotony that gets to me," Smith says before defiantly declaring, "I'm going to get out of here."

### *Horses* LP November 10, 1975 (Arista AL 4066) (USA)

*Horses* does not contain the short, garage band structure of other proto-punk music. But it would have plenty of punk attitude. And it showed a literary quality coupled with street poetry. Although it would be an important album for punk, it also was significant in post-punk with its multiplicity of musical styles and the literary quality. With her charismatic stage presence, Smith was one of the most influential and important figures of the punk and post-punk era. In many ways, female punk singers are all Patti's children.

As if to seize rock music and bring it into a new generation, the album starts with a reworking of the 1960s garage band song "Gloria," with Smith adding her own lyrics for most of the song. She can deliver raging, punk-like songs such as the second part of "Free Money." In the epic "Land," she hijacks the R&B song "Land of 1,000 Dances" and makes it her own.

"Redondo Beach," about the suicide of a young woman on a beach, is an early incorporation of reggae musical styles into the punk era. Like the Velvet Underground, many of Smith's songs on this album are about a search for transcendence, whether it's the vision of a spaceship after a death in "Birdland," financial liberation and the change it will bring in "Free Money," or the angelic visitation in "Break It Up."

**Genre:** Proto-punk/Proto Post-punk

## The Stooges

***The Stooges* LP August 5, 1969 (Elektra EKS 74051) (USA)**

This album is the great leap out of garage rock into proto-punk. The production by the Velvet Underground's John Cale uses more complicated layering of sound different from 1960s lo-fi garage band songs. Ron Asheton's guitar has some 1960s hard rock influences, but there's also some *White Light/White Heat* feel at times too. Sometimes there's a wah-wah guitar sound that sounds like later 1960s psychedelic rock. But there's also a dirty, heavy, gritty sound different from garage band songs.

A major reason this album is proto-punk is because of singer Iggy Pop. The attitude in the lyrics is coming from a very different perspective than most 1960s music. There isn't the utopian, hippie perspective, and there aren't the more conventional love song lyrics of 1960s garage bands.

Patti Smith's lyrics were both literary and street level, often with a visionary, spiritual, transcendental quality. This made her one of the most important figures during the proto-punk, punk, and post-punk eras (Gijsbert Hanekroot/Alamy).

One of the subjects is malaise and boredom. "Another year with nothing to do," Pop says over the Bo Diddley–inspired beat in "1969." In "No Fun," the singer doesn't know what to do when "there's no fun to hang around feeling that same old way." Iggy Pop gave proto-punk one of its most punk-like viewpoints: boredom resulting from feeling alienated from the culture. Some of the album also has a primal quality, like "Little Doll," "Not Right," and "I Wanna Be Your Dog," which is enhanced by sleigh bells and piano that give the song somewhat of a Velvet Underground quality.

*Fun House* LP July 7, 1970 (Elektra EKS-74071) (USA)

This is one of the most dangerous-sounding albums ever made. Doing their best to capture the spirit of the Stooges' raucous live performances, this album is dirtier and sludgier than the first album. The first side is more straight-ahead proto-punk songs, while the second side is more experimental. This is proto-punk, so there isn't the tight structure of full-fledged punk songs. There are long guitar solos and parts of songs that sound like improvised jams. Between Pop's voice and Asheton's guitar sound, however, there's a tension and energy that inspired punk music.

The most straight-ahead proto-punk songs are the first three songs: "Down on the Street," "Loose," and "T.V. Eye," one of the most energetic opening three songs on any album. These songs are both exciting and menacing. With Pop's screams and sound on "T.V. Eye," it almost sounds like an animal prowling the streets. There's a feeling of something being out of control and an aura of anarchy that would continue into punk music.

On the second side, "1970" starts with a "1969"-type Bo Diddley beat but then turns into a jam with a long guitar solo and later an extended free jazz–style saxophone part. "Fun House" also features a saxophone and extended jam sections, while "L.A. Blues" is all pretty much noise punk with Pop's growls over the proto-punk version of chaotic, free-form jazz. Overlooked at the time, the album would prove to be influential on punk, noise punk, and even heavy metal and hard rock.

*Raw Power* LP February 7, 1973 (Columbia KC 32111) (USA)

After the free-form manic energy of *Fun House*, the Stooges' third album is more tightly structured. And there's a change in sound with James Williamson taking over on guitar with Ron Asheton switching to bass. This Stooges album is closer to what will come with full-fledged punk than their first two albums, which were still steeped in a 1960s garage band–influenced sound.

Iggy Pop has such a strong onstage persona and commanding tone in his singing that it's easy to overlook how much he is a street poet. While Lou Reed and Patti Smith gave a literary quality to proto-punk, Pop's lyrics were simple punk poetry. In many ways Iggy Pop created the raw attitude of punk, the quality of a prophetic outsider becoming empowered that became a central component of the punk perspective.

In "Search and Destroy" he describes himself as "the world's forgotten boy" and uses soldier imagery to describe how he will live. "Raw Power" is a masterpiece of energy within a churning beat where raw power is like a mystical primal force that has "a healing hand" but can also "destroy a man." The future of horror punk and even Goth can be heard in the eerie vocals in "Penetration."

**Genre:** Proto-punk

# Television

**"Little Johnny Jewel" 45 August 18, 1975 (ORK 81975) (USA)**

Sometimes jokingly called the Grateful Dead of punk, Television's first record was so long it had to be separated into two sides of a 45. What really separates it from the jam-based songs popular in the pre-punk era is the chaotic, almost avant-guitar sounds. In 1975, this sounds like it's coming from an entirely different place called the future. And it was an enormous influence on the post-punk sensibility.

**Genre:** Proto Post-punk

## Upsetters

### 14 Dub Blackboard Jungle LP October 1973 (Upsetter none) (Jamaica)

The album starts with this Rastafari-like announcement: "Calling the meek and the humble, welcome to blackboard jungle, so don't you fumble, just be humble." And from there a new sound begins. A subgenre of reggae, dub music was originally instrumental versions of songs that a toaster, a reggae predecessor to a rapper, would talk over. Sometimes sound effects were added. Or instrumentation dropped away. But it used an echo-like reverb sound that was influential on punk, post-punk, and second wave ska.

It's arguable what the first dub album was, but this was an important one. It was masterminded by Lee "Scratch" Perry and King Tubby, who would become giants in the dub genre.

**Genre**: Proto–Second Wave Ska/Proto Post-punk influence

## Various Artists

### The Harder They Come Soundtrack LP July 7, 1972 (Island ILPS 9202) (UK)

During an era of midnight cult films, *The Harder They Come* movie was a regular feature in movie theaters. In the film, Jimmy Cliff plays the role of Ivan, who moves from the country to the city and falls victim to a criminal underworld while trying to be a reggae singer. But many audiences went to see the movie for the music. And the film's soundtrack served as the gateway to reggae and Jamaican music for non–Jamaican audiences.

These songs offer different perspectives on oppression that had a thematic connection to punk. "Rivers of Babylon" by the Melodians is largely a musical adaptation of Psalm 137 about the pain and homesickness of being in exile. "Johnny Too Bad" by the Slickers is the story of a criminal who would find no options or redemption in the end with its ominous line "where you gonna run to?" Desmond Dekker's "007 (Shanty Town)" is also about a criminal who will ultimately self-destruct.

But of all the songs, the title track might have been the most influential song from this soundtrack. Jimmy Cliff sings about defining the spiritual life as wanting justice corrected in this life, not in the afterlife. The Clash would mention the movie in "Guns of Brixton," and they covered "Pressure Drop" by Toots and the Maytals, which is also on the soundtrack.

**Genre:** Proto–Second Wave Ska

## The Velvet Underground

### The Velvet Underground and Nico LP March 12, 1967 (Verve V-5008) (USA)

Famously called the first modern rock album by legendary rock critic Lester Bangs, this album shows a punk-like spirit because it focuses on the dark side of the 1960s, urban life, and being an outsider. Released just a few months before the Summer of Love and the Beatles' *Sgt. Pepper's Lonely Hearts Club Band*, this album demystified the drugs that were such a central part of the 1960s hippie subculture. "Waiting for the Man" is an unglamorous view of trying to score drugs, while "Heroin" is about addiction and the reason for wanting to get high, which is to obliviate pain. The song is more about escapism rather than the pseudo-transcendence of 1960s rock drug culture.

The Velvet Underground—(clockwise from top left) Lou Reed, Sterling Morrison, John Cale, Moe Tucker, and Nico—changed the perspective and subject matter of 1960s music. The band shattered hippie utopianism and expanded what rock music could encompass. This created what later came to be called proto-punk, the precursor to both punk and post-punk (PBH Images/Alamy).

But ultimately, this album was more influential on post-punk, no wave, and noise punk, all genres more than a decade in the future when this album was released. Reed called his guitar tone and tuning "ostrich guitar," and it was a sound that later many post-punk and no wave bands would emulate. And there simply never were songs released like "Black Angel Death Song," with its discordant viola part played by John Cale. There's a sense of the experimental and avant-garde injected into rock music. And if that wasn't enough, Goth music has its roots here too. In "All Tomorrow's Parties," Nico's haunting vocals point to a Goth-like vocal tone and the song's lyrics are about the superficiality of wearing costumes and clothes that don't reflect the inner self.

### *White Light/White Heat* LP January 30, 1968 (Verve V6–5046) (USA)

The band is at its most experimental, unconventional, and avant-garde. "The Gift" predates horror punk with its spoken-word narrative about a man mailing himself in a large box to his college girlfriend, a stunt that ends in violence. "Lady Godiva's Operation" is a disturbing song about brain surgery (perhaps a lobotomy) gone wrong. These songs opened up the subject matter for horror punk, post-punk, and Goth music.

"White Light/White Heat," with its churning vibrant music, is about shooting up on drugs, which continues the dark side of drug use from their first album. "I Heard Her Call My Name" features a shrieking, free-form guitar solo over a pounding rhythm that combines into a virtual blueprint for noise rock. It ends with the 17-minute "Sister Ray," a journey through several characters indulging in drugs, sex, and prostitution. There's some swirling organ at times by John Cale, frantic rhythm guitars, and more screeching lead guitar. Overall, there's a relentless unsettling sordid quality to the album about an underworld of characters following their misguided impulses.

### *The Velvet Underground* LP March 13, 1969 (MGM SE-4167) (USA)

With John Cale no longer in the band, the avant-garde and experimental quality is reduced to "The Murder Mystery," a nine-minute song with mostly spoken-word pieces read out of each channel. Otherwise, this album is the Sunday morning to the Saturday night of *White Light/White Heat*. While there was a lack of consciousness to many of the characters on *White Light/White Heat*, here there's a desire for spiritual-like self-reflection and contemplation. That starts with the beautiful "Candy Says," which is about a yearning for self-knowledge once a false identity is shed ("what do you think I'd see if I could walk away from me?")

Much of this album features a meditative minimalism. For punks and post-punks, however, the guitar sound on "What Goes On" is particularly influential with a church-like organ added. It features a guitar solo that's a subdued version of the screeching guitar from *White Light*'s "I Heard Her Call My Name." That chunky guitar rhythm that would be associated with jangle punk is also in "Beginning to See the Light." The album-ending "After Hours" features the innocent, appealingly amateurish vocals of drummer Maureen Tucker. It's not a punk-sounding song, but the vocals are so unconventional that it's in the DIY spirit of punk. Anyone can do it, the song seems to say, even the most introverted.

### *VU* LP (recorded 1968, released February 1985) (Verve 422–823 721-1) (USA)

Post-punk bands like the Feelies, the Fall, and Swell Maps would sometimes play what came to be called jangle punk. The so-called jangle guitar was previously associated with the Beatles, the Byrds, and the Searchers. But what's sometimes called jangle punk connects back more to the dirtier, faster, and chunky rhythm guitar the Velvet Underground used. That started with "There She Goes Again" from the first Velvet Underground album. But it's expanded in the outtakes released on *VU*, such as "I Can't Stand It" and "Foggy Notion."

The album also includes one of their best songs, "Stephanie Says," which was recorded after the release of *White Light/White Heat*. By the time of their next album John Cale was out of the band, so perhaps that's why it wasn't released eariler. But it's one of the band's best songs, a beautiful song about the effects of pain and isolation.

### *Loaded* LP November 15, 1970 (Cotillion SD 9034) (USA)

The title of this album reportedly refers to being "loaded" with hits that would finally give them chart success (which didn't happen). This attempt to be more accessible is their most pop-oriented album. But there's enough of the solid Velvet Underground sound here to make it essential proto-punk.

That comes across especially in two songs. "Rock & Roll" is about an affluent suburban girl who rejects the materialism around her and finds salvation in music so much that "her life was saved by rock and roll." This is a thematic prelude to the Ramones song "Sheena Is a Punk Rocker," another song about a girl liberated from oppression by the right music. The search for salvation (sometimes in misguided adventures in sex and drugs) is something consistent in the Velvet Underground's songs. It's also there in "Sweet Jane," which argues against nihilism with the life-affirming realization that one must not hate whatever part one has been given in life.

**Genre:** Proto Punk/Post-punk/Goth/No Wave/Noise Punk

# Chapter Notes

## Introduction

1. Jean Twenge, *Generations: The Real Differences Between Gen Z, Millennials, Gen X, Boomers, and Silents and What They Mean for America's Future* (Simon & Schuster, 2023), 78.
2. Twenge, *Generations*, 5.
3. Jeffrey J. Williams, "Not My Generation," *The Chronicle of Higher Education*, March 31, 2014, https://www.chronicle.com/article/not-my-generation-145569/.
4. Williams, "Not My Generation."
5. Jeffrey J. Williams, "The Generation in Between: An Interview with Jonathan Pontell," *Symplokē* 23, no. 1–2 (2015): 493.
6. Williams, "The Generation in Between," 488.
7. Williams, "The Generation in Between," 496.
8. Williams, "The Generation in Between," 496.
9. Mimi Haddon, *What Is Post-Punk?* (University of Michigan Press, 2023), 42.
10. Dave Laing, *One Chord Wonders: Power and Meaning in Punk Rock* (PM Press, 2015), 38.
11. Laing, *One Chord Wonders*, 80.
12. Laing, *One Chord Wonders*, 80.
13. Greil Marcus, *Lipstick Traces: A Secret History of the 20th Century* (Harvard University Press, 1989), 2.
14. Marcus, *Lipstick Traces*, 2, 5.
15. Laing, *One Chord Wonders*, 48.
16. Nicholas H. Smith, "Punk as Praxis," in *Punk Rock and Philosophy*, ed. Joshua Heter and Richard Greene (Open Universe, 2022), 33.
17. Gerfried Ambrosch, *The Poetry of Punk: The Meaning Behind Punk Rock and Hardcore Lyrics* (Routledge, 2018), 10.
18. Gerfried Ambrosch, "American Punk: The Relations between Punk Rock, Hardcore, and American Culture," *American Studies* 60, no. 2/3 (2015): 229.
19. Steve Waksman, *This Ain't the Summer of Love: Conflict and Crossover in Heavy Metal and Punk* (University of California Press, 2009), 264.
20. Waksman, *This Ain't the Summer of Love*, 264–5.
21. Waksman, *This Ain't the Summer of Love*, 265.
22. Tiffany Montoya, "Punk Consciousness and Class Consciousness," in *Punk Rock and Philosophy*, ed. Joseph Heter and Richard Greene (Open Universe, 2022), 188.
23. Montoya, "Punk Consciousness and Class Consciousness," 189.
24. Waksman, *This Ain't the Summer of Love*, 198.
25. Waksman, *This Ain't the Summer of Love*, 150.
26. Haddon, *What Is Post-Punk?*, 31.
27. Simon Reynolds, *Rip It Up and Start Again: Postpunk 1978-1984* (Penguin, 2005), 3.
28. Simon Reynolds, *Totally Wired: Postpunk Interviews and Overviews* (Soft Skull Press, 2010), 419.
29. Reynolds, *Rip It Up and Start Again*, 6.
30. Haddon, *What Is Post-Punk?*, 4.
31. Haddon, *What Is Post-Punk?*, 161–2.
32. Lol Tolhurst, *Goth: A History* (Hachette, 2023), 5.
33. Tolhurst, *Goth: A History*, 23–6.
34. Reynolds, *Rip It Up and Start Again*, 354.
35. Reynolds, *Rip It Up and Start Again*, 423.
36. Reynolds, *Rip It Up and Start Again*, 140.
37. Mimi Haddon, "Dub is the New Black: Modes of Identification and Tendencies of Appropriation in Late 1970s Post-Punk," *Popular Music* 36, no. 2 (May 2017): 284.
38. Haddon, "Dub is the New Black," 286.
39. Haddon, *What Is Post-Punk?*, 59.
40. Paul Kauppila, "From Memphis to Kingston: An Investigation into the Origin of Jamaican Ska," *Social and Economic Studies* 55, no. 1/2 (2006): 75.
41. Kauppila, "From Memphis to Kingston," 75.
42. Reynolds, *Rip It Up and Start Again*, 18.
43. Reynolds, *Rip It Up and Start Again*, 231.
44. Haddon, *What Is Post-Punk?*, 147.
45. Nick_Rhodes_Tye, "Duran Duran First Interview," October 5, 2022, YouTube video, 1:35, https://www.youtube.com/watch?v=4dN4GI-diu0.
46. Dabatube, "Duran Duran First Known Interview," January 20, 2011, YouTube video, 3:35, 7:45, https://www.youtube.com/watch?v=xSkCc3iO9qA&t=308.
47. Reynolds, *Rip It Up and Start Again*, 338.
48. Reynolds, *Totally Wired*, 425–6.
49. Dave Rimmer, *Like Punk Never Happened: Culture Club and the New Pop* (Faber & Faber, 2023), 15.

# Bibliography

## History/Critical Essays

33⅓ series. These short books from Bloomsbury Publishing address specific albums with a variety of approaches, but many emphasize critical analysis. Those that are from the proto-punk/punk/post-punk and second wave ska era are Joy Division's *Unknown Pleasures*; the Velvet Underground's *The Velvet Underground and Nico*; the Ramones' *Ramones*; Captain Beefheart's *Trout Mask Replica*; Patti Smith's *Horses*; Wire's *Pink Flag*; Madness's *One Step Beyond*; Television's *Marquee Moon*; Talking Heads' *Fear of Music*; Gang of Four's *Entertainment!*; Dead Kennedys' *Fresh Fruit for Rotting Vegetables*; Blondie's *Parallel Lines*; the Modern Lovers' *The Modern Lovers*; Young Marble Giants' *Colossal Youth*; the Raincoats' *The Raincoats*; Suicide's *Suicide*; and ESG's *Come Away with ESG*.

Ambrosch, Gerfried. "American Punk: The Relations between Punk Rock, Hardcore, and American Culture." *American Studies* 60, no. ⅔ (2015): 215–33.

Ambrosch, Gerfried. *The Poetry of Punk: The Meaning Behind Punk Rock and Hardcore Lyrics*. Routledge, 2018.

Augustyn, Heather. *Ska: The Rhythm of Liberation*. Scarecrow Press, 2013.

Azerrad, Michael. *Our Band Could Be Your Life: Scenes from the American Indie Underground 1981-1991*. Little, Brown and Company, 2001.

Bangs, Lester. *Main Lines, Blood Feasts, and Bad Taste: A Lester Bangs Reader*. Anchor Books, 2003.

Bangs, Lester. *Psychotic Reactions and Carburetor Dung*. Alfred A. Knopf, 1987.

Blake, Mark. *Punk: The Whole Story*. DK Publishing, 2006.

Brown, Rodger Lyle. *Party Out of Bounds: The B-52's, R.E.M., and the Kids Who Rocked Athens, Georgia*. University of Georgia Press, 1991.

Butt, Gavin. *No Machos or Pop Stars: When the Leeds Art Experiment Went Punk*. Duke University Press, 2022.

Cogan, Brian. *The Encyclopedia of Punk Music and Culture*. Sterling, 2006.

Coon, Caroline. *1988: The New Wave Punk Rock Explosion*. Omnibus, 1982.

Ensminger, David. *The Politics of Punk: Protest and Revolt from the Streets*. Rowman & Littlefield, 2016.

Ensminger, David. *Punk Women: 40 Years of Musicians Who Built Punk Rock*. Microcosm, 2021.

Gaines, Donna. *Why the Ramones Matter*. University of Texas Press, 2018.

Gimarc, George. *Punk Diary: The Ultimate Trainspotter's Guide to Underground Rock, 1970-1982*. Backbeat, 2005.

Glasper, Ian. *Burning Britain: The History of UK Punk 1980-1984*. PM Press, 2014.

Glasper, Ian. *The Day the Country Died: A History of Anarcho Punk 1980-1984*. PM Press, 2014.

Goldman, Vivien. *Revenge of the She-Punks: A Feminist Music History from Poly Styrene to Pussy Riot*. University of Texas Press, 2019.

Haddon, Mimi. "Dub Is the New Black: Modes of Identification and Tendencies of Appropriation in Late 1970s Post-Punk." *Popular Music* 36, no. 2 (May 2017): 283–301.

Haddon, Mimi. *What Is Post-Punk?* University of Michigan Press, 2023.

Heter, Joshua, and Richard Greene. *Post-Punk Philosophy: Rip It Up and Think Again*. Open Universe, 2024.

Heter, Joshua, and Richard Greene. *Punk Rock and Philosophy*. Open Universe, 2022.

Heylin, Clinton. *Babylon's Burning: From Punk to Grunge*. Viking, 2007.

Heylin, Clinton. *From the Velvets to the Voidoids: The Birth of American Punk Rock*. Chicago Review Press, 2005.

Hurchalla, George. *Going Underground: American Punk 1979-1989*. PM Press, 2016.

Kauppila, Paul. "From Memphis to Kingston: An Investigation Into the Origin of Jamaican Ska." *Social and Economic Studies* 55, nos. 1–2 (2006): 75–91.

Kuhn, Gabriel. *Sober Living for the Revolution: Hardcore Punk, Straight Edge, and Radical Politics*. PM Press, 2010.

Laing, Dave. *One Chord Wonders: Power and Meaning in Punk Rock*. PM Press, 2015.

Larson, Jen B. *Hit Girls: Women of Punk in the USA, 1975-1983*. Feral House, 2023.

MacLeod, Dewar. *Kids of the Black Hole: Punk Rock in Postsuburban California*. University of Oklahoma Press, 2010.

Marcus, Greil. *Lipstick Traces: A Secret History of the 20th Century*. Harvard University Press, 1989.

Masters, Marc. *No Wave*. Black Dog Publishing, 2007.
Mattson, Kevin. *We're Not Here to Entertain: Punk Rock, Ronald Reagan, and the Real Culture War of 1980s America*. Oxford University Press, 2020.
Moore, Thurston, and Byron Coley. *No Wave: Post-Punk. Underground. New York. 1976–1980*. Abrams Image, 2008.
O'Shea, Mick. *The Sex Pistols Invade America: The Fateful U.S. Tour, Jan. 1978*. McFarland, 2008.
Rachel, Daniel. *Too Much Too Young, the 2 Tone Records Story: Rude Boys, Racism, and the Soundtrack of a Generation*. Akashic, 2024.
Reddington, Helen. *The Lost Women of Rock Music: Female Musicians of the Punk Era*. Routledge, 2007.
Reynolds, Simon. *Rip It Up and Start Again: Postpunk 1978–1984*. Penguin, 2005.
Reynolds, Simon. *Shock and Awe: Glam Rock and Its Legacy, from the Seventies to the Twenty-First Century*. Dey Street Books, 2016.
Reynolds, Simon. *Totally Wired: Postpunk Interviews and Overviews*. Soft Skull, 2010.
Rimmer, Dave. *Like Punk Never Happened: Culture Club and the New Pop*. Faber & Faber, 2023.
Robb, John. *The Art of Darkness: The History of Goth*. Manchester University Press, 2023.
Robbins, Ira, ed. *The New Trouser Press Record Guide*. Charles Scribner's Sons, 1985.
Rombes, Nicholas. *A Cultural Dictionary of Punk 1974–1982*. Continuum, 2009.
Rose, Caryn. *Why Patti Smith Matters*. University of Texas Press, 2022.
Ruland, Jim. *Corporate Rock Sucks: The Rise and Fall of SST Records*. Hachette Books, 2022.
Sabin, Roger, ed. *Punk Rock: So What?* Routledge, 1999.
Spence, Simon. *What Have We Got: The Turbulent Story of Oi!* Omnibus, 2023.
Strong, M.C. *The Great Indie Discography*. Canongate, 1999.
Tolhurst, Lol. *Goth: A History*. Hachette, 2023.
Unsworth, Cathi. *Season of the Witch: The Book of Goth*. Nine Eight Books, 2023.
Waksman, Steve. *This Ain't the Summer of Love: Conflict and Crossover in Heavy Metal and Punk*. University of California Press, 2009.
Weidman, Rich. *Punk: The Definitive Guide to the Blank Generation and Beyond*. Backbeat, 2023.
Wells, Steven. *Punk: Loud, Young and Snotty: The Stories Behind Every Song*. Thunder's Mouth Press, 2004.
Worley, Matthew. *No Future: Punk, Politics and British Youth Culture, 1976–1984*. Cambridge University Press, 2017.

## Oral Histories

Abrams, Howie, and James Lathos. *Finding Joseph I: An Oral History of H.R. from Bad Brains*. Post Hill Press, 2019.
Adams, Chris. *Turquoise Days: The Weird World of Echo & the Bunnymen*. Soft Skull, 2002.
Augustyn, Heather. *Ska: An Oral History*. McFarland, 2010.
Blush, Steven. *American Hardcore: A Tribal History*. Feral House, 2010.
Boulware, Jack, and Silke Tudor. *Gimme Something Better: The Profound, Progressive, and Occasionally Pointless History of Bay Area Punk from Dead Kennedys to Green Day*. Penguin, 2009.
Colgrave, Stephen, and Chris Sullivan. *Punk: The Definitive Record of a Revolution*. Thunder's Mouth Press, 2005.
Crawford, Scott. *Spoke: Images and Stories from the 1980s Washington, D.C. Punk Scene*. Akashic Books, 2017.
Doe, John, and Tom DeSavia. *Under the Big Black Sun: A Personal History of L.A. Punk*. Da Capo Press, 2016.
Ensminger, David. *Left of the Dial: Conversations with Punk Icons*. PM Press, 2013.
Gold, Jeff, and Iggy Pop. *Total Chaos: The Story of the Stooges as Told by Iggy Pop*. Third Man Books, 2016.
Jones, Dylan. *Loaded: The Life (and Afterlife) of the Velvet Underground*. Grand Central Publishing, 2023.
Lydon, John. *Rotten: No Irish, No Blacks, No Dogs*. Picador, 2008.
Malkin, John. *Punk Revolution!: An Oral History of Punk Rock Politics and Activism*. Rowman & Littlefield, 2023.
McCormick, Neil, and U2. *U2 by U2*. It Books, 2009.
McNeil, Legs. *Please Kill Me: The Uncensored Oral History of Punk*. Penguin, 1996.
Mullen, Brendan. *Lexicon Devil: The Fast Times and Short Life of Darby Crash and the Germs*. Feral House, 2002.
O'Hagan, Sean, and Nick Cave. *Faith, Hope and Carnage*. Picador, 2022.
Partridge, Andy. *Complicated Game: Inside the Songs of XTC*. Jawbone, 2016.
Rettman, Tony. *NYHC: New York Hardcore 1980–1990*. Bazillion Points, 2014.
Rettman, Tony. *Straight Edge: A Clear-Headed Hardcore Punk History*. Bazillion Points, 2017.
Robb, John. *Punk Rock: An Oral History*. PM Press, 2012.
Russo, Stacy. *We Were Going to Change the World: Interviews with Women from the 1970s and 1980s Southern California Punk Rock Scene*. Santa Monica Press, 2017.
Savage, Jon. *This Searing Light, The Sun and Everything Else: Joy Division, the Oral History*. Faber & Faber, 2020.
Sex Pistols. *1977: The Bollocks Diaries*. Cassell, 2018.
Spitz, Marc, and Brendan Mullen. *We Got the Neutron Bomb: The Untold Story of L.A. Punk*. Three Rivers Press, 2001.
York, Will. *Who Cares Anyway: Post-Punk San Francisco and the End of the Analog Age*. Headpress, 2023.

## Memoirs

Alvertine, Viv. *Clothes, Clothes, Clothes. Music, Music, Music. Boys, Boys, Boys.* Thomas Dunne Books, 2014.
Bag, Alice. *Violence to Hollywood Stage, a Chicana Punk Story Girl: East L.A. Rage.* Feral House, 2011.
Black, Pauline. *Black by Design.* Serpent's Tail, 2012.
Bono. *Surrender: 40 Songs, One Story.* Alfred Knopf, 2022.
Bradley, Michael. *Teenage Kicks: My Life as an Undertone.* Omnibus, 2016.
Dictor, Dave. *MDC: Memoir from a Damaged Civilization: Stories of Punk, Fear, and Redemption.* Manic D Press, 2016.
Diggle, Steve. *Autonomy: Portrait of a Buzzcock.* Omnibus, 2024.
Frantz, Chris. *Remain in Love: Talking Heads, Tom Tom Club, Tina.* St. Martin's Press, 2010.
Gordon, Kim. *Girl in a Band: A Memoir.* Dey Street Books, 2015.
Graffin, Greg. *Punk Paradox: A Memoir.* Hachette Books, 2022.
Harry, Deborah. *Face It: A Memoir.* Dey Street Books, 2019.
Hell, Richard. *I Dreamed I Was a Very Clean Tramp: An Autobiography.* Ecco, 2014.
Hook, Peter. *Unknown Pleasures: Inside Joy Division.* It Books, 2013.
Hynde, Chrissie. *Reckless: My Life as a Pretender.* Anchor Books, 2016.
Ignorant, Steve. *The Rest Is Propaganda.* Southern Records, 2010.
Jones, Steve. *Lonely Boy: Tales from a Sex Pistol.* Da Capo Press, 2017.
Keithley, Joey. *I, Shithead: A Life in Punk.* Arsenal Pulp Press, 2004.
Lomas, Ross. *City Baby: Surviving in Leather, Bristles, Studs, Punk Rock, and G.B.H.* Bazillion Points, 2015.
Lydon, John. *Anger Is an Energy: My Life Uncensored.* Dey Street Books, 2016.
Matlock, Glen. *I Was a Teenage Sex Pistol.* Faber & Faber, 1990.
Miret, Roger. *My Riot: Agnostic Front, Grit, Guts & Glory.* Post Hill Press, 2019.
Moore, Thurston. *Sonic Life: A Memoir.* Doubleday, 2023.
Morris, Keith. *My Damage.* Da Capo Press, 2017.
Morris, Stephen. *Confessions of a Post-Punk Percussionist: The Joy Division Years.* Constable & Robinson, 2022.
Morrissey. *Autobiography.* Penguin, 2014.
Mould, Bob. *See a Little Light: The Trail of Rage and Melody.* Little, Brown and Company, 2011.
Panter, Horace. *Ska'd for Life: A Personal Journey with The Specials.* Pan Books, 2008.
Ramone, Dee Dee. *Legend of a Rock Star: A Memoir: The Last Testament of Dee Dee Ramone.* Da Capo Press, 2003.
Ramone, Johnny. *Commando: The Autobiography of Johnny Ramone.* Harry N. Abrams, 2012.
Ramone, Marky. *Punk Rock Blitzkrieg: My Life as a Ramone.* Touchstone, 2015.
Roger, Ranking. *I Just Can't Stop It: My Life in The Beat.* Omnibus Press, 2021.
Rollins, Henry. *Get in the Van: On the Road with Black Flag.* 2.13.61, 1994.
Sargeant, Will. *Bunnyman: Post-War Kid to Post-Punk Guitarist of Echo and the Bunnymen.* Third Man Books, 2022.
Smith, Mark E. *Renegade: The Lives and Tales of Mark E. Smith.* Penguin, 2009.
Stein, Chris. *Under a Rock.* St. Martin's Press, 2024.
Suggs. *That Close.* Quercus, 2013.
Sumner, Bernard. *Chapter and Verse: New Order, Joy Division and Me.* Transworld, 2015.
Tolhurst, Lol. *Cured: The Tale of Two Imaginary Boys.* Da Capo Press, 2017.
Turner, Jeff. *Cockney Reject.* John Blake Publishing, 2010.
Valentine, Gary. *New York Rocker: My Life in the Blank Generation with Blondie, Iggy Pop, and Others, 1974–1981.* Da Capo Press, 2006.

## Biographies

Andrews, Mark. *Paint My Name in Black and Gold: The Rise of the Sisters of Mercy.* Unbound, 2023.
Apter, Jeff. *The Story of the Cure.* Omnibus, 2009.
Bad Religion, and Jim Ruland. *Do What You Want: The Story of Bad Religion.* Hachette, 2021.
Berger, George. *The Story of Crass.* PM Press, 2009.
Bockris, Victor, and Roberta Bayley. *Patti Smith: An Unauthorized Biography.* Simon & Schuster, 1999.
Chick, Stevie. *Spray Paint the Walls: The Story of Black Flag.* PM Press, 2011.
Davis-Chanin, Laura. *Infinite Dreams: The Life of Alan Vega.* Backbeat, 2024.
Dellinger, Jade, and David Giffels. *Are We Not Men? We Are Devo.* SAF Publishing, 2003.
Earles, Andrew. *Hüsker Dü: The Story of the Noise-Pop Pioneers Who Launched Modern Rock.* Voyageur Press, 2010.
Foege, Alec. *Confusion Is Next: The Sonic Youth Story.* St. Martin's Press, 1994.
Gilbert, Pat. *Passion Is a Fashion: The Real Story of the Clash.* Da Capo Press, 2005.
Graham, Bill. *U2: The Early Days.* Dell Publishing, 1989.
Hewitt, Paolo. *The Jam: A Beat Concerto—The Authorized Biography.* Book Sales Ltd., 1983.
Howe, Zoe Street. *Typical Girls?: The Story of the Slits.* Omnibus, 2009.
Lester, Paul. *Gang of Four: Damaged Gods.* Omnibus, 2008.
Link, Roland. *Kicking Up a Racket: The Story of Stiff Little Fingers 1977–1983.* Appletree, 2009.
Mathur, Paul. *Siouxsie and the Banshees: The Authorized Biography.* Sanctuary Publishing Ltd., 2003.
McGartland, Tony. *Buzzcocks: The Complete History.* Music Press Books, 2017.

Mehr, Bob. *Trouble Boys: The True Story of the Replacements*. Da Capo Press, 2016.

Myers, Ben. *John Lydon: The Sex Pistols, PiL, and Anti-Celebrity*. Independent Music Press, 2004.

Ogg, Alex. *Dead Kennedys: Fresh Fruit for Rotting Vegetables, The Early Years*. PM Press, 2014.

Porter, Dick. *Journey to the Centre of The Cramps*. Omnibus, 2015.

Savage, Jon. *England's Dreaming: Anarchy, Sex Pistols, Punk Rock, and Beyond*. St. Martin's Press, 2001.

Trowell, Ian. *Throbbing Gristle: An Endless Discontent*. Intellect Ltd., 2023.

True, Everett. *Hey Ho Let's Go: The Story of the Ramones*. Omnibus, 2002.

Trynka, Paul. *Iggy Pop: Open Up and Bleed: A Biography*. Broadway Books, 2007.

Williams, Paul. *You're Wondering Now: The Specials from Conception to Reunion*. Cherry Red Books, 2009.

## Generations

Twenge, Jean. *Generations: The Real Differences Between Gen Z, Millennials, Gen X, Boomers, and Silents and What They Mean for America's Future*. Simon & Schuster, 2023.

Williams, Jeffrey J. "The Generation in Between: An Interview with Jonathan Pontell." *Symplokē* 23, no. 1–2 (2015): 485–511.

Williams, Jeffery J. "Not My Generation." *The Chronicle of Higher Education*, March 31, 2014. https://www.chronicle.com/article/not-my-generation-145569/.

# Index

Action Pact! 14
Adam and the Ants 36
Adamson, Stuart 28–29, 155, 156
The Adicts 15
The Adolescents 15, 17
Advert, Gaye 16
The Adverts 16–17, 179
Agent Orange 17
Agnostic Front 17–18, 184
Akrylykz 18
The Alarm 18
Albini, Steve 28, 29
*Alice in Wonderland* 154
Allen, Dave 87
Alley Cats 18–19
Altered Images 19–20, 188
The American Dream 3, 192
Andersen, Hans Christian 153
Anderson, Leesa 143
Angelic Upstarts 20
Anti-Pasti 20
Antidote 20, 184
apocalyptic imagery 10, 15, 16, 21, 26, 28, 34, 45, 46, 49, 64, 70, 71, 73, 75, 85, 88, 89, 95, 102, 140, 141, 142, 157, 160, 164, 170, 174, 180, 186, 189, 193, 199, 201, 203
Armstrong, Louis 30, 89
Articles of Faith 20–21
Artificial Peace 184
Asheton, Ron 65, 66, 210, 211
Ashman, Matthew 36
Aspinall, Vicky 133
The Associates 21
Au Pairs 21–22
Avengers (band) 22, 69, 120
*The Avengers* (TV show) 177

B-52s 17, 23–24, 131, 186, 187, 206
baby boomer generation 3, 4, 89, 92, 133, 134
Bad Brains 24–25, 112, 184
Bad Manners 25, 1840
Bad Religion 25–26
Bags, Alice 26
The Bags 26

*The Banana Splits* 68
Bane, Honey 26, 83
Bangs, Lester 212
Barile, Al 164
Barson, Mike 106
Basement 5 26
Bators, Stiv 61
Bauhaus 9, 27–28, 30
Beach Boys 192
The Beatles 10, 46, 134, 212, 214
Beckett, Samuel 187
Bedford, Mark 106
Beefheart, Captain 85, 108, 115, 124, 202
Bernhardt, Sarah 191
Beshara 28
Biafra, Jello 62, 63
Big Black 10, 28–29, 90, 119, 170, 171
Big Boys 29
Big Country 29–30, 156
The Birthday Party 9, 30–31, 37, 85; *see also* The Boys Next Door
Black, Pauline 146
Black Flag 31–33, 112, 137, 165, 194
Black Sabbath 68
The Blasters 85
Blitz 33
Blondie 23, 33–35, 150, 196
Blue Orchids 35
Blue Oyster Cult 48
Bobby Fuller Four 48
The Bodysnatchers 35, 57, 184
Bondage, Beki 186
Bono 180
Boon, D. 115
Bow Wow Wow 36, 38, 124
Bowie, David 21, 36–37, 73, 125, 127, 186, 201
The Boys Next Door 30; *see also* Birthday Party
Bradbury, John 162
Branca, Glenn 10, 37–38, 175, 178
Brannon, John 120
The Breeders 28
Brewer, Jack 143

Briscoe, Vanessa 131
Brown, James 72, 161, 185
Brown, Jerry 61
Buck, Peter 137
Buckler, Rick 94
Budgie 55, 152, 153
Burg, China 109
Burgess, Mark 38
Burke, Clem 35
Burundi drumming 36, 38, 124
Bush, Kate 38
The Bush Tetras 38, 131
Buster, Prince 75, 105, 107, 162, 209
Butler, Richard 129
The Buzzcocks 6, 8, 15, 39–41, 44, 65, 98, 104, 108, 149, 175, 182, 196
The Byrds 10, 158, 214
Byrne, David 23, 41, 172, 173, 174

Cabaret Voltaire 11, 41–42
Cagney, James 148
Cale, John 210, 214, 215
Campbell, Stan 164
Camus, Albert 56
Can 201–202
Captain Sensible 58
Carlier, Ramona 118
The Cars 25
Casey, Jayne 124
Cave, Nick 30, 31, 37
A Certain Ratio 42
Cervenka, Exene 193
Chai, Dianne 18–19
The Chameleons 42–43, 51
Chance, James 185
Chandra 43–44
Channel 3 44
Chaos U.K. 44
Chelsea 44–45
Chevron, Philip 132
Circle Jerks 31, 33, 45–46
Clark, Petula 23
The Clash 11, 13, 21, 44, 46–49, 50, 54, 58, 69, 105, 113, 143, 166, 177, 183, 188, 200, 204, 212
Cliff, Jimmy 212

223

*A Clockwork Orange* 144
Cock Sparrer 49–50
Cockney Rejects 7, 29, 50
Cocteau Twins 38, 50–51
Cold War 16, 35, 44, 54, 63, 71, 102, 117, 144, 148, 149, 155, 163, 168, 169, 179, 188, 197
Comsat Angels 51
Conflict 51–52
The Contortions 10, 38, 185
Cooper, Alice 73, 202
Corboy, Dave 143
Corman, Roger 136
Costello, Elvis 52–53, 93
County, Wayne 53
The Cramps 8, 30, 53–54
Crash, Darby 89
Crass 54–55, 83, 90, 185, 200
Crass Record Label 26, 51, 54, 55, 125, 200
The Cravats 55
Cream 7
The Creatures 27, 55–56, 153
*Crime and Punishment* 109
Crossover Thrash: formation of 7; in music 14, 44, 45, 69, 70, 78, 88, 93, 115, 183, 187
The Cult 139
Culture Club 11
The Cure 9, 56–57
Currie, Cherie 141
Curtis, Ian 72, 99, 100, 101, 120, 121

D-beat 70, 139, 185
Dakar, Rhoda 35, 57, 163, 164
The Damned 46, 58–61, 143, 204
Damners, Jerry 162
The Dance 60–61
Dangerhouse record label 18, 22, 26, 64, 69, 78, 188
Da Silva, Ana 133
Dave Clark Five 139
The Dead Boys 61
Dead Kennedys 61–64, 110
Dead Man's Shadow 14
Deadline 184
Death 202–203
The Death Cult 139
Deep Purple 7
Deep Wound 64
Dekker, Desmond 212
Delta 5 64
The Descendents 6, 64–65, 68
Desjardins, Chris 85
Desperate Bicycles 65
Destroy All Monsters 65–66
De Vivre, Joy 55
Devo 8, 11, 52, 185
DeVoto, Howard 8, 39, 108, 175
Dickens, Charles 20
The Dickies 65, 68
The Dicks 68–69

Diddley, Bo 210, 211
The Dils 69
Dinger, Klaus 205
Discharge 44, 69–70, 185
Dischord record label 78, 90, 113, 120, 145, 164, 165, 175, 184, 187
Disco 1, 12, 35, 43, 112, 114, 130, 136, 194, 196, 200
Diserio, Eugenie 61
Disorder 70
DNA 10, 70, 185
D.O.A. 7, 70–71, 194
Dr. Feelgood 72, 203
Doe, John 85, 193
Donahue, Patty 187, 188
Dostoevsky, Fyodor 109
Dub 8, 11, 26, 27, 42, 76, 83, 127, 128, 170, 178, 212
Du Plenty, Tomata 145
Duran Duran 12
Duritti Column 71–72
Dury, Ian 72, 106, 107
Dylan, Bob 196
dystopian themes 15, 16, 26, 32, 44, 51, 59, 61, 77, 95, 102, 110, 137, 144, 163, 168, 169, 173, 177, 181

The Eagles 192
East Bay Ray 62
Eater 72–73
Echo and the Bunnymen 73–74
Eddy, Duane 53
The Edge 179, 180
The Effigies 74–75
electronic/electronic/electric punk 28, 35, 36, 41, 42, 66, 145, 149, 169, 179, 194, 205
The English Beat 75–76, 146, 184
Eno, Brian 10, 36, 41, 67, 68, 173, 174, 185, 208
ESG 76
Essential Logic 76–77, 137
Evans, Judy 89
The Exploited 7, 52
Eyes 78

Factory record label 42, 71, 100, 101, 120, 121, 188
The Faith 78–79, 145
The Fakes 79
The Fall 35, 79–82, 187, 214
Fancy Rosy 82
Fang 83
Farren, Mick 83
Fast Product record label 84, 86, 110, 144
Fatal Microbes 26, 83
Fear 83–84
The Feelies 10, 84, 112, 137, 214
Fine Young Cannibals 18

The Fire Engines 10, 84–85
Flanagan, Harley 167
Fleetwood Mac 139
Flesh Eaters 85
Fleshtones 85
Flipper 85–86
Flouride, Klaus 62
The Flowers 86
Foreman, Chris 106
45 Grave 13
Foster, Jodie 97
4AD Record Label 27, 30, 31, 50, 51, 118, 194
4 Skins 97
Foxton, Bruce 94, 95
Frantz, Chris 173
Fraser, Elizabeth 50, 51
The Freeze 185

Gang Green 185
Gang of Four 8, 28, 84, 86–87, 108, 185, 200
The Gangsters 88
Garvey, Steve 175
GBH 88–89
Generation Jones 3, 4, 5, 8, 9, 11, 12, 15, 26, 32, 35, 43, 49, 57, 61, 64, 71, 77, 83, 90, 94, 110, 111, 114, 119, 123, 133, 134, 150, 155, 159, 160, 161, 172, 181, 187, 192, 193, 195, 196, 197, 199
Generation X 4
Generation X (band) 89
*Georgy Girl* 15
The Germs 89
Gerry and the Pacemakers 139
Gift, Roland 18
Gill, Andy 86, 87
Ginn, Greg 33
Gira, Michael 272
Glam Rock 7, 12, 27, 48, 73, 97, 148, 182, 205, 208
Glitter, Gary 208
Gogol, Nikolai 149
Golding, Lynval 162
Gordon, Kim 160, 161, 187
The Gordons 90
Goth: formation of sub-genre of post-punk 9; in music 16, 17, 19, 27, 28, 30, 31, 42, 45, 50, 51, 53, 55, 58, 59, 60, 69, 80, 82, 85, 100, 101, 108, 115, 119, 128, 129, 139, 149, 150, 151, 152, 154, 159, 170, 171, 179, 186, 194, 206, 211, 214
Government Issue 90–91, 184
Grandmaster Flash 104
The Grateful Dead 175, 211
*The Great Rock and Roll Swindle* 148
Grogan, Claire 19
Grundy, Bill 177
Guevara, Che 170
The Gun Club 9, 18, 91

Hackney, David 203
Hagen, Nina 91
Hall, Terry 162, 163
Hannett, Martin 76, 100, 129
*A Hard Day's Night* 15
hardcore punk 4, formation of 6; 7, in songs 13, 14, 15, 17, 18, 19, 21, 24, 25, 26, 29, 31, 32, 33, 44, 45, 46, 51, 58, 59, 62, 63, 64, 65, 68, 69, 70, 71, 77, 78, 79, 83, 84, 88, 89, 90, 92, 93, 97, 103, 110, 112, 113, 114, 115, 117, 118, 120, 137, 138, 145, 150, 159, 160, 164, 165, 168, 169, 175, 179, 181, 183, 184, 185, 187, 189, 190, 193, 199, 200, 202, 203, 204
*The Harder They Come* 212
Harper, Charlie 181
Harrison, Jerry 173, 204
Harry, Debbie 34
Hart, Grant 92
Harvey, PJ 28
Head, Jowe 162
Headon, Topper 47
Hearst, Patty 115
Heartbreakers 92
heavy metal 7, 8, 18, 21, 25, 32, 44, 46, 48, 69, 78, 83, 84, 85, 86, 88, 89, 90, 102, 115, 137, 164, 183, 185, 187, 189, 202, 204, 211
Hell, Richard 92, 132
Hendrix, Jimi 7
Hess, Rudolph 100
Hetston, Greg 137
Hill, Napoleon 24
Hinckley, John, Jr. 97
hippie culture and punk reaction 3, 4, 6, 15, 23, 31, 46, 59, 61, 69, 78, 93, 113, 136, 186, 200, 202, 210, 212, 213
Hitler, Adolf 100
Honeyman-Scott, James 128
Hook, Peter 121
horror Punk: formation of 8; in music 14, 18, 53, 54, 59, 83, 85, 115, 117, 134, 135, 170, 179, 187, 189, 202, 211, 214
Houston, Penelope 22
H.R. 24
The Human League 145
Husker Du 92–93, 138
Huwe, Anja 194
Hynde, Chrissie 128

Idol, Billy 89
industrial music 26, 35, 36, 41, 66, 67, 79, 100, 102, 126, 154, 170, 178, 188, 191, 194
Inflatable Boy Clams 93

Jackson, Joe 93
The Jam 44, 69, 94–97, 122, 204

James, Brian 58
jangle punk/post-punk 10, 21, 64, 80, 84, 98, 104, 109, 111, 112, 119, 138, 152, 171, 172, 214
Jerry's Kids 185
Jett, Joan 89, 97, 141
JFA 97, 110
JJ All Stars 97
Jobson, Richard 155
Johansen, David 205
Johnny Moped 97
Johnson, Robert 91
Johnson, Wilko 72, 203
The Jolt 97–98
Jones, Mick 47, 177
Josef K 10, 84, 98, 123, 158
Joy Division 9, 29, 67, 72, 76, 99–101, 120, 121, 188
Judge Dread 101–102

Kafka, Franz 98
Kennedy, John F. 66, 115
Kerr, Jim 150
Killing Joke 102
The Kinks 128
Kleenex 102–103, 149
Kraftwerk 11, 205
Kraut 103

Lanfeld, Julie 150
LeBon, Simon 12
Led Zeppelin 7, 71
Lee, Christopher 116
Lee, Peggy 112
Lee, Sara 87
Lennon, John 19, 147, 200, 206
Letts, Don 26
Levene, Keith 129, 130
Lewis, Jerry Lee 193
Libertine, Eve 55
LiLiPUT 102, 103–104, 149
Linsey, Arto 185
Liquid Liquid 104
Lloyd, Richard 176
Logic, Lara 76, 133, 137
The Lone Ranger 190
*Lord of the Flies* 15
Los Lobos 85
Lovich, Lene 92
Lucas, George 116
Luddites 82
Ludus 104–105
Lunch, Lydia 176, 185
The Lurkers 105
Lwin, Annabella 36
Lydon, John 129, 130, 147, 148; see also Rotten, Johnny

Maby, Graham 93
MacGowan, Shane 121
Mackay, John 150, 153
MacKaye, Alec 78, 79, 175, 184
MacKaye, Ian 78, 113, 120, 175, 184

Mackenzie, Billy 21
Macnee, Patrick 177
Madness 18, 25, 75, 105–108, 146, 155, 175, 184
Magazine 8, 76, 104, 108–109, 175
Marcus, J. 64
Marie et les Garçons 109
Marley, Bob 26, 203–204
Marr, Johnny 158
Mars 10, 109, 185
Mason, Nick 59
Maximum Joy 110
Mayfield, Curtis 194
McCulloch, Ian 73, 74
MC5 202, 204, 205
McGeoch, John 108, 109, 152, 153
McLaren, Malcolm 92, 148
MDC 110
The Mekons 110–111
The Melodians 212
The Members 111
The Membranes 112
Mercedes, Denise 167
Mercier Descloux. Lizzy 112, 140
Method Actors 112
The Middle Class 112
Miller, Roger 117
Minor Threat 46, 113–114, 120, 145, 175, 184, 190, 199
The Minutemen 29, 114–115, 194
The Misfits 8, 115–117, 182
Mission of Burma 117–118, 131
Mo-dettes 118
Modern English 118
Modern Lovers 109, 204–205
Mofungo 119
The Monkees 113, 184
Monochrome Set 119
Morgan, Dennis 26
Morris, Keith 31, 33, 45, 46
Morrison, Hilary 86
Morrison, Sterling 213
Morrissey 104, 158, 159
The Mothers of Invention 19
Motorik 205
Mould, Bob 92
MTV 4, 12, 145
Murray, Pauline 123
Murvin, Junior 48
Mussolini, Benito 87

Necros 120
Negative Approach 120
Negative Trend 120
Nelson, Ricky 53
The Nerves 35
Ness, Mike 160
Neu! 205
New Order 76, 120–121
New Romantics replacing punk era 11–12; 14, 21, 36, 45

New Wave 4, 9, 16, 19, 20, 23, 41, 51, 52, 78, 90, 91, 131, 167, 179, 186, 187, 194, 196, 205
New York Dolls 205–206
Niagra 65, 66
Nico 206, 212, 213, 214; *see also* The Velvet Underground
999 14
The Nips 121–122
Nirvana 28, 83, 189
Nixon, Richard 72
No Wave: formation of sub-genre of post-punk 9–10; in music 30, 37, 38, 43, 44, 60, 65, 66, 70, 72, 104, 109, 112, 119, 124, 128, 129, 130, 140, 149, 158, 160, 161, 169, 170, 171, 175, 176, 178, 185, 198, 202, 206, 208, 213, 215
Noise Rock/Punk: formation of sub-genre 10; in music 28, 37, 66, 70, 82, 84, 90, 160, 170, 171, 176, 178, 189, 191, 206, 211, 213, 214, 215
Nolan, Jerry 92
nuclear war 1, 4, 17, 26, 46, 51, 54, 57, 77, 78, 102, 114, 117, 141, 144, 145, 159, 163, 168, 169, 170, 178, 180, 181, 186, 188, 197, 199
Nylon, Judy 159

Ocasek, Ric 25
The Offs 122
Oh-OK 122
Oi!: formation of 7; in music 15, 20, 33, 45, 50, 54, 78, 88, 93, 97, 117, 148, 181, 183, 199
Ono, Yoko 23, 91, 206
Opus 122
Orange Juice 84, 122–123
Orwell, George 153, 169
outsider persona 15, 45, 50, 54, 59, 60, 61, 63, 80, 83, 88, 93, 95, 104, 114, 117, 123, 132, 135, 136, 142, 143, 147, 148, 158, 160, 167, 171, 182, 189, 190, 201, 207, 211, 212
Owen, Malcolm 142

Palladin, Patti 159
Palmolive 133, 157
Panter, Horace 162
Partridge, Andy 196, 197, 198
Pearlman, Sandy 48
Peel, John 70, 98, 156, 157
Peligro, D.H. 62
Penetration 123
Pere Ubu 8, 123–124, 131
Perry, Lee "Scratch" 212
Pigbag 124
Pierce, Jeffrey Lee 91
Pierson, Kate 23
Pink Floyd, 59
Pink Military 124–125

*Plan 9 from Outer Space* 59, 117
Plastic Bertrand 83, 125, 149
Poe, Edgar Allan 152
The Pogues 121, 132
Poison Girls 83, 125, 140
police harassment 32, 44, 45, 46, 47, 49, 61, 68, 71, 94, 110, 164, 181, 184
political/social themes 2, 3, 4, 5, 6, 7, 8, 11, 14, 15, 22, 25, 32, 33, 44, 45, 44, 48, 51, 53, 58, 61, 62, 63, 65, 67, 69, 71, 72, 73, 75, 78, 81, 84, 86, 87, 88, 92, 95, 96, 97, 100, 102, 105, 110, 111, 114, 120, 123, 129, 132, 133, 134, 137, 139, 140, 142, 143, 144, 146, 147, 151, 163, 164, 165, 166, 167, 181, 182, 185, 189, 190, 191, 193, 197, 200, 202, 203, 204, 205, 208
Pollock, Jackson 158
Pontell, Jonathan 3
Pop, Iggy 28, 35, 125–127, 207, 210, 211; *see also* The Stooges
The Pop Group 127–128, 157
pop punk: formation of 6: in songs 14, 15, 16, 19, 33, 34, 35, 37, 39, 40, 41, 53, 59, 60, 64, 65, 68, 71, 73, 78, 85, 90, 93, 98, 105, 108, 115, 116, 117, 119, 121, 122, 131, 132, 133, 134, 135, 136, 137, 138, 139, 140, 141, 142, 143, 144, 149, 167, 168, 171, 177, 179, 181, 182, 183, 184, 189, 190, 194, 196, 197, 200, 204
Posh Boy record label 17, 44, 137, 159, 172, 179
post-punk 2, 4, 5, 6; formation of 8; jangle post-punk 10; mixing with traditionalism 9; in music 11, 12, 13, 17, 18, 19, 21, 22, 23, 24, 26, 27, 28, 29, 30, 31, 33, 35, 36, 37, 38, 39, 40, 41, 42, 43, 44, 45, 49, 50, 51, 54, 55, 56, 57, 59, 60, 61, 64, 65, 66, 67, 68, 70, 71, 72, 73, 74, 76, 77, 79, 80, 81, 82, 83, 84, 85, 86, 87, 90, 91, 92, 96, 98, 99, 100, 101, 102, 103, 104, 105, 108, 109, 110, 111, 112, 113, 114, 115, 117, 118, 119, 121, 122, 123, 133, 125, 126, 127, 128, 129, 130, 131, 132, 133, 134, 137, 138, 139, 141, 142, 143, 144, 145, 146, 149, 150, 151, 152, 153, 154, 155, 156, 157, 158, 160, 161, 162, 167, 168, 169, 170, 171, 172, 173, 175, 176, 177, 178, 179, 180, 185, 186, 187, 188, 189, 190, 191, 192, 193, 194, 196, 197, 198, 199, 200, 202, 203, 205, 206, 208, 209, 211, 212, 213, 214
Postcard record label 79, 84, 98, 122–123

Presley, Elvis 46, 194
The Pretenders 128
Pretty Maid Company 82
*The Prisoner* 48
The Proletariat 185
The Psychedelic Furs 128–129
*Psycho* 116
Psychobilly 8, 53, 54, 189
pub rock 72, 97, 106, 132, 181, 203
Public Image Ltd. 8, 29, 38, 108, 129–130, 192
Purple Hearts 130–131
Pylon 131–132

racism 7, 13, 20, 110, 113, 136, 142, 164, 203
Radiation, Roddy 162
The Radiators/Radiators From Space 132
Radio Birdman 132–133
The Raincoats 93, 103, 133–134, 137, 198
Ramone, Dee Dee 92, 135
Ramone, Joey 135
Ramone, Johnny 5, 33, 88, 135, 137, 201
Ramone, Marky 136
The Ramones 5, 6, 7, 20, 24, 33, 49, 53, 61, 73, 92, 100, 116, 134–137, 143, 147, 149, 182, 196, 201, 204, 215
Rankine, Alan 21
rap 4, 14, 24, 28, 49, 61, 104, 106, 107, 114, 165, 199
Rastafarianism 11, 25, 142, 203
Reagan, Ronald 12, 63, 96, 114, 147, 179, 189
Red C 184
Red Crayola 137
Red Cross 137
The Redskins 137
Reed, Lou 72, 205, 207–208, 211, 213; *see also* The Velvet Underground
reggae 8, 11, 20, 21, 24, 25, 26, 27, 28, 38, 42, 45, 47, 48, 49, 52, 75, 76, 91, 93, 101, 102, 107, 112, 119, 127, 128, 129, 142, 145, 146, 157, 163, 165, 166, 168, 170, 181, 192, 203, 204, 209, 212
Reilly, Vini 71
R.E.M. 10, 112, 122, 131, 132, 137–138
The Replacements 137–138
Rev, Martin 170
The Revillos 17, 139
The Rezillos 139
Reyes, Ron 31, 137
Richman, Jonathan 205
Rimmer, Dave 12
Ritual 139
Robinson, Smokey 75
Robinson, Tom 140

# Index

*Rock 'N' Roll High School* 204
Rocksteady 10, 11, 36
*The Rocky Horror Picture Show* 53
Roger, Ranking 75
The Rolling Stones 46, 67
Rollins, Henry 32, 33, 165, 184
Romero, George 116
Rosa Yemen 112, 140
Ross, Malcolm 98
Rotten, Johnny 5, 14, 147, 148; see also Lydon, John
Rough Trade record label 35, 41, 64, 76, 81, 82, 103, 119, 128, 133, 134, 137, 157, 158, 159, 162, 165, 171, 177, 178, 186, 192, 199
Roxy Music 208
Rubella Ballet 140
Rudi 141
Ruefrex 141
The Runaways 97, 141
Russell, Arthur 172
The Ruts 141–142
The Ruts D.C. 142

Saccharine Trust 143
Sado-Nation 143
Sage, Greg 143, 189, 190
The Saints 143–144
Savage Republic 144
Scabies, Rat 58
The Scars 144
Schneider, Fred 23
Scream 145
The Screamers 145, 169
Scritti Politti 145
The Searchers 214
The Selecter 11, 75, 146–147, 184
7 Seconds 13
Sex Pistols 5, 6, 7, 24, 26, 46, 54, 58, 92, 100, 108, 116, 129, 143, 147–148, 150, 177
The Shaggs 202, 208–209
Shakespeare, William 110
Sham 69 7, 20, 29, 142, 148–149
Sharkey, Feargal 183
Sharp, Elliot 119
Shelley, Pete 39, 40
Sherman. Allen 116
*The Silence of the Lambs* 82
Simenon, Paul 47
Simple Minds 149–150
SIN 34 150
Siouxie, Sioux 55, 56, 150, 151, 152, 153
Siouxsie and the Banshees 8, 9, 55, 56, 108, 109, 150–154
Sisters of Mercy 9, 154
Ska 2, 5, 10–11, 12, 18, 25, 26, 28, 36, 49, 52, 57, 75, 76, 88, 93, 97, 101, 102, 105, 106, 107, 108, 118, 119, 122, 124, 142, 146, 147, 155, 162, 163, 164, 175, 183, 184, 197, 203, 204, 207, 209, 212

Ska-Downs 155
Skatalites 209
The Skids 29, 155–156
Slade 208
Slash Records 83, 89, 192
The Slickers 212
The Slits 103, 133, 156–157
Smash, Chas 106
Smith, Brix 82
Smith, Mark E. 79, 80, 81, 82, 187
Smith, Patti 54, 157–158, 209–210
Smith, Robert 57
Smith, T.V. 179
The Smiths 10, 104, 123, 158–159
Snatch 159
*The Snow Queen* 153
Social Distortion 159–160
Sonic Youth 10, 90, 120, 160–161, 170, 171, 187, 189
The Sound 160, 161
Soundtracks & Head 162
soundtracks: epic 162, 171
Spandau Ballet 11
*Spartacus* 72
Special AKA 57
The Specials 11, 52, 75, 146, 162–164, 183, 184
Spector, Phil 128, 136
spiritual themes 5, 9, 11, 16, 25, 27, 31, 35, 38, 39, 44, 50, 74, 86, 91, 101, 127, 143, 148, 153, 154, 157, 158, 161, 162, 174, 176, 180, 188, 201, 206, 207, 210, 212, 214
Springa 164
Spungen, Nancy 116
SS Decontrol 164
SST records 31, 32, 33, 114, 115, 143
Stabb, John 90
Staple, Neville 162
State of Alert (S.O.A.) 165, 184
Statton, Alison 198
Steele, Bobby 182
Sterling, Linder 104, 105
Stiff Little Fingers 44, 50, 69, 132, 165–167, 188, 200
The Stimulators 167
Stinson, Bob 137
Stipe, Lynda 122
Stipe, Michael 122, 137, 138
Stodola, Randy 19
The Stooges 53, 65, 66, 88, 89, 120, 124, 125, 127, 132, 160, 171, 184, 205, 206, 207, 210–211
*The Stranger* 56
The Stranglers 167–168
Street Punk 7, 20, 70, 78, 88, 89, 181, 183
Strummer, Joe 45, 47, 48, 181, 200
Styrene, Poly 194, 195

Subhumans 168–169
Suburban Lawns 169
Subversa, Vi 125, 140
Subway Sect 169
Sudden, Nikki 171
Suggs 106
Suicide 169–170
Sumner, Bernard 120, 121
Supertramp 90
The Swans 10, 90, 170–171
Swell Maps 137, 162, 171–172, 214
Symbol Six 172
Synth-pop 11, 21, 44, 51, 67, 145, 178, 205

T. Rex 27, 208
Talking Heads 8, 28, 41, 42, 172–174, 183, 185, 204
Taylor, John 12
The Teardrops 175
Teen Idles 113, 175, 184
Teenage Film Stars 175
Teenage Jesus and the Jerks 10, 175–176, 185, 198
television 8, 92, 109, 176–177, 186, 211
television personalities 175, 177
*The Texas Chain Saw Massacre* 134
Thatcher, Margaret 12, 55, 75, 96
Theater of Hate 177
Theodorakis, Mikis 144
Theoretical Girls 178
This Heat 178
Thomas, David 123, 124
Throbbing Gristle 11, 178–179
Thunders, Johnny 92
*THX 1138* 116
Tilton, Martha 42
Tissue, Su 169
Toasting 18, 75, 93, 157, 207, 212
Toots and the Maytalls 162, 212
*Top of the Pops* 52, 139
*The Trial* 98
Trotsky, Leon 137
T.S.O.L. 179
Tubby, King 212
Tucker, Maureen 213, 214
Tuxedomoon 179
23 Skidoo 13
Twiggy 177
Two Tone 25, 36, 57, 75, 93, 105, 122, 142, 146, 147, 162, 163, 164, 183, 184, 207

U2 51, 179–180
UK 82 7, 44, 51, 77, 168, 181, 183
U.K. Subs 180–181
The Undead 182
The Undertones 39, 65, 182–183, 196

# Index

The Untouchables (punk band) 185
The Untouchables (ska band) 183
Up, Ari 156, 157
Uproar 183
Upsetters 211
*Urban Cowboy* 90
Urban Waste 184

Vampira 59
Van Halen 90
Vanian, Dave 58, 59
Varukers 185
Vega, Alan 170
The Velvet Underground 30, 73, 109, 119, 123, 133, 160, 171, 176, 189, 191, 201, 204, 205, 206, 210, 212–215
Verlaine, Tom 176, 186
Vice Squad 186
Vicious, Sid 116, 148
violence 14, 15, 16, 25, 48, 57, 61, 63, 82, 83, 86, 87, 96, 105, 113, 114, 116, 125, 148, 163, 164, 165, 168, 171, 187, 194, 200, 214
Virgin Prunes 186
Visage 11
Visconti, Tony 36
The Void 184, 187

The Wake 188
Wakeling, Dave 75
The Waitresses 186
The Wall 188
Watson, Chris 42
Watt, Mike 114
The Weirdos 188–189
Weller, Paul 94, 95, 96, 122
*West Side Story* 33
Westerberg, Paul 137, 138
Weymouth, Tina 173
The Who 89
Williams, Andy 75
Williamson, James 127, 207, 211
Wilson, Cindy 23
Wilson, Ricky 186
The Wipers 92, 143
Wire 8, 108, 184, 188–189
Wobble, Jah 129, 130, 192
Wood, Ed 59
Woodgate, Daniel 106
Woods, Lesley 22
Wynette, Tammy 194

X 9, 18, 19, 85, 91, 192–194
Xmal Deutschland 9, 30, 194
X-Ray Spex 76, 194–196
XTC 156, 167, 196–198

Y Pants 198
Young Marble Giants 198–199
Youth Brigade 184, 199

Z 144
Zero Boys 200
Zoom, Billy 193
The Zounds 200

www.ingramcontent.com/pod-product-compliance
Lightning Source LLC
Chambersburg PA
CBHW060342010526
44117CB00017B/2926